Cross-Language Studies of Learning to Read and Spell

NATO ASI Series

Advanced Science Institutes Series

A Series presenting the results of activities sponsored by the NATO Science Committee, which aims at the dissemination of advanced scientific and technological knowledge, with a view to strengthening links between scientific communities.

The Series is published by an international board of publishers in conjunction with the NATO Scientific Affairs Division

A	**Life Sciences**	Plenum Publishing Corporation
B	**Physics**	London and New York
C	**Mathematical and Physical Sciences**	Kluwer Academic Publishers
D	**Behavioural and Social Sciences**	Dordrecht, Boston and London
E	**Applied Sciences**	
F	**Computer and Systems Sciences**	Springer-Verlag
G	**Ecological Sciences**	Berlin, Heidelberg, New York, London,
H	**Cell Biology**	Paris and Tokyo
I	**Global Environmental Change**	

PARTNERSHIP SUB-SERIES

1.	**Disarmament Technologies**	Kluwer Academic Publishers
2.	**Environment**	Springer-Verlag / Kluwer Academic Publishers
3.	**High Technology**	Kluwer Academic Publishers
4.	**Science and Technology Policy**	Kluwer Academic Publishers
5.	**Computer Networking**	Kluwer Academic Publishers

The Partnership Sub-Series incorporates activities undertaken in collaboration with NATO's Cooperation Partners, the countries of the CIS and Central and Eastern Europe, in Priority Areas of concern to those countries.

NATO-PCO-DATA BASE

The electronic index to the NATO ASI Series provides full bibliographical references (with keywords and/or abstracts) to more than 50000 contributions from international scientists published in all sections of the NATO ASI Series.
Access to the NATO-PCO-DATA BASE is possible in two ways:

– via online FILE 128 (NATO-PCO-DATA BASE) hosted by ESRIN,
Via Galileo Galilei, I-00044 Frascati, Italy.

– via CD-ROM "NATO-PCO-DATA BASE" with user-friendly retrieval software in English, French and German (© WTV GmbH and DATAWARE Technologies Inc. 1989).

The CD-ROM can be ordered through any member of the Board of Publishers or through NATO-PCO, Overijse, Belgium.

Series D: Behavioural and Social Sciences – Vol. 87

Cross-Language Studies of Learning to Read and Spell

Phonologic and Orthographic Processing

edited by

Che Kan Leong
University of Saskatchewan,
Canada

and

R. Malatesha Joshi
Oklahoma State University,
U.S.A.

Kluwer Academic Publishers

Dordrecht / Boston / London

Published in cooperation with NATO Scientific Affairs Division

Proceedings of the NATO Advanced Study Institute on
Cognitive and Linguistic Bases of Reading, Writing and Spelling
Praia de Alvor, Algarve, Portugal
September 1994

A C.I.P. Catalogue record for this book is available from the Library of Congress.

ISBN 0-7923-4457-X

Published by Kluwer Academic Publishers,
P.O. Box 17, 3300 AA Dordrecht, The Netherlands.

Kluwer Academic Publishers incorporates the publishing programmes of
D. Reidel, Martinus Nijhoff, Dr W. Junk and MTP Press.

Sold and distributed in the U.S.A. and Canada
by Kluwer Academic Publishers,
101 Philip Drive, Norwell, MA 02061, U.S.A.

In all other countries, sold and distributed
by Kluwer Academic Publishers Group,
P.O. Box 322, 3300 AH Dordrecht, The Netherlands.

Printed on acid-free paper

TABLE OF CONTENTS

vi

Chinese

PREFACE

The present volume is based on the proceedings of the Advanced Study Institute (ASI) sponsored by the North Atlantic Treaty Organization (NATO) held in Alvor, Algarve, Portugal. A number of scholars from different countries participated in the two-week institute on Cognitive and linguistic aspects of reading, writing, and spelling. The present papers are further versions with modifications and refinements from those presented at the Advanced Study Institute.

Several people and organizations have helped us in this endeavor and their assistance is gratefully acknowledged. Our special thanks are to: the Scientific Affairs division of NATO for providing the major portions of the financial support, Dr. L.V. da Cunha of NATO and Dr. Tilo Kester and Mrs. Barbara Kester of the International Transfer of Science and Technology (ITST) for their help and support of the various aspects of the institute; and the staff of Hotel Alvor Praia for making our stay a pleasant one by helping us to run the institute smoothly.

This volume contains twenty chapters, grouped by languages (English, German, Dutch, Nordic, and Chinese), on phonologic and orhtographic processing in learning to read and spell in a cross-language perspective. The integrative theme is the importance of metalinguistic awareness and also orthographic factors in learning to read and spell in alphabetic language systems. Phonological processing reinforces orhtographic processing, and is in turn bolstered by the latter in emergent literacy. The interplay of these factors is stressed in the various chapters. Areas such as phonological processing subserving metalinguistic awareness are seen as worthy of further investigation.

The volume should be of interest to researchers, clinicians and post-graduate students interested in the psychology of reading and spelling within the broad cross-language framework. The fairly detailed treatment of metalinguistic awareness and orthographic processing and their interactive effects of reading and spelling in different language systems advances our understanding of early literacy.

With the constraint of camera-ready publishing to conserve time and resources, the authors and the coeditors in their various editorial capacities have endeavored to keep the book to a high publication quality. We beg the indulgence of the readers should they come across typographical errors.

Che Kan Leong, University of Saskatchewan, Canada
R. Malatesha Joshi, Oklahoma State University, USA
October 1996

LIST OF CONTRIBUTORS

ASSINK, E.M.H.   *Department of Psychology, University of Utrecht, Heidelberglaan 2, 3584 CS Utrecht, The Netherlands*

BRUCK, M.   *Department of Psychology, McGill University, Montreal, Canada H3A 1B1*

CATTS, H.   *Speech-Language-Hearing: Sciences and Disorders, University of Kansas, 3031 Dole, Lawrence, Kansas, 66045-2181, USA*

COENEN, M.J.W.L., *Dept. of Special Education, University of Nijmegen, PO Box 9104, 6500 HE Nijmegen, The Netherlands*

DODD, B.*   *Dept. of Speech and Hearing, University of Queensland, Brisbane, Queensland 4072, Australia*

GILLON, G.   *Dept. of Speech and Hearing, University of Queensland, Brisbane, Queensland 4072, Australia*

HANLEY, J.R.   *Dept. of Psychology, University of Liverpool, PO Box 147, Liverpool, L69 3BX, UK*

HUANG, H.S.   *Dept. of Special Education, National Tainan Teachers College, Tainan, Taiwan*

JANSEN, H.   *Department of Psychology, Univeristy of Bielefeld, D-33501, Bielefeld, Germany*

JOSHI, R.M.   *Dept. of Curriculum and Instruction, College of Education, 252 Willard Hall, Oklahoma State University, Stillwater, OK. 74078, USA*

KORKEAMÄKI, R.-L.   *Department of Education, University of Oulu, Fin-90570, Oulu, Finland*

LANDERL, K.   *Institute of Psychology, University of Salzburg, Hellbrunnerstraße, A-5020 Salzburg, Austria*

LARRIVEE, L.S.   *Speech-Language-Hearing: Sciences and Disorders, University of Kansas, 3031 Dole, Lawrence, Kansas, 66045-2181, USA*

LEONG, C.K.   *College of Education, University of Saskatchewan, 28 Campus Drive, Saskatoon, Saskatchewan, Canada S7N 0X1*

LYSTER, S.-A.H.   *Institute for Special Education, University of Oslo, Postbox 1140, Blindern, 0317 Oslo, Norway*

MANNHAUPT, G. *Department of Psychology, Univeristy of Bielefeld, D-33501, Bielefeld, Germany*

MARX, H.   *Department of Psychology, Univeristy of Bielefeld, D-33501, Bielefeld, Germany*

NÄSLUND, J.C.**   *College of Education, University of New Mexico, Albuquerque, New Mexico, 87131, USA*

NIEDERSØE, J.   *Office of School Psychology, Bornholm, Denmark*

OLOFSSON, Å.   *Dept. of Psychology, University of Umeå, S-901 87 Umeå Sweden*

REITSMA, P. *Paedologisch Instituut - Vrije Universiteit Amsterdam, PO Box 303, 1115 ZG Duivendrecht, The Netherlands*
SCHNEIDER, W. *Department of Psychology, University of Würzburg, Willelsbacherplatz 1, D-97074 Würzburg, Germany*
SCHREUDER, R. *Interfaculty Research Unit for Language and Speech, University of Nijmegen, PO Box 9104, 6500 HE Nijmegen, The Netherlands*
SCHWARTZ, S. *Montreal Children's Hospital, Montreal, Quebec, Canada H3H 1P3*
SCOTT, V.G. *Speech-Language-Hearing: Sciences and Disorders, University of Kansas,, 3031 Dole, Lawrence, Kansas, 66045-2181, USA*
SPELBERG, H.C.L. *Dept. of Special Education, Rijksuniversiteit Groningen, Grote Rozenstraat 38, 9712 TJ Groningen, The Netherlands*
UHRY, J.K. *Graduate School of Education, Fordham University, 113 West 60th Street, New York, New York 10023-7478, USA*
VALTIN, R. *Humboldt Universität Berlin, Institut für Schulpädagogik, Unter den Linden 6, 10099 Berlin, Germany*
VAN BON, W.H.J. *Dept. of Special Education, University of Nijmegen, PO Box 9104, 6500 HE Nijmegen, The Netherlands*
VAN DEN BOS, K.P. *Dept. of Special Education, Rijksuniversiteit Groningen, Grote Rozenstraat 38, 9712 TJ Groningen, The Netherlands*
VAN DEN BROEK, P. *Dept. of Educational Psychology, University of Minnesota, Minneapolis, MN 55455, USA*
WENTINK, H.W.M.J. *Dept. of Special Education, University of Nijmegen, PO Box 9104, 6500 HE Nijmegen, The Netherlands*
WILCOX, K.A., *Speech-Language-Hearing: Sciences and Disorders, University of Kansas, 3031 Dole, Lawrence, Kansas, 66045-2181, USA*
WOOD-JACKSON, C. *Speech-Language-Hearing: Sciences and Disorders, University of Kansas, 3031 Dole, Lawrence, Kansas, 66045-2181, USA*

* Present Address: *Dept. of Speech, The University of Newcastle-upon-Tyne, Newcastle-upon-Tyne, NE1 7RU, UK*

** Present Address: *Dept. of Applied Behavioral Studies in Education, College of Education, 426 Willard Hall, Oklahoma State University, Stillwater, OK. 74078, USA*

RELATING PHONOLOGIC AND ORTHOGRAPHIC PROCESSING TO LEARNING TO READ AND SPELL

CHE KAN LEONG
College of Education
University of Saskatchewan
28 Campus Drive
Saskatoon, Saskatchewan
Canada. S7N 0X1

R. MALATESHA JOSHI
College of Education
252 Willard Hall
Oklahoma State University
Stillwater, OK. 74078-0146
U.S.A.

Abstract: This chapter serves a dual purpose. It attempts to set forth our views on phonological and orthographic processing in learning to read and spell in a cross-language perspective; and to highlight the various chapters, which are grouped by languages (English, German, Dutch, Nordic, & Chinese). While metalinguistic awareness plays an important role in reading alphabetic language systems, we suggest that orthographic factors are also important. Phonological processing reinforces orthographic processing, and is in turn bolstered by the latter in emergent literacy. The interplay of these factors provides an integrative theme for the volume, and the various chapters are discussed within this broad framework. Several areas such as phonological processing subserving phonemic awareness are seen as important for continued investigation.

It is with considerable trepidation that we title this volume: **Cross-Language Studies of Learning to Read and Spell: Phonologic and Orthographic Processing.** For one thing, our intent is not to compare different languages in relation to emergent literacy. Nor should we try, because language systems differ, even though there is "diverse oneness of writing systems" (DeFrancis, 1989). For another thing, we do not seek to represent even the main language systems as this is a daunting task, if not an impossible one.

Diversity and "Oneness"

According to Gelb (1963), language/writing systems may be broadly grouped according to whether they are alphabetic (English being an obvious example), morphemic (e.g., Chinese), or syllabic (e.g., Japanese). The Japanese syllabary, which incorporates both the alphabetic kana (hiragana and katakana), and the morphemic kanji, is not represented in this volume. The two chapters on Chinese address mainly the role of "phonemic awareness" and the "paradigmatic analysis" in Chinese word reading and spelling. For the alphabetic language systems represented here (English, German, Dutch, and Nordic languages), they vary considerably from "deep" to "shallow" in the grapheme-phoneme or phoneme-grapheme

1

C.K. Leong and R.M. Joshi (Eds.), Cross-Language Studies of Learning to Read and Spell, 1–29.
© 1997 Kluwer Academic Publishers. Printed in the Netherlands.

correspondences continuum and this differential mapping has an effect on early literacy.

Even for our very moderate coverage of alphabetic language systems, we do not, for example, deal with modern Greek language, the first fully and a relatively "pure" alphabetized system. We have no coverage for Romance languages (Spanish, Italian and Portuguese), which are written with much higher transparent orthography than English. Nor are we able to deal with Hebrew, which signals most vowels with small diacritical marks, and the letters carry mainly consonantal information. Thus the "cross-language" aspects should bear with these omissions.

Given the necessarily restricted coverage, we take heart from the fact that there are other volumes covering various facets of different language/writing systems with reference to literacy acquisition including reading. An earlier anthology **Comparative Reading** edited by Downing (1973) describes children's reading behavior in learning to read in different language/writing systems in fourteen countries. A later volume **Orthography, Reading, and Dyslexia** (Kavanagh & Venezky, 1980) discusses the role of writing systems on reading and its difficulties.

A recent volume **Scripts and Literacy** edited by Taylor and Olson (1995) examines in some detail the inter-related aspects of scripts and literacy such as cognitive processes, word recognition and learning to read generally. The nature of writing systems is discussed at some length and the language/writing systems represented include: Chinese, Japanese, Korean, Hebrew, and others in addition to English. Another in-depth explication of learning to read and reading difficulties in different orthographic systems is provided by Aaron and Joshi (1989). A recent special issue in the journal **Reading and Writing** asks the specific question if phonological and orthographic characteristics of different Romance languages influence the onset of literacy, and examines the interactions of these effects (Morais, 1995). The present volume continues with this theme, but with different alphabetic language and writing systems and with Chinese.

Even from the selective coverage, it is clear that attempts to understand phonological and orthographic coding in different languages should inform both researchers and practitioners of the structure of language/writing systems and of their effects on written word representation.

Aim and scope of this volume

Given our limited coverage of even the major language/writing systems in relation to early literacy, our aim is a modest one. Our intent is to examine underlying mechanisms of processing shallow (transparent) and deep (opaque) alphabetic language systems, and the disparate (from the vantage point of alphabetic systems) Chinese language in learning to read and to spell. It is our hope that out of the diversity of languages, some broad, unified theme may emerge. This theme should relate to making contact from listening and speaking, that most children already know, with what the written symbols in different writing systems or orthographies represent.

The simple view is that the need for humans to communicate necessitates listening and speaking, and that the use of acoustic and articulatory speech signals entails phonological processing. While this view is obvious, we need to be more explicit. We would like to know the more precise nature of the phonological processing, the underlying speech perception and production mechanisms and their effects on early literacy. In particular, we need to know the different levels at which verbal messages are represented by writing systems and the ways in which these systems constrain the mapping of the spoken language.

The English orthography, for example, is morphophonemic and is represented by phonemes, syllables with their onsets and rimes and other sublexical units. In the case of a different orthography, that of the bi-scriptal Japanese syllabary, each Japanese kana symbol represents a speech unit known as "mora", which is more of a subsyllabic and a timing unit on which the rhythm of the Japanese language is based (Leong & Tamaoka, 1995; Otake, Hatano, Cutler, & Mehler, 1993). Japanese morae are pronounced with approximately equal durations. Thus, if it is thought that phonological awareness is central to learning to read Japanese (at least for the hiragana and katakana script), then the study of morae as units of segment of speech in both speech perception and production becomes important (Leong, 1995).

In the case of Chinese, the language/writing system is morphosyllabic, which incorporates a phonological basis in analytic word reading as shown in both psycholinguistic and psychological analyses (DeFrancis, 1989; Leong, 1995, this volume). However, the phonological processing may not involve segmental analyses of phonemes and morphophonemes, as in the case of alphabetic languages; and the nature and size of the linguistic segments are constrained by the morphosyllabic characteristics of Chinese.

Indeed, for alphabetic and syllabic language/writing systems, there is an interplay in both phonologic and orthographic processes in learning to read. There is general agreement from research that phonology is integral to the access to the linguistic structure by learners, and this phonological involvement is constrained only by variations in language or orthography systems (Frost & Katz, 1992).

This chapter first discusses the role of phonological and orthographic including morphological processing in emergent literacy to provide the framework. It then comments on the various chapters and attempts to draw out their integration within this broad theme. The chapter ends with some suggestions for areas of further investigation.

Phonological Processing

For the purpose of this overview and commentary, we will use the terms linguistic awareness, metalinguistic awareness interchangeably. This broad concept of phonological awareness also includes phonemic awareness, as discussed by a number of our contributors in this volume.

Metalinguistic awareness generally refers to the ability to progress from the transparent to the opaque forms of language and to attend to these forms in and of themselves. It is the gradual shift of attention from meaning to structure or from linguistic content to linguistic forms; and denotes implicit knowledge that is made explicit. Specifically, metalinguistic awareness refers to the ability to conceptualize, reflect on, and manipulate sublexical segments of spoken language such as phonemes, onsets and rimes, syllables and related units; and this reflective ability facilitates literacy learning.

Theory-based long-term research and training studies on metalinguistic awareness in young children have been carried out these twenty years or so by the Haskins group, the Oxford group, the Brussels group, the Austin, Texas group, the Australia-New Zealand group, and the Umeå group. These different research groups provide convergent evidence on the importance of metalinguistic awareness in early reading instruction and in preventing reading failure (see also Downing & Valtin, 1984; Sawyer & Fox, 1991).

Metalinguistic Awareness

We would like to think the Umeå group of Lundberg, Åke Olofsson and Margit Torneus as among the first to carry out in the 1970s a theory-based, long-term study to understand the nature of metalinguistic awareness, and also among the first to institute successful training programs with young children. Moreover, the group is among the first to use sophisticated linear structural equation modeling (LISREL) technique to tease out the direct and indirect effects of the various metalinguistic variables on reading and spelling. While Lundberg and his colleagues may not like to be given prime of place in their research and training enterprise, their long-term studies also show the benefit of examining language systems other than, or in addition to, English.

Writing in 1978, Lundberg suggested that: "The central aspect of linguistic awareness is an **attention shift** from content to form, the ability to make language forms opaque." (p. 87, original emphasis). Working with Åke Olofsson and others, he showed in the 1980s that phonemic awareness as represented by rhyme recognition, segmental analysis, phoneme deletion and addition, phonemic synthesis, can be developed in prereaders outside the context of formal reading instruction (Olofsson & Lundberg, 1983). Furthermore, phonemic training contributes to the long-term development of accurate concepts of reading in the preschool child and to the cognitive clarity of formal reading instruction in school (Olofsson & Lundberg, 1985).

In their much quoted large-scale training study, Lundberg, Frost, and Petersen (1988) provided an extensive training program over an eight-month period for stimulating metalinguistic awareness (word segmentation, syllable synthesis, syllable segmentation, initial phoneme, phoneme segmentation, phoneme synthesis) in 235 six-year-old Danish children (schooling begins at age 7 in Denmark), compared with a control group of 155 children. Lundberg et al. found small but significant effects on rhyming tasks, on tasks involving word and syllable manipulation, and dramatic increase in phonemic segmentation in the target group of children. Furthermore, the sustained, systematic and explicit training also had a facilitating effect on the target children's reading and spelling and this positive effect persisted till grade two.

The series of training studies by the Umeå group has shown that metalinguistic awareness facilitates reading and spelling, that segmentation ability does not develop spontaneously, and that these metalinguistic abilities can be trained in young children. There are several questions that we would like to comment on.

Rhyming. One question pertains to rhyming ability. This ability, or what José Morais, Bertelson, Cary, and Alegria (1986) term "sensitivity to sound similarity", does not seem to be strongly dependent on formal training. In a recent report with two studies, Høien, Lundberg, Stanovich and Bjaalid (1995) show that phonological awareness is a separate component from phonological short-term memory and naming speed. This work by Høien et al. also reminds us of the work of Maryanne Wolf (1986, 1991) and others on naming speed or rapid automatized naming as a predictor of reading disorder.

Furthermore, the phonological awareness component seems to yield separate syllabic, rhyme, and phonemic awareness subcomponents. This separability may explain the observation by Morais (1991a) on rhyming and alliteration in an illiterate poet. If further confirmed of the separability of these phonologic subcomponents, there are implications for training of children to develop sensitivity and mastery of these subskills.

Task analysis. There is a need for careful task analysis of the different aspects of metalinguistic awareness. Take, as an example, an often used task of asking children to repeat "just a little" of an utterance. This metalinguistic task may not deal directly with segmental analysis of words. This is shown in the answer of "half a dollar" when children are asked to elide the second syllable from "dollar".

Furthermore, metalinguistic tasks in many studies vary in complexity, even though they show reasonably high internal consistency. The phoneme deletion task, especially for initial phonemes ("If you take away the /n/ sound from the word NICE, what word is left?"), has been shown to be the most difficult, but is a moderately good predictor for first-grade reading. The sound isolation task ("What is the first sound in 'rose'?") and the medial phoneme deletion task ("What word will be left if /t/ were taken away from the middle of STAND?") have been shown by Yopp (1988) to explain some 62% of the variance denoted by her kindergartners' "learning rate".

Onset and rime. The other question is the contribution of intermediate segments of the onset and rime. Onset refers to the syllable's initial consonant or consonant cluster and rime refers to that part of the syllable beginning with a vowel and any consonants coming after it. Examples of onsets and rimes are TH//ING in THING, R//AIN in RAIN, GR//AIN in GRAIN, TR//AIN in Train. An important feature of rimes is that they are often repeated in words with similar pronunciations.

Goswami (1986, 1988a, 1988b, 1990), Treiman (1985; Treiman, Goswami, & Bruck, 1990) and others have shown that onsets and rimes of printed words are also natural units in helping children to make **analogies** to pronounce unknown words with the same rimes. Analogies are predicated on making inferences that two or more words with similar spelling patterns will be similar in pronunciation (e.g., CARE, DARE, BEWARE; VAGUE, PLAGUE). Rime families cue vowel pronunciations and serve as building blocks for monosyllabic words in both reading and spelling. Those children skilled in making phonological judgments about rimes also tend to be good at making analogies between the spelling patterns of rimes when reading. Conversely, children learning to read unfamiliar words by analogy with known words also require some knowledge of grapheme-phoneme correspondences and phonological recoding skills (Ehri & Robbins, 1992).

This reciprocal relationship is helped by the high degree of overlap between regularity and consistency of orthographic neighbors of rime families. This is shown by Stanback (1992) in her analyses of 824 different orthographic rimes from 17,602 English words (e.g., AT as pronounced in CAT in 265 words and as in WHAT in only six words). The studies of Goswami and Treiman and the "type-token" analysis of Stanback point to the usefulness in teaching rime families to beginning readers/spellers and those children "at risk" for developing literacy. As examples, rime-based training has been found to have an effect on initial reading (Bruck & Treiman, 1992; Peterson & Haines, 1992), although considerable practice is needed for retention effects. Moreover, rime-based analogies as compared with smaller, nonrime-based analogies present less difficulties to poor readers and these readers can be trained to use analogies to learn unfamiliar words (Greaney & Tunmer, 1996).

Summary Statement on Phonological Awareness

Summarizing from available research evidence, educed from the Haskins Laboratories, the Umeå group, the Brussels and other research teams, we suggest segmentation and categorization processes are important in mapping alphabetic symbols onto speech sounds (phonology). These are the prerequisite conditions:

(1) The segments must be reasonably distinguishable in the acoustic speech signals, which form a continuous stream because of coarticulation. More than one segment of information may be encoded in the same place of the speech signal; and similar acoustic properties may lead to the perception of more than one segment (Liberman, Cooper, Shankweiler, & Studdert-Kennedy, 1967).

(2) The segments must correspond in some reliable way to sublexical or lexical units.

(3) Categorization relates surface phonetic renderings to deep phonological categories of the language. This process involves learning the phonetic or allophonic variations and the linguistic contexts in which they occur (e.g., the English phonological category of /p/ contains the voiced allophones [p] and the unvoiced [p] varying according to the speech environment).

Different linear speech units such as phonemes with their allophones and hierarchical structures of sublexical units such as syllables with their onsets and rimes play an important role in reading acquisition. The contribution of this role may vary according to the age and reading level of learners. In general, there is a superiority of onsets over phonemes that constitute them in speech sound similarity judgment (e.g., PACT-PEEL judged as more similar phonetically than PLAN-PROW) (Treiman & Zukowski, 1996, Experiment 1). In their experiments 2 through 5 Treiman and Zukowski (1996) test the linguistic status of the syllable with syllables and nonsyllabic stimulus units containing the same number of phonemes, and show that phonological similarity is more prominent when based on shared full syllables than when based on parts of the syllable.

To conclude this part of the discussion of metalinguistic awareness, we are well reminded of the seminal work on "phonemic hearing" and phonematic analysis of the Russian psychologist Daniel Borisovich Elkonin (1973). Elkonin emphasizes that nothing must confuse the child's understanding of the features of speech. Writing in **Comparative Reading** (Downing, 1973), Elkonin stated that: "May it not be sufficient to teach literacy simply by building on the level of phonematic hearing the child developed before entering school in the process of mastering the reception and production of spoken language?... It [Phonemic hearing] is a matter of helping children to understand the way in which language behaves in spoken and written form -- the sound structure, the grammar, the orthography..." (Elkonin, 1973, pp. 553-556). Even allowing for the shallow Cyrillic language systems in mapping speech sound onto graphic symbols, these statements apply with equal force to other alphabetic language systems.

Orthographic Processing

While the centrality of phonemic awareness in early reading and reading disorders is well documented and not disputed, we should also pause to reflect if there are other linguistic components which contribute to acquiring reading and spelling. Recently, an **integrative** view of the development of phonological and orthographic processes linking reading and spelling is favored by a number of researchers such as Adams (1990), Ehri (1992), and Foorman (1994, 1995).

What then is orthographic processing? These are some of the notions: (1) "... orthographic form ... as a sequence of letters bearing systematic relationships to phonological properties of the word." (Ehri, 1980, p. 313). (2) "... orthographic form ... is the identity of the letters in the sentence and their systematic relationship to sound which is important." (Goswami, 1990, p. 324).

In several insightful papers, Foorman (1994, 1995) has raised the question if phonological and orthographic processes are separate but equal. She further argues for the reinforcement of phonological representation by systematically analyzing orthographic units or sublexical units. In her ongoing studies of spelling and reading, Ehri (1992) proposes an integrative view of "amalgamating" phonological and orthographic processing.

The emphasis on the **morphophonemic** forms of the underlying, abstract representation of the internal lexicon can be seen from several theoretical perspectives. One is computational linguistic or linguistic, the other is psychological, and the third is educational.

Different Perspectives

From the linguistic perspective, Bybee (1995) argues for the interdependence of form (morphology and phonology) and meaning, and the importance of lexical strength and lexical connections. From the computational linguistic perspective, Venezky (1970) emphasizes the morphophonemic nature of English in his seminal computational analysis of the underlying patterns of the English orthography.

From the psychological perspective, more precise lexical representation is explained by Shankweiler and Lundquist (1992, p.43) as follows: "The evidence supports the expectation that both phonologic and morphologic aspects of linguistic awareness are relevant to success in spelling and reading." From the education perspective, Henry and the contributors to her Special Issue on **The Role of Decoding on Reading Research and Instruction** all converge on the relations between phonological and orthographic knowledge subserving both spelling and word recognition (Henry, 1993).

Related Principles

Elbro and Arnbak (1996) emphasize the principle of **transparency** and **productivity** in enhancing word knowledge, especially morphologically complex words. The first principle of transparency to opacity provides a range of morphological depth both for our understanding of the nature of morphology and also in mapping out systematic teaching programs. The second principle of productivity in morphology is a relative concept and refers to the processing of possible new words, including possible but non-occurring words. Productivity depends, among other things, on the morphological class of words. For example, the suffixation #NESS is semantically more transparent than the suffixation +ITY and tends to be more productive (Aronoff, 1976).

We would like to add two related notions as important for developing the abstract internal lexicon. These are the notions of **redundancy** and **precision** as discussed by Perfetti (1991, 1992). Redundancy refers to providing or using multiple coding systems, phonologic and orthographic to promote word knowledge. Precision refers to increasingly more refined knowledge of words. Both notions work hand-in-hand and help children to enhance the productivity of the internal lexicon. Moreover, automaticity also plays a role in lexical representation in reading English (Wolf, 1986, 1991), and more so in a more regular writing system such as German (Wimmer, 1993, 1996).

We should note the multiple tasks that Elbro and Arnbak have used to tap morphological processing. These tasks include: sentence analysis, inflection and compounding, reversal of roots of compound words, morpheme synthesis, and morphological completion tasks. These tasks are not easy to design and we will do well to note the ingenuity of Elbro and Arnbak in coming to grips with both the rationale and the actual design of the tasks.

Interplay of Phonologic and Orthographic Processing

There are several research and practical issues. One is the question of the possible contribution of phonological awareness to morphological awareness and the need to tease out some of the overlapping aspects. It is possible that phonologically complex conditions may be morphological in nature. It could be argued just as forcefully the other way round. Thus the teasing out of the confounding phonologic, orthographic and morphologic conditions should provide areas for further exploration.

One reason why the Elbro and Arnbak training study of morphological awareness with 10 to 12 year old dyslexics did not give "impressive" results could be due to the moderate level of general ability as shown on the Raven's Progressive Matrices (Raven percentile of 53 for the target group and 42 for the control group). The understanding of the internal structure of words and their relation does require a certain level of cognitive ability. Having said this, we agree with Elbro and Arnbak that "it **is** possible to train morphological awareness even in dyslexic students." Indeed, their results show that the target students are more aware of word formation rules, even in making "sound-preserving errors". It is further significant to note that the target students make better use of their decoding skills, and that the morphological awareness training shows greater effect on spelling than on reading. In agreement with Shankweiler and Lundquist (1992), we suggest the exploration of the relationship between morphology and spelling may yield even more insight into spelling than the morphology and reading relationship.

We would like to end this part in providing the framework for the volume by referring to Adams (1990, p. 416) that: "... deep and thorough knowledge of spelling patterns, and words, and of the phonological translations..., are of inescapable importance to both skillful reading and its acquisition."

Integrating Phonological and Orthographic Processing

Research programs carried out these two decades or so at the Haskins Laboratories, Oxford, Umeå, Brussels, Texas, Pittsburgh and elsewhere have shown the central role of phonological processing in reading acquisition and in preventing reading disabilities (see Goswami & Bryant, 1990; Leong, 1991; Share, 1995, for details). It has further been demonstrated that systematic, explicit metalinguistic training stimulates phonological awareness in preschool or grade one children and that such training facilitates subsequent reading and spelling performance (Foorman & Francis, 1994; Lundberg, Frost & Petersen, 1988).

While the central role of phonological processing is well documented in alphabetic languages, we should ask if this role is also reinforced by orthographic processing; and if the phonological involvement varies according to the dimension from the more transparent to the more opaque alphabetic language systems. We should also ask if similar involvement applies to morphosyllabic or syllabic languages such as Chinese and Japanese.

Phonological Processing Subserving Phonemic Awareness

In the Section dealing with the English language, the theme of inadequate phonological representation in emergent readers/spellers as explanatory for phonemic awareness performance runs through several of the chapters. **Catts, Wilcox, Wood-Jackson, Larrivee, and Scott** examine the construct of phonemic awareness and the measures used to assess this aspect of phonological awareness within the categories of phoneme segmentation, phoneme synthesis and sound comparison. From their phoneme oddity task with items contrasting maximally and minimally in the place of articulation, manner of articulation, and voicing, Catts et al. find that children perform significantly better with phonetically dissimilar than phonetically similar items and are more accurate in their oddity judgment with later stimulus trials. These authors suggest that sensitivity to, and knowledge of, the sound structure of language relate to the deeper knowledge of phonological processing.

The effect of the complex relationship between speech sounds and graphemes on poor readers' ability to decode unfamiliar letter strings is discussed by **Dodd and Gillon**. These authors suggest that training phonological processing skills, rather than semantic-syntactic skills, helps improve reading accuracy. Their targeting phoneme-grapheme rules in intervention will be the most effective when regularity and consistency overlap in such relationship. We would like to think that their suggestion of poor readers' inefficiency in "rule" abstraction not being "specific to linguistic behavior" may be interpreted within the finding of Dodd, Leahy and Hambly (1989) of context-dependent rules.

The chapters by Catts et al., and by Dodd and Gillon, in different ways, are reminiscent of the elegant study of Shankweiler and Liberman (1972) of the child's misreadings and their relation to speech. Shankweiler and Liberman's advocacy for the comparative study of speech perception and production, phonological development and reading is explicated in recent works by Fowler (1991), and Morais and Mousty (1992).

In her insightful probing into the development of phoneme awareness, Fowler (1991, p. 101) suggests that failure to gain access to such awareness is associated with a host of subtle "phonological deficits, involving the formation, retrieval, and maintenance of phonological representations." Consonant with the findings of infants' perception of phonetic change despite overlap among tokens of vowels (Kuhl, 1983), and the notion of phonological development as "innately guided learning process" proposed by Jusczyk and Bertoncini (1988), Fowler posits articulatory gestures, and not so much phonemes, as the fundamental units of speech perception and production. The scope of gestural representations maybe more salient with syllables, then subsyllabic units such as onsets and rimes and to phonemic segments.

In tune with the view of Fowler (1991), Morais and Mousty (1992) emphasize that phonemic manipulation may be subserved by more primary phonological representations of speech. Developmental changes of phonemic awareness relate to complex interactions of phonologic sensitivity, phonological awareness and segmental analysis of speech. Phonological sensitivity is explained as "...the capacity to distinguish between phonologically similar words while listening for meaning"; and phonological awareness "implies attention to the phonological forms of utterances" (Morais & Mousty, 1992, p. 206). The move from less segmental toward more segmental analysis (e.g., prereaders' differential performance on segmentation of fricatives as compared with stop consonants) helps in recovering the representations of new words, multisyllabic words and pseudowords.

Temporal Integration and Rapid-Naming

The explication of "causes" of phonemic awareness by Fowler(1991), and Morais and Mousty (1992) further substantiates the studies by Catts et al. and by Dodd and Gillon. Moreover, the subtle and broad array of phonological deficits in poor readers may extend to such tasks as rapid automatized naming (R.A.N.) (Denckla & Rudel, 1976; Wolf, 1986, 1991), pseudoword repetition, sentence repetition and related tasks involving complex lexical items and word strings. The chapter by **Schwartz and Bruck** is cast within the framework of temporal processing for children with "central auditory processing" disorder.

Earlier, Tallal (1980) showed that children with developmental dysphasia and with developmental dyslexia were inefficient in responding to rapidly presented verbal and nonverbal acoustic stimuli. The therapeutic "stretching" technique of extending initial formant transitions of, say, stop consonants while maintaining the total duration of the consonants was found to be effective in helping these children to discriminate speech sounds previously found to be indiscriminable.

In her extensive series of studies of children with language and reading impairment, Tallal has emphasized the importance of investigating the detection, temporal integration, discrimination, sequencing, rate processing, and serial memory of complex acoustic spectra of speech. She and her colleagues have provided a physiological basis to explain the significant deficit of language-impaired children in discriminating, sequencing and remembering very brief speech signals followed by very rapid succession in terms of "tens of milliseconds" by other stimuli. Tallal, Miller, and Fitch (1993) state that speech perception and production would be particularly vulnerable to this type of fine-grained temporal processing disorders in the range of tens of milliseconds; and that "language- and reading-impaired children, due to their basic auditory temporal processing deficit, are unable to establish stable and invariant phonemic representations." (p.   37).   These researchers are careful to point out that while their data suggest that reading acquisition may be disrupted by auditory temporal phonological deficits, "... the deficits in the other modalities, such as the transient visual system, may not in themselves affect reading directly" (Tallal et al., 1993, p. 37).

Related to the notion of rapid auditory processing is the suggestion of rapid serial retrieval difficulty and the amelioration of children with dyslexia in reading accuracy, but not in the rate of reading.   These are the main findings of Uhry's case studies of training older dyslexics in reading "nonsense" words.   These findings lend support to the "double deficit" hypothesis of Wolf (1986, 1991; Wolf, Pfeil, Lotz, & Biddle, 1994) to explain the deficiencies of dyslexics in phonological processes such as segmentation tasks and naming-speed with serial and continuous tasks. The double deficit hypothesis upholds the important role of phonological processing, but also points to the naming-speed deficit as further explanations of the heterogeneous nature of reading disorders and extending into other alphabetic language systems.

The notion of speed of reading real and psuedowords was one of the hypotheses tested in emergent readers in Germany and the U.S.A. in the chapter by **Näslund, Schneider, and van den Broek**. These authors examine phonemic segmentation, word and pseudoword decoding in first and second grade German and U.S. children and also reading comprehension (second grade only). One finding was that the German children were more accurate in phoneme manipulation. Another finding was that these children read pseudowords about as quickly as real words, although there was considerable individual variation. This latter finding may be explained by the more regular German orthography with more consistent grapheme-phoneme correspondence, but should also be interpreted within the broader context that severely reading disordered children are impaired in both phonological processes and naming speed.

Reading Speed and Phonological Awareness in Learning to Read/Spell German

The question of whether or not a consistent orthography such as German is helpful to dyslexics is studied by **Landerl**. Using very "similar" one-, two- and three-syllable English and German words of high and low frequency and also nonwords, Landerl provides a detailed analysis of the reading strategies between English dyslexics and "German" dyslexics (Austrian children learning German) of comparable age (twelve-year-old) and non-verbal general ability. Her general finding is that the German dyslexics read accurately but slowly, while their English counterparts show low reading accuracy and considerably lower reading speed (except for one-syllable high frequency words). Word frequency, word length and lexicality also affect English dyslexics, more they do German dyslexics.

Context of Reading Speed and Phonemic Awareness

The Landerl study may be compared with the series of studies by Wimmer (1993, 1996). Wimmer (1993) finds a much lower rate of reading error in German-speaking dyslexics at the end of grade 2 and a farther drop at the end of grade 4, as compared with English dyslexics. This should be interpreted within the broader context of the fairly rapid acquisition of word decoding and phonemic awareness by normally progressing German children, but not by German children with reading difficulties. In a recent study of nonword reading of ten-year old German dyslexics, Wimmer (1996) uses a "double match" research design by matching words with nonwords and a reading age (RA) control matched on reading speed and accuracy with the dyslexics. Wimmer finds that the dyslexics read the nonwords at slower speed and with slightly lower accuracy than the RA match, but the German dyslexics read the nonwords rather accurately, as compared with English dyslexics as reported in the research literature.

Taken together, the studies of German-speaking children by the Salzburg group of Wimmer and Landerl (also Wimmer, Landerl, Linortner & Hummer, 1991) reinforce the notion of the central role of phonemic awareness in learning to read and spell, as is shown consistently in the research literature on emergent literacy in English. The observation by Landerl (this volume) that one advantage of a consistent orthography such as German is that it should help children to become "self-reliant readers." This self-teaching approach results from refined phonological knowledge, which reinforces orthographic knowledge, and is in turn bolstered by the latter. Similar arguments have also been put forward forcefully by Share (1995) in his detailed review of reading acquisition issues. In a recent study with English children, Landerl, Frith, and Wimmer (1996) further show that phonological and orthographic representations of words are closely intertwined and activated in normal readers; whereas these connections are much less strong and with less phonological underpinning in dyslexics as compared with their spelling age controls. Where speed of processing is important is in facilitating grapheme-phoneme conversion.

In their prospective Munich longitudinal study of 210 German children from about ages six, **Schneider and Näsland** report on the inter-relation of "phonological awareness", verbal and nonverbal general ability, memory span and "early literacy" (e.g., letter knowledge) in predicting decoding speed, reading comprehension and speed. While all four domains contribute significantly to reading and spelling as assessed from grade two on, that of both broad-band and narrow-band phonological awareness (rhyming, syllable segmentation, sound matching and sound blending) is shown to be the most predictive of reading and spelling. This is followed by early literacy variables, then memory span tasks, and much less so "intelligence".

The findings of the Munich prospective study of phonemic awareness as the major determinant of emergent literacy, and not so much general verbal or nonverbal intelligence, are in line with the position of Morais, Alegria, and Content (1987). The Munich findings also support the efficacy in training phonological awareness both for instruction and intervention of children "at risk" for reading and spelling, as demonstrated in the Lundberg, Frost, and Petersen (1988) training and intervention study.

Rapid Bypass of Logographic Phase of Emergent Literacy in German

The Bielefeld Longitudinal Study of **Mannhaupt, Jansen, and Marx** deals with beginning literacy instruction of 187 German children. The findings point to the bypass of the "logographic" phase of reading/spelling as discussed in the English literature (e.g., Frith, 1985), and the fairly rapid acquisition of grapheme-phoneme correspondence by German readers/spellers. This latter finding is in line with the results of the fairly rapid acquisition of word decoding and phonemic awareness by normally progressing German-speaking children (though not for those "at-risk" for reading) of the Salzburg group (Landerl, this volume; Wimmer, 1993,1996), thus accentuating the role of naming speed for German readers.

Mannhaupt et al. suggest that stage models of early literacy acquisition developed for English-speaking children may not apply with equal force to a different language and culture. However, it should be pointed out that the first or logographic phase of reading should not be interpreted as confined to picture-like recognition of symbols, as early readers at this stage use some letter-sound knowledge and attempt to analyze segments of spoken words (Ehri, 1987; Stuart & Coltheart, 1988).

The use of reading/spelling strategies by learners of the more consistent German language is detailed in some case studies of young children by **Valtin**. In agreement with Mannhaupt et al., she also suggests that the logographic phase proposed by Frith (1985) for learning to read/spell English is bypassed rapidly by normally progressing German children in learning German. The fairly regular grapheme-phoneme correspondence of the German orthography facilitates the rapid move by learners into the alphabetic phase of reading/spelling, as shown by Landerl (this volume) and Wimmer (1993, 1996). Valtin's observation of young German children's "phonemic spelling" further reinforces the central role of phonemic awareness in emergent literacy, even though individuals vary considerably.

Developing Orthographic and Phonologic Knowledge in Learning to Read/Spell Dutch

In a volume on the basic processes of learning to read/spell Dutch, Reitsma and Verhoeven (1990) discuss the highly regular correspondence between graphemes and phonemes in the Dutch language with fairly consistent pronunciation of most native Dutch words, and the need for segmentation into appropriate morphemic units for polysyllabic words. Their analysis of initial reading instruction in Dutch schools shows intensive teaching and learning of basic decoding principles for regularly written Dutch words within the first "four or five months" of formal reading instruction. There is heavy emphasis on the "structuur" method of teaching clusters of letters, spelling patterns, and word families to enhance the discovery of the basic principle of the written language. While phonological processing including phonological awareness and letter-name knowledge is important and integral for learning to read and spell Dutch, orthographic knowledge is acquired early by Dutch children and is "indispensable" for competency in emergent literacy in Dutch (Reitsma, 1990).

Orthographic Representation

It is within the above context and also the earlier Section on Orthographic Processing that the chapters on learning to read/spell Dutch should be examined. **Wentink, van Bon and Schreuder** study the role of rapid and accurate vocalization processes of "syllable-bound" monosyllabic Dutch pseudowords with varying orthographic structures of consonant-vowel-consonant (CVC), CCVC/CVCC and CCVCC. Their results show that beginning Dutch readers depend more on grapheme-phoneme correspondence rules, while competent readers also incorporate syllable-bound strategies in decoding.

The theme of using "multiletter recognition units" and learning more about "orthographic representation" by emergent Dutch readers is discussed by **Reitsma**. In an experiment with seven-year-old beginning Dutch readers, Reitsma corroborates his earlier findings (e.g., Reitsma, 1990) of the important role of practice to gain automaticity in decoding and to enhance "specific orthographic representation" with transfer effects to analogous untrained words (e.g., with similar rime units). Reitsma's emphasis on the development of orthographic knowledge is consonant with Perfetti's(1992) notion of redundancy and precision to enhance lexical representation, as discussed in earlier sections and in Leong (this volume).

The interaction of phonemic and graphemic processing is studied by **Assink** with twelve-year-old poor Dutch readers, compared with their reading age controls, in a series of Stroop-like computerized experiments on visual matching of real and pseudo Dutch words in congruent or incongruent alternating upper and lower cases, digit symbols and visual shapes in congruent or incongruent font sizes. The poor readers were found to be slower in reaction times than their controls on letter and digit matching, but not on visual figure matching. This slower performance by the poor readers with letter strings of evolving orthographic and phonologic complexity suggests an inefficiency in accessing graphemic and phonological cues. Assink proposes that studies of lettercase alternation at the graphemic level may shed light on the more precise role of orthographic knowledge in reading Dutch, as discussed by Reitsma (1990, this volume).

If Assink's data do not yield unequivocal answers on the role of orthographic processing in reading/spelling Dutch, **Coenen, van Bon and Schreuder** address specifically the issue of orthographic knowledge used by first and second grade Dutch readers/spellers. Coenen et al. also ask if such knowledge is used in reading prior to its use in spelling.

Making use of the linguistic principle that the Dutch phoneme /ɛi/ is almost always represented by the grapheme <ij> and the phoneme /ɑu/ is almost always represented by the grapheme <ou>, Coenen et al. examine the naming and spelling of computer-displayed words, pseudohomophones and pseudowords containing the Dutch /ɛi/ or /ɑu/ phonemes by these young Dutch readers/spellers. The logic of their study is that an advantage (shorter reaction times) of naming words over pseudowords might suggest the use of phonological representation; whereas an advantage of naming words over pseudohomophones might further implicate orthographic knowledge. Coenen et al. find some evidence that beginning readers of Dutch use grapheme-phoneme conversion rules, while competent readers show "parallel progress" in using syllable units to decode words as well.

The results of the Coenen et al. investigation of Dutch first and second graders' reading aloud and spelling of words seem compatible with the more current dual-route model of processing from print to speech, the dual-route cascaded (DRC) model of Coltheart, Curtis, Atkins, and Haller (1993). In this updated, modular, computational DRC version of the dual-route architecture, grapheme-phoneme conversion can go on in parallel with the lexical look-up in cascading processes rather than in threshold or discrete fashions. Cascading in an interactive-activation model of visual word recognition and naming emphasizes the immediate activation, through excitatory and inhibitory processes, of different levels of information (graphemic, phonemic and semantic).

This current dual-route cascaded (DRC) model of Coltheart et al. better explains the indirect and tentative findings of the two studies of **van den Bos and Spelberg** that real words and pseudowords are not differentially sensitive to different processing routes. These authors' suggestion of the need for readers to establish orthographic recognition units of different sizes for words with phonological underpinning is in line with Goswami's (1993) interactive-analogy model of reading development. This interactive-developmental approach also explains the inability of children with reading difficulties to use their inadequate phonological knowledge to facilitate orthographic analysis, and hence adding to their difficulties.

Phonological Development in Reading/Spelling Nordic Languages

In a longitudinal project with 248 Danish children, **Olofsson and Niedersøe** study the relative strengths of early language measures including speech comprehension and inflectional morphology at age 3 in predicting phonological awareness in kindergarten and word decoding in grade 2. Path analysis results show phonology in speech production, word memory and syllable and phoneme awareness as predictive of word reading and also considerable direct effect of the morphology variable. These results point to the importance of phonological training, as discussed by Catts et al., Dodd and Gillon, and others in this volume and elsewhere.

The "metalinguistic intervention programs" carried out by **Lyster** with 273 Norwegian preschool children emphasize internal sound structures (onsets and rimes) and morphological constituents (affixation and compounding). Her training results show that the target groups receiving metaphonological and metamorphological training benefit in their spelling, as compared with a control group, but there are differential effects of the kinds of training in relation to the education background of the mothers of the children.

The Lyster intervention programs with the inclusion of metamorphological training adds to the earlier, detailed research programs of Skjelfjord (1987a, 1987b), which provide explicit, systematic and "sequential" phonemic awareness and segmentation training to young Norwegian children in realistic school settings. Skjelfjord's emphasis on articulatory features in connection with the classification of phonemic segments is well supported by the theoretical position of phonemic manipulation underpinned by phonological representation (Fowler, 1991; Morais & Mousty, 1992), as discussed in earlier sections.

A different approach to training is used by **Korkeamäki** in her three qualitative studies with kindergarten and preschool Finnish children to instill the alphabetic principle of letter-sound correspondences in the context of child-centered, meaningful reading and writing through stories, nursery rhymes and games. We would agree with Korkeamäki's suggestion that involvement in meaningful literacy activities helps children to learn more about the written language, but would also emphasize the need for systematic training in phonological awareness especially for children "at risk", as shown by the effective training program of Lundberg et al. (1988). Both synthetic and analytic approaches in meaningful contexts are needed to promote literacy.

Phonemic Awareness in Word Reading in Chinese

The preceding chapters in the various sections have all shown the central role of phonemic awareness in learning to read/spell alphabetic languages ranging from the more transparent (e.g., Finnish) to the more opaque (e.g., English) in grapheme-phoneme correspondences. For more regular alphabetic languages such as Dutch, orthographic processing with multiletter units assumes an increasingly important role for older and more skilled readers. What about the case of Chinese word reading? Is phonological processing involved in reading Chinese characters and words, and if so in what way? These are some of the questions addressed in the chapter by Hanley and Huang.

Drawing on the earlier work of Read, Zhang, Nie and Ding (1986) on speech sounds manipulation of Chinese adults, **Hanley and Huang** examine the effects of phonological awareness (rhyming and alliteration) in spoken words, phoneme deletion tasks and visual skills on the reading ability of eight-year-old Chinese children in Taiwan and Hong Kong, compared with English children learning to read English in England.

One main finding of Hanley and Huang is that when vocabulary and non-verbal general ability were partialled out, the performance of the Chinese children in phoneme segmentation did not relate significantly to their reading. Similar results were obtained with a group of six-year-old Taiwanese children. The other main finding is that the Chinese children outperformed their British age-peers in deleting the initial phonemes from CCVC words with consonant clusters, but did worse than their controls in deleting the initial phonemes from CVCC words starting with single consonants. These results are explained by Hanley and Huang in terms of the syllable structure of Chinese characters and the way this knowledge may affect the performance of the children.

Spurred on by the much-quoted Read et al. study (1986) and the Hanley and Huang work and drawing on his research (e.g., Leong, 1986, 1995; Leong, Cheng, & Mulcahy, 1987; Leong & Hsia, 1996), Leong attempts to explain the way in which Chinese children come to understand and learn Chinese characters and words in "analytic reading" of Chinese. The emphasis is on the productivity of the language system to enable learners to transcribe new or possible lexical items (characters and words) to access the speech sound, internal structure and meaning of these items.

Leong discusses the morphosyllabic characteristic of Chinese and the inherent use of the "'universal' phonological principle" in accessing the internal lexicon (Perfetti & Zhang, 1995; Perfetti, Zhang, & Berent, 1992). He emphasizes the need in studies of learning to read/spell Chinese to examine linguistic variables, especially the internal structure of the Chinese syllable of initial (onset) and final (rime) further decomposable into peak and coda; and also prosodic elements of Chinese tone assignments in autosegmental phonology. His analysis of initial reading materials and actual classroom practices shows a clear multi-faceted approach of integrating the learning of speech sounds, configurations and meanings of Chinese characters and words. The approach to emergent literacy is one of analysis and synthesis through such activities as rhyme, alliteration, speech games, character/word recognition through graphemic parsing, and reading coupled with writing (spelling) reinforced with practice to gain automatic processing of these related subskills.

Summary and Prospect

As with any edited book, what may not be achieved completely in unity may be more than compensated for by the richness and diversity of the different studies with different approaches.   The present volume is no exception especially as diverse languages and orthographies are represented. In fact, careful reading of the various chapters reveals a fairly integrative theme running through them.   This is the theme of phonologic and orthographic processing, which is the subtitle of this volume.   Within this broad framework certain areas or topics emerge as worthy of continuing or further investigation.

One area is the more precise delineation of phonological processing as it relates to language and reading/spelling.   Sensitivity to the internal phonological structure of words provides a "bridge between language and literacy" (Morais, 1991b).   Now that this "bridge" is fairly well cemented as the result of some twenty years of research, the foundation or the underlying representation for the surface phonetic forms needs to be further consolidated.

Speech Perception and Production

Some of these aspects may relate to "articulatory awareness" (Morais, 1991b, p. 35) such as the effect of coarticulation on the development of segmental analysis (e.g., easier isolation of fricatives than stops); the role of stress assignment (e.g., the illiterates studied by the Brussels group being more sensitive to the stress part of the syllable than to the unstressed part); and the effect of phonetic categories on intervocalic rhythms (Treiman & Danis, 1988), among other aspects.

The spoken word as the "prosodic word" with its segments and features entails the study of the syllable with its constituents of onsets and rimes, as discussed in earlier sections and also by Macken (1992).   Macken argues forcefully for the learning of superordinate principles in phonology, which explain the properties of individual phonetic segments (e.g., /tr/ in TRAIN with the surface phonetic form of [tr]).

There are practical applications for instruction and remediation derived from the detailed study of speech perception and production.   As an example, the Lindamood-Bell Auditory Conceptualization Test-Revised (LACT-R) makes use of the "comparator function" in comparing phonological structures such as where and how syllables differ and the conceptualization of these differences (Lindamood, Bell, & Lindamood, 1992). These authors have provided print and interactive videodisc materials to enhance phonological awareness. The Skjelfjord (1987a, 1987b) training program with Norwegian children is another example of systematic training of the articulatory features and the concepts of the prosodic word. Awareness of articulatory gestures was part of the training program to tease out the effects of syllable and phoneme "supraphonemic" training in two longitudinal studies of preliterate Portuguese-speaking children (Cary & Verhaeghe, 1994). Cary and Verhaeghe confirmed the efficacy of training with phonemic and supraphonemic units in enhancing metaphonological ability, but did not find transfer of training in the non-linguistic visual area to the linguistic domain.

Graphemic Parsing in Orthographic Processing

The other aspect is the continued investigation of the nature and the role of orthographic processing in relation to emergent literacy. As discussed earlier, it is not easy to disentangle orthographic processing from phonological processing, and ways of assessing orthographic processing typically include such tasks as pseudohomophone-word choice (e.g., RUME-ROOM), exception word spelling (e.g., DENY) and the like, which also contain phonological elements (Foorman, 1994). Graphemic parsing is a necessary mechanism, though not a sufficient one, in converting print to sound.

As minimum contrastive units in writing, graphemes are analogous to, but not strictly parallel with, phonemes in spoken language (Venezky, 1970). Not dissimilar to phonemes with different phonetic realizations because of coarticulation effects, graphemes can assume different canonical forms in different orthographic environments (e.g., spelling for /sh/ palatalized as <t> as in NATION). Thus awareness of graphemic units such as the correct parsing of DEAF as <d> + <ea> + <f> or WINDY as WIND_Y is needed to reinforce phonological processing. In the case of morphologically complex words, knowledge of their internal, hierarchical structure is important. The ability to "see" the inner form of EQUALITY as being predictable from the base form EQUAL with vowel alternation and vowel reduction, and the lexical relatedness of SEPARATE and PARE is particularly critical for older readers/spellers. Leong and Parkinson (1995) have shown in four experiments with poor readers compared with their controls that such knowledge of lexical relatedness in derivational morphology is productive and is a possible source of reading difficulty.

We would agree with Ehri (1992) and Foorman (1994, 1995) that an integrative view of phonologic and orthographic processing is essential for the understanding of learning to read/spell. In his chapter in this volume, Leong offers some evidence for paradigmatic analysis in Chinese word reading and emphasizes the multi-level approach involving understanding of the speech sounds of words, their internal structure and their meaning in context in learning to read/spell Chinese. Even in the case of the transparent Spanish language there is some evidence that those learners who rely exclusively on grapheme-phoneme translation have great difficulties with long words, as Spanish has very few monosyllabic words (Sebastián-Gallés, 1991).

Making Connections

We would also like to think that conceptually the integrative view of learning to read/spell can be accommodated within the updated dual-route cascaded (DRC) model of reading of Coltheart et al. (1993) as the DRC architecture is computational and incorporates parallel-distributed processing approaches. Another viable theoretical model is the restrictive-interactive (R-I) model of Perfetti (1991, 1992). This model emphasizes the use of multiple sources of information in parallel in word identification and is a process "in which word representations acquire rich connections between phonemic and graphemic segments (redundancy) with reliable precise spellings (precision) uninformed by rules" (Perfetti, 1991, p. 43).

The integrative approach of phonologic and orthographic processing applies to both reading and spelling in young children as shown in the study of individual growth curve analysis of 80 first graders by Foorman, Francis, Novy, and Liberman (1991).There is also some suggestion that poor mastery of "phoneme-grapheme relational rules" may characterize spelling difficulties as shown by Joshi and Aaron (1991) in their detailed case studies of college students with "poor spelling".

Theoretically, reading and spelling may arise from the same lexical representative, although they differ in processing details, as delineated in the restrictive-interactive (R-I) model of reading of Perfetti (1991, 1992, in press). Furthermore, spelling is seen as a manifestation of high quality lexical representation (Perfetti, in press). Writing on the relations between learning to read and learning to spell, Shankweiler and Lundquist (1992) state that "both phonologic and morphologic aspects of linguistic awareness are relevant to success in spelling and reading" (p.182). Even though the reference here is to alphabetic languages, this statement applies with equal force to other language systems as well.

It could be expected that studies of the cognitive processes of spelling and their relationship to the cognitive processes of reading are fruitful endeavors for researchers and practitioners (see Brown & Ellis, 1994, for details). It could be further expected that studies of language and orthography systems in addition to English will add to our understanding of reading and spelling and their difficulties. As an example, research studies of the morphologically "rich" European languages such as Italian, Dutch and Swedish show that there are different clusters stored (stems for Italian, morphemes for Dutch) in the lexicon in lexical look-up and affixation in word formation (Jarvella, 1995). Productive roots also have a special status in Hebrew where infixation of vowel patterns between the consonants of the root morpheme brings about changes in orthographic and phonological structure (Frost & Katz, 1992). These are some of the findings to show that the interactive nature of orthography, phonology, morphology and meaning in different orthographies (Berninger, 1994, 1995; Frost & Katz, 1992) merits further intensive, detailed investigation.

Acknowledgment: We thank our authors for their contribution to this volume and for stimulating our thinking on learning to read and spell. The writing of this chapter is assisted in part by the Social Sciences and Humanities Research Council of Canada through SSHRC Research Grant No. 410-96-0186 awarded to Che Kan Leong. This assistance is gratefully acknowledged.

References

Aaron, P.G., & Joshi, R.M. (Eds.). (1989). *Reading and writing disorders in different orthographic systems.* Dordrecht: Kluwer Academic Publishers.

Adams, M.J. (1990). *Beginning to read: Thinking and learning about print.* Cambridge, MA: The MIT Press.

Aronoff, M. (1976). *Word formation in generative grammar.* Cambridge, MA: The MIT Press.

Berninger, V.W. (Ed.). (1994). *The varieties of orthographic knowledge. I: Theoretical and developmental issues.* Dordrecht: Kluwer Academic Publishers.

Berninger, V.W. (Ed.). (1995). *The varieties of orthographic knowledge. II: Relationships to phonology, reading, and writing.* Dordrecht: Kluwer Academic Publishers.

Brown, G.D.A., & Ellis, N.C. (Eds.). (1994). *Handbook of spelling: Theory, process and intervention.* Chichester: John Wiley.

Bruck, M., & Treiman, R. (1992). Learning to pronounce words: The limitations of analogies. *Reading Research Quarterly, 27,* 374-389.

Bybee, J. (1995). Diachronic and typological properties of morphology and their implications for representation. In L.B. Feldman (Ed.), *Morphological aspects of language processing* (pp. 225-246). Hillsdale, NJ: Lawrence Erlbaum.

Cary, L., & Verhaeghe, A. (1994). Promoting phonemic analysis ability among kindergartners. *Reading and Writing: An Interdisciplinary Journal, 6,* 251-278.

Coltheart, M., Curtis, B., Atkins, P., & Haller, M. (1993). Models of reading aloud: dual-route and parallel-distributed-processing approaches. *Psychological Review, 100,* 589-608.

DeFrancis, J. (1989). *Visible speech: The diverse oneness of writing systems.* Honolulu: University of Hawaii Press.

Denckla, M.B., & Rudel, R.G. (1976). Rapid automatized naming (R.A.N.): Dyslexia differentiated from other learning disabilities. *Neuropsychologia, 14,* 471-479.

Dodd, B., Leahy, J., & Hambly, G. (1989). Phonological disorders in children: Underlying cognitive deficits. *British Journal of Developmental Psychology, 7,* 55-71.

Downing, J. (Ed.). (1973). *Comparative reading.* New York: Macmillan.

Downing, J., & Valtin, R. (Eds.). (1984). *Language awareness and learning to read.* New York: Springer-Verlag.

Ehri, L.C. (1980). The development of orthographic images. In U. Frith (Ed.), *Cognitive processes in spelling* (pp. 311-338). London: Academic Press.

Ehri, L.C. (1987). Learning to read and spell words. *Journal of Reading Behavior, 19,* 5-31.

Ehri, L.C. (1992). Reconceptualizing the development of sight word reading and its relationship to recoding. In P.B. Gough, L.C. Ehri, & R. Treiman (Eds.), *Reading acquisition* (pp. 107-143). Hillsdale, NJ: Lawrence Erlbaum.

Ehri, L. C., & Robbins, C. (1992). Beginners need some decoding skill to read by analogy. *Reading Research Quarterly, 27,* 13-26.

Elbro, C., & Arnbak, E. (1996). The role of morpheme recognition and morphological awareness in dyslexia. *Annals of Dyslexia, 46,* (in press)

Elkonin, D.B. (1973). USSR. In J. Downing (Ed.), *Comparative reading* (pp. 551-579). New York: Macmillan.

Foorman, B.R. (1994). Phonological and orthographic processing: Separate but equal? In V.W. Berninger (Ed.), *The varieties of orthographic knowledge. I: Theoretical and developmental issues* (pp. 321-357). Dordrecht: Kluwer Academic Publishers.

Foorman, B.R. (1995). Practiced connections of orthographic and phonological processing. In V.W. Berninger (Ed.), *The varieties of orthographic knowledge. II: Relationships to phonology, reading, and writing* (pp. 377-419). Dordrecht: Kluwer Academic Publishers.

Foorman, B.R., & Francis, D.J. (1994). Exploring connections among reading, spelling, and phonemic segmentation during first grade. *Reading and Writing: An Interdisciplinary Journal, 6,* 65-91.

Foorman, B.R., Francis, D.J., Novy, D., & Liberman, D.(1991). How letter-sound instruction mediates progress in first-grade reading and spelling. *Journal of Educational Psychology, 83,* 456-469.

Fowler, A. E. (1991). How early phonological development might set the stage for phoneme awareness. In S.A. Brady & D.P. Shankweiler (Eds.), *Phonological processes in literacy: A tribute to Isabelle Y. Liberman* (pp. 97-117). Hillsdale, NJ: Lawrence Erlbaum.

Frith, U. (1985). Beneath the surface of developmental dyslexia. In K.E. Patterson, J.C. Marshall, & M. Coltheart (Eds.), *Surface dyslexia: Neuropsychological and cognitive studies of phonological reading* (pp. 301-330). London: Lawrence Erlbaum.

Frost, R., & Katz, L. (Eds.). (1992). *Orthography, phonology, morphology, and meaning.* Amsterdam: North-Holland.

Gelb, I.J. (1963). *A study of writing.* Chicago: University of Chicago Press.

Goswami, U. (1986). Children's use of analogy in learning to read: A developmental study. *Journal of Experimental Child Psychology, 42*, 73-83.

Goswami, U. (1988a). Orthographic analogies and reading development. *Quarterly Journal of Experimental Psychology, 40A*, 239-268.

Goswami, U. (1988b). Children's use of analogy in learning to spell. *British Journal of Developmental Psychology, 6*, 21-33.

Goswami, U. (1990). Phonological priming and orthographic analogies in reading. *Journal of Experimental Child Psychology, 49*, 323-340.

Goswami, U. (1993). Toward an interactive analogy model of reading development: Decoding vowel graphemes in beginning reading. *Journal of Experimental Child Psychology, 56*, 443-475.

Goswami, U., & Bryant, P. (1990). *Phonological skills and learning to read.* Hillsdale, NJ: Lawrence Erlbaum.

Greaney, K.T., & Tunmer, W.E. (1996). Onset/rime sensitivity and orthographic analogies in normal and poor readers. *Applied Psycholinguistics, 17*, 15-40.

Henry, M. K. (Ed.). (1993). The role of decoding in reading research and instruction [Special issue]. *Reading and Writing: An Interdisciplinary Journal, 5(2)*.

Høien, T., Lundberg, I., Stanovich, K.E., & Bjaalid, I.-K.(1995). Components of phonological awareness. *Reading and Writing: An Interdisciplinary Journal, 7*, 171-188.

Jarvella, R.J. (1995). Morphology in skilled word recognition. In C.K. Leong & R.M. Joshi (Eds.), *Developmental and acquired dyslexia: Neuropsychological and neurolinguistic perspectives* (pp. 221-236). Dordrecht: Kluwer Academic Publishers.

Joshi, R.M., & Aaron, P.G. (1991). Developmental reading and spelling disabilities: Are these dissociable? In R.M. Joshi (Ed.), *Written language disorders* (pp. 1-24). Dordrecht: Kluwer Academic Publishers.

Jusczyk, P.W., & Bertoncini, J. (1988). Viewing the development of speech perception as an innately guided learning process. *Language and Speech, 31*, 217-238.

Kavanagh, J.F., & Venezky, R.L. (Eds.), (1980). *Orthography, reading, and dyslexia*. Baltimore: University Park Press.

Kuhl, P. K. (1983). Perception of auditory equivalence classes for speech in early infancy. *Infant Behavior and Development, 6*, 263-285.

Landerl, K., Frith, U., & Wimmer, H. (1996). Intrusion of orthographic knowledge on phoneme awareness: Strong in normal readers, weak in dyslexic readers. *Applied Psycholinguistics, 17*, 1-14.

Leong, C.K. (1986). What does accessing a morphemic script tell us about reading and reading disorders in an alphabetic script? *Annals of Dyslexia, 36*, 82-102.

Leong, C.K. (1991). From phonemic awareness to phonological processing to language access in children developing reading proficiency. In D.J. Sawyer & B.J. Fox (Eds.), *Phonological awareness in reading: The evolution of current perspectives* (pp. 217-254). New York: Springer-Verlag.

Leong, C.K. (1995). Orthographic and psycholinguistic considerations in developing literacy in Chinese. In I. Taylor & D.R. Olson (Eds.), *Scripts and literacy: Reading, and learning to read alphabets, syllabaries and characters* (pp. 163-183).Dordrecht: Kluwer Academic Publishers.

Leong, C.K., Cheng, P. W., & Mulcahy, R. (1987). Automatic processing of morphemic orthography by mature readers. *Language and Speech, 30,* 181-197.

Leong, C.K., & Hsia, S. (1996). Cross-linguistic constraints on Chinese students learning English. In M.H. Bond (Ed.), *The handbook of Chinese psychology* (pp. 63-78 + ref.). New York: Oxford University Press.

Leong, C.K., & Parkinson, M.E. (1995). Processing of English morphological structure by poor readers. In C.K. Leong & R.M. Joshi (Eds.), *Developmental and acquired dyslexia: Neuropsychological and neurolinguistic perspectives* (pp. 237-261).Dordrecht: Kluwer Academic Publishers.

Leong, C.K., & Tamaoka, K. (1995). Use of phonological information in processing kanji and katakana by skilled and less skilled Japanese readers. *Reading and Writing: An Interdisciplinary Journal, 7,* 377-393.

Liberman, A.M., Cooper, F.S., Shankweiler, D.P., & Studdert-Kennedy, M. (1967). Perception of the speech code. *Psychological Review, 74,* 431-461.

Lindamood, P.C., Bell, N., & Lindamood, P. (1992). Issues in phonological awareness assessment. *Annals of Dyslexia, 42,* 242-259.

Lundberg, I. (1978). Aspects of linguistic awareness related to reading. In A. Sinclair, R.J. Jarvella, & W.J.M. Levelt (Eds.), *The child's conception of language* (pp. 83-96). New York: Springer-Verlag.

Lundberg, I., Frost, J., & Petersen, O.-P. (1988). Effects of an extensive program for stimulating phonological awareness in preschool children. *Reading Research Quarterly, 23,* 263-284.

Macken, M.A. (1992). Where's phonology? In C.A. Ferguson, L. Menn, & C. Stoel-Gammon (Eds.), *Phonological development: Models, research, implications* (pp. 249-269). Timonium, MD: York Press.

Morais, J. (1991a). Constraints on the development of phonemic awareness. In S.A. Brady & D.P. Shankweiler (Eds.), *Phonological processes in literacy: A tribute to Isabelle Y. Liberman* (pp. 5-27). Hillsdale, NJ: Lawrence Erlbaum.

Morais, J. (1991b). Phonological awareness: A bridge between language and literacy. In D.J. Sawyer & B.J. Fox (Eds.), *Phonological awareness in reading: The evolution of current perspectives* (pp. 31-71). New York: Springer-Verlag.

Morais, J. (Ed.). (1995). Literacy onset in Romance language [Special issue]. *Reading and Writing: An Interdisciplinary Journal, 7 (1).*

Morais, J., Alegria, J., & Content, A. (1987). The relationships between segmental analysis and alphabetic literacy: An interactive view. *Cahiers de Psychologie Cognitive, 7,* 415-438.

Morais, J., Bertelson, P., Cary, L., & Alegria, J. (1986).Literacy training and speech segmentation. *Cognition, 24,* 45-64.

Morais, J., & Mousty, P. (1992). The causes of phonemic awareness. In J. Alegria, D. Holender, J.J. de Morais, & M. Radeau (Eds.), *Analytic approaches to human cognition* (pp. 193-212).Amsterdam: North-Holland.

Olofsson, Å., & Lundberg, I. (1983). Can phonemic awareness be trained in kindergarten? *Scandinavian Journal of Psychology, 24,* 35-44.

Olofsson, Å., & Lundberg, I. (1985). Evaluation of long term effects of phonemic awareness training in kindergarten. Illustrations of some methodological problems in evaluation research. *Scandinavian Journal of Psychology, 26*, 21-34.

Otake, T., Hatano, G., Cutler, A., & Mehler, J. (1993). Mora or syllable? Speech segmentation in Japanese. *Journal of Memory and Language, 32*, 258-278.

Perfetti, C.A. (1991). Representations and awareness in the acquisition of reading competence. In L. Rieben & C.A. Perfetti (Eds.), *Learning to read: Basic research and its implications* (pp. 33-44). Hillsdale, NJ: Lawrence Erlbaum.

Perfetti, C.A. (1992). The representation problem in reading acquisition. In P.B. Gough, L.C. Ehri, & R. Treiman (Eds.), *Reading acquisition* (pp. 145-174). Hillsdale, NJ: Lawrence Erlbaum.

Perfetti, C. A. (in press). The psycholinguistics of spelling and reading. In C.A. Perfetti, L. Rieben, & M. Fayo (Eds.), *Learning to spell*. Hillsdale, NJ: Lawrence Erlbaum.

Perfetti, C.A., & Zhang, S. (1995). Very early phonological activation in Chinese reading. *Journal of Experimental Psychology: Learning, Memory and Cognition, 21*, 24-33.

Perfetti, C.A., Zhang, S., & Berent, I. (1992). Reading in English and Chinese: Evidence for a "universal" phonological principle. In R. Frost & L. Katz (Eds.), *Orthography, phonology, morphology, and meaning* (pp. 227-248). Amsterdam: North-Holland.

Peterson, M.E., & Haines, L.P. (1992). Orthographic analogy training with kindergarten children: Effects on analogy use, phonemic segmentation, and letter-sound knowledge. *Journal of Reading Behavior, 24*, 109-127.

Read, C., Zhang, Y.-F., Nie, H.-Y., & Ding, B.-W. (1986). The ability to manipulate speech sounds depends on knowing alphabetic writing. *Cognition, 24*, 31-44.

Reitsma, P. (1990). Development of orthographic knowledge. In P. Reitsma & L. Verhoeven (Eds.), *Acquisition of reading in Dutch* (pp. 43-64). Dordrecht: Foris Publications.

Reitsma, P., & Verhoeven, L. (1990). *Acquisition of reading in Dutch*. Dordrecht: Foris Publications.

Sawyer, D.J., & Fox, B.J. (Eds.). (1991). *Phonological awareness in reading: The evolution of current perspectives*. New York: Springer-Verlag.

Sebastián-Gallés, N. (1991). Reading by analogy in a shallow orthography. *Journal of Experimental Psychology: Human Perception and Performance, 17*, 471-477.

Shankweiler, D., & Liberman, I.Y. (1972). Misreading: A search for causes. In J.F. Kavanagh & I.G. Mattingly (Eds.), *Language by ear and by eye: The relationships between speech and reading* (pp. 293-317). Cambridge, MA: The MIT Press.

Shankweiler, D., & Lundquist, E. (1992). On the relations between learning to spell and learning to read. In R. Frost & L. Katz (eds.), *Orthography, phonology, and meaning* (pp. 179-192). Amsterdam: North-Holland.

Share, D. (1995). Phonological recoding and self-teaching: Sine qua non of reading acquisition. *Cognition, 55*, 151-218.

Skjelfjord, V.J. (1987a). Phonemic segmentation. An important subskill in learning to read: I. *Scandinavian Journal of Educational Research, 31*, 41-57.

Skjelfjord, V.J. (1987b). Phonemic segmentation. An important subskill in learning to read: II. *Scandinavian Journal of Educational Research, 31*, 81-98.

Stanback, M.L. (1992). Syllable and rime patterns for teaching reading: Analysis of a frequency-based vocabulary of 17,602 words. *Annals of Dyslexia, 42*, 196-221.

Stuart, M., & Coltheart, M. (1988). Does reading develop in a sequence of stages? *Cognition, 30*, 139-181.

Tallal, P. (1980). Auditory temporal perception, phonics, and reading disabilities in children. *Brain and Language, 9*, 182-198.

Tallal, P., Miller, S., & Fitch, R.H. (1993). Neurobiological basis of speech: A case for the preeminence of temporal processing. In P. Tallal, A.M. Galaburda, R.R. Llinás, & C. von Euler (Eds.), Temporal information processing in the nervous system: Special reference to dyslexia and dysphasia. *Annals of the New York Academy of Sciences, 682*, 27-47.

Taylor, I., & Olson, D.R. (Eds.). (1995). *Scripts and literacy: Reading and learning to read alphabets, syllabaries and characters.* Dordrecht: Kluwer Academic Publishers.

Treiman, R. (1985). Onsets and rimes as units of spoken syllables: Evidence from children. *Journal of Experimental Child Psychology, 39*, 161-181.

Treiman, R., & Danis, C. (1988). Syllabification of intervocalic consonants. *Journal of Memory and Language, 27*, 87-104.

Treiman, R., Goswami, U., & Bruck, M. (1990). Not all nonwords are alike: Implications for reading development and theory. *Memory and Cognition, 18*, 559-567.

Treiman, R., & Zukowski, A. (1996). Children's sensitivity to syllables, onsets, rimes, and phonemes. *Journal of Experimental Child Psychology, 61*, 193-215.

Venezky, R.L. (1970). *The sound structure of English orthography.* The Hague: Mouton.

Wimmer, H. (1993). Characteristics of developmental dyslexia in a regular writing system. *Applied Psycholinguistics, 14*, 1-33.

Wimmer, H. (1996). The nonword reading deficit in developmental dyslexia: Evidence from children learning to read German. *Journal of Experimental Child Psychology, 61*, 80-90.

Wimmer, H., Landerl, K., Linortner, R., & Hummer, P. (1991).The relationship of phonemic awareness to reading acquisition: More consequence than precondition but still important. *Cognition, 40*, 219-249.

Wolf, M. (1986). Rapid alternating stimulus naming in the developmental dyslexias. *Brain and Language, 27*, 360-379.

Wolf, M. (1991). Naming-speed and reading: The contribution of the cognitive neurosciences. *Reading Research Quarterly, 26*, 123-141.

Wolf, M., Pfeil, C., Lotz, R., & Biddle, K. (1994). Towards a more universal understanding of the developmental dyslexias: The contribution of orthographic factors. In V.W. Berninger (Ed.), *The varieties of orthographic knowledge I: Theoretical and developmental issues* (pp. 137-171). Dordrecht: Kluwer Academic Publishers.

Yopp, H.K. (1988). The validity and reliability of phonemic awareness tests. *Reading Research Quarterly, 23*, 159-177.

TOWARD AN UNDERSTANDING OF PHONOLOGICAL AWARENESS

HUGH W. CATTS, KIM A. WILCOX, CARLA WOOD-JACKSON, LINDA S. LARRIVEE, AND VICTORIA G. SCOTT
Speech-Language-Hearing: Sciences and Disorders
University of Kansas
3031 Dole
Lawrence, Kansas 66045-2181

ABSTRACT: Numerous studies have documented a relationship between phonological awareness and reading achievement. Despite this work, phonological awareness and its development are not well understood. This chapter examines phonological awareness, first by considering how it has been measured, and then, by studying factors related to performance on a frequently used measure of phonological awareness. A review of the literature showed that numerous tasks have been used to measure children's awareness of phonemes. These can be divided into phoneme segmentation, phoneme blending, and sound comparison tasks. It is proposed that performance on phoneme segmentation and phoneme blending tasks is heavily influenced by experience with an alphabetic writing system. An investigation of a commonly used sound comparison task, the oddity task, suggested that performance on this task was dependent in part on chidren's perceptual and memory abilities.

During the last 20 years, the construct of phonological awareness has received considerable attention in the psychological and educational literature (Golinkoff, 1978; Liberman & Shankweiler, 1985; Sawyer & Fox, 1991; Stanovich, 1988; Tunmer, Pratt, & Herriman, 1984; Wagner & Torgesen, 1987). For the most part, this attention is the consequence of the strong association that has been found between phonological awareness and early reading ability. Numerous studies have shown a relationship between the awareness of speech sounds and reading achievement (e.g., Bradley & Bryant, 1983; Fox & Routh, 1975; Juel, Griffith, & Gough, 1986; Liberman, Shankweiler, Fischer, & Carter, 1974; Morais, Bertelson, Cary, & Alegria, 1986; Treiman & Baron, 1981; Tunmer & Nesdale, 1985). Many investigations have further provided evidence that phonological awareness plays a causal role in learning to read an alphabetic orthography (e.g., Bradley & Bryant, 1985; Lundberg, Frost, & Petersen, 1988; Mann & Liberman, 1984; Stanovich, Cunningham, & Cramer, 1984; Torgesen, Wagner, & Rashotte, 1994).

Despite the emphasis placed on phonological awareness, the nature of this construct remains somewhat elusive. Presently, there is little consensus in the literature on how best to define phonological awareness. Definitions

C.K. Leong and R.M. Joshi (Eds.), Cross-Language Studies of Learning to Read and Spell, 31–52.
© 1997 *Kluwer Academic Publishers. Printed in the Netherlands.*

often include such subjective terms as "sensitivity," "reflection", or "conscious awareness" of speech sounds. Furthermore, speech sounds may include allophones, phonemes, onsets and rimes, syllables, or words. With such imprecise definitions, it is difficult to determine what phonological awareness encompasses and how specifically it is related to reading. In this paper, we address the question of what phonological awareness is, first by considering how it has been measured, and then by examining factors related to performance on a common measure of phonological awareness.

Measuring Phonological Awareness

One way of gaining insight into the nature of phonological awareness is by examining the manner in which phonological awareness has been assessed (Lewkowicz, 1980; Nesdale, Herriman, & Tunmer, 1984; Stahl & Murray, 1994; Yopp, 1988). Recently, Catts and Scott (1994) reviewed approximately 100 investigations for the last 30 years in which phonological awareness was assessed. Reports of these investigations appeared in 31 professional journals and 11 books. They involved subjects who spoke a variety of languages including English (Bradley & Bryant, 1983), Italian (Cossu, Shankweiler, Liberman, Katz, & Tola, 1988), Hebrew (Bentin & Leshem, 1993), German (Wimmer, Landerl, Linortner, & Hummer, 1991), Portuguese (Morais, Cary, Alegria, & Bertelson, 1979), Swedish (Lundberg, Olofsson, & Wall, 1980), Norwegian (Skjelfjord, 1987), and Mandarin (Read, Zhang, Nie, & Ding, 1986).

Our review indicated that numerous tasks have been employed to assess phonological awareness. In these tasks, participants have been asked to segment, manipulate, produce, or make judgments about speech sound units varying in size and level of abstraction. In this paper, we will focus on only those tasks which involve the apparent awareness of phoneme-size units (i.e., phoneme awareness). As a result, we exclude tasks used to measure awareness of rhyme, syllables, or words (e.g., phonological length).

The results of our review indicated that over 20 tasks have been employed to measure awareness of phonemes. These tasks can be divided into three broad categories: phoneme segmentation, phoneme synthesis, and sound comparison. Descriptions of these tasks are included in Appendix A, along with a short list of relevant citations (see Catts & Scott, 1994 for further citations).

Phoneme Segmentation

The first category of measures consists of tasks that require subjects to count, produce, or somehow denote (tapping, representing them with a token) the number of phonemes in words (see Table 1). Variations on this format include deleting, adding, subtracting, or reversing phonemes. What these various tasks have in common is the need for subjects to segment a syllable or word into phonemes. In other words, in order to complete these tasks subjects must be able to explicitly extract and attend to sub-syllabic phonetic units roughly corresponding to a phoneme. Such a level of awareness is generally necessary in order to delete these units, count them, or represent them with tokens. This awareness has been referred to as segmental awareness (Morais, 1991), phoneme analysis (Torgesen, Morgan, & Davis, 1992), or phoneme segmentation (Liberman & Shankweiler, 1979).

Table 1. Categories of phoneme awareness tasks

Phoneme Awareness Tasks

Phoneme Segmentation

- Tapping
- Counting
- Tokens
- Say Sounds
- Deletion
- Addition
- Reversal
- Metathesis
- Substitution
- Pig Latin
- Invented Spelling

Phoneme Blending

- Synthesis

Sound Comparison

- Same/Different
- Match to Sample
- Oddity
- Sound Detection
- Alliteration

Phoneme segmentation, as described above, does not seem to come naturally to most young children. Phonemes are inherently abstract units. In most linguistic theories, the phoneme is the abstract element responsible for distinguishing meaning (Bloomfield, 1933). Although important as a unit at this tacit, representational level, the phoneme does not exist as a discrete element in articulation or in the speech signal (Liberman, Cooper, Shankweiler, & Studdert-Kennedy, 1967). Phonemes are realized in speech as part of coarticulated syllabic segments. Thus, one cannot simply divide articulation or the resultant acoustic signal into phonemes. One can, however, given the appropriate experience or training, come to appreciate the existence of speech sound units or articulatory gestures roughly equivalent to phonemes. For example, children may have their attention repeatedly drawn to the fact that words begin/end in the same way, and as a result, come to assign a unit value (phoneme) to these beginnings and endings. Such a realization, however, does not generally emerge from the everyday use of speech. Children produce and perceive phonemes with little explicit attention given to these language units. For most children, awareness of phonemes seems to come as a result of learning an alphabetic orthography (Stuart & Coltheart, 1988). An alphabetic writing system is based on the principle that graphemes in print represent phonemes (actually, phonetic segments) in speech. Learning grapheme-phoneme correspondence requires children to extract and attend to the phonemes that graphemes represent. Therefore, in a sense, graphemes serve as the medium by which most children come to appreciate phonemes (Morais, 1991). Without this alphabetic experience, children may not reach this level of speech sound awareness. Indeed, research has documented the difficulties prereaders (Lundberg & Hoien, 1991; Stahl & Murray, 1994), illiterates (Morais et al., 1979), and readers of a nonalphabetic orthography (Read et al., 1986) have with phoneme segmentation tasks.

It is not surprising that performance on phoneme segmentation tasks will be heavily influenced by children's literacy experiences. Children who have had more exposure to grapheme-phoneme correspondence, either through formal instruction or informal literacy activities, will likely have a greater appreciation of phonemes and will perform better on phoneme segmentation tasks than will children with less literacy experience. It is also possible that for some children the feedback provided during the instruction and initial phases of many phoneme segmentation tasks (e.g., Lindamood & Lindamood, 1975) may serve as training in phoneme awareness. Thus, performance on some phoneme segmentation tasks, those in which feedback is provided, may be an indication of children's ability to learn to explicitly segment phonemes. Therefore, individual differences in children's literacy experiences and their ability to benefit from phoneme-level feedback may account for much of the variability in the performance observed in phoneme segmentation tasks. By extension, phoneme segmentation tasks that provide explicit feedback may be especially effective for the prediction of later reading ability. Children who perform well on these tasks would be expected to acquire reading and spelling skills more easily than those children who perform poorly.

Phoneme Blending

The second category of phoneme awareness tasks consists essentially of one type of measure, the phoneme synthesis or phoneme blending task. In this task, children are presented with spoken allophones (or syllables) and are asked to blend these units together to produce a word or nonword (Chall, Roswell, & Blumenthal, 1963; Perfetti, Beck, Bell, & Hughes, 1988; Torneus,

1984; Yopp, 1988). The linguistic and cognitive demands of this measure of phoneme awareness are not well understood. Presumably, children need to have some rudimentary knowledge of the phoneme as a unit of speech in order to perform the task. Phoneme blending seems to require that the child be able to assign a phoneme value to each allophone and then combine these at some abstract level in order to form the targeted word. Evidence that this task requires segmental knowledge comes from studies showing that prereaders are generally unsuccessful in phoneme blending tasks (e.g., Lundberg & Hoien, 1991). Furthermore, other studies show a dramatic increase in children's performance on phoneme blending tasks between the ages of 6 and 7 years (Torgesen & Morgan, 1990; Torgesen, Wagner, Balthazar, Davis, Morgan, Simmons, Stage, & Zips, 1989). This, of course, corresponds with beginning reading instruction which, as noted above, facilitates phoneme segmentation ability.

Sound Comparison

The third category of phoneme awareness tasks consists of measures involving sound comparisons. Included in this category, are tasks that require children to judge the similarities/differences in the phonemes of words in a same-different, match-to-sample, or oddity format. Other tasks in this category require children to judge if a target sound is contained in a word or to produce a word that contains a target sound. What these tasks seem to have in common is the need for children to make comparisons between the sounds of words. Such sound comparison is clearly necessary in the same-different, match-to-sample, oddity, and sound detection tasks. In the sound production task, sound comparison is also a likely component. In order to produce a word that begins/ends with a target sound, children may compare the phonetic structure of words in their lexicon with the target sound until a match is found.[1]

There is an important difference between phoneme awareness tasks in this third category and those in the first two categories. Segmentation and blending tasks require children to appreciate the phoneme as a unit of speech and to be able to segment or blend phonetic units corresponding to phonemes. While phoneme segmentation skills are potentially useful to children in sound comparison tasks, they are not necessary for successful completion of these tasks. To make judgments about the similarities/differences in the sounds of words, children do not have to segment these sounds. Instead, children can make comparisons based on

---

[1] Other strategies are also available to the child. For example, a child may use his/her orthographic knowledge by selecting a word from his/her lexicon that begins with the letter representing the target sound.

unanalyzed forms. For example, to judge if "sit" and "soap" begin with the same sound, children need not have a segmented representation of each word available to them. Rather, they need only make a similarity judgment about whether these unanalyzed forms begin in a similar phonetic (or acoustic) manner. The same is true in the sound detection task. To detect if a given word begins with a target sound, children are required only to compare the target sound to the phonetic form of the given word. Again, children do not have to explicitly segment the word in order to recognize that it contains the target phonetic unit.

Further evidence that sound comparison tasks may not require phoneme segmentation abilities comes from research that has employed these tasks with nonreaders. This work has shown that adult illiterates (Morais, 1991) and children with very little literacy experience (Maclean, Bryant, & Bradley, 1988) can perform successfully on the sound detection and/or the oddity tasks. Given that nonreaders do not generally have phoneme segmentation abilities, it is likely that the participants in these studies were using other strategies to successfully perform these tasks. It is our contention that they were making speech sound judgments on the basis of unanalyzed forms.

Unlike phoneme segmentation which appears, in part, to be a consequence of initial instruction in reading, the ability to make speech sound comparisons may be an important antecedent for learning to read. Clearly, the ability of children to accurately and quickly make judgments concerning sound similarity/difference could be an asset in learning the alphabetic code. For example, children who can easily identify that words begin in the same manner, may more readily learn to represent these words with the same letter. Several lines of research also support this contention. For example, numerous studies have shown that young children's performance on sound comparison tasks are predictive of later reading ability (Maclean, et al., 1988; Stanovich, et al., 1984). In addition, research shows that training in sound comparison activities may influence reading ability. Specifically, Byrne and Fielding-Barnsley (1990) found that teaching prereaders to recognize similarities in the beginning sounds of words facilitated their acquisition of the alphabetic principle. Interestingly, this training was shown to be more successful in facilitating reading than was training in phoneme segmentation.

In the past, sound comparison tasks have simply been accepted as measures of phonological awareness with little attention given to the parameters or variables that might influence performance on these tasks (but see Treiman & Zukowski, 1991). However, to understand these tasks and their relationship to cognitive and reading abilities, we need to identify the variables that influence performance. In the study described below, we investigated some of the variables related to performance on one sound comparison task, the phoneme oddity task.

Factors Influencing Phoneme Oddity Performance

The phoneme oddity task is one of the most frequently used measures of phonological awareness in young children (Bradley & Bryant, 1983; Felton & Brown, 1990; Mann, 1993; Torgesen & Bryant, 1994). In this task, a child is asked to choose among three (or four) spoken words, the word that begins/ends with a different phoneme (i.e., odd word) than the other words (i.e., like words). This task requires skills in phonological perception in order to make phonological distinctions between the target sounds in the stimulus words. The task also appears to be a memory task. It requires participants to hold a series of words in memory and compare the initial or final segments (as noted above, not necessarily phonemic segments) in order to discern which one differs from the others. In this initial study, we investigated the role of phonological perception factors in explaining individual differences in children's performance on the oddity task. We reasoned that if phonological perception ability was an important component of the oddity task, then factors related to this ability would influence performance. For example, it is well documented that the phonetic similarity between speech sounds plays a role in subjects' ability to make perceptual distinctions (Wang & Bilger, 1973). If the stimuli in the oddity task were controlled such that the target phoneme of the odd word differed minimally from that of the like words, then subjects might be expected to perform less well than if it differed maximally.

To investigate the above hypothesis, we administered a phoneme oddity task to 30 children between the ages of 5 years, 8 months and 6 years, 9 months (mean age = 6 years, 2 months). None of the children had a history of speech, language, or hearing problems and all performed within normal limits on tests of speech sound production, vocabulary, and grammar. Subjects were tested during the second half of their kindergarten school year.

A phoneme oddity task, consisting of 3 practice and 16 test trials, was constructed for this investigation (see Appendix B). The phonological characteristics of the initial phonemes in the stimulus words were manipulated to create 2 levels of phonological contrast across trials. These levels were defined as maximally contrasted and minimally contrasted. For each of the eight maximally contrasted trials, the initial phonemes in the like words contrasted with the initial phoneme of the odd word by place of articulation, manner of articulation, and voicing (Shriberg & Kent, 1982). Also, these initial phoneme contrasts exhibited a subjective rating of 4.5 or higher on a 5.0 dissimilarity scale (Singh, Woods, & Becker, 1972) and evidenced few confusions in noise by adult listeners (Wang & Bilger, 1973). The other eight trials were designated as minimally contrasted trials. On each of these trials, the initial phonemes of the like words contrasted with the initial phoneme of the odd word by only one feature (place, manner, or voicing). These contrasts were further found to have a subjective rating of less than 4.0 on a 5.0 dissimilarity scale (Singh, et al., 1972) and evidenced frequent confusions in noise by adult listeners (Wang & Bilger, 1973).

Previous research has suggested that some young children may rely on global similarities/differences in the stimulus words when performing the oddity task rather than just using the acoustic/phonetic cues of the initial phoneme (Byrne & Fielding-Barnsley, 1993; Treiman & Breaux, 1982). To control for possible effects of global similarity, dissimilarity rating scales (Singh & Woods, 1971; Singh, et al., 1972) were used to ensure that the vowel and final consonant of the like words were not disproportionately more similar to each other than they were to the vowel and consonant of the odd word. Stimulus words in the oddity task were also selected such that items on minimally contrasted trials had a similar frequency of occurrence in English to items on the maximally contrasted trials (Frances & Kucera, 1982).

During testing, subjects were shown a picture of each of the stimulus words as the examiner individually produced the words. Following presentation of the third item in the triad, subjects were asked to point to the picture of the word that began with a different sound than the others. The examiner provided feedback only on the practice trials. Stimulus trials were presented to subjects in a fixed quasi-random order. For both maximally and minimally contrasted trials, the odd word occurred 2 times in the first position of the stimulus triad, 3 times in the second position, and 3 times in the third position.

Our results demonstrated that children did well overall on the phoneme oddity task, achieving an average of 70.1% correct. However, participants performed differently on the maximally and minimally contrasted trials. As predicted, the children scored significantly better (p. <.01) on the maximally contrasted trials (mean = 77.9%, SD = 23.1%) than they did on the minimally contrasted trials (mean = 64.6%, SD = 25.2%). This finding supports our hypothesis that phonological perception influences performance on the phoneme oddity task.

Whereas our prediction concerning phonological perception held true, our findings may be a bit surprising to some, especially those familiar with developmental speech perception research. This research indicates that very young children are able to make fine perceptual distinctions between the initial sounds of words, including those of the type found in our minimally contrasted set (Eilers & Minifie, 1975; Eimas, 1975; Morse, 1972). So why then do the children in this study fail some items on the oddity task and why do they exhibit differences in performance on maximally and minimally contrasted items? The answer may lie in differences in both the stimuli and in the procedures used in phonological awareness tasks versus those used in speech perception measures.

In most speech perception studies involving initial consonant judgments, the vowel or vowel-consonant context of the stimuli is held constant, so that stimulus items vary only in the initial consonant (e.g., ba vs. pa). This simplifies perceptual judgments by reducing the allophonic variation across stimulus items. By contrast, in the present study and in most other studies of phonological awareness, the vowel-consonant context varies considerably. Thus, the variability resulting from different vowel-consonants may increase the difficulty of the entire protocol. This by itself, however, would not seem to account for the inconsistency in the findings of our study and those of speech perception studies. Kuhl (1980), for example, has shown that infants can make discriminations of perceptually similar consonants even when the vowel context is allowed to vary.

Another stimulus variable might also contribute to the present findings. Most studies that have employed the oddity task as a measure of phonological awareness have used real words as stimuli. Speech perception research, on the other hand, has generally employed nonsense syllables as stimuli. Perhaps the activation of semantic meaning in the tasks diverts the listener's attention away from the phonetic detail available in the stimuli and thus decreases performance. To test this hypothesis, future studies might compare children's performance on the oddity task using phonetically comparable stimuli which are both real and nonsense words.

A more likely explanation for the discrepancies between the findings of our study and those of speech perception research concerns the manner in which phonetic contrasts are presented. Previous work (Burns & Ward, 1978; Carney, Widin, & Viemeister, 1977) has shown that performance is affected by the degree of listener uncertainty concerning the stimuli employed in a task. Specifically, this research indicates that listeners perform significantly better when the same stimulus contrast is repeatedly presented than when stimulus contrasts vary from trial to trial. In most developmental speech perception studies, numerous trials are devoted to a small number of phonetic contrasts. In fact, an entire study may be centered around one phonetic contrast. As a result, the participants have ample opportunity to focus their attention on the phonetic contrast of concern and on the specific acoustic cues which signify that contrast. In our study and other studies of phonological awareness, numerous phonetic contrasts are tested in a single assessment. In addition, as few as one trial may be devoted to each contrast. The participants are, thus, given little chance to focus on a particular phonetic contrast. Rather, they must constantly change their frame of reference from one trial to the next. This lack of stimulus consistency across trials may make the oddity task as used in phonological awareness research more difficult than that used in speech perception research.

The differences in performance noted in phonological awareness and speech perception testing might also be a reflection of the number of responses analyzed. It is not unusual to collect hundreds of responses from each subject (and perhaps for each contrast) in studies of speech perception. By contrast, most studies of phonological awareness rely on responses to ten to fifteen trials. Thus, it is possible that data from phonological awareness tasks do not represent asymptotic performance by listeners. Instead, listeners may still be learning the task and improving their performance when the testing session ends. The likelihood that these tasks yield non-asymptotic performance is increased by the level of stimulus uncertainty presented to listeners in phonological awareness tasks.

Recall, that memory abilities may also play a role in children's performance on the oddity task. Although memory factors were not targeted directly for investigation, our results suggest that children's memory does affect their performance on the oddity task. Our findings indicated that subjects' performance was influenced by the position of the odd word in the stimulus triad. Results showed that subjects performed significantly better when the odd word was in the third position (mean = 87.7%) than when it was in the first (mean = 50.8%) or second position (mean = 67.0%). There was also a significant difference between subjects' performance when the odd word was in the first than when it was in the second position. Figure 1 shows this pattern was similar for both maximally and minimally contrasted trials. The difference between maximally and minimally contrasted trials was somewhat smaller in the final position. However, the interaction between level of contrast and position was not found to be statistically significant. These results are suggestive of a recency effect in children's performance. That is, the more recent the occurrence of the odd word, the more accurate the response. This effect may be interpreted as indicating that children's memory for the odd word fades over the length of the stimulus triad. This suggests, therefore, that individual differences in memory ability may account for some of the variability in children's performance on the oddity task. Conclusions concerning the role of memory in the oddity task should be considered to be tentative at this time. The present study was not designed specifically to address this issue. Only limited opportunities were available for evaluating children's performance across triad positions. Future studies will need to consider more specifically the role of memory abilities in the oddity task.

Implications and Conclusions

Our findings demonstrated ·that phonological perceptual factors influenced children's performance on the phoneme oddity task. Children performed significantly better when oddity judgments involved phonetically dissimilar contrasts than when these judgments involved phonetically similar contrasts. In addition, children were increasingly more accurate in their sound judgments as the correct response occurred later in the stimulus triad. The latter results suggest that memory factors contribute to children's performance on the oddity task.

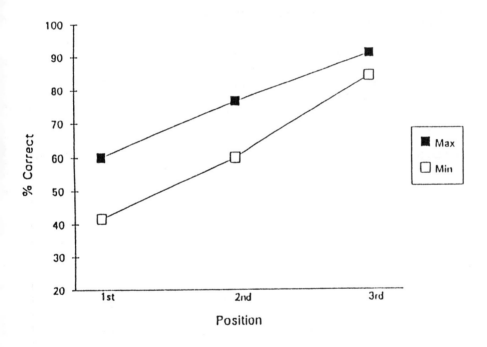

Figure 1. Percentage correct for participants on the maximally and minimally contrasted trials across each position of occurrence of the odd word.

The results of this study are important because they contribute to our understanding of both phonological awareness and the tasks that are commonly used to measure this awareness. In the past, the phoneme oddity task and many other sound awareness tasks have been taken on face value as measures of phonological awareness with little examination of the factors that underlie performance on these tasks. As a result, phonological awareness has remained an elusive construct. The systematic investigation of sound awareness tasks may help take away some of the mystery that surrounds phonological awareness and brings this construct in line with other psychological constructs (e.g., hearing sensitivity or pitch perception) that have been systematically described and investigated. Furthermore, a detailed analysis of these tasks should help us refine their format and increase their diagnostic sensitivity or applicability (e.g., allow us to set and control the ceiling or basal performance levels). Knowing which variables affect performance on phonological awareness tasks may also provide us with insight into the origins or developmental precursors of phonological awareness. The present study, for instance, suggests that early development of phonological perception and memory may be related to later phonological awareness. Furthermore, systematic research of phonological awareness tasks may provide us with valuable information concerning the relationship between phonological awareness and early reading achievement. For example, we may find that certain variables associated with phonological awareness tasks are more closely related to reading than others.

In sum, it is hoped that this work stimulates further investigation of the stimuli and paradigms used in phonological awareness testing. Such investigation will help to provide a better understanding of the construct of phonological awareness and the measures used to assess it.

REFERENCES

Bloomfield, L. (1933). *Language.* New York: Holt, Rinehart, &Winston.

Bentin, S., & Leshem, H. (1993).   On the interaction between phonological awareness and reading acquisition: It's a two way street. *Annals of Dyslexia, 43,* 125-148.

Bradley, L., & Bryant, P. (1983).   Categorizing sounds and learning to read: A causal connection. *Nature, 301,* 419-421.

Bradley, L., & Bryant, P. (1985).   Rhyme and reason in reading and spelling.   Ann Arbor, MI.: University of Michigan Press.

Burns, E., & Ward, W. (1978).   Categorical perception-phenomenon or epiphenomenon: Evidence from experiments in the perception of melodic musical intervals. *Journal of the Acoustical Society of America, 63,* 456-468.

Byrne, B., & Fielding-Barnsley, R. (1990). Acquiring the alphabetic principle: A case for teaching recognition of phoneme identity. *Journal of Educational Psychology, 82*, 805-812.

Byrne, B., & Fielding-Barnsley, R. (1991). Evaluation of a program to teach phonemic awareness to young children. *Journal of Educational Psychology, 83*, 451-455.

Byrne, B., & Fielding-Barnsley, R. (1993). Recognition of phoneme invariance by beginning readers. *Reading and Writing: An Interdisciplinary Journal, 5*, 315-324.

Byrne, B., & Ledz, J., (1983). Phonological awareness in reading-disabled adults. *Australian Journal of Psychology, 35*, 185-197.

Carney, A., Widin, G., & Viemeister, N. (1977). Noncategorical perception of stop consonants differing in VOT. *Journal of the Acoustical Society of America, 62.* 961-970.

Catts, H. (1993). The relationship between speech-language impairments and reading disabilities. *Journal of Speech and Hearing Research, 36*, 948-958.

Catts, H., & Scott, V. (1994). *Measuring phonological awareness.* Working paper of the Kansas Early Childhood Research Institute. University of Kansas.

Chall, J., Roswell, F., & Blumenthal, S. (1963). Auditory blending ability: A factor of success in beginning reading. *Reading Teacher, 17*, 113-118.

Cossu, G., Shankweiler, D., Liberman, I., Katz, L., & Tolar, G. (1988). Awareness of phonological segments and reading ability in Italian children. *Applied Psycholinguistics, 9*, 1-16.

Ehri, L. (1989). The development of spelling knowledge and its role in reading acquisition and reading disability. *Journal of Learning Disabilities, 22*, 356-364.

Ehri, L., Wilce, L., & Taylor, B. (1988). Children's categorization of short vowels in words and the influence of spellings. In K. Stanovich (Ed.), *Children's reading and the development of phonological awareness.* (pp.149-177). Detroit: Wayne State University Press.

Eilers, R., & Minifie, F. (1975). Fricative discrimination in early infancy. *Journal of Speech and Hearing Research, 18*, 158-167.

Eimas, P. (1975). Auditory and phonetic coding of the cues for speech: Discrimination of the [r-1] distinction by young infants. *Perception & Psychophysics, 18*, 341-347.

Felton, R., & Brown, I. (1990). Phonological processing as predictors of specific reading skills in at risk for reading failure. *Reading and Writing: An Interdisciplinary Journal, 2*, 39-59.

Foster, K., Erickson, G., Foster, D., Brinkman, D., & Torgesen. J. (1994). Computer administered instruction in phonological awareness: Evaluation of the DaisyQuest Program. *Journal of Research and Development in Education, 17*, 126-137.

Fox, B., & Routh, D. (1975). Analyzing language into words, syllables, and phonemes: A developmental study. *Journal of Psychological Research, 4*, 331-342.

Frances, W., & Kucera, H. (1982). *Frequency analysis of English usage: Lexicon and grammar.* Boston: Houghton Mifflin Company.

Golinkoff, R. (1978). Critique: Phonemic awareness skills and reading achievement. In F. Murray & J. Pikulski (Eds.), *The acquisition of reading: Cognition, linguistic, and perceptual prerequisites* (pp. 23-41). Baltimore: University Park Press.

Juel, C., Griffith, P., & Gough, P. (1986). Acquisition of literacy: A longitudinal study of children in first and second grades. *Journal of Educational Psychology, 78,* 243-255.

Kamhi, A., & Catts, H. (1986). Toward an understanding of developmental language and reading disorders. *Journal of Speech and Hearing Disorders, 51,* 337-347.

Kuhl, P. (1980). Perceptual constancy for speech-sound categories in early infancy. In G. Yeni-Komshian, J. Kavanagh, & C. Ferguson (Eds.), *Child Phonology: Vol. 2. Perception* (pp. 41-66). New York: Academic Press.

Lenchner, O., Gerber, M., & Routh, D. (1990). Phonological awareness tasks as predictors of decoding ability: Beyond segmentation. *Journal of Learning Disabilities, 23,* 240-247.

Lewis, B. & Freebairn, L. (1992). Residual effects of preschool phonology disorders in grade school, adolescence, and adulthood. *Journal of Speech and Hearing Research, 35,* 819-831.

Lewkowicz, M. (1980). Phonemic awareness training: What to teach and how to teach it. *Journal of Educational Psychology, 72,* 686-700.

Liberman, A., Cooper, F., Shankweiler, D., & Studdert-Kennedy, M. (1967). Perception of the speech code. *Psychological Review, 24,* 431-461.

Liberman, I.Y., & Shankweiler, D. (1979). Speech, the alphabet, and teaching to read. In L. Resnick & P. Weaver (eds.) *Theory and practice of early reading.* (vol 2, pp. 109-132). Hillsdale, New Jersey: Lawrence Erlbaum Associates.

Liberman, I.Y., & Shankweiler, D, (1985). Phonology and the problems of learning to read and write. *Remedial and Special Education, 6,* 8-17.

Liberman, I.Y., Shankweiler, D., Fischer, F., & Carter, B. (1974). Explicit syllable and phoneme segmentation in young children. *Journal of Experimental Child Psychology, 18,* 201-212.

Lindamood, C. & Lindamood, P. (1975). *The A.D.D. program: Auditory discrimination in depth.* (2nd ed.) Allen, TX: DLM, Inc.

Lundberg, I., Frost, J., & Petersen, O. (1988). Effects of an extensive program for stimulating phonological awareness in preschool children. *Reading Research Quarterly, 23,* 263-284.

Lundberg, I., & Hoien, T. (1991). Initial enabling knowledge and skills in reading acquisition: Print awareness and phonological segmentation. In D. Sawyer & B. Fox (Eds.), *Phonological awareness in reading: The evolution of current perspectives* (pp. 73-95). New York: Springer-Verlag.

Lundberg, I., Olofsson, A., & Wall. S. (1980). Reading and spelling skills in the first school years predicted from phonemic awareness skills in kindergarten. *Scandinavian Journal of Psychology, 21,* 159-173.

Maclean, M., Bryant, P., & Bradley, L. (1988). Rhymes, nursery rhymes and reading in early childhood. In K. Stanovich (Ed.), *Children's reading and the development of phonological awareness* (pp. 11-37). Detroit: Wayne State University Press.

Mann, V. (1993). Phoneme awareness and future reading ability. *Journal of Learning Disabilities, 26,* 259-269.

Mann, V., & Liberman, I. (1984). Phonological awareness and verbal short term memory. *Journal of Learning Disabilities, 17,* 592-599.

Mann, V., Tobin, P., & Wilson, R. (1987). Measuring phonological awareness through the invented spellings of kindergarten children. *Merrill-Palmer Quarterly, 33,* 365-391.

Marsh, G., & Mineo, R. (1977). Training preschool children to recognize phonemes in words. *Journal of Educational Psychology, 69,* 748-753.

Morais, J. (1991). Phonological awareness: A bridge between language and literacy. In D.J. Sawyer & B.J. Fox (Eds.), *Phonological awareness in reading.* (pp. 31-71). New York: Springer-Verlag.

Morais, J., Bertelson, P., Cary, L., & Alegria, J. (1986). Literacy training and speech segmentation. *Cognition, 24,* 45-64.

Morais, J., Cary, L., Alegria, J., & Bertelson, P. (1979). Does awareness of speech as a sequence of phones arise spontaneously? *Cognition, 7,* 323-331.

Morse, P. (1972). The discrimination of speech and nonspeech stimuli in early infancy. *Journal of Experimental Child Psychology, 14,* 477-492.

Näslund, J., & Schneider, W. (1991). Longitudinal effects of verbal ability, memory capacity, and phonological awareness in reading performance. *European Journal of Psychology, 6,* 375-392.

Nesdale, A., Herriman, M., & Tunmer, W. (1984). Phonological awareness in children. In W. Tunmer, C. Pratt, & M. Herriman (Eds.), *Metalinguistic awareness in children: Theory, research and implications* (pp. 36-54). New York: Springer-Verlag.

Olson, R., Wise, B., Conners, F., Rack, J., & Fulker, D. (1989). Specific deficits in component reading and language skills: Genetic and experimental influences. *Journal of Learning Disability, 22,* 339-348.

Perfetti, C., Beck, I., Bell, L., & Hughes, C. (1988). Phonemic knowledge and learning to read are reciprocal: A longitudinal study of first grade children. In K. Stanovich (Ed.), *Children's reading and the development of phonological awareness.* (pp. 39-75). Detroit: Wayne State University Press.

Perin, D. (1983). Phonemic segmentation in spelling. *British Journal of Psychology, 74,* 129-144.

Read, C., & Ruyter, L. (1985). Reading and spelling skills in adults of low literacy. *Remedial and Special Education, 6,* 43-52.

Read, C., Zhang, Y., Nie, H., & Ding, B. (1986). The ability to manipulate speech sound depends on knowing alphabetic reading. *Cognition, 24,* 21-34.

Rosner, J., & Simon, D. (1971). The auditory analysis test: An initial report. *Journal of Learning Disabilities, 4,* 40-48.

Sawyer, D. (1987). *Test of awareness of language segements.* Austin, TX: Pro-Ed.

Sawyer, D.J., & Fox, B.J. (1991). *Phonological awareness in reading: The evolution of current perspectives* New York: Springer-Verlag.

Share, D., Jorm, A., MacLean, R., & Matthews, R. (1984). Sources of individual differences in reading acquisition. *Journal of Educational Psychology, 6,* 1309-1324.

Shriberg, L., & Kent, R. (1982). *Clinical phonetics.* New York: John Wiley & Sons.

Singh, S., & Woods, D. (1971). Perceptual structure of 12 American English vowels. *The Journal of the Acoustical Society of America, 46,* 1861-1866.

Singh, S., Woods., & Becker, G. (1972). Perceptual structure of 22 prevocalic English consonants. *The Journal of the Acoustical Society of America, 52,* 1698-1711.

Skjelfjord, V. (1987). Phonemic segmentation: An important subskill in learning to read: 1. *Scandinavian Journal of Educational Research, 31,* 41-57.

Stahl, S., & Murray, B. (1994). Defining phonological awareness and its relationship to early reading. *Journal of Educational Psychology, 86,* 221-234.

Stanovich, K. (Ed.). (1988). *Children's reading and the development of phonological awareness.* Detroit: Wayne State University Press.

Stanovich, K., Cunningham, A., & Cramer, B. (1984). Assessing phonological awareness in kindergarten children: Issues of task comparability. *Journal of Experimental Child Psychology, 38,* 175-190.

Stuart, M., & Coltheart, M. (1988). Does reading develop in a sequence of stages? *Cognition, 30,* 139-181.

Torgesen, J., & Bryant, B. (1994). *Test of phonological awareness.* Austin, Texas: Pro-Ed.

Torgesen, J., & Morgan, S. (1990). Phonological synthesis tasks: A developmental, functional, and componential analysis. In L. Swanson & B. Keogh (Eds.) *Learning disabilities: Theoretical and research issues* (pp. 263-276). Hillsdale, NJ: Lawrence Erlbaum Associates.

Torgesen, J., Morgan, S., & Davis, C. (1992). Effects of two types of phonological awareness training on word learning in kindergarten children. *Journal of Educational Psychology, 84,* 364-370.

Torgesen, J., Wagner, R., Balthazar, M., Davis, C., Morgan, S., Simmons, K., Stage, S., & Zips, F. (1989). Development and individual differences in performance on phonological synthesis tasks. *Journal of Experimental Child Psychology, 47,* 491-505.

Torgesen, J., Wagner, R., & Rashotte, C. (1994). Longitudinal studies of phonological processing and reading. *Journal of Learning Disabilities, 27,* 276-286.

Tornéus, M. (1984). Phonological awareness and reading: A chicken and egg problem? *Journal of Educational Psychology, 76,* 1346-1358.

Treiman, R., & Baron, J. (1981). Segmental analysis ability: Development and relationship to reading. In G.E. MacKinnon & T.G. Waller (Eds.), *Reading research: Advances in theory and practice,* (Vol. 3) , (pp. 159-196). New York: Academic Press.

Treiman, R., & Baron, J. (1983). Phonemic-analysis training helps children benefit from spelling-sound rules. *Memory and Cognition, 11,* 382-389.

Treiman, R., & Breaux, A. (1982). Common phoneme and overall similarity relations among spoken syllables: Their use by children and adults. *Journal of Psycholinguistic Research, 11,* 569-598.

Treiman, R., & Zukowski, A. (1991). Levels of phonological awareness. In S. Brady & D.Shankweiler (Eds.) *Phonological processes in literacy* (pp. 67-83). Hillsdale, NJ: Lawrence Erlbaum Associates.

Tunmer, W., & Nesdale, A. (1985). Phonemic segmentation skill and beginning reading. *Journal of Educational Psychology, 77*, 417-427.

Tunmer, W., Pratt, C., & Herriman, M. (Eds.) (1984). *Metalinguistic awareness in children: Theory, research and implications.* New York: Springer-Verlag.

Vellutino, F., & Scanlon, D. (1988). Phonological coding, phonological awareness and reading ability: Evidence from a longitudinal and experimental study. In K. Stanovich (Ed.), *Children's reading and the development of phonological awareness* (pp. 77-119). Detroit: Wayne State University.

Wagner, R., & Torgesen, J. (1987). The nature of phonological processing and its causal role in the acquisition of reading skills. *Psychological Bulletin, 101*, 192-212.

Wang, M., & Bilger, R. (1973). Consonant confusions in noise: A study of perceptual features. *Journal of the Acoustical Society of America, 54*, 1248-1266.

Wallach, L., Wallach, M., Dozier, M., & Kaplan, N. (1977). Poor children learning to read do not have trouble with auditory discrimination but do have trouble with phoneme recognition. *Journal of Educational Psychology, 69*, 36-39.

Wimmer, H., Landerl, K. Linortner, R., & Hummer, P. (1991). The relationship of phonological awareness to reading acquisition: More consequence than precondition but still important. *Cognition, 40*, 219-249.

Yopp, H. (1988). The validity and reliability of phonemic awareness tests. *Reading Research Quarterly, 23*, 159-177.

Zifcak, M. (1981). Phonological awareness and reading acquisition. *Contemporary Educational Psychology, 6*, 117-126.

APPENDIX A. MEASURES OF PHONOLOGICAL AWARENESS

PHONEME SEGMENTATION

Tapping

Subject is asked to tap a dowel rod or clap hands for each sound in a word.

Lenchner, Gerber, & Routh, 1990; Liberman, Shankweiler, Fischer, & Carter, 1974; Perfetti, Beck, Bell, & Hughes, 1988; Tunmer & Nesdale, 1982; Yopp, 1988.

Counting

Subject is asked to count the sounds in a word.

Lencher, Gerber, & Routh, 1990; Read & Ruyter, 1985; Vellutino & Scanlon, 1988.

Subject is asked if a word has a given number of sounds.

Foster, Erickson, Foster, Brinkman, & Torgesen,1994.

Tokens

Subject is asked to represent the sounds in words with tokens.

Felton & Brown, 1990; Lindamood & Lindamood, 1975; Lundberg, Olofsson, & Wall, 1980; Sawyer, 1987; Treiman & Baron, 1981; Tornéus, 1984.

Say Sounds

Subject is asked to say each of the sounds in a word.

Juel, Griffith, & Gough, 1986; Read & Ruyter, 1985; Share, Jorm, Maclean, & Matthews, 1984; Yopp, 1988.

Subject is asked to say the sound at the beginning, middle, or end of a word, or the sound that comes after a particular sound in a word.

Read & Ruyter, 1985; Stanovich, Cunningham, & Cramer, 1984; Torneus 1984; Wallach, Wallach, Dozier, & Kaplan, 1977; Yopp 1988.

Subject is asked to say a little bit of a word.

Fox & Routh, 1975; Kamhi & Catts, 1986; Maclean, Bryant, & Bradley, 1988; Morais, Bertelson, Cary, & Alegria, 1986.

Deletion

Subject is asked to say a word after deleting a target sound.

Catts, 1993; Juel, Griffith, & Gough, 1986; Lenchner, Gerber, & Routh, 1990; Morais, Bertelson, Cary, & Alegria, 1986; Perfetti, Beck, Bell, & Hughes 1988; Rosner & Simon, 1971; Stanovich, Cunningham, & Cramer, 1984; Yopp, 1988.

Subject is asked to identify a sound deleted from a word. "What sound do you take away from sit to get it?"

Stanovich, Cunningham, & Cramer, 1984; Tornéus, 1984.

Addition

Subject is asked to pronounce a syllable or word after adding a target sound.

Morais, Cary, Alegria, & Bertelson, 1979; Read & Ruyter, 1985.

Reversal

Subject is asked to say a word after reversing the sounds. "Say the word tack backwards."

Byrne & Ledz, 1983; Lundberg, Olofsson, & Wall, 1980; Yopp, 1988.

Metathesis

Subject is asked to say a two-word phrase after reversing the initial sounds of the words. "Say the phrase sea shells after reversing the initial sounds." Or subject is asked to correct a metathesized phrase, e.g., dot hog.

Näslund & Schneider, 1991; Perin, 1983.

Substitution

Subject is asked to say a word after substituting a target sound for another sound in a word.

Juel, Griffith, & Gough, 1986; Lenchner, Gerber, & Routh, 1990; Näslund & Schneider, 1991; Stanovich, Cunningham, & Cramer, 1984.

Pig Latin

Subject is asked to say a word after moving the initial sound to the end of a word and adding ay.

Lewis & Freebairn, 1992; Olson, Wise, Conners, Rack, & Fulker, 1989.

Invented Spelling

Subject is asked to spell, as best he/she can, a spoken word.

Ehri, 1989; Mann, Tobin, & Wilson, 1987; Zifcak, 1981.

PHONEME BLENDING

Synthesis

Subject is asked to blend a series of sounds together to form a word.

Catts, 1993; Chall, Roswell, & Blumenthal, 1963; Lenchner, Gerber, & Routh, 1990; Lundberg, Olofsson, & Wall, 1980; Perfetti, Beck, Bell, & Hughes, 1988; Torneus, 1984; Yopp, 1988.

Subject is asked if a target word is made up of a series of phonemes. "Is cat made up of /k/ /a/ /t/ ?"

Foster, Erickson, Foster, Brinkman, & Torgesen (1994).

SOUND   COMPARISON

Same/Different

Subject is asked to judge whether or not word pairs begin, end, or share the same sound.

Foster, Erickson, Foster, Brinkman, & Torgesen, 1994; Treiman & Zukowski, 1991; Wallach, Wallach, Dozier, & Kaplan, 1977; Yopp, 1988.

Match-to-Sample

Subject is presented with a target word and asked to choose which of two (or more) words begins, ends, or shares the same sound as the target word.

Byrne & Fielding-Barnsley, 1991; Maclean, Bryant & Bradley, 1988; Stanovich, Cunningham, & Cramer, 1984; Torgesen & Bryant, 1994.

Subject is presented with three words and asked to choose the two words that start the same.

Treiman & Breaux, 1982.

Subject is asked to sort a group of pictures into categories based on initial sounds or choose from groups of pictures, pictures that start with a target sound.

Ehri, Wilce, & Taylor, 1988; Read & Ruyter, 1985; Treiman & Breaux, 1982.

Oddity

Subject is presented with three (or more) words and asked to choose the word that does not begin, end, or share the same sound as the others.

Bradley & Bryant, 1983; Felton & Brown, 1990; Foster, Erickson, Foster, Brinkman, & Torgesen, 1994; Maclean, Bryant, & Bradley, 1988; Stanovich, Cunningham, & Cramer, 1984; Torgesen & Bryant, 1994; Yopp, 1988.

Sound   Detection

Subject is asked if a word contains a target sound or if a target sound is in a word. "Is there a /s/ in soap?" Subject may be asked if a target sound is at the beginning or ending of a word.

Lundberg, Olofsson, & Wall, 1980; Marsh & Mineo, 1977; Morais, Bertelson, Cary, & Alegria, 1986; Read & Ruyter, 1985.

Alliteration

Subject is asked to say a word that starts with a target sound or the same sound as a target word.

Maclean, Bryant, & Bradley, 1988; Read & Ruyter, 1985.

APPENDIX B. PHONOLOGICAL ODDITY TASK

Practice items:

bat	ear	bus
web	goat	gun
seal	safe	shirt

Test items:

1.	net	nose	pig
2.	cheese	mop	moon
3.	tag	ten	cup
4.	gate	sun	soap
5.	fan	thumb	five
6.	chain	cheese	ship
7.	gas	fish	gum
8.	nine	mouse	nut
9.	bone	boot	shell
10.	sock	thumb	thief
11.	duck	sheep	dog
12.	fish	van	foot
13.	cake	pot	pig
14.	jeep	jug	fan
15.	hat	nine	house
16.	bed	book	pin

THE NATURE OF THE PHONOLOGICAL DEFICIT UNDERLYING DISORDERS OF SPOKEN AND WRITTEN LANGUAGE

BARBARA DODD & GAIL GILLON
Department of Speech and Hearing Disorders
University of Queensland
Brisbane, Queensland 4072
Australia

ABSTRACT: There is now considerable evidence that the deficit underlying literacy disorders is a phonological one (Rack, Snowling & Olson, 1992). This hypothesis fits with research that has shown that the spelling and reading abilities of children who have a current spoken phonological disorder, as opposed to delay, perform more poorly than controls on standard measures of reading and spelling. Further, phonologically disordered children would appear to have particular difficulty spelling those words where a rule (e.g. final 'e' lengthens the preceding vowel) needs to be applied. These studies suggest that one deficit underlying difficulties in the acquisition of spoken and written language might be an impaired ability to abstract and use phonological rules. Two experiments are described that compare the ability of groups of children with specific reading disability and reading-age matched controls to abstract non-linguistic and phoneme-grapheme rules. The findings indicated a specific deficit in rule abstraction in that children with specific reading disability had difficulties in dealing with rule flexibility. This conclusion is supported by the efficacy of intervention programs that targeted poor readers phoneme-grapheme rule use. It was concluded that at least some children who are identified as having specific reading disability have a general underlying deficit affecting the ability to derive complex rules.

There is now strong evidence that inadequate knowledge of the sound structure of language, due to phonological processing deficits, constrains the acquisition of literacy skills. Rack, Snowling & Olson (1992) concluded that many dyslexics have a specific deficit in phonological reading, as evidenced by poor performance when reading non-words (e.g., Fox, 1994; Snowling, 1981). The deficit appears to limit the ability to decode text using grapheme-phoneme conversion rules. This hypothesis raises the issue of the nature of the deficit in rule abstraction and/or use. A number of questions can be asked:

Is the deficit specific to written language, or is it also apparent in spoken language?

Is the impaired ability to abstract and use rules specific to linguistic behaviour?

Does complexity of the rule influence its abstraction and use?

C.K. Leong and R.M. Joshi (Eds.), Cross-Language Studies of Learning to Read and Spell, 53–70.

Does targeting phoneme-grapheme rule abstraction and use in an intervention program result in remediation of reading disability?

This report provides some evidence bearing on these questions, from previous reports in the literature and two new experiments.

Is the Deficit Specific to Written Language, or Is It also Apparent in Spoken Language?

One way of investigating whether an impaired ability to abstract and use rules is specific to written language is to describe the literacy skills of children who have delayed phonological acquisition and children with a phonological disorder characterised by atypical (non-developmental) rules. Those children who have difficulty abstracting the rules that govern spoken phonology would be expected to have more difficulty acquiring the rules governing phoneme-grapheme correspondences than children whose acquisition of spoken phonology is merely delayed.

Dodd, Gillon, Oerlemans, Russell, Syrmis & Wilson (1995) compared groups of phonologically delayed, disordered and a matched control groups' ability to read and spell using standardised tests. Children with delayed phonological development did not differ from age-matched controls in their ability to spell the real words in the South Australian Spelling Test (Westwood, 1979), although they made fewer phonologically plausible spelling errors. The phonologically disordered group performed poorly in comparison with both the control and delayed groups on the spelling measures. Assessment of the children's reading ability indicated that the normally speaking control group and the delayed group did not differ quantitatively in their ability to read non-words (Woodcock Reading Mastery Battery, 1987) or on their performance on the accuracy and comprehension measures of the Neale Analysis of Reading Ability (Neale, 1988). Those children whose speech errors were atypical of normal development differed from the control group on all three measures. These results, summarised in Table 1 and Figure 1, indicate that children whose speech is characterised by the use of atypical phonological rules also appear to have difficulty in abstracting and using rules for reading and spelling.

In another experiment (Dodd & Cockerill, 1985), the ability of phonologically disordered children and reading-age matched controls to spell three types of words was compared. Thirteen words had strict one-to-one phoneme-grapheme correspondence (e.g. rent, trips); 13 were examples of rare spellings that have to be learned since they cannot be generated by phoneme-grapheme conversion rules alone (e.g. yacht, ocean); and 13 were rule governed i.e. require the operation of spelling rules to generate correct spelling (e.g. bake, buzz). The results showed that the two groups did not

Table 1. Control, delayed and consistent groups' spelling performance
(Mean raw score, ± SD, Range)

	Control	Delayed	Consistent
South Australian	25.6	15.5	1.8
Spelling Test	± 11	± 16	± 3.2
(Total possible = 70)	12–43	0–37	0–10
% Phonologically	67.4	27.3	2.0
Plausible Errors	± 29.7	± 32.5	± 6.7
	22–100	0–75	0–22

differ in terms of the number of errors made when spelling words that had a strict one-to-one phoneme-grapheme correspondence or words that had rare spellings. However, there was a significant difference in the groups' ability to spell words where a spelling rule needed to be applied, with the speech disordered children making more errors. These results indicated that while the phonologically disordered children had mastered simple one-phoneme-one-grapheme rules, they had difficulty with more complex relationships between sound and orthography e.g. final *e* lengthens the preceding vowel, /k/ after a short vowel is represented as *ck*.

The findings of the experiments summarised (Dodd & Cockerill, 1985; Dodd et al., 1994) suggest that a deficit in rule abstraction and use has consequences that do not seem to be restricted to written language. Other research, showing that poor readers with no concurrent speech difficulties make more errors when asked to imitate unfamiliar polysyllabic words (Snowling, 1987), provides further evidence that a single deficit might underlie difficulties in speaking, spelling and reading. Further, poor readers' impaired rule abstraction and use does not seem to be restricted to the phonological language domain. Difficulties acquiring knowledge of morphological and syntactic rules are also apparent (Gillon and Dodd, 1993; Siegal and Ryan, 1984; Vogel, 1974). These findings suggest that the deficit underlying poor phonological rule abstraction and use may reflect a more general impairment in using rules to aid the learning process. Savage (1982) demonstrated that poor readers' performance was inferior to age-matched good readers when they were required to learn artificial symbol-word correspondences which varied in terms of consistency and rule application. (e.g. recognising the symbol ->. as representing the word "boy"). Poor readers showed particular difficulty when learning involved the use of an inconsistent rule.   These results were sustained even when differences in reading experience were ruled out (Manis & Morrison, 1985). All the research studies discussed, however, have involved linguistic processing.   Could the deficit affect non-linguistic behaviour?

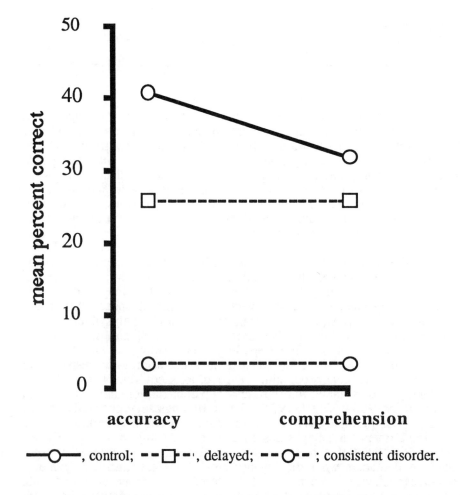

Figure 1. Children with a current spoken phonological disorder: Text reading.

Is the Impaired Ability to Abstract and Use Rules Specific to Linguistic Behaviour?

The ability to abstract rules is a cognitive one involving pattern recognition. While an impaired ability to abstract rules would be particularly apparent during language acquisition because linguistic systems are highly rule governed, a more pervasive impairment may exist. The experiment reported below investigated subjects' performance on a non-linguistic rule governed task. There were three groups of subjects: poor readers; chronological-age matched normal readers (to control for cognitive knowledge and experience); and reading-age matched average readers (to control for the possibility that experience in grapheme-phoneme rule conversion may generally enhance a child's ability to abstract rules).

Experiment One

SUBJECTS

All subjects attended main-stream primary schools in a metropolitan area were from families with average or above average socio-economic status and were native monolingual speakers of English. The 'poor readers' were identified as having specific reading disability using exclusionary criteria. That is, they had significant difficulty in acquiring efficient and fluent reading skills in the absence of: neurological disorder, emotional or behavioural disorder, sensory impairment, previously diagnosed spoken language difficulties (e.g. delayed comprehension), inadequate educational opportunities, or below average intellectual ability (as evidenced by psychologist's reports). Thus, all children included in the experimental groups had unexpected reading difficulties in view of their other abilities.

The Neale Analysis of Reading Ability Revised (Neale, 1988) was used to obtain measures of students' reading accuracy and comprehension. This test, which has been standardised on an Australian population, consists of a series of graded prose passages that are read aloud, plus comprehension questions. The experimental subjects' reading accuracy performance was at least two years below that appropriate for their chronological age. Control subjects' performance was between three months below and 12 months above the level appropriate for their chronological age. All students performed within the average or above average range on the Test of Non Verbal Intelligence -2 (TONI). There were 15 subjects in each group. The poor readers also showed significant phonological processing deficits as evidenced by poor performance on The Lindamood Auditory Conceptualisation Test (LAC) (Lindamood & Lindamood, 1979) and phoneme-grapheme conversion rule deficits as indicated by poor performance on a non-word reading task. The CA control group were drawn from the same classes as the poor readers. The examiner was unaware of who the good and poor readers were when administering the experimental task. Group characteristics are shown in Table 2.

Table 2. Experiment One: Group Characteristics

	Chronological Age*	Reading Age		TONI
		Accuracy	Comp.	
Poor Readers				
Mean	11.4	7.8	8.3	100
SD	0.89	0.52	0.84	9.1
Chronological-Age Matched Controls				
Mean	11.3	11.8	11.8	100
SD	0.78	0.94	0.8	8.7
Reading-Age Matched Controls				
Mean	7.7	7.8	7.7	104
SD	0.82	0.81	0.75	9.2

* Age expressed in years.

METHOD

The rule/nonrule governed learning task from the Muma Assessment Program (MAP) (Muma & Muma, 1979) was used in this experiment. This is a descriptive assessment procedure which examines children's ability to extract rules and assesses their flexibility in shifting from one rule orientation to another. The task was presented individually to each subject. Cards from a pack of 50 were shown to the subject one at a time. Each card had two pictures of the same common object (e.g. apple). The pictures of the objects differed according to size and colour (e.g. one big red apple and one small blue apple). The subject was instructed to guess which one of the two pictures the examiner was thinking of and to point to that picture. The examiner indicated yes or no depending on whether the choice was correct or incorrect. The cards were presented as fast as possible and the subject was only allowed one choice per card. Initially, the examiner was thinking of all the red objects (referred to as the initial set of items). After the subject had responded correctly on eight consecutive cards the examiners' choice changed to selecting all the blue objects (referred to as the reversal shift). Following eight consecutive correct responses the examiner changed to selecting all the big objects (termed non-reversal shift). The task was not interrupted when changes were made from one shift to another.

RESULTS

The number of trials (cards) it took to gain 8 consecutive correct responses was recorded for each subject for each of the three conditions (initial, reversal and nonreversal). Some subjects took a great number of trials (e.g. 169) to demonstrate rule learning. To avoid statistical problems caused by outlying scores, the scores of two subjects were deleted (according to Wilkinson, 1992).

A two-factor ANOVA (condition x group) revealed a significant difference between groups ($F(2,40) = 4.863$, $P < 0.025$). The conditions term was also significant ($F(2,80) = 14.372$, $P < 0.001$). As shown in Figure 2, the experimental and CA-matched control groups needed more trials to derive the rule for the nonreversal shift. The interaction term was significant ($F(4,80) = 2.947$, $P = 0.025$). *Post-hoc* Bonferroni corrected Fisher's least significant difference tests showed no significant difference between the groups' performance for the initial and reversal conditions, but a significant difference between the experimental and CA control groups ($LSD(40) = 23.0$, $P < 0.05$) and the experimental and RA control groups ($LSD(40) = 35.6$, $P < 0.001$) for the nonreversal set. Figure 2 shows the poor readers took more trials to extract the rule governing the nonreversal set.

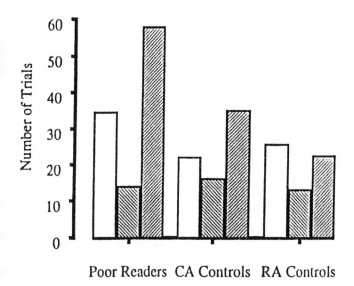

Poor Readers CA Controls RA Controls

Figure 2. Mean number of trials for rule abstraction.

DISCUSSION

The results suggest that poor readers' difficulty in abstracting rules was not restricted to linguistic tasks. Rather, they seem to have particular difficulty with rule flexibility in general. While shifting from one salient aspect to another within the same category (e.g. colour: from red to blue) provided no difficulty, they were less able than the two control groups to switch categories of salience (e.g. from colour to size). These findings suggest that the nature of some poor readers' rule abstraction impairment may be a lack of flexibility in the application of rules which are either irregular or complex.

Does Complexity of the Rule Influence its Abstraction and Use?

The complexity of non-words has already been raised as an important issue in identifying the nature of poor readers difficulties. Rack et al's (1992) review discussed how both phonological complexity (with regards to number of phonemes) and visual similarity to real words can contribute to success or failure on non-word tasks. However, the complexity of rule knowledge required to decode non-words is not directly often addressed. Studies usually employ a variety of non-words; some items can be decoded by one-to-one rule correspondence (e.g., lut), other items require knowledge of additional rules such as 'e' marking the lengthening of the vowel (e.g., strale) (Olson, Wise, Conners, Rack & Fulker, 1989). Analysis of the effects of these different types of rule knowledge has received little attention.

Morrison (1984) described a series of studies that investigated the characteristics of rules that may pose problems for poor readers. The studies assessed the effects on word pronunciation by normal and disabled readers, of: rule consistency (*ee* as in *keep* and *queen* as opposed to *o* in *both* and *moth*); word consistency (opportunity to use analogy so that a known word, e.g. *meal*, can inform the spelling of unknown words such as *deal* and *seal*); and rule conditionality. Conditional grapheme-phoneme correspondences were defined as those orthographic units whose pronunciation depended upon its graphemic environment (e.g., the presence of a final *e* lengthens the preceding vowel). In contrast, unconditional correspondences "do not vary in pronunciation as a function of identifiable contingencies in the graphemic environment (e.g., *ea* in great, breath, breather)" (Morrison, 1984, p. 21). The findings indicated that rule consistency and conditionality had a greater influence on disabled readers performance compared to that of the controls. Morrison (1984, p. 23) concluded that "one source of the disabled reader's problem lies in the complex, irregular system of rules governing symbol-sound correspondences in the English language". However, the stimulus words used in the experiments described by Morrison (1984) were real words. The results may have been influenced by the use of visual recognition strategies in decoding, making generalisations from the studies problematic. There is a need then for studies that investigate the influence of rule complexity on reading and spelling, using non-words.

Experiment 2

The experiment described below used a reading-age match design and extends the work reported by Morrison (1984). Its aim was to identify phoneme-grapheme conversion rules that poor readers find particularly difficult.

SUBJECTS

Ten poor readers and 10 normal readers, matched for ability on the Neale Analysis of Reading Ability Revised (Neale, 1988) participated in this study.   A two-factor ANOVA (reading measure x group) indicated no significant difference between the groups' reading accuracy and reading comprehension performance. The poor readers were identified as having specific reading disability according to the same criteria used in Experiment 1. All subjects were from mainstream primary schools in an Australian metropolitan area and were native monolingual speakers of English. Group characteristics are reported in Table 3.

Table 3. Experiment 2 : Group Characteristics

	Chronological Age*	Reading Age		TONI
		Accuracy	Comp.	
Poor Readers				
Mean	10.3	7.2	7.5	96
SD	1.06	0.68	1.14	6.25
Reading-Age Matched Controls				
Mean	7.53	7.73	7.63	100
SD	0.96	1.05	1.13	7.25

* Age expressed in years.

METHOD

Students were trained to accurately name a set of pictures. They were then presented with eight pictures, one at a time. Each picture had six "words" written under it. One of these words was the correct spelling (e.g., train), one was an incorrect spelling, but when decoded sounded the same as the real word (described as a target non-word e.g., trane), and four other words were distractors. The distractors included a close approximation which may be mistaken for the target non-word if rule knowledge was not applied (e.g., tran). Other distractors were jumbled up letters (e.g., trne). The students were instructed to indicate (by ticking) which two words said the name of the picture. They were told one was the real spelling and one was not the correct spelling but sounded like the real word. They were told they must tick two words on each page. There were three practice items.

One set of target non-words (unconditional) could be read by direct one-to-one phoneme-graheme conversion strategies i.e., *chirch* (church), *klown* (clown), *koin* (coin), and *krowd* (crowd). These words contained vowels that could be represented in more than one way (e.g., *ir, ur, er; ow, ou; oi, oy*). The second set (conditional) depended on knowledge of a vowel rule i.e., *kone* (cone) *trane* (train) *fone* (phone) and *cheze* (cheese).

RESULTS

The measure used was the percentage of correct responses for the real words and the target non-words for each of the conditional and unconditional rule sets.

Real words: Consistent with the reading-age match design, no significant difference was obtained between groups for the real words using a two factor ANOVA (group x conditions). The within subjects terms were also insignificant indicating similar performance on both sets of real words.

Target Non-words: A two-factor ANOVA for the target non-words showed that the difference between groups was not significant ($F(1,18) = 4.074$, $P = 0.059$), although there was a trend for the poor readers to perform less well than the reading-age matched controls. The conditions term was significant ($F(1,18) = 44.596$, $P < 0.001$). Both groups performed better on the unconditional non-words as shown in Figure 3. A significant interaction term was also obtained ($F(1,18) = 12.236$, $P < 0.01$). *Post-hoc* independent *t*-tests indicated no significant difference between groups for the conditional set of words, but a significant difference between groups for the unconditional sets ($t(18) = 3.669$, $P < 0.01$) as shown in Figure 3. Paired *t*-testing indicated that the poor readers' performance did not differ significantly between conditional and unconditional sets. However, the reading-age matched control group performed significantly better on the unconditional set than they did on the conditional set ($t(9) = 9.798$, $P < 0.001$).

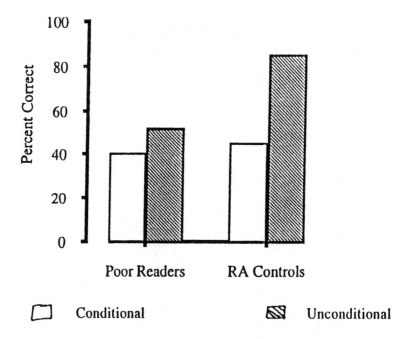

Figure 3. Nonword reading of conditinal and unconditional words: Percent correct.

DISCUSSION

These results have a number of implications. First, the results demonstrated the need to use non-words in order to tease out differences between reading-age matched normal and poor readers. Poor readers are likely to adopt a visual whole-word recognition strategy because of their phonological coding impairment. Consequently, experiments only employing real words are confounded by individual children's sight vocabularies. The findings also indicated that while the good readers performed better on the unconditional non-words than the non-words where a rule had to be known, the reading disabled children performed equally on both conditions. That is, relative to the control group they had particular difficulty when identifying words where the phoneme-grapheme relationship is inconsistent. For example /k/ can be represented orthographically as either c, k or ck, /ɜ/ can be represented variously as *ur* (church), *ir* (bird), *or* (word), *er* (herd), *ear* (heard). Thus the complexity of the relationship between speech sound and orthographic representation influences poor readers ability to decode unfamiliar letter strings.

Does Targeting Phoneme-Grapheme Rule Use in an Intervention Program Result in Remediation of the Reading Disability?

While few research studies have described the efficacy of phonological processing skills training for children with reading disorder, results from intervention studies are important because they not only enhance our understanding of reading disability from a theoretical perspective, but guide educators in the practicalities of program implementation. A recent study by Gillon and Dodd (1995) investigated the effects of training phonological, semantic and syntactic processing skills in spoken language on reading ability. Ten subjects aged between 10 and 12 years identified as having a specific reading disability participated in the study. The results indicated that the reading disabled students had the language learning capacity to improve their spoken language skills to age appropriate levels. Training phonological processing skills had a greater impact on improving *reading accuracy* than training semantic-syntactic skills. The subject group showed an average improvement of approximately 15 months in reading accuracy age following their participation in a 12 hour phonological processing skills program over a three month period. This improvement was notable compared to a pattern of very limited growth in the subjects' reading performance in the two years prior to the phonological intervention program (despite children receiving individual remedial tuition at school). While examination of the effects of intervention on *reading comprehension* indicated that semantic syntactic skill training was equally important as the phonological processing skills program, there was a trend for this effect to vary according to severity of the subjects' reading deficit. The weakest readers in the subject group showed no significant gains in reading performance following the semantic-syntactic training program.

This study raised a number of important issues.

Length of training program. Gillon and Dodd's (1995) study demonstrated significant improvement in the subjects' phonological processing skills after only 12 hours of training (2 hours per week for a six week period). Would a program of longer duration produce even greater improvement and transfer effects to reading performance? Other researchers investigating effects of phonological skill training have argued that subjects benefit from an extended treatment period (Hurford, 1989; Lovett, 1991). Alternatively, a short intensive period of explicit intervention may be all that is required to establish the base skills for improvement.

Severity of disorder. Information related to training effects for students with particularly severe reading deficits is limited. As recognised by McCormick (1994), the performance of severely disabled readers is often masked in research reports by the lack of reading performance homogeneity in the populations studied.

Model of intervention. Most training studies with older students have utilised student participation in laboratory classrooms or specialised clinics away from the students' schools. These models most often use individual or pair training by qualified professionals. However, the realities of busy caseloads warrant the investigation of models of phonological processing skill programs which include group work and the involvement of agents of therapy.

A series of efficacy studies were designed to provide insight into these three issues. Children aged between 9-14 years, identified as having a specific reading disability, participated in three intervention programs. The programs were adapted from the Tracking Speech Sounds section of the Auditory Discrimination in Depth Program Revised Edition (A.D.D) (Lindamood & Lindamood, 1975), excluding the use of the alternate letter sound classification system. Rather, traditional sound names were used. The Tracking Speech Sounds section of the program specifically teaches segmentation, manipulation and blending of speech sounds in syllables. The metalinguistic approach to discussing the changes in syllables described in the ADD manual was emphasised during the current training program. This included the colour encoding activity to teach students to use coloured blocks to represent sounds. They were required to identify the number, order, sameness or difference of the sounds in the syllables heard by arranging and manipulating blocks. One block represented one sound. A problem solving approach was adopted and the students were required to alter the block pattern according to the changes they heard in the speech pattern.

Once the students became confident with encoding using colored blocks, they were taught to encode the syllables (non-words) heard with the letter tiles and letter cards provided with the program. The next step developed the students' ability to read simple and complex syllables. The students were required to change the letter tile patterns as the spoken pattern changed. When the students gained confidence in reading and spelling the non-words, transfer of skills to real words was made. The real words were selected from the schools' spelling lists, consistent spelling rules were made explicit, and unconditional vowel sound-letter relationships were exemplified.

The results indicated that intervention targeting poor readers' phonological processing skills led to a dramatic improvement in their reading accuracy and reading comprehension performance. Increasing length of training time significantly improved transfer effects to the reading process for readers matched for severity of delay pre-program (see Figure 4). Children with particularly severe phonological processing skill deficits benefited from an extended training period (see Figure 5). Both individual and group intervention models for phonological processing training proved successful (see Figure 6).

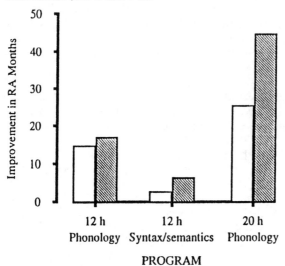

Figure 4. Effect of intervention: Length and content of program.

□ Accuracy   ▨ Comprehension

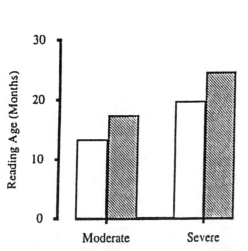

Figure 5. Effect of intervention: Spacing severity.

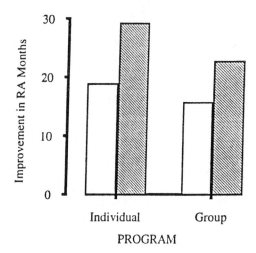

Figure 6. Effect of intervention: Service-Delivery model.

Conclusion

Four questions were posed in the introduction concerning the nature of poor readers' impaired ability to abstract and use grapheme-phoneme conversion rules. The evidence presented allows some preliminary conclusions to be drawn.

The deficit is not specific to written language; it is also apparent in spoken language. Children who have a concurrent spoken phonological disorder in that they use non-developmental phonological rules also perform poorly on standard reading and spelling assessments. They appear to have particular difficulty spelling words where knowledge of a complex rule is required as compared to words that can be spelled by one-to-one phoneme-grapheme matching. Further, children identified as poor readers also have difficulty with spoken phonology (unfamiliar polysyllabic word repetition) and perform more poorly than controls on tasks assessing some aspects of syntax and semantics. These findings indicate that poor reading and spelling may be considered as symptoms of a more general linguistic deficit . While some aspects of their poor spoken language may be a consequence of their limited exposure to written language, evidence identifying specific difficulties with rules suggests that low literacy is not the sole explanation for spoken language difficulties.

The impaired ability to abstract rules is not specific to linguistic behaviour. The results of an experiment comparing normal and poor readers ability to abstract non-linguistic rules showed a poorer performance by the poor readers. What was particularly interesting was that while shifting from one salient aspect to another within the same category provided no great difficulty, they were less able to switch categories of salience. This finding is consistent with the nature of some poor readers' rule abstraction impairment being a lack of flexibility in the application of rules which are either irregular or complex.

The complexity/regularity of the rule influences its abstraction and use. In comparison with controls, poor readers were shown to have relative difficulty reading non-words whose orthographic form included letters that have more than one realisation when spoken (e.g., *ow* pronounced as in cow and low), or speech sounds that have more than one orthographic representation (/k/ as in *c, k, ck*). Thus, poor readers seem to have particular difficulty coping with the irregularities of English orthography.

Targeting phoneme-grapheme rule use in an intervention program results in improved reading ability. The evaluation of intervention programs for poor readers is important because it provides the best test of any hypothesis concerning the nature of underlying deficit. The results of the programs described indicated that substantial gains in reading accuracy could be obtained when children were exposed to an intervention focussing on the relationships governing phoneme-grapheme correspondences. Evidence that it was the content of the program that was important came from studies showing that improvement was independent of the initial degree of reading delay and program delivery model. Further, increasing the length of the intervention increased its efficacy. These results demonstrate that poor readers in the later primary school years, who had already been exposed to remediation available in their schools to little effect, improved rapidly when exposed to very specific intervention focussing on phoneme-grapheme relationships.

Thus, poor readers seem to have a difficulty abstracting rules in general (both linguistic and non-linguistic) and a particular difficulty with complex or irregular orthographic representations of words. However, once a rule or phoneme-grapheme relationship is learned, its use can be generalised. That is, the deficit underlying some poor readers difficulties appears to be one of abstraction or identification of patterns rather than application of that knowledge. These findings fit with the conclusions of Vellutino and Scanlon (1984, p.41) who argued that reading disabled children's difficulty may be attributed to a learning style characterised by "the tendency to process letters, words, or information of any kind at a global and superficial level, with little inclination to discriminate in a fine grained or flexible manner".

REFERENCES

Dodd, B. & Cockerill, H. (1985). Phonologically disordered children's sp. lling abilities. In J.E. Clark (Ed.), *The cultivated Australian, Beitrage zur phonetik und linguistik.* (pp. 404–415). Hamburg: Helmut Buske Verlag.

Dodd, B., Gillon, G., Oerlemans, M., Russell, T., Syrmis. M., & Wilson, H. (1995). Phonological disorder and the acquisition of literacy. In B. Dodd (Ed.), *Differential diagnosis and treatment of speech disordered children.* (pp. 125-146) London: Whurr.

Fox, E. (1994). Grapheme-phoneme correspondence in dyslexic and matched control readers. *British Journal of Psychology, 85,* 41-53.

Gillon, G., & Dodd, B. (1993). The communication skills of children with specific reading disability. *Australian Journal of Human Communication Disorders, 21,* 86–102.

Gillon, G., & Dodd, B. (1995). The effects of training phonological, semantic and syntactic processing skills in spoken language on reading ability. *Language, Speech and Hearing Services in Schools, 26,* 58-68.

Hurford, H. (1989). Training phonemic segmentation ability with a phoneme discrimination intervention in second and third grade children with reading disabilities. *Journal of Learning Disabilities, 23,* 564–569.

Lindamood, C., & Lindamood, P. (1975). *Auditory Discrimination in Depth Revised Edition.* Allen, TX: DLM Teaching Resources.

Lindamood, C., & Lindamood, P. (1979). *Lindamood Auditory Conceptualization Test.* Allen, TX: DLM Teaching Resources.

Lovett, M. (1991). Reading, writing and remediation: Perspectives on the dyslexic learning disability from remedial outcome data. *Learning and Individual Differences 3,* 295–305.

Manis, F., & Morrison, F. (1985). Reading disability: A deficit in rule learning? In L. Siegal & F. Morrison (Eds.), *Cognitive development in atypical children. Progress in cognitive development research.* (pp. 1-26) New York: Springer-Verlag.

McCormick, S. (1994). A non-reader becomes a reader: A case study of literacy acquisition by a severely disabled reader. *Reading Research Quarterly , 29,* 157–176.

Morrison, F. (1984). Word decoding and rule learning in normal and disabled readers. *Remedial and Special Education, 5,* 20–27.

Muma, J., & Muma, D. (1979). *Muma Assessment Program.* Lubbock, TX: Natural Child Publishing Company.

Neale, M. (1988). *Neale Analysis of Reading Ability-Revised.* Hawthorn: Australian Council for Educational Research Limited.

Olson, R., Wise, B., Connors, F., Rack, J., & Fulker, D. (1989). Specific deficits in component reading and language skills: Genetic and environmental influences. *Journal of Learning Disabilities, 22,* 339–348.

Rack, J., Snowling, M., & Olson, R. (1992). The nonword reading deficit in developmental dyslexia: a review. *Reading Research Quarterly, 27,* 29–53.

Savage, P. (1982). *Symbol-word correspondence learning and symbol-sound correspondence knowledge in normal and disabled readers.* Unpublished doctoral dissertation. University of Minnesota, Minneapolis.

Siegal, L., & Ryan, E. (1984). Reading disability as a language disorder. *Reading and Special Education, 5,* 28–33.

Snowling, M. (1981). Phonetic deficits in phonological dyslexia. *Psychological Research, 43,* 219–234.

Snowling, M. (1987). *Dyslexia: A cognitive developmental perspective.* Oxford: Blackwell.

Vellutino, F., & Scanlon, D. (1984). Converging perspectives in the study of the reading process: Reactions to the papers presented by Morrison, Siegal and Ryan and Stanovich. *Remedial and Special Education, 5,* 39–44.

Vogel, S. (1974). Syntactic abilities in normal and dyslexic children. *Journal of Learning Disabilities, 7,* 103–109.

Wilkinson, L. (1992). *SYSTAT: The System For Statistics.* Evanston, IL: Systat.

Westwood, P. (1979). *South Australian Spelling Test.* Education Department of South Australia: Adelaide.

Woodcock, R. W. (1987). *Woodcock Reading Mastery Test – Revised.* Circle-Pines, MN: American Guidance Service.

CASE STUDIES OF DYSLEXIA: YOUNG READERS WITH RAPID SERIAL NAMING DEFICITS

JOANNA K. UHRY
Graduate School of Education
Fordham University
New York, New York 10023

ABSTRACT: This study follows three girls with phonological awareness deficits and reading disorder from early identification through the end of their second year of tutoring during the third-grade school year. Tutoring in a university setting included letter-sound training, segmenting and spelling to increase phonological awareness, as well as practice reading both phonetically and narratively controlled text. It was hypothesized that training would provide reading accuracy and prevent a relative deficit in nonsense word reading. It was also hypothesized that concomitant deficits in rapid serial naming would interfere with remediation of reading rate and this turned out to be the case. An oral reading transcript, used for analysis of reading strategies, is used as evidence that traces of phonological awareness deficits remain.

Recent research links the word-level reading deficits that are characteristic of dyslexia with deficits in phonological processing (see Stanovich, 1986). The two aspects of phonological processing which are of particular interest here involve phonological awareness and rapid naming. Phonological awareness is typically measured by a hierarchy of tasks involving sound matching, blending, segmenting, and deleting phonemes in spoken words (Adams, 1990). The level of ease with which a child perceives the identity and relative location of phonemes in spoken language appears to affect the ease with which she or he relates these phonemes to letters in written words. Thus children with weak phonological awareness struggle to make full and appropriate use of letter-sound associations when they read, and their reading is often characterized by difficulty in using word attack skills to decode phonetically regular nonsense words (Felton & Wood, 1992; Rack, Snowling, & Olson, 1992).

A second aspect of phonological processing involves "rapid automatized naming" (Denckla & Rudel, 1976), or "phonological recoding in working memory" (Wagner & Torgesen, 1987). This is typically measured by asking the child to name serial stimuli as rapidly as possible By calling this "rapid serial naming," it is contrasted with what Wolf (1991) calls "discrete-trial naming" which is not as directly related to word reading (Stanovich, 1981). Rapid serial naming is so close to what beginning readers do as they move along a line of print retrieving letter sounds or words that it

C.K. Leong and R.M. Joshi (Eds.), Cross-Language Studies of Learning to Read and Spell, 71–88.
© *1997 Kluwer Academic Publishers. Printed in the Netherlands.*

is easy to see how the task taps a process which affects success in learning to read.

Fortunately, children who are at risk for reading disorder can be identified early through screening instruments that use phonological tasks (Stanovich, Cunningham, & Cramer, 1984; Uhry, 1993a). While there is little evidence that deficits in rapid serial naming can be remediated, there is strong evidence that phonological awareness training can be effectively carried out with prereaders (Ball & Blachman, 1991; Bradley & Bryant, 1983, Lundberg, Frost, & Petersen, 1988), beginning readers (Felton, 1993; Uhry & Shepherd, 1993, Shepherd & Uhry, 1993), and older remedial readers (Alexander, Andersen, Heilman, Voeller, & Torgesen, 1991).

It has been argued that children with dyslexia can be taught to recognize specific words through repeated readings, but that even after remediation they will continue to have difficulty with phonological processing and, thus, in using word attack skills to read unfamiliar words or nonsense words (Bradley & Bryant, 1978; Snowling, 1980; Snowling & Hulme, 1989). There is evidence, however, that this is not necessarily the case provided that remediation involves systematic training in phonological awareness. For example, Alexander et al. (1991) used the Auditory Discrimination in Depth Program (Lindamood & Lindamood, 1975) to train ten children with dyslexia who ranged in age from 7 through 12. The children were encouraged to use sensory feedback from oral mechanisms, and later to segment and represent sounds in spoken words with small blocks and then with letters. After training, these children demonstrated significant growth in reading both real words and nonsense words. Rather than being deficient, their nonsense word standard scores were 15 points higher than word reading scores.

In my own work (Uhry, 1993b), three children with dyslexia, ages 9 and 10, were trained to read nonsense words effectively. Baseline instruction in letter sounds and in sounding out and blending words increased word reading without increasing nonsense word reading over a baseline period, a finding consistent with most existing literature. However, the introduction of phonological awareness training consisting of sound analysis (i.e., segmenting and phonological spelling) had a dramatic impact on the ability of these children to read nonsense words.

It was reasoned that if older children with dyslexia could be taught to read nonsense words, then similar training would facilitate decoding and prevent the nonsense word deficit in young children at risk for dyslexia. A longitudinal training study was undertaken with the hypothesis that training would alleviate some of the symptoms of dyslexia and that there would be individual variation in response to treatment (Shepherd & Uhry, 1993). The present study reports on the second year of this project.

In the first year, 12 children at risk for dyslexia were provided with training in phonics knowledge, phonological awareness, and text reading (Shepherd & Uhry, 1993). The discrepancy between word reading, viewed in the literature as remediable, and nonsense word reading, viewed as a chronic deficit, did not develop. After training, mean scores in nonsense word reading were higher than those in word reading, consistent with findings from Alexander et al. (1991). In fact, for several children, there was little or no progress in standard scores on word reading, despite dramatic progress in ability to read nonsense words. A case history of one such child was embedded in our earlier report (Shepherd & Uhry, 1993). KM earned a standard score of 78 in word reading at the time of entry into the study at the end of first grade, and this remained at 78 after five months of tutoring. By contrast, her nonsense word reading score rose from 61 to 94 over this same period of time. KM was able to sound out words but not to recognize them quickly when she read. One plausible explanation was found in her extraordinary deficits in rapid serial naming. While she had been drilled on letter sounds, and thus could use this knowledge to sound out words, we thought she would need drill on letter units and words before she would be able to retrieve them quickly enough to enable fluent reading. Her program was modified to include linguistic readers and drill with word cards.

The present study is a report of the effects of these modifications in KM's treatment over the course of a second year of tutoring. In order to test generalizability of the findings, results are included for KM and for two other children who were also very weak in rapid serial naming. The hypothesis of the present study is based on work by Wood and Felton (1994) suggesting that degree of rapid serial naming difficulty is a good predictor of remediation of phonologically based reading disorder. We expected that these children eventually would read quite accurately, but that they would read more slowly than other children their age. The research design combines case histories of three poor readers in terms of analysis of individual scores over time, as well as a micro-analysis of a videotaped reading session.

Method

Three at-risk beginning readers were observed over a two-year period during tutoring in a university clinic. The object was to document individual response to treatment through both test scores and observations. The subjects were tested and treated over a two year period with first year group data reported in a previous study (Shepherd & Uhry, 1993).

Subjects: Subjects were three girls who were just finishing the third-grade school year at the time of final data collection after two years of tutoring. They were of middle-to-high socioeconomic status (SES) as determined by parent education level; all parents had attended college or graduate school. Criteria for inclusion in our original study was a full scale as well as Verbal scale IQ of at least 90, a significant discrepancy between reading level and IQ, and deficits in phonological awareness or rapid serial naming or both. The children who were selected for this follow-up study were chosen from the original group of 12 subjects because of their severe rapid serial naming deficits.

KM and MD attended the same independent school in New York City. The third girl, MR, initially attended a public school program for gifted children, but during third grade moved to another school because she could no longer keep up with her peers because of her reading difficulty. Her new school was what is known as an "alternative" or experimental public school. Their schools were alike in that classes were relatively small (under 20) and teachers were dedicated and attentive to individual needs. The schools were progressive rather than traditional in structure, and reading was taught using a whole language rather than code-based approach. However, all three received some direct instruction in code skills during first or second grade, and other children in their classes read and wrote extremely well, often two to three years above grade expectations.

Treatment

Year 1: The university clinic-based remedial program for all twelve participants in the original study involved a four-part, hour-long tutoring lesson twice a week. This was based on components from an earlier training study of first-grade children in whole language classrooms (Uhry & Shepherd, 1993) and is similar to a program used by Blachman (Blachman, Ball, Black, & Tangel, 1994). The goal for the first three activities was to teach a code-based reading strategy using direct instruction techniques. This strategy appears to be neglected by children with dyslexia; they tend to overuse context and prior knowledge. For example, when KM was first seen at the university clinic she almost never kept her eyes on a word as she tried to figure out how to decode it. Instead, she looked away from the text and then provided a word with a contextual association. Even after 35 tutoring sessions, her tutor needed to remind her to use letter cues.

The four-part lesson used the following sequence of activities:

1. Letter-sound responses were practised using the Orton-Gillingham based Initial Reading Deck (IRD, Cox, 1971), a set of key-word pictures and letters (e.g., a picture of a table and the letter *t*).

2. Phonological awareness was practised using words made up of phonemes introduced using the IRD. A word was said aloud by the tutor, and then segmented into parts by the student, who initially represented each sound with a 2 cm colored wooden block, with blue for consonants and red for vowels. Once segmentation of consonant-vowel-consonant (cvc) words with short /a/ was mastered, segments were spelled with the IRD cards (Uhry & Shepherd, 1993).

3. In the third activity, synthetic phonics readers (Makar, 1985) were used to practise text with words which had already been spelled and read in isolation. Students were encouraged to read using a left-to-right, letter-by-letter, sounding out and blending strategy, usually called an "alphabetic" (Frith, 1985) or "cipher" strategy (Gough & Tunmer, 1986).

4. In the fourth activity, meaning-emphasis or narratively controlled trade books were read. This text usually contained a word or pattern already read during that lesson in the code-emphasis text. The rationale for combining a meaning-based and code-based approach comes from a study by Iverson and Tunmer (1993) in which the Reading Recovery remedial program (Clay, 1993) was combined with code instruction. Tunmer (1994) presents evidence that letter cues are a more productive strategy for poor readers than context cues. During this portion of the lesson, the tutor actively coached the child to use letter cue as well as context cue strategies.

Year 2: Training activities from the first year were retained with one modification. Synthetic phonics readers were replaced by the Merrill Linguistic Readers. When a new letter-sound was introduced it was segmented and spelled as before, but reading practice focused on using units of letters. The rationale for retaining direct instruction in new phonetic patterns comes from Ehri and Robbin's (1992) finding that children do better at analogy reading given phonetic knowledge and strategies as a precursor. A rationale for analogy instruction can be found in Goswami's work (1986).

Measures

IQ-reading and listening-reading discrepancies: An IQ versus reading comparison was made using scores from the Wechsler scales and reading subtests from the Wechsler Individual Achievement Test (WIAT). Both

Siegel (1989) and Stanovich (1991) criticize the use of IQ based discrepancies. While IQ is believed to affect reading level, reading level can arguably be considered an influence on the development of cognitive skills over time. While IQ for these children was measured prior to the point at which reading level could be expected to affect IQ, a listening comprehension measure (WIAT) was also used. It was hypothesized that so long as decoding is weaker than IQ, reading comprehension will be affected to some extent by poor decoding, and reading comprehension will be lower than listening comprehension. A measure of verbal knowledge was also taken. The General Information subtest of the Peabody Individual Achievement Test (PIAT) was used as a second way of looking at the difference between word reading and verbal ability. Both the listening and the knowledge measures were collected at posttest.

Comparisons of real word with nonsense word reading: Deficits in nonsense word reading are considered symptomatic of dyslexia. Because the WIAT does not contain a nonsense word reading task, a second word reading task was administered. The Woodcock Reading Mastery Test (WRMT-R) has both a Word Identification test, comprised of real words in lists, and a Word Attack test, comprised of nonsense words such as *ift* and *straced*.

Rate versus accuracy: The hypothesis of the study is that phonological awareness training can increase reading accuracy but that reading rate will remain slow after treatment. The Gray Oral Reading Test (GORT-3) graded passages provide a standard score for both accuracy and rate. A second measure of reading rate was taken because we wanted one which used more naturalistic, literature-based passages than those provided by the GORT-3. The Houghton-Mifflin (H-M) Pupil Placement Tests provide graded passages and a formula for figuring whether the student is reading within an average range of speed for grade level.

Measures of phonological processing: Phonological awareness was measured by three tests in order to sample abilities at several levels on a hierarchy described by Adams (1990) in which blending is considered a relatively easier and earlier-developing skill than either segmenting or phoneme manipulation. The Sound Blending test from the Illinois Test of Psycholinguistic Abilities (ITPA) was chosen because it includes the sorts of long words (e.g., *telephone*) and unfamiliar words (i.e., nonsense words such as *opasto*) that third-grade children are expected to blend and read.

Both Rosner's Test of Auditory Awareness Skills (TAAS) and the Lindamood Auditory Conceptualization Test (LAC) measure ability to analyze sounds in spoken words. The LAC measures phoneme distinctions, phoneme location, and phoneme manipulation, but includes only one item in which consonant clusters are manipulated. On the higher level LAC items the examiner says, "If that says *ups*, show me *usp*" and the child is expected to change a wooden block sequence (e.g., red-green-yellow to red-yellow-green). A child can score at third-grade criterion level without being successful on the item in which a consonant cluster is manipulated. Because consonant clusters are difficult for children with dyslexia (Bruck & Treiman, 1990) the TAAS was used here as well. There are four consonant cluster items on the TAAS in which one consonant is deleted. For example, the examiner says, "Say *smack*. Now say it again but don't say /m/."

The Rapid Automatized Naming Test (RAN) was used to measure rapid serial naming and the Boston Naming Test was used for discrete-trial naming. Norms for the latter were developed on an SES matched group of New York City children.

Procedures

Tutoring was provided twice a week for the two year period. Children came to a university-based tutoring center where trained graduate students provided tutoring under observation through a one-way mirror. Posttest data (Shepherd & Uhry, 1993) were collected in early March of the first year, and in late April of the second. Case histories using documentation from standardized testing as well as descriptions of strategies (Snowling & Hulme, 1989) provided a model for descriptive aspects of this study. Videotapes were used to confirm scorings and were also used to prepare written transcripts of reading episodes roughly modeled on the oral language transcript "dialogue boxes" used by Bloom (Bloom & Lahey, 1978, p. 107). Here they were used to produce a record of reading miscues and strategies.

First Year Results

Initial identification: KM and MD, who attended the same school, were first identified as being at risk when their school administered a kindergarten screening test, the Early Reading Screening (Uhry, 1993a). At the end of the kindergarten year they were unable to blend phonemes into words, to segment oral words into phonemes, or to provide invented spellings as well as other children in their classes. They could read fewer of their classmates' names and could identify almost no other words. Their teachers were surprised because they seemed so bright. KM's IQ was 130 and MD's was 126, as measured by the WPPSI. Neither child was referred for outside help, but extra attention was provided within their first-grade whole language classrooms. When they could read only a few words by the end of that year, both were referred to a university clinic for educational evaluations and tutoring, and became participants in our longitudinal study (Shepherd & Uhry, 1993).

MR attended a special program for gifted children in a public school. Reading progress during first grade was unexpectedly poor and she was referred to the school-based evaluation team for psychological and educational testing. These school-generated reports revealed an IQ of 126 as measured by the Wechsler Intelligence Scales for Children (WISC-III), very poor blending skills, and inability to read any words at all. At the end of her first-grade year, MR was referred to us by her public school resource room teacher who thought that she was dyslexic.

Additional evaluation at the onset of the study for the three children confirmed discrepantly poor reading, with scores well below their high IQ's and at least a standard deviation below national norms on the WIAT. Word reading scores ranged from 60 (MR) to 78 (KM) and IQ-reading discrepancies ranged from 52 (KM) to 66 (MR). All three had deficient phonological awareness skills and extremely slow naming rates on the RAN. See Table 1 for this data.

Initial changes in reading skills. By March of the first year, group results (Shepherd & Uhry, 1993) were consistent with findings from Alexander et al. (1991). See Table 2 for WRMT-R scores. At that point KM had a gain score for this initial instructional period of 33 points on the Word Attack (nonsense word) test and was able to blend and delete phonemes within the normal range using a set of norms especially developed for her high achieving school class. However, she demonstrated no standard score growth at all on the Word Identification test; this remained at 78. Although KM could now sound out some new words, she was not building a lexicon of sight words which she recognized easily. For example, she could read the nonsense word *nan* on the Word Attack test , but failed to recognize it when reading about a character named *Nan* whose name occurred over and over in a book. This was not the case for MD and MR who had improved dramatically in word reading as well as in phoneme manipulation ability on the TAAS. MD had entered with some ability to read nonsense words and all three were now relatively strong at this. If all three could read nonsense words and manipulate phonemes, why could only two of these girls retain sight words?

There were several hypotheses about why this was the case. The first was that either psychological or attentional issues were interfering with learning; it was hard to engage KM's attention during tutoring. She was referred for an outside psychological evaluation, but the psychologist simply confirmed her high IQ and her reading disorder, and failed to find attentional problems in non-reading areas. KM was extremely high functioning in math. The second hypothesis was that while there was evidence from the ITPA, the Rosner, and the Word Attack test that phonological awareness deficits seemed remediated, KM's extremely slow naming rate on the RAN might be interfering with ability to retrieve words quickly while reading. The argument for this was built on the fact that KM had received repeated drill on letter sounds through use of the Initial Reading Deck cards. We reasoned that with this drill she was now able to retrieve phonemes quickly, but that she would need practice with larger units (see LaBerge, 1979). However, MR and MD were doing well at word reading and they, too, were slow at serial naming.

We also wondered if, over time, KM's advantage in phonetic sounding-out skills would facilitate word recognition. This hypothesis is consistent with Ehri's (1992) model of sight words as underpinned by phonetic knowledge. It is also consistent with an earlier study of ours (Uhry & Shepherd, 1993) in which segmenting and spelling training was used with beginning readers. After four months of training they had an advantage over controls in nonsense word reading, but not until another two months of training did they outdistance controls in word reading. These results led to the prediction that KM's new skills in phonetic decoding would eventually facilitate the development of a stronger sight vocabulary.

Table 1. Descriptive data at onset of treatment at the beginning of grade 2.

ID	Age in Mos.	IQ	WId	Discrep. IQ-WId	Dys. in Family	Deficit in PA	RAN* Col	Num	Obj	Let
KM	85	130	78	52	father	yes	- - - - - - - -		0	- - -
MD	84	126	65	61	no	yes	- - - - - - -		0	- - -
MR	86	126	60	66	mother	yes	0	- - -	0	-

- Note: A negative score on the RAN indicates a naming time that is slower than the normal range. Two minus signs indicate a time that is two standard deviations slower than age norms.

Table 2. Woodcock Reading Mastery Test subtest scores at onset, and after 35 hours of treatment, and then at posttest, after 90 hours of treatment, with significant discrepancies between Word Identification (WId)and Word Attack (WA).

	Onset			35 Hours			90 Hours		
	Wid	WA	Discrep.	WId	WA	Discrep.	WId	WA	Discrep.
KM	78	61	WId>WA	78	94	WId<WA	95	99	0
MD	65	99	WId<WA	88	102	0	100	105	0
MR	60	75	WId<WA	78	101	WId<WA	87	97	0

Second Year Results

It was the hypothesis of the present study that reading accuracy could be improved for these three phonologically impaired children through instruction in letter-based phonological awareness training, together with reading instruction emphasizing both letters and units of letters. It was also hypothesized that because of concomitant deficits in rapid serial naming, their rate of reading would continue to be problematic in comparison with reading accuracy. Test data at the end of the second year of treatment support the two-part hypothesis.

Word Reading Accuracy: See Tables 2 and 3 for posttest achievement test scores for the three subjects. Their scores were remarkably similar by the end of the second year of treatment. Word reading was within the average range for all three, with WIAT and WRMT-R word-reading scores quite close in each case. Again, as with our earlier studies (Shepherd & Uhry, 1993; Uhry, 1993b), and consistent with findings by Alexander et al. (1991), there was no nonsense word deficit relative to word recognition ability. Training in listening carefully to the sounds in spoken words and building a carefully constructed model of letter-sound associations through segmenting and spelling activities appears to be effective. This is consistent with the literature (Ehri & Wilce, 1987; Uhry & Shepherd, 1993) indicating that spelling can be used effectively as a form of beginning reading instruction.

Table 3. Achievement test scores at posttest, after 90 hours of treatment at the end of grade 3.

ID	WIAT			PIAT	
	Sp.	Word Rdg.	Rdg. Comp.	List. Comp.	Gen. Info.
KM	94	94	103	120*	138
MD	86	97	109	128*	107
MR	90	90	105	112*	120

Note: * A standard score difference of 15 points represents a significant discrepancy between subtests on the WIAT.

It is difficult to interpret the cause of KM's dramatic improvement in word reading, but it is consistent with our earlier finding that growth in nonsense word reading precedes growth in word reading (Uhry & Shepherd, 1993). It is also possible that changes in her remedial program played a role, and that instruction using linguistic readers encouraged more rapid processing of letter units.

Lower versus Higher Level Skills: Bruck (1994) presents a profile of adult dyslexics in which rote, low level phonological skills are less well developed than higher level thinking skills. Even though KM's spelling, nonsense word, and word reading were much improved, they were still discrepantly lower than verbal comprehension skills and IQ. Her WIAT scores in spelling and word recognition were somewhat lower than scores in reading comprehension, and significantly lower than scores in listening comprehension. This pattern held for all three girls. For KM and MR this contrast held for decoding versus general information as well. Note that KM's score on the the PIAT General Information test was 138. Her strength in listening and in verbal knowledge indicate that her decoding, while in the average range, was still below levels predicted by her strong verbal skills. While the discrepancy was reduced, the scores remain hierarchically nested.

Word Reading Rate: Another hypothesis was that while reading accuracy could be remediated, which was the case here at least to the extent that these children were reading at grade-level expectations, their slowness with serial naming would adversely affect their reading rate. It was expected that rate would be less well developed than accuracy, and this was the case. See results for rate in Table 4. In all three cases the standard score was significantly higher for accuracy than for rate on the GORT-3. While reading accuracy was in the normal range, rate was below average for KM and MD, and just at the bottom edge of the average range for MR. When this comparison was made using the more contextualized and naturalistic Houghton-Mifflin passages, the results were similar. All three children read at a third-grade instructional level on this informal inventory. Using a formula for figuring words-per-minute supplied by the publisher, all three of the subjects read more slowly than the criterion rate for third grade. They read roughly 65 words-per-minute, while the publisher's criterion rate is between 100 and 130 words-per-minute.

Table 4. Reading rate comparisons at the end of grade 3 on graded reading passages

ID	GORT-3		H-M Grade 3 Passage		
	Accur.	Rate	Accur. g.e.	wpm	average wpm for Grade 3
KM	11	7*	3rd	64	100-130
MD	10	7*	3rd	67	100-130
MR	11	8*	3rd	63	100-130

Note:* A standard score difference of 3 points represents a significant discrepancy between accuracy and rate on the GORT-R.

Phonological Processing Results

Results from the posttest phonological processing measures are not surprising given the above results (see Table 5). On the phonological awareness measures all three subjects demonstrated strong auditory blending skills. KM also did well on the other two measures, which had been true at the end of the first year. MD did well on the TAAS, and did less well on the

LAC where she scored below third-grade criterion and struggled with sequences of sounds. MR did well on the LAC, but poorly on the TAAS where she failed to segment and delete consonant clusters, a characteristic of dyslexia according to Bruck and Treiman (1990). RAN scores, however, indicate that for all three children, rapid serial naming continued to be slow.

These results suggest that KM's phonological awareness has been well remediated, with consequent improvement first in nonsense word reading, and later, during the second year of treatment, in word reading. They suggest, too, that rapid serial naming was still an issue for KM and that the underlying process measured by this test continues to adversely affect her rate of reading.

Table 5. Phonological processing scores at posttest after approximately 90 hours of treatment at the end of grade 3.

	Phonological Awareness			Rapid Serial Naming			
	Lind.	Rosner	ITPA		RAN		
ID	LAC*	TAAS	Blend	Col	Num	Obj	Let
KM	90/81	12/13	30/32	0	--	-	-
MD	74/81	13/13	29/32	--	---	0	--
MR	94/81	9/13	30/32	0	-	0	-

Note: Phonological awareness scores are presented with the child's score over the criterion score for age or grade. A negative score on the RAN indicates a naming rate which is a standard deviation lower than normal.

Transcript of KM's Reading

While the GORT-3 results indicate normal accuracy and below normal rate of reading, transcripts of videotaped reading episodes make the relationship appear far more complex than test scores suggest. The following transcript presents the text on the left as written, and on the right, as read aloud by KM. The underlined words tell us that she misread 9 out of 104 words, or with an accuracy rate of roughly 91 percent, considered an appropriate error rate for instructional text. A glance at the transcript informs us that there are many pauses while reading, an expected outcome if rapid naming is an issue. However, it is also clear from the much larger mass of text on the right than the left that decodings through sounding out, misreadings, and repeated readings have made a large contribution to the time it took KM to read this text. KM was not simply retrieving words slowly; she was stopping and starting and rereading and struggling with decoding as well.

Table 6. Text and transcript from a videotape of km's reading of a GORT-3 passage.

GORT-3 Text	KM's Reading
The era of the cowboy came to	The <u>urra</u> of the cowboy came to
an end as a result of changes	an ... end as <u>the</u> results of changes
in the cattle business. When	in the cat-tle business. When
cows roamed the	cows roamed ... (deep sigh) ... the
vast	/v/ ... vast ... va ... vast
ranges of the Southwest,	ranges of the Southwest, ...
the herd could not be rounded up	the herd ... could not be ... rounded up
without skilled riders on horseback.	<u>with</u> skilled ... riders on horseback.
But with the	But with the ... what? ... But with the
invention of	<u>on-drigion</u> of
	... um ... pri ... bri ... brarring ...
	bearing ... (whispering) what's it called?
	(looking away from text very
	intently and then, suddenly)
barbed wire	<u>breeding</u>! ... write ... white ... <u>write</u>
great stretches of	great ... /s-t-r/ etches of ... wha?
ranchland	lanch ... ranch ... land ... <u>lanchland</u>
were fenced into smaller ranches.	were fenced into smaller ranches.
Then the roundup was no	Then, the ... <u>groupup</u> was no
longer a major event and	longer a major ... eve ... event and
cowboys became less important.	cowboys became less important.
The long trail	The long trail
drives	div ... dri ... driv ... drives
to the north, in which the cowboy's	to the north, in which the cowboy's
skill at herding cattle	skill at hear ... herding cattle
was	was ... what?
essential	es ... ez ... en ... <u>tal</u> ... was what? blank.
also became a thing of the past. With	also became a thing of the past. With
the coming of the railroad, cattle could	the coming of the railroad ... cattle could
be shipped directly to market.	be shipped ... directly to market.

One interesting episode here involves KM's attempts to sound out the words *barbed wire*. Her struggle to retrieve a word (i.e., "What's it called?") and then the look of relief and triumph as she finally thought of the word are characteristic of confrontational naming difficulties. Had she followed " ... pri ... bri ... brarring ... bearing" with "barbed" at this point, it would have provided good anecdotal evidence of the relationship between naming and reading difficulties. However, after seeming to agonize over retrieval and then "get it," she confidently produced the word "breeding" rather than "barbed." Retrieval is not the only issue here. KM appears to be using what Ehri (Ehri & Wilce, 1987) describes as a partial cue strategy rather than the full blown cipher strategy. There is some overlap in letters and sounds. The sounds /b/ and /r/ are common to both *barbed* and *breeding*. KM sounded out the beginning of *barbed* and then appeared to try to find a contextually related topic (horse breeding) as a lexical match rather than using all available letter cues. During the first year of tutoring she had frequently looked away from a printed word to carry out a contextual search, and she underutilized letter cues or failed to use them at all. Reading on this passage represents great progress for KM. She could read several lines at a time with accuracy, appropriate phrasing, and good expression. It is true that her reading rate is slow, but reading rate for connected text cannot be isolated from reading accuracy. KM's struggle with phonetic decoding appears to be slowing her down. The relationship between accuracy and rate seems to me to be highly complex.

Conclusions

The hypothesis of this study is that reading accuracy can be remediated, but that rate cannot. Evidence confirming this hypothesis was found in significantly discrepant accuracy and rate scores for these three very bright children with dyslexia. However, transcription of a representative reading episode provides evidence that the relationship between accuracy and rate is complex, and that, for these children, the cipher strategy and the acquisition of sight vocabulary remain incompletely remediated.

The implications for instruction are that the symptoms of dyslexia can be ameliorated using a combination approach which includes phonics drill, phonological awareness training using letters, and a great deal of practice actually using these skills and strategies in reading text. Overall, results are encouraging in terms of the progress these three children have made over a two year period of remediation. Despite pervasive serial naming problems, as well as initial phonological awareness problems which appear to be reduced but still present to a greater degree than test results would indicate, KM has acquired phonetic strategies, a sight vocabulary, and the ability to read with some fluency.

REFERENCES

Adams, M. J. (1990). Beginning to read: Thinking and learning about print. Cambridge, MA: MIT Press.

Alexander, A. W., Andersen, H. G., Heilman, P. C., Voeller, K. K. S., & Torgesen, J. K. (1991). Phonological awareness training and remediation of analytic decoding deficits in a group of severe dyslexics. *Annals of Dyslexia, 41*, 193-206.

Ball, E. W., & Blachman, B. A. (1991). Does phoneme segmentation training in kindergarten make a difference in early word recognition and developmental spelling? *Reading Research Quarterly, 26*, 49-66.

Blachman, B. A., Ball, E. W., Black, R. S., & Tangel, D. M. (1994). Kindergarten teachers develop phoneme awareness in low-income, inner-city classrooms: Does it make a difference? *Reading and Writing: An Interdisciplinary Journal, 6*, 1-18.

Bloom, L. & Lahey, M. (1978). *Language development and language disorder.* New York: Macmillan.

Bradley, L., & Bryant, P. E. (1978). Difficulties in auditory organization as a possible cause of reading backwardness. *Nature, 271*, 746-747.

Bradley, L. & Bryant, P. E. (1983). Categorizing sounds and learning to read: A causal connection. *Nature, 301*, 419-21.

Bruck, M. (1994, October). *Outcomes of adults with childhood histories of dyslexia.* Paper presented at NATO Advanced Study Institute in Alvor, Portugal.

Bruck, M. & Treiman, R. (1990). Phonological awareness and spelling in normal children and dyslexics: The case of initial consonant clusters. *Journal of Experimental Child Psychology, 50*, 156-178.

Clay, M. M. (1993). Reading recovery: A guidebook for teachers in training. Portsmouth, NH: Heineman.

Cox, A. (1971). *Initial reading deck.* Cambridge, MA: Educators Publishing Service.

Denckla, M. B., & Rudel, R. G. (1976). Rapid Automatized Naming (R.A.N.): Dyslexia differentiated from other learning disabilities. *Neuropsychologia, 14*, 471-479.

Ehri, L. C. (1992). Reconceptualizing the development of sight word reading and its relationship to recoding. In P. B. Gough, L. C. Ehri & R. Treiman (Eds.), *Reading acquisition* (pp. 107-143). Hillsdale, NJ: Lawrence Erlbaum Associates.

Ehri, L. C., & Robbins, C. (1992). Beginners need some decoding skill to read words by analogy. *Reading Research Quarterly, 27*, 12-26.

Ehri, L. C., & Wilce, L. C. (1987). Does learning to spell help beginners learn to read words? *Reading Research Quarterly, 18*, 47-65.

Felton, R. H. (1993). Impact of instruction on word identification skills in children with phonological processing problems. In R. M. Joshi & C. K. Leong (Eds.), *Reading disabilities: Diagnosis and component processes* (pp. 267-278). Dordrecht, Netherlands: Kluwer Academic Publishers.

Felton, R. H., & Wood, F. B. (1992). A reading level match study of nonword reading skills in poor readers with varying IQ. *Journal of Learning Disabilities, 25*, 318-326.

Frith, U. (1985). Beneath the surface of developmental dyslexia. In K. E. Patterson, J. C. Marshall, & M. Coltheart (Eds.), *Surface dyslexia: Neuropsychological and cognitive studies of phonological reading* (pp. 301-330). London: Lawrence Erlbaum Associates, Ltd.

Goswami, U. (1986). Children's use of analogy in learning to read: A developmental study. *Journal of Experimental Child Psychology, 42,* 73-83.

Gough, P. B., & Tunmer, W. E. (1986). Decoding, reading, and reading disability. *Remedial and Special Education, 7,* 6-10.

Iverson, S., Tunmer, W. E. (1993). Phonological processing skills and the reading recovery program. *Journal of Educational Psychology, 85,* 112-126.

LaBerge, D. (1979). Perception of units in reading. In L. B. Resnick & P. A. Weaver (Eds.), *Theory and practice of early reading,* (Vol. 3, pp. 31-51). Hillsdale, NJ: Erlbaum.

Lindamood, C. H., & Lindamood, P. C. (1975). *Auditory Discrimination in Depth.* Allen, TX: DLM/Teaching Resources.

Lundberg, I., Frost, J., & Petersen, O. P. (1988). Effects of an extensive program for stimulating phonological awareness in preschool children. *Reading Research Quarterly, 23,* 263-284.

Makar, B. W. (1985). *The tin man.* Cambridge, MA: Educators Publishing Service.

Rack, J. P., Snowling, M. J., & Olson, R. K. (1992). The nonword reading deficit in developmental dyslexia: A review. *Reading Research Quarterly, 27,* 28-53.

Shepherd, M. J. & Uhry, J. K. (1993, April). *Phonological awareness training: Case studies of children at-risk for dyslexia.* Paper presented at a symposium on phonological awareness at the annual meeting of the American Educational Research Association in Atlanta.

Siegel, L. S. (1989). IQ is irrelevant to the definition of learning disabilities. *Journal of Learning Disabilities, 22,* 469-478.

Snowling, M. J. (1980). The development of grapheme-phoneme correspondences in normal and dyslexic readers. *Journal of Experimental Child Psychology, 29,* 294-305.

Snowling, M. J. & Hulme, C. (1989). A longitudinal case study of developmental phonological dyslexia. *Cognitive Neuropsychology, 6,* 379-401.

Stanovich, K. E. (1981). Relationships between word decoding speed, general name-retrieval ability, and reading progress in first-grade children. *Journal of Educational Psychology, 73,* 309-315.

Stanovich, K. E. (1986). Matthew effects in reading: Some consequences of individual differences in the acquisition of literacy. *Reading Research Quarterly, 21,* 360-406.

Stanovich, K. E. (1991). Discrepancy definitions of reading disability: Has intelligence led us astray? *Reading Research Quarterly, 26,* 7-29.

Stanovich, K. E., Cunningham, A. E., Cramer, B. (1984). Assessing phonological awareness in kindergarten children: Issues of task comparability. *Journal of Experimental Child Psychology, 38,* 175-190.

Tunmer, W. E. (1994, October). *Language prediction skill, phonological recoding ability, and beginning reading.* Paper presented at NATO Advanced Study Institute in Alvor, Portugal.

Uhry, J. K. (1993a). Predicting reading from print awareness and phonological awareness skills: An early reading screening. *Educational Assessment, 1,* 349-368.

Uhry, J. K. (1993b). The spelling/reading connection and dyslexia: Can spelling be used to teach the alphabetic strategy? In R. M. Joshi & C. K. Leong (Eds.), *Reading disabilities: Diagnosis and component processes* (pp. 253-266). Dordrecht, Netherlands: Kluwer Academic Publishers.

Uhry, J. K., & Shepherd, M. J. (1993). Segmentation/spelling instruction as part of a first grade reading program: Effects on several measures of reading. *Reading Research Quarterly, 28,* 218-233.

Wagner, R.K., & Torgesen, J.K. (1987). The nature of phonological processing and its causal role in the acquisition of reading skills. *Psychological Bulletin, 101,* 192-212.

Wolf, M. (1991). Naming speed and reading: The contribution of the cognitive neurosciences. *Reading Research Quarterly, 26,* 123-141.

Wood, F. B., & Felton, R. H. (1994). Separate linguistic and attentional factors in the development of reading. *Topics in Language Disorders, 14,* 42-57.

THE RELATIONSHIP OF CENTRAL AUDITORY PROCESSING DISORDER AND LEARNING PROBLEMS

SYBIL SCHWARTZ
Montreal Children's Hospital
Montreal, Quebec
Canada, H3H 1P3

MAGGIE BRUCK
Department of Psychology
McGill University
Montreal, Canada H3A 1B1

ABSTRACT: Children with Learning Disabilities with a positive Central Auditory Processing deficit diagnosis (CAP+); children with Learning Disabilities with a negative Central Auditory Processing diagnosis (CAP-); and children with no school problems and no difficulty with Central Auditory Processing were compared on measures of Intelligence, Language, Memory, Attention, Phonological Awareness, Reading and Spelling in order to elucidate the nature of CAP deficits. The differences found between the CAP+ and CAP-groups shed some light on the nature of a CAP deficit and the additional burden imposed on children with Learning Disabilities. The similarities raise important issues regarding remediation and assumptions regarding the effect of a CAP deficit on learning.

Central auditory processing is defined as the analysis and use of sound signals by the central auditory system. Central auditory tests, which were originally developed to identify lesions in the central nervous system of adults, have recently been adopted to identify central auditory processing problems in children with language or learning problems.

Diagnosis of a Central Auditory Processing (CAP) disorder is based on abnormal CAP test battery results. The audiologist uses different tests to verify the integrity of CAP. Patterned or distorted stimuli are presented to one or both ears. Poor function on these tests is assumed to be related to dysfunction or disruption of the auditory pathways at a more central level. Thus evaluation of the child's ability to process auditory information in situations of reduced signal redundancy should reveal subtle dysfunction of central processing. However the validity and reliability of the tests and test batteries used with children have not been firmly established.

Furthermore, the concept of CAP dysfunction in children is not universally accepted. There are strong believers and those who have serious doubts. Some question whether the symptoms commonly

C.K. Leong and R.M. Joshi (Eds.), Cross-Language Studies of Learning to Read and Spell, 89–101.
© 1997 *Kluwer Academic Publishers. Printed in the Netherlands.*

attributed to CAP disorders could equally be attributed to other disorders. Gascon, Johnson, and Burd, (1986) question the existence of a CAP disorder as an entity separate from attention deficit disorder. In a study investigating the relationship of attention deficit disorder (ADD) and CAP, all of the ADD children who had normal language and reading skills were found to have significant CAP difficulties.

Rees (1973,1981) has also questioned the validity of a CAP disorder. She concluded that specific auditory difficulties are symptoms of a general language disorder. However, those who support the concept of CAP developmental disorders conceive of them as an impairment of auditory processing as opposed to linguistic processing. Sloan (1986) defines an auditory processing disorder as "difficulty in processing the acoustic speech signal that interferes with accurate and efficient perception of speech" (p. 35). She cautions that the manifestations of CAP dysfunction may be confused with linguistic processing disorders.

Several studies have attempted to investigate the relationship between learning disabilities (LD) and CAP disorders (Ferrre & Wilber, 1986, Jerger, Martin, & Jerger, 1987, Roush & Tait, 1984). Most of the studies investigating the relationship between LD and CAP have compared a group of LD children and Normals on CAP test performance. A major difficulty in interpreting the research is the inconsistent and often unclear criteria used for subject selection. The LD sample is provided by the school and few, if any, details are given.

A recent pilot study by Peck, Gessard, and Hellerman (1991) found no clinically significant correlations between CAP scores, data from other disciplines, or behavioral characteristics as described by parents and teachers. They concluded that more research is needed to define exactly what CAP testing is measuring and what its clinical significance is in the pediatric population (see Kamhi & Beasley, 1985 for similar conclusions).

To date, no study has carefully looked at the linguistic, cognitive and academic profiles of children diagnosed as having CAP deficits who also have significant learning disabilities. In the present study we compared the profiles of children who have both learning problems and CAP deficits to those who have learning problems but no CAP deficits. We examined children's performance in a number of domains. These were intelligence, language, memory, written language skills, phonological processing, and attention.

Methods

SUBJECTS

Three groups of subjects were tested; Children with LD and CAP (CAP+), children with LD and normal CAP functioning (CAP-) and a group of normals (N). Children in CAP+ and CAP- were selected from patients in the Audiology Department of a children's hospital who had undergone CAP testing to clarify the nature of their learning problems. Subjects who received CAP testing and met the following criteria were included:

i)   average IQ as measured by four subtests of the WISC-R
ii) performance on a standardized reading comprehension or standardized word recognition test was below 30%, and
iii) the child was between 8-10 years old

Children were further divided into CAP+ and CAP- on the basis of their performance on the CAP tests. If a child failed one or more of the CAP tests, they were considered to have a CAP deficit. The normal control group was chosen from local schools on the basis of performance on the academic tests, teacher ratings, and normal functioning on the same CAP testing undergone by the experimental groups (See Table 1).

Table 1. Subject characteristics.

	CAP+ (N=25)	CAP- (N=21)	NORMALS (N=25)	F TEST/ BONFERRONI
Age(mos.)	109	110	112	NS
IQ(WISC-R)	107	115	122	N>CAP+=CAP-**
Word recog. (%)	13	11	81	N>CAP+=CAP-**
Word attack (%)	14	11	73	N>CAP+=CAP-**
Reading comp.(%)	10	20	52	N>CAP+=CAP-*
Spelling (%)	9	8	65	N>CAP+=CAP-**

*p<.05; **p<.001

TESTS

Children who were found to have normal peripheral hearing were administered the following CAP tests: Staggered Spondaic Word Test (S.S.W.), (Katz, 1977); Competing Sentences, (Willeford, 1978); Competing Environmental Sounds (Katz, 1981); Pitch Pattern (Pinheiro, 1977); Phonemic Synthesis (Katz, 1981); and Auditory Figure-Ground, (Keith, 1986).

Subjects were compared on tests of:

(1). Intelligence:
Wechsler Intelligence Scale For Children- Revised (WISC-R) (partial) (Wechsler, 1974).

(2). Language:
Expressive One-Word Picture Vocabulary Test-Revised, (EOWPVT-R) (Gardner, 1990); Peabody Picture Vocabulary Test-Revised (PPVT-R) (Dunn & Dunn, 1981); Test for Reception of Grammar (TROG) (Bishop, 1982); Vocabulary (subtest WISC-R) (Wechsler, 1974); Golick Sentence Repetition Test (Golick, 1977); The Token Test for Children (DiSimoni, 1978); Pseudoword Repetition Test (PSWRT) (Taylor, Lean, & Schwartz, 1989); Syllable Deletion Tasks.

(3). Memory:
Children's Auditory Verbal Learning Test (CAVLT) (Talley, 1989); Digit Span (WISC-R) (Wechsler,1974).

(4). Written language-
Woodcock 1. Word Identification, 2. Word Attack; (Woodcock, 1987) Gray Oral Reading test-Revised (GORT-R) 1. Listening comprehension, 2. Reading Comprehension, (Wiederholt & Bryant, 1986); Wide Range Achievement Test (WRAT-R) Spelling (Jastak & Wilkinson, 1984).

(5). Phonological Processing
Phonological Deletion tasks; Phoneme Counting

(6). Attention
Continuous Performance Test (CPT); Conners' Parent Checklist (Conners, 1973).

PROCEDURE

Prior to participation, all subjects passed tests of peripheral hearing: pure tone audiometry within 10 db. from 250 to 8000 Hz; normal discrimination in quiet PBK (40db S.L.); contralateral and ipsilateral acoustic reflexes; and tone decay above reflex thresholds. Subjects were then administered the CAP tests. The tests were administered by two Audiologists in a sound treated room using a clinical diagnostic audiometer and a tape recorder. The experimental tests (intelligence, language, memory, written language, phonological processing, and attention) were administered by the first author, a Speech-Language Pathologist and trained research assistants who were blind to subject grouping.

RESULTS

One way ANOVA's with Bonferroni corrections were carried out on each of the measures.

Intelligence. All subjects were in the normal range of intelligence. The CAP+ group was significantly below the Normals.

Written Language. Both CAP+ and CAP- had serious problems in reading and spelling. According to many definitions - normal intelligence with serious delays in written language skills, these two groups would be classified as having learning disabilities. The two CAP groups did not differ significantly on either reading or spelling but were significantly below the Normals.

Language. CAP+ and CAP- did not differ significantly on any of the vocabulary measures (EOWPVT-R, PPVT-R, WISC-R Vocabulary). Scores were in the average range but were significantly below the Normals. Significant differences were found between CAP+ and CAP- on five language measures- the TROG, PSWRT, Sentence Repetition, the Token Test, and Syllable Deletion. In each instance CAP+ and CAP- were significantly below the Normals. (See Figures 1-5)

Memory. Scores were in the normal range for CAP+ and CAP- on Immediate Memory, Level of Learning, Immediate Recall and Delayed Recall. The differences between CAP+ and CAP- were nonsignificant. Both groups differed significantly from the Normals on all measures except Immediate Recall.

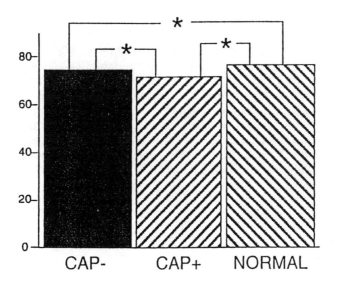

Figure 1. Mean scores on TROG.

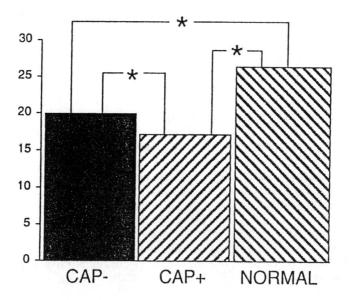

Figure 2. Mean scores on pseudoword repetition test.

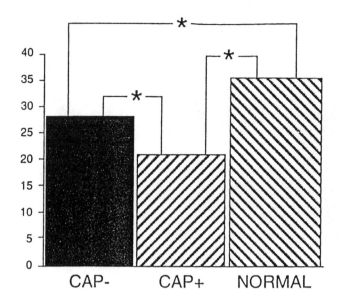

Figure 3. Mean scores on sentence repetition test.

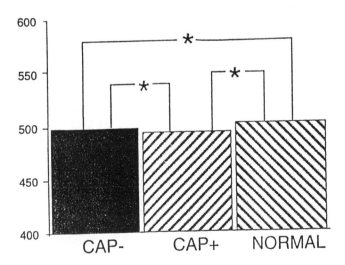

Figure 4. Mean standard scores on Token test.

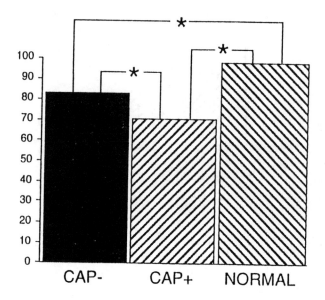

Figure 5. Mean % correct scores on syllable deletion.

Phonological processing. CAP+ and CAP- did not differ on Phoneme Counting or Phoneme Deletion. On Phoneme Counting CAP+ performed significantly below the Normal group. On Phoneme Deletion both CAP+ and CAP- were significantly below the Normals.

Attention. Significant difference were found between the CAP+ and CAP- on the Conners' Parent Checklist. The CAP+ were significantly different from the Normals (See Figure 6). On the CPT no differences were found between CAP+ and CAP- on either omissions or commissions. The CAP+ were significantly below the Normals on commissions.

DISCUSSION

Many similarities were found between the two groups of children with learning problems. They did not differ significantly on Intelligence, Memory or on any of the three vocabulary measures - expressive (EOWPVT-R), receptive (PPVT-R), or defining (WISC-R Vocabulary).

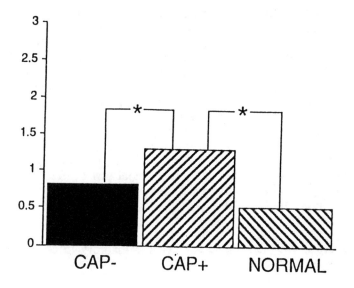

Figure 6. Mean scores on Conners Parent Rating Scale.

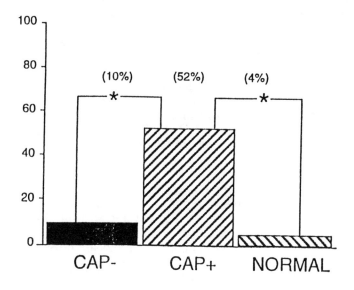

Figure 7. Percent scores >1.5 on Conners Parent Rating Scale.

The differences found offer some insight into the type of difficulty experienced by those with CAP deficits. CAP+ and CAP- differed significantly on five language measures: the TROG which is a receptive test of grammatic and syntactic sensitivity; the Golick Sentence Repetition Test which taps the ability to retain and repeat syntactic and semantic information; the Pseudoword Repetition Test which tests the ability to remember and repeat polysyllabic words; the Token Test which taps the ability to follow commands of increasing length and complexity; and Syllable Deletion which tests the ability to manipulate syllables within a pseudoword. These five tests all require rapid, accurate temporal processing. Two of the five require repetition. Does the CAP+ represent a special group of children with Specific Language Impairment (SLI) and, if so, is there an underlying cognitive impairment which could account for their particular linguistic deficits?

Leonard (1989) has suggested that the inability to cope with lack of saliency is responsible for much of the difficulty encountered by children with specific language disorders (SLI). He found that SLI children miss segments of the signal- in particular the unstressed segments which are shorter and less intense. On the TROG all the nuances must be processed accurately and in the correct temporal order. In many instances syntactic cues are at the ends of words or in unstressed segments and are therefore less salient. The bisyllabic and multisyllabic pseudowords in the Pseudoword Repetition Test and Syllable Deletion tests also involve the processing of unstressed syllables, as does the Sentence Repetition Test.

Tallal (1980, 1984) found that developmental language impaired and reading impaired children had CAP deficits. Both groups exhibited a profound deficit in processing rapidly presented acoustic information. She concluded that a basic temporal processing impairment underlies their inability to integrate sensory information that converges in rapid succession in the central nervous system and also affects motor output in the millisecond time frame. A recent study of dyslexic children pinpointed a fundamental brain flaw in the left hemisphere that handles rapidly flowing auditory information. There is some evidence of changes in the number and volume of the magnocellular regions of the lateral and medial geniculate (Galaburda, Menard, & Rosen, 1994). Gathercole and Baddeley (1990) found that children with SLI were significantly impaired on tests of verbal short term memory and concluded that a primary deficit in phonological short term memory was the basis of the language deficit. In all of these theories as to the nature of the underlying deficit, it remains unclear as to whether the deficit is a cause or a consequence of the disorder.

Another possibility is that CAP+ and CAP- children share similar underlying difficulties but those of the CAP+ children are more severe. Certainly clinicians find that the CAP+ children are more disabled and slower in their response to remediation. A treatment study would help to determine the validity of this clinical impression.

There was a relationship between the observational data for Attention Deficit Disorder obtained by the Conners' Parent Checklist and CAP test results. Significant differences were found between CAP+ and CAP-. These results are in keeping with those found by other researchers (Gascon et al., 1986; Ludlow, Cudahy and Bassich, 1983). Gascon et al. (1986) hypothesized several explanations to account for the attentional deficits found in children with CAP deficits. They felt it would be necessary to test for attention in other modalities than the auditory domain to ascertain whether the CAP deficits might be causing or contributing to the attention deficits. No differences were found between the CAP+ and CAP- groups on the CPT, a measure of visual attention. The attentional differences noted were not part of a generic attention deficit so one might assume that they were specific to the auditory modality.

The similarities between the CAP+ and CAP- groups raise some questions as well. Advocates for Central Auditory Processing disorders believe that the phonological processing problems often associated with learning difficulties are a result of the Central Auditory Processing Disorder. The finding that CAP+ and CAP- did not differ on the Phonological Processing tests suggests that phonological processing problems are related to learning disabilities. Many, if not most, children with reading and spelling difficulties have problems with phonological processing whether or not they test positively on CAP tests. Audiologists involved in CAP testing often make suggestions or offer remedial activities related to the reading-phonic difficulty. CAP testing does not provide sufficient information to decide on the best remedial academic strategy. Such suggestions would best be made in conjunction with other professionals, who know about the reading process, the acquisition of literacy, and the range of deficits associated with learning disabilities.

Central auditory processing disorders in children have only recently been linked to any neurological or anatomical abnormality. Further study with the newer and more sensitive radiologic investigative methods, or neurophysiological and neurochemical tests might increase our knowledge of the cause or causes of CAP disorders.

REFERENCES

Bishop, D.V.M. (1982). *Test for Reception of Grammar* (TROG). Available from the author at University of Manchester, Department of Psychology, Manchester, England.

Conners, C.K. (1973). Rating scales for use in drug studies with children. *Psychopharmacology Bulletin, 1,* 24-28.

DiSimoni, F. (1978). *The Token Test for Children.* Boston: Teaching Resources Corporation.

Dunn, L., & Dunn, L. (1981). *The Peabody Picture Vocabulary Test-Revised.* Circle Pines, MN: American Guidance Service.

Ferre, J.M., & Wilber, L.A. (1986). Normal and learning disabled children's central auditory processing skills: an experimental test battery. *Ear and Hearing, 7,* 336-343.

Galaburda, A.M., Menard, M.T., & Rosen, G.D. (1994). Evidence for aberrant auditory anatomy in developmental dyslexia. *Proceedings of the National Academy of Sciences, USA, 91,* 8010-8013.

Gardner, M.F. (1990). *Expressive One-Word Picture Vocabulary Test-Revised.* Novato, CA: Academic Therapy Publications.

Gascon, G., Johnson,R., & Burd, L. (1986). Central auditory processing and attention deficit disorders. *Journal of Child Neurology, 1,* 27-33.

Gathercole, S.E.,& Baddeley,A.D. (1990). Phonological memory deficits in language-disordered children: A longitudinal study. *Journal of Memory and Language, 29,* 336-360.

Golick, M., (1977). *Language development in children- A linguistic analysis.* Unpublished doctoral dissertation, McGill University.

Jastak, S., & Wilkinson,G. (1984). *Wide Range Achievement Test-Revised.* Wilimington, DE: Jastak Associates.

Jerger, S., Martin, R.C., & Jerger, J. (1987). Specific auditory perceptual dysfunction in a learning disabled child, *Ear and Hearing, 8,* 78-86.

Kamhi, A.G., & Beasley, D.S. (1985). Central auditory processing disorders: Is it a meaningful construct in the 20th century? *Journal of Children's Communication Disorders, 9,* 5-13.

Katz, J. (1977). The Staggered Spondaic Word Test. In R. W. Keith (Ed.), *Central Auditory Dysfunction.* (PP. 103-127). New York: Grune & Stratton.

Katz, J. (1981). Phonemic synthesis: Testing and training. In R.W. Keith (Ed.) *Central auditory and language disorders in children.* (pp. 145-159) Houston: College Hill Press.

Keith, R. (1986). SCAN: *A screening test for auditory processing disorders.* San Diego: The Psychological Corporation.

Leonard, L.B. (1989).   Language learnability and specific language impairment in children. *Applied Psycholinguistics, 10,* 179-202.

Ludlow, C.L., Cudahy, E.A., & Bassich, C. (1983). Auditory processing skills of hyperactive, language impaired, and reading disabled boys. In E.Z. Lasky and J. Katz (Eds.), *Central Auditory processing Disorders.* (pp. 163-184). Baltimore: University Park Press.

Peck, D., Gressard, R., & Hellerman, S.   (1991).   Central auditory processing in the school-aged child: Is it clinically relevant? *Developmental and Behavioral Pediatrics, 12,* 324-326.

Pinheiro, M.L. (1977).   Tests of central auditory function in children with learning disabilities. In R. Keith (Ed.), *Central Auditory Dysfunction.* (pp. 223-254). New York: Grune & Stratton.

Rees, N.S. (1973).   Auditory processing factors in language disorders: The view from Procrustes' bed. *Journal of Speech and Hearing Disorders, 38,* 304-315.

Rees, N.S. (1981).   Saying more than we know: Is auditory processing disorder a meaningful concept? In R.W. Keith (Ed.) *Central auditory and language disorders in children,* (pp. 94-120).   San Diego, CA: College Hill Press.

Roush, J. & Tait, C. (1984).   Binaural fusion, masking level differences, and auditory brain stem responses in children with language-learning disabilties. *Ear and Hearing, 5,* 37-44.

Sloan, C. (1986). *Treating auditory processing difficulties in children.* San Diego: College Hill Press.

Tallal, P. (1980).   Language and reading: Some perceptual prerequisites. *Bulletin of the Orton Society, 30,* 170-178

Tallal, P. (1984).   Temporal or phonetic processing deficit in dyslexia? That is the question. *Applied Psycholinguistics, 10,* 167-169.

Talley, J.L. (1989). *Children's auditory verbal learning test.* Odessa, Fl: Psychological Assessment Resources.

Taylor, H.G., Lean, D., & Schwartz, S. (1989).   Pseudoword repetition ability in learning disabled children. *Applied Psycholinguistics, 10,* 203-219.

Wechsler, D. (1974). *Wechsler Intelligence Scale for Children-Revised.* New York: Psychological Corporation.

Wiederholt, J.L., & Bryant, B.R. (1986). *Gray Oral Reading Test-Revised.* Austin: Pro-Ed.

Willeford, J. (1977).   Assessing central auditory behaviour in children. A test battery approach. In R.W. Keith, (Ed.) *Central Auditory Dysfunction.* (pp. 43-72). New York: Grune & Stratton.

Woodcock, R. (1987). *Woodcock Reading Mastery Tests-Revised.* Circle Pines, MN: American Guidance Service.

BEGINNING READING IN GERMANY AND THE U.S.: A COMPARISON OF PHONOLOGICAL SEGMENTATION, DECODING, LEXICAL ACCESS, AND COMPREHENSION

J. C. NÄSLUND
College of Education
University of New Mexico
Albuquerque, N.M. 87131
U.S.A.

W. SCHNEIDER AND
Dept. of Psychology
University of Würzburg
W-8700 Würzburg
Germany

PAUL VAN DEN BROEK
Dept. of Educ. Psychology
University of Minnesota
Minneapolis, MN 55455
U.S.A.

ABSTRACT. First and second grade German and American children were compared on three phonological awareness tasks, lexical access speed, decoding of words and pseudowords, and reading comprehension in order to assess the relationship of linguistic and reading (decoding and comprehension) measures in both language groups. No significant differences were found between German and American children in either grade in pseudoword decoding accuracy, word decoding speed, and the phoneme take-away task. Word decoding accuracy was similar for first grade children, but second grade American children were significantly more accurate than children in the German second grade. German children in both first and second grade were significantly more accurate in phoneme manipulation tasks and faster at decoding pseudowords. The patterns of errors in the phoneme take-away task were similar between language groups. Pseudoword decoding performance indicated that American children made more errors in decoding vowels than did German children in both grades. Phonemic tasks were significantly related to reading measures for both German and American children. The latter group showed a greater relationship between reading measures and lexical access speed than did German children. Differences in orthography and lessened vowel consistency in English may give rise to differences in phonemic representations of vowels and an increased reliance on lexical access cues in reading for the American children. This might explain why German children do not differ as much as American children in their speed of word decoding as compared with decoding pseudowords.

International researchers have demonstrated the universal importance of several linguistic factors affecting early reading acquisition. One of the most important of these factors appears to be a young reader's efficient access to phonemic representations. A significant relationship between awareness of and automatic access to phonemic representations and reading proficiency has been found in many languages with orthographies that vary in their degree of transparency of grapheme to phoneme (symbol to sound) representation. Past and current research in English, Czech, German, Danish, Italian and other languages suggests that regardless of the orthography, an individual learning to read will benefit from a good perceptual and cognitive representation of the phonemes present in the language they are learning to

C.K. Leong and R.M. Joshi (Eds.), Cross-Language Studies of Learning to Read and Spell, 103–120.
© 1997 Kluwer Academic Publishers. Printed in the Netherlands.

read (Bradley & Bryant, 1983; Caravolas & Bruck, 1993; Cossu, Shankweiler, Liberman, Katz & Tola, 1988; Lundberg, Olofsson, & Wall, 1980; Näslund & Schneider, 1991; Stanovich, Cunningham & Feeman, 1984).

Another variable of importance to reading researchers is the degree of automatic lexical access one demonstrates. Denckla and Rudel (1976) introduced the Rapid Automatic Naming paradigm to investigate the relationship between automatic access of lexical representations (e.g., the "name" associated with an object, letter, or an attribute, such as color) and reading acquisition and proficiency. Recently, Hulme and Tordoff (1989) have offered an additional component of this paradigm. Speech rate, in general, also appears to relate significantly to reading proficiency. These processes might be related to Tallal and colleagues' observations (see review by Tallal, Miller & Fitch, 1993; Bowers & Wolf, 1993; Wolf, 1991) that suggest a neurophysiological basis for a "precise timing mechanism" in both phonemic recoding and sound representations in general. Although this theory has received recent media recognition, other prominent researchers in the field remain skeptical that such a specifically defined neurological explanation can be demonstrated. However, the relationship between speed and efficiency of naming (as a measure of lexical access) is fairly accepted among researchers in reading.

It is still an open question as to whether the degree of transparency between graphemes and phonemes in a language might facilitate or hinder a beginning reader's efforts to decipher the code of words in print and reach an automatic efficiency in decoding. Thus far, results are not altogether clear concerning the relative contribution of type of orthography to the presence or absence of reading problems. There is some evidence that phonemic awareness is of equal importance to transparent and less transparent orthographies, as shown in German, Czech, English, Danish, and Italian studies referenced earlier. Phonemic awareness predicted reading performance in German, Danish, and Italian children similarly to how it predicted reading in studies of American children (Cossu et al., 1988; Lundberg et al. 1980; Näslund & Schneider, 1991). German and Italian orthography are both considered significantly more transparent in grapheme to phoneme correspondence than English.

In a longitudinal study, German children were tested in memory, phonemic awareness, and lexical access speed and accuracy in kindergarten (Näslund & Schneider, 1991). These measures were used as predictors of later reading comprehension and decoding ability in second grade. German children apparently benefited from the high degree of transparency in their language, making few errors in decoding words and non-words. However, those with poorer phonemic awareness performance in kindergarten, and in second grade, were poorer at comprehension, and slower at decoding than those with better phonemic awareness performance. The efficiency of decoding was likely affected by level of phonemic awareness. Accessing lexical representations to serve in comprehension might be also affected negatively by low levels of phonemic awareness. Orthographic transparency might aid in accuracy of letter to sound mapping for certain language groups. However, without a supportive system of phonemic representation, the mapping of letter strings to lexical representations might be hindered.

Not all researchers agree with this interpretation of results. Cossu, Rossini and Marshall(1993) have provided disconfirming evidence of this seemingly straightforward relationship between phonemic representations and reading performance in studies of various Italian populations. Some Down Syndrome children, who demonstrate little ability to use phonemic representations, nevertheless learned to read proficiently in Italian (as expected by their ability levels). Cossu et al. (1988) also provide evidence that phonemic awareness tasks are easier for Italian children learning to read, given the great transparency of their language. In addition, the word decoding errors made in Italian differ, and are less in number than those made by American children at similar reading levels (see also Thorstad, 1991).

A recent study that directly compares Czech and English-Canadian children further examines the impact of language structure on children's phonemic representations and the degree to which transparency of orthography effects early spelling, which is a good indicator of children's understanding of the relationship between orthography and phonological properties (Caravolas & Bruck, 1993). Czech has a more complex consonant onset structure than English, German, or Italian. Onset consonant clusters are more frequent, and have numerous possible linguistically "legal" combinations. Czech children performed better overall than Canadian English speakers in pre-kindergarten, kindergarten, and first grade phonemic awareness tasks. However, Czech children's superiority appeared only in tasks reflecting consonant structure found frequently in Czech (e.g., CCV syllables were more easily segmented that CVC syllables). Caravolas and Bruck (1993) interpret their results as supporting a linguistic input effect on the strength and type of phonemic representations. The superior performance of Czech children was specific to their own language, especially given the English-Canadian speaking children's superiority in tasks requiring segmentation of singleton consonant onsets from their rime units, which might be interpreted as a less complex task than segmenting consonant clusters.

The present study compares American and German children. The syllable structure of these languages is not as variant as either Italian or Czech and English.   German children might benefit from a more transparent orthography in comparison to English. In addition, German vowels have less spoken variants than the American-English system. Most long-to-short vowel changes in German are markerd, such as tense or pluralization (i.e., anfangen-fängt an; Maus-Mäuser), whereas such variations in English vowels are not standardized to "long" and "short" vowel forms (i.e., run-ran; win-won; begin-began; mouse-mice, etc.). The pronunciation of German vowels does not usually vary dependent on orthographic environment, as in English (i.e., pat-part; dip-dirt; calendar-colander). The consistency of consonantal sounds does not vary to a great extent between languages. These comparisons in German and English are advantageous to studying cross-linguistic differences in phonology and orthography that may or may not contribute to differences in phonemic awareness and reading tasks.

Näslund & Schneider (1991) found a low level of variance accounted for in decoding and comprehension by the lexical access measures in their earlier German sample. These results were discrepant in comparison with American studies, which indicated a strong relationship of lexical access and reading proficiency (see Wolf, 1991, for review). Lexical access should be compared directly with other variables (such as phonemic awareness) between language groups in order to test the possibility that lexical access differentially affects learning to read in various orthographies. Given the lower level of transparency in English orthography, children learning to read in English might rely on an interaction of phonemic and lexical representations in reading more so than readers of more transparent orthographies.

The influential model of dual route processing (Coltheart, 1978) suggested two actual routes for reading. One route was phonemic, the other was direct lexical representation. The route of word recognition depended upon the level of familiarity with the word read. Most researchers today agree that a direct lexical route without some level of phonemic representations is not likely. The original proposal of this dual-process theory may have been influenced by the orthographic properties of English. Readers of English must use contextual cues (morphological and orthographic) to recognize correctly the phonetic properties of many words. Strong phonemic representations are necessary in the reading of English. However, in somewhat of a contrast to more transparent orthographies, the efficiency (speed and accuracy) of lexical representations, especially at the morphological level, may significantly enhance word decoding efficiency in less transparent orthographies.

The study presented here attempts to address some of these questions with a direct comparison of first and second grade children in Germany and the U.S.. The study was conducted simultaneously in Würzburg, Minnesota, and Wisconsin. The school districts chosen were matched roughly in size and economic range. Children in the study reported here received the same tasks, directly translated when appropriate. Non-words used for decoding and some phonemic tasks were identical, chosen for their legality in German and English orthography, and for similarity of difficulty level.

Method

SUBJECTS

Seventy-four German children (30 in the first grade and 44 in the second grade) and 67 American children (35 in the first grade and 32 in the second grade) completed all tasks with proper data recording. The original sample of German children was 88 (43 in first grade and 45 in second grade) and the original sample for the U.S. group was 154 (74 in first grade and 80 in second grade). Errors in timing data were minimal for the German sample. Unfortunately, in the U.S. sample, a few of the teachers collecting data did not use the standardized procedures of timing responses. Tape recordings of all sessions allowed screening of improper timing. This led to a great reduction in data for the U.S. group in speed measures.

PROCEDURES AND MATERIALS

No teachers used a "whole language" approach in their reading instruction. Districts were chosen for a match in socio-economic conditions in both countries. School principals were solicited as to their interest in participation. From those schools in agreement, an equal number of first and second grade children from each school was randomly selected to be in the study. Due to absences on the days of group reading comprehension tests and improper timing data reported, not all children are included in the analyses.

TASK DESCRIPTIONS

All tasks were conducted in children's schools and practice items were presented for each task (except for reading comprehension). All sessions were recorded on audio cassette.

Phonemic Take-Away: Fifteen items were used, eight of which produced a non-word when the first sound was taken away (i.e., English: felt-elt; German: gelb-elb), and seven that produced a word after the first sound was removed (i.e., English: pink-ink; German: Post- Ost). Children were instructed to say what was left of a word after the first sound was removed. A fixed order was used, with the items that produced a word response presented after the item that produced a pseudoword.

Phonemic recognition: Nine items require child to listen to two pseudowords (two and three syllables) and determine if the two are different or the same. The item is played again (if answer is "different"), and the child is asked to indicate the sounds that differ. There is at most one sound change in any word. The same items are used in English and German, with intonation and accent adjusted (i.e., LOMAFI & LOMAPI). *Part two*: Twelve items require children to replace one sound in a pseudoword (one or two syllables) with another sound. The same items are used for both language groups, with intonation and accent adjusted (e.g., RATU changed to RATO).

Word and pseudoword decoding: Speed and accuracy were assessed for six lists of four items each for both words and pseudowords (24 items each set). All words and pseudowords were one syllable, and words were high frequency words at the first and second grade level for both languages. Words were translated directly. All pseudowords used regular spelling. The pseudowords were the same for both language groups for purposes of direct comparison. Children practised reading three lists of words and pseudowords different from those used in the study before measures were recorded. Lists were used instead of single items in order to increase accuracy of experimenter measures of speed.

Reading comprehension: An 18-item comprehension test consisting of seven short stories was used in both countries. Items were multiple choice questions requiring children to infer information from the story. Vocabulary was intended to be familiar to children.

Lexical access speed and accuracy: *Colors of objects*: Black and white drawings of five familiar items were presented to children, and they were asked to indicate the usual color of the object ("yellow" for a LEMON, "red" for a TOMATO, "green" for a LEAF, etc.). Children were then presented with a sequence of five cards, each with the same five objects in a row in fixed random order. Children were instructed to name the color of each object as quickly and accurately as possible. *Object names*: After the task of naming colors of objects, each child was shown a card with black and white drawings of ten familiar objects (i.e., horse, comb, chair, ring, train, shoe, etc.). After the experimenter was certain the child agreed on the same name of each object, a sequence of five cards was presented, each card with a row of five of the ten objects named in the practice session. The child was again instructed to name the items as quickly and accurately as possible. Given the average number of errors for all children in the study was .03 items over all colors and items, accuracy measures are not compared in this study. Variance in speed is assessed.

Results and Discussion

DIFFERENCES IN TASK PERFORMANCE.

This study compared German and American children on tasks of phonological segmentation, word and pseudoword decoding, and reading comprehension (in second grade, only). Table 1 provides the means and standard deviations, and the significance level of the Bonferroni adjusted t-test for each task. German and American children were similar in each grade on a task of removing the first sound in a target word, but in the second grade, German children outperformed Americans in the more complex phonemic manipulation task ($p=0.001$). In first grade, these groups did not differ in word reading accuracy, word reading speed, phoneme manipulation, or in pseudoword reading accuracy, but did differ in pseudoword reading time ($p<0.0001$), which was much slower for Americans than Germans. A similar pattern was found for the second grade comparisons, except that American second graders were better at word decoding accuracy than Germans, and Germans were better in reading comprehension in second grade ($p's<0.05$).

Table 1. German and U.S. means, standard deviations, and t-test results.

Task	Grade	German mean (s.d.)	U.S. mean (s.d.)	p of t
Word decoding	1	16.50 (1.85)	17.78 (5.22)	.18
Pseudoword decoding	1	14.91 (2.39)	13.83 (6.79)	.38
Decoding difference	1	1.59 (1.86)	3.94 (4.36)	.005*
Word decoding speed	1	901 ms (511 ms)	1271 ms (965 ms)	.052
Pseudoword decoding speed	1	847 ms (546 ms)	2083 ms (1064 ms)	.0001*
Decoding speed difference	1	(-54 ms) (284 ms)	766 ms (749 ms)	.0001*
Word span	1	3.97 (.74)	4.38 (.92)	.051
Lexical access speed	1	644 ms (167 ms)	706 ms (163 ms)	.13

Table 1. (Continued)

Task	Grade	German mean (s.d.)	U.S. mean (s.d.)	p of t
Phoneme recognition	1	4.35 (2.65)	2.39 (2.36)	.004
Phoneme take-away	1	9.41 (5.36)	11.19 (4.71)	.15
Phoneme manipulation	1	3.75 (2.38)	3.00 (1.77)	.14
Reading comprehension	1	8.62 (4.55)	8.86 (3.99)	.82
Word decoding	2	18.16 (1.82)	22.97 (1.27)	.0001*
Pseudoword decoding	2	16.09 (2.79)	17.43 (4.66)	.14
Decoding difference	2	2.07 (1.94)	5.54 (3.92)	.0001*
Word decoding speed	2	363 ms (183 ms)	354 ms (134 ms)	.81
Pseudoword decoding speed	2	486 ms (234 ms)	946 ms (573 ms)	.0001*
Decoding speed difference	2	123 ms (199 ms)	593 ms (508 ms)	.0001*
Word span	2	4.03 (.73)	4.40 (.95)	.054
Lexical access speed	2	593 ms (154 ms)	641 ms (182 ms)	.21
Phoneme recognition	2	5.35 (2.71)	3.09 (2.17)	.0001*
Phoneme take-away	2	13.29 (2.82)	12.94 (3.24)	.61
Phoneme manipulation	2	5.20 (2.37)	3.46 (2.23)	.0012*
Reading comprehension	2	11.67 (4.86)	8.69 (3.94)	.0042

* Note: * t-tests Bonferroni adjustment for experimentwise error (p<.05=p<.0033).
     ms = time in milliseconds

In both grades, the difference in reading speed for pseudowords and words indicated that German children did not differ in these tasks, reading pseudowords just about as quickly as real words. American children, however, differed significantly in reading speed between these sets of stimuli. One possible explanation is the differences in experience with orthographies. English is not as shallow an orthography as German. German readers appear to be reading pseudowords with much more ease, employing a "word attack" approach, whereas American children appear to look at pseudowords as items they "do not know", and take more time employing decoding strategies.

Correlations among tasks. Correlations presented in Tables 2, 3, 4, & 5 indicate the strength of relationship among the phonological tasks and reading/decoding measures in both countries, for both grades. For the first grade, all measures were significantly correlated for the U.S. sample. The correlations were not as high for the German first grade group as for the American children. Lexical access speed was not as significantly related to decoding measures for Germans as compared to Americans. The phoneme take away tasks were significantly related to almost all decoding tasks. The phoneme manipulation task was only significantly related to two of the decoding tasks for Americans. Lexical access appeared more related to reading and decoding for the American children than the German children in first grade.

Table 2. Correlations for German first grade (N=32).

Reading Tasks	Reading comp.	Word decoding	pseudoword decoding	word deco. speed	p-word deco. speed
Reading Comp.		.35	.33	-.57***	-.51***
Word Decoding			.71**	-.59**	-.56**
Pseudoword deco.				-.34	-.18
Word decoding speed					.88**
Linguistic tasks					
Lexical access speed	-.20	-.08	.11	-.01	.16
Word span	.13	.04	.01	.01	.06
Phoneme Recogn.	.29	.36*	.24	-.43*	-.23
Phoneme Take-away	.58*	.31	.36*	-.60***	-.53***
Phoneme manipulation	.34	.30	.25	-.31	-.26

* p<.05, ** p<.01, *** p<.001.

Table 3. Correlations for U.S. first grade (N=35).

Reading Tasks	Reading comp.	Word decoding	pseudoword decoding	word decoding speed	p-word decoding speed
Reading Comp.		.63***	.59***	-.74***	-.52***
Word Decoding			.84***	.71***	-.59**
Pseudoword decoding				-.58***	-.50***
Word decoding speed					.71***
Linguistic tasks					
Lexical access speed	-.25	.43**	-.45**	.43**	.32
Word span	.46**	.45**	.46**	.32	.31
Phoneme recognition	.24	.26	.23	-.36*	-.26
Phoneme Take-away	.37*	.74***	.71***	.52***	-.40*
Phoneme manipulation	.47**	.62***	.63	-.39*	-.40*

* $p<.05$, ** $p<.01$, *** $p<.001$.

Correlations in the second grade (see Tables 4 & 5) indicate weaker relationship between reading and the lexical access tasks for the German children as compared with the American children. A similar pattern is found for the phoneme tasks between the American and German second grade groups.

Error patterns. Patterns of responses in the 'initial sound take-away' task did not differ substantially for Germans and Americans (see Table 6), and in neither grade were accuracy rates significantly different. German children in each grade outperformed American children in the more difficult phonemic manipulation tasks. Performance of this particular task might be less difficult if children can easily make use of sound representations, which might explain why children with a shallower orthography would be able to represent the sounds and manipulate them more easily than children manipulating sounds in English.

Table 4. Correlations for German second grade (N=44).

Reading Tasks	Reading comp.	Word decoding	pseudoword decoding	word decoding speed	p-word decoding speed
Reading Comp.		.23	.29	-.59***	-.43**
Word Decoding			.72***	-.31*	-.31*
Pseudoword decoding				-.37*	-.27
Word decoding speed					.57***

Linguistic tasks

Lexical access speed	-.32*	.22	-.16	.26	.39**
Word span	.25	.05	.01	-.18	-.12
Phoneme recognition	.33*	.09	.33*	-.30	-.26
Phoneme Take-away	.45**	.09	.26	-.54***	-.54***
Phoneme manipulation	.49**	.26	.27	-.37*	-.28*

* p<.05,   ** p<.01,   *** p<.001.

Table 5. Correlations for U.S. second grade (N=32).

Reading Tasks	Reading comp.	Word decoding	pseudoword decoding	word decoding speed	p-word decoding speed
Reading Comp.		.52**	.57***	-.88***	-.48**
Word Decoding			.68***	-.61***	-.41*
Pseudoword decoding				-.66***	-.66***
Word decoding speed					.60***
Linguistic tasks					
Lexical access speed	-.54**	-.30	-.29	.48**	.50**
Word span	.44*	.23	.36*	-.46**	-.25
Phoneme recognition	.25	.16	.32	-.37*	-.27
Phoneme Take-away	.56***	.22	.36*	-.56***	-.33
Phoneme manipulation	.37*	.51**	.45**	-.53**	-.44**

* p<.05, ** p<.01, *** p<.001.

Table 6. Phoneme take-away task error analysis: Proportions correct, non-responses, and types of errors. N's are total possiblle responses for each Country and Grade.

Country	First Grade		Second Grade	
	U.S.	Germany	U.S.	Germany
Total responses:	1100	645	1200	675
Proportion of total errors	.40	.53	.10	.12
Total errors	(440)	(342)	(120)	(81)

Type of response error
Proportion of Total Responses
(Proportion of Errors)

No response	.01	.005	.01	0
	(.025)	(.01)	(.10)	
Repeat item, add to word	.05	.04	.01	.01
	(.125)	(.075)	(.10)	(.085)
Single sound in target	.02	.03	.01	.005
	(.125)	(.075)	(.10)	(.085)
Change, shift, delete middle	.21	.20	.02	.05
or end of word	(.125)	(.075)	(.10)	(.085)
Change first sound or remove	.11	.24	.04	.04
consonant cluster	(.125)	(.075)	(.10)	(.085)
Segmentation correct, but off	.01	.03	.001	.01
by one sound elsewhere	(.125)	(.075)	(.10)	(.085)

Error patterns for the pseudoword decoding task are directly comparable between countries, given the same items were used. Results of chi-square analyses of error data indicate a significant difference in error patters between German and American children (see Tables 7 & 8). In both grades, German children had proportionately fewer vowel errors, and mixed vowel-consonant errors, in comparison to consonant errors than did American children. For all groups, in both grades and countries, consonant errors were the most frequent. Errors were not counted in this analysis if these were the results of dialect (i.e., the Franken-German dialect does not distinguish between /p/ and /b/ phonemes, and /t/ and /d/ in final positions are not as distinguishable as in the initial position in German), or if responses reflected an inability to distinguish between 'long' and 'short' variations of vowels in English. The majority of errors in German appeared to reflect minimal pair confusions (/g/ and /k/, /d/ and /t/ in the initial position), and some stops (/b/ and /d/). American errors indicated, in both grades, more misreading not attributable to minimal pair or stop confusions. Changing the order of consonants (i.e., 'flad' to 'fald') was a common consonant error in both language groups.

Table 7. Pseudoword decoding errors in first grade.

| | Error type | | | |
	consonant	vowel	mixed	total
Country				
U.S.	185	84	156	425
Germany	112	21	20	153
Total	297	105	176	578

Chi Square = 42.17, df = 2, p<.001

Note: Errors are partitioned between vowel, consonant, and mixed (vowel & consonant) errors.

Table 8. Pseudoword decoding errors for second grade.

| | Error type | | | |
	consonant	vowel	mixed	total
Country				
U.S.	105	78	47	230
Germany	104	6	6	116
Total	209	84	53	346

Chi Square = 62.68, df = 2, p<.001

Note: Errors are partitioned between vowel, consonant, and mixed (vowel & consonant) errors.

Conclusions

This study was not intended to indicate which nation produced better readers, but investigated differences in orthographic constraints of both languages that might give rise to different decoding and reading habits. German and American samples were compared directly in their performance of reading comprehension, decoding speed and accuracy (words and pseudowords), phonemic awareness and recoding ability, and lexical access speed. The relation of phonemic tasks and lexical access to reading measures (comprehension and decoding) was found to differ between the two language groups in both first grade and second grade. Phonemic tasks correlated with reading tasks in both countries. However, lexical access performance was also significant for the American group, but not as much so for the German group.

Error patterns indicate similarities in performance of the phoneme take-away task, which requires phonemic representations. Analyses on the two other phonemic tasks are in progress. Strategies in the phonemic take-away task were the most readily interpretable among the three phonemic tasks. Decoding of pseudowords demonstrated differences in the types of errors made by German and American first and second graders. Although no significant differences were found in the proportion of errors between the two language groups, experience in learning to read in languages differing in orthographic transparency might explain the differences found in the types of errors made. All children made more consonant than vowel errors. However, the American children demonstrated proportionately more vowel errors than did German children. This difference might reflect the ambiguity of English vowels in comparison with the German vowel system, which has more orthographic representations of vowels, but less variation in pronunciation than English vowels.

The universal importance of phonemic representations in learning to read was supported in this comparative study. An additional influence of lexical access speed was discovered for the American children. This influence was particularly strong for the American group. This results, in combination with the findings of vowel errors, might lead to proposing an additional step required in decoding in less transparent orthographies, such as English. Where the vowel structure is more ambiguous in its representation, readers may rely on lexical access (particularly at the morphological level) to support phonemic representations in the process of accurate decoding.

One possible explanation for the difference between the Cossu et al. (1988) results and those from American and German studies is that Italian not only has a more transparent orthography than English, but has a syllable structure that is more "open" than both English and German. Italian has less

Consonant-Vowel-Consonant (CVC) syllables than either English or German. Deciphering strings of CV and CCV syllables (onset-rime units minus end consonants, or "codas"), acoustically and orthographically, might be less complex than strings of CVC, CCVC, and CVCC syllables. This lessened phonic complexity might explain why Cossu finds Italian children more proficient in phonemic awareness tasks, and faster in learning to read than American children. Syllable structure might also lead to a partial explanation of why German, American, and Scandinavian children vary so much in phonemic awareness, and that this awareness has a significant influence on their reading ability.

Cossu et al. (1988) did not directly compare American and Italian children. The Italian children in the study were compared to a previous study completed 14 years previously (Liberman, Shankweiler, Fischer, & Carter, 1974). Thorstad (1991) directly compared English and Italian children, and controlled for orthographic transparency. Some English children learned to read and spell with a traditional orthography (t.o.) and some with a phonetically transparent writing system called the "initial teaching alphabet" (i.t.a.) designed as an experimental system to facilitate early attempts to read in English (see Pitman, 1969). The English children using i.t.a. and Italian children were similar in first grade reading performance, and both groups outperformed the English t.o. group. Spelling did not show the same results. Both English groups were similar, but were significantly lower in performance as compared to the Italian first grade children. Thorstad (1991) and Caravolas and Bruck (1993) are two of the few studies that directly compare language groups on phoneme awareness and reading or writing. Both studies suggest that a simpler vowel and syllable structure, as found in Italian, would not explain the difference in ease of learning to read and write (as Cossu et al. 1988 claim) any more than would the affordance of a transparent orthography. In addition, Caravolas and Bruck (1993) demonstrated superiority in some phonemic awareness tasks for Czech children due to an increased exposure to a complex syllable structure, which also counters interpretations of Cossu et al. (1988). Reading models that compare transparent and less transparent orthographies should be assessed further with additional languages to further our understanding of possible language structure differences in learning to read efficiently.

REFERENCES

Bowers, P.G. & Wolf, M. (1993). Theoretical links among naming speed, precise timing mechanisms and orthographic skill in dyslexia. *Reading and Writing: An Interdisciplinary Journal, 5,* 69-86.

Bradley, L. & Bryant, P.E. (1983). Categorizing sounds and learning to read--A causal connection. *Nature, 301,* 419-421.

Caravolas, M. & Bruck, M. (1993). The effect of oral and written language input on children's phonological awareness: A cross-linguistic study. *Journal of Experimental Child Psychology, 55,* 1-30.

Coltheart, M. (1978). Lexical access in simple reading tasks. In G. Underwood (Ed.) *Strategies of information processing* (pp. 151-216). San Diego, CA: Academic Press.

Cossu, G., Rossini, F., & Marshall, J.C. (1993). When reading is acquired but phonemic awareness is not: A study of literacy in Down's syndrome. *Cognition, 46,* 129-138.

Cossu, G., Shankweiler, D., Liberman, I.Y., Katz, L.E., & Tola, G. (1988). Awareness of phonological segments and reading ability in Italian children. *Applied Psycholinguistics, 9,* 1-16.

Denckla, M.B. & Rudel, R. (1976). Rapid automatic naming (RAN): Dyslexia differentiated from other learning disabilities. *Neuropsychologia, 14,* 471-479.

Hulme, C. & Tordoff, V. (1989). Working memory development: The effects of speech rate, word length and acoustic similarity on serial recall. *Journal of Experimental Child Psychology, 47,* 72-87.

Liberman, I.Y., Shankweiler, D., Fischer, W., & Carter, B. (1974). Explicit syllable and phoneme segmentation in the young child. *Journal of Experimental Child Psychology, 18,* 201-212.

Lundberg, I., Olofsson, Å, & Wall, S. (1980). Reading and spelling skills in the first grade school years predicted from phonemic awareness sills in kindergarten. *Scandinavian Journal of Psychology, 21,* 159-173.

Näslund, J.C. & Schneider, W. (1991). Longitudinal effects of verbal ability, memory capacity, and phonological awareness on reading performance. *European Journal of Psychology of Education, 6,* 375-392.

Pitman, J. (1961). Learning to read: An experiment. *Journal of Royal Society of Arts, 109,* 149-180.

Stanovich, K.E., Cunningham, A.E., & Feeman, D.J. (1984). Intelligence, cognitive skills, and early reading progress. *Reading Research Quarterly, 19,* 278-303.

Tallal, P., Miller, S., & Fitch, R.H. (1993). Neurological basis of speech: A case for the preeminence of temporal processing. *Annals of the New York Academy of Science, 682,* 27-47.

Thorstad, G. (1991). The effect of orthography of the acquisition of literacy skills. *British Journal of Psychology, 82,* 527-537.

Wolf, M. (1991). Naming speed and reading: The contribution of the cognitive neuroscience. *Reading Research Quarterly, 26,* 123-141.

NOTE: Project Assistants: Karin Lenz and Antonie Doll (Germany) and Gail Jordan (USA) Project supported by the Alexander-von-Humboldt Stiftung and an NIMH post-doctoral training grant from the University of Minnesota.

WORD RECOGNITION IN ENGLISH AND GERMAN DYSLEXICS: A DIRECT COMPARISON

KARIN LANDERL
Institute of Psychology
University of Salzburg
Hellbrunnerstraße
A-5020 Salzburg, Austria

ABSTRACT. According to current cognitive theories, classic dyslexia is caused by a deficit in phonological processing. Different orthographies represent different ways of realizing the phonological properties of a language. German orthography represents the relationships between phonemes and graphemes in a much more consistent and transparent fashion than English orthography with its many exceptional and irregular spellings. The present study compared the word and nonword reading abilities of 12 year old English and German speaking dyslexic children. A word and a nonword reading task was developed which allowed a direct comparison of the two language groups. One, two and three syllable words which are similar in English and German and corresponding nonwords were presented. While the consistency of German orthography allows dyslexic chidren to acquire considerable though not sufficient knowledge about the relationships between spoken and written words, the complexity of English orthography poses an additional problem for dyslexic children. German dyslexics read slowly but accurately, while English dyslexics showed low reading accuracy and low reading speed. Word frequency, item length and lexicality had a stronger influence on English dyslexics' performance than on performance of the German chidren.

For many years psychological research on reading acquisition examined the causes and symptoms of dyslexia, a specific deficit in the development of reading abilities. The main question was, which of the cognitive processes relevant in reading acquisition are not functioning properly in dyslexics. The major outcome of the research of the last two decades is that deficits in phonological processing are related to reading failure in a large number of otherwise normally developing children (Stanovich, 1994). Such a phonological deficit is assumed to be responsible for difficulties in the process of phonological coding which plays an important role in the acquisition of word recognition abilities. Phonological coding is the process of transforming letters and letter patterns into phonological codes which allow access to word pronunciation and meaning. This process is especially important for reading of nonwords for which pronunciations cannot be accessed but must be assembled. As a matter of fact, specific difficulties with reading of nonwords were found to be the main diagnostic indication of the impaired phonological coding component of word recognition in dyslexics (Rack, Snowling & Olson, 1992).

C.K. Leong and R.M. Joshi (Eds.), Cross-Language Studies of Learning to Read and Spell, 121–137.
© *1997 Kluwer Academic Publishers. Printed in the Netherlands.*

Phonological coding is not only relevant for nonword reading, but also for the development of word recognition abilities. The acquisition of phonological coding allows the child to use grapheme-phoneme correspondences in a systematic way to read the many words which are encountered for the first time. In Frith's (1985) model of reading development, this ability is termed "alphabetic strategy". The ability to tackle new words is obviously critical for further reading development as it functions as a self-teaching mechanism for building up memory representations for word spellings (Jorm & Share, 1983).

The major limitation of these findings is that they are mainly based on studies with English speaking children. English orthography is characterized by many ambiguous and irregular spellings and a rather low degree of consistency of grapheme-phoneme correspondences. It can be assumed that, due to the complex relationships between written and spoken language in English, phonological coding is difficult. The special characteristics of English orthography may therefore be responsible for the fact that a deficit in phonological processing has a disastrous effect on reading acquisition. However, many orthographies are not as complex as English, that is, the relationships between written and spoken language are much more straightforward. The question is, if the conception of a deficit in phonological coding as the main symptom of dyslexia holds for children acquiring a consistent orthography as well as for children acquiring the complex orthography of English.

Learning to read German

A typical example of an orthography with high grapheme-phoneme consistency and only a restricted number of irregular or exception spellings is German. The consistency of German orthography is very high for grapheme-phoneme correspondences, that is, there is usually only one way to pronounce a certain grapheme. For example, in the English words *hand, ball* and *garden* the grapheme *a* is pronounced differently, in the German equivalents *Hand, Ball* and *Garten*, however, the grapheme *a* is always pronounced /a/. There are several context sensitive rules, e.g., that the letter *s* is usually pronounced /s/ but in certain grapheme sequences like *st* or *sp*, it is pronounced /ʃ/. However, the number of these context sensitive rules is limited and quite often a slow sounding out strategy by ignoring those context sensitive rules nevertheless results in word preforms which enable recognition of the particular word. For example, if a child sounds out /stat/ instead of /ʃtat/ for the grapheme sequence *Stadt*, he or she will still be able to recognize the German word for 'city'. The consistency of phoneme-grapheme correspondences, however, is not as high as for grapheme-phoneme correspondences.

The high consistency of the German writing system may be responsible for the fact that a phonics teaching approach is preferred. The goal of reading instruction in grades one and two is to introduce slowly and systematically all grapheme-phoneme correspondences and to teach and practise word recognition via phoneme blending. To introduce blending, children first learn letters for vowels and continuants, so that blending can be easily demonstrated and practiced with words like *im, am, Oma, Mama* and so on. In the beginning, the blending ritual results in word preforms, which characteristically have artificially lengthened phonemes and incorrect stress assignments. However, these preforms are normally close enough to the target pronunciation to allow recognition. The important aspects of this approach are that the straightforward grapheme-phoneme correspondences do not have to be detected, but are systematically presented and that heavy emphasis is placed on how to assemble word pronunciations via grapheme-phoneme conversion.

It was demonstrated that this combination of a consistent orthographic system and a straightforward phonics teaching approach helps young readers to acquire the ability of phonological coding. In a direct comparison of the reading abilities of 7-, 8- and 9-year old English and German readers, Wimmer and Goswami (1994) showed that English and German children's abilities to read short, high frequency words was comparably good. However, the German children outperformed the English children on a nonword reading task. For their word reading task, Wimmer and Goswami used numberwords between *two* and *twelve*, which are very similar in English and German so that differences in visual processing were limited (e.g., *three - drei*). The nonwords were derived from the numberwords by exchanging the consonantal onsets (e.g., *thro* was derived from *three* and *two*), so that the nonwords consisted of the same graphemes as the words and, most importantly, the onset and rime clusters of the numberwords were kept intact. Although the nonwords allowed reading by analogy with existing words, the English children of all three grade levels needed considerably more time than the German children to read the nonwords and they committed more than twice as many errors.

Being Dyslexic in English and German

If German children with normally developed phonological processing abilities are able to acquire phonological coding quite easily, then it might be argued that even children who have a deficit in phonological processing might be able to do so. As a matter of fact, Wimmer (1993) found that German dyslexics in grades two, three and four showed surprisingly high reading accuracy in a nonword reading task. However, although the dyslexics made only few reading errors, their reading speed was deficient.

The nonwords that Wimmer used in this study are somewhat problematic since their structure was rather untypical for German grapheme sequences. In a recent study, Wimmer (1996) used nonwords that consisted of grapheme sequences which corresponded to onset and rime segments of high frequency words. Once again, German dyslexics at the end of grade four committed hardly any reading errors, but their reading speed was very low. Interestingly, dyslexics' reading speed for nonwords was even lower than that of reading age matched control children. Thus, although a specific nonword reading deficit cannot be found in German dyslexics with respect to reading accuracy, such a deficit does exist with respect to reading speed.

Obviously, studies with German dyslexics provide results that are different from results with English dyslexics. An important further step in the analysis of English and German dyslexics' reading strategies is a direct comparison of the two orthography groups instead of between studies comparisons. There exist many words which are very similar in English and German so that differences in visual and semantic processing can be minimized. Such a direct comparison also allows a more detailed analysis of the differences in reading strategies between English and German dyslexics. In the present study we were especially interested in the effects of word frequency, lexicality and word length. Effects of word frequency are interesting with respect to children's direct word recognition abilities. If the dyslexics read directly, then one would expect that performance on high frequency words should be considerably better than on low frequency words. Nonwords cannot be read directly but must be read indirectly. Therefore, a strong effect of lexicality would indicate a deficit in indirect reading. Effects of item length are also interesting with respect to indirect reading. Dyslexics with a deficit in indirect reading will find long items more difficult to read than short items.

One, two and three syllable words, half of high and the other half of low frequency, and nonwords which were derived from these words were presented. Only words were used that are similar in English and German (e.g., *boat - Boot, motor - Motor, quality - Qualität*), so that a direct comparison of the two orthography groups was possible. To ensure that the nonwords did not include any uncommon grapheme sequences, they were derived from the words. The one and two syllable nonwords were derived by exchanging the consonantal onsets (e.g., *hoat - Hoot, potor - Potor*) so that the onset and rime segments of the nonwords were exactly the same as in the words. For the three syllable nonwords, the syllables of the words were rearranged (e.g., *ralective - Ralektiv, pepratic - Pfefratisch*). The items were presented one after the other on a computer screen. Both reading errors and reading speed for each item were recorded.

Eighteen English and 18 German dyslexic children participated in this comparison. The subject details of these children can be seen in Table 1.

Table 1. Mean age, reading level and nonverbal intelligence of English and German dyslexic children (Ranges in parenthesis)

	N (% boys)	Age	Reading Level (percentile)	Nonverbal IQ
English	18 (83)	12:3 (10:9-13:11)	8.4 (2-19)	103 (91-121)
German	18 (78)	11:7 (10:7-12:7)	9.5 (1-36)	103 (85-145)

The English children were officially diagnosed children with special needs. Ten children attended a special school for dyslexic children, four got intensive remediation in dyslexia centers associated with their school and two were enrolled in special remediation programs in their schools. Their reading ability was assessed by BAS word recognition test (Elliot, Murray, & Pearson, 1983). As can be seen in Table 1, the dyslexics' word recognition abilities are below percentile 19 in comparison to normal readers of the same age. Their mean reading age is 8:3 (7:3-10:9), therefore, their reading abilities are about four years below their chronological age.

The German dyslexics were recruited from two longitudinal studies conducted in our laboratory in Salzburg[1]. Their reading difficulties were first assessed at the end of grade one and grade two respectively and their reading development was observed over the following years. The reading test that we used to assess children's current reading abilities was a test which we developed in our lab (Landerl, Wimmer, & Moser, 1996). Although this test is only standardized for children up to eleven years of age, it was given preference over German reading tests for children older than 10 years, which are tests of reading comprehension throughout. Unlike the BAS word recognition test which is a test of reading accuracy, the main diagnostic

---

[1] As the Austrian children from Salzburg were learning to read in German, they are referred to as "German" children throughout this paper for ease of exposition.

criterion of the German reading test is reading speed. It will be demonstrated that German dyslexics usually do not commit many reading errors. However, their reading speed is considerably lower than that of normal readers. On a combined score of reading speed for a short text and a list of quite complex compound words like *Obststand* or *Krankenschwester*, the dyslexics of the present study on average showed a reading speed which was below percentile 10 in comparison to 10 to 11 year old children. Obviously, their reading speed must be even more deficient in comparison to 12 year old normal readers. Table 1 also shows that both English and German dyslexics' nonverbal intelligence assessed by Raven's Standard Progressive Matrices (Raven, 1987) was normal.

Effects of Word Frequency

To examine the effects of word frequency we compared English and German dyslexics' ability to read words of high and of low frequency according to Thorndike and Lorge (1944). Figure 1 presents the mean percentages of correct responses for these items separately for the three word lengths (max=16).

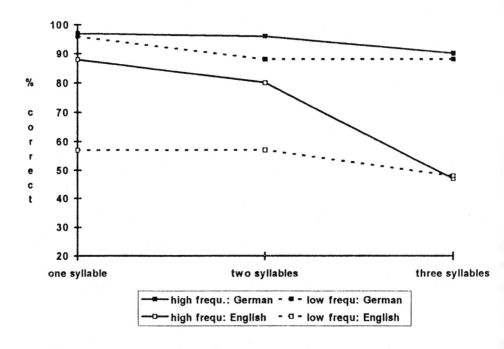

Figure 1. Percentage of correct readings for high and low frequency words.

From Figure 1, it is evident that the German dyslexics showed very high reading accuracy both for the high and for the low freuquency items of all three word lengths. Obviously, word frequency does not have much effect on their reading accuracy.

On the other hand, word frequency has a strong effect on English dyslexics' reading accuracy. While they could produce correct readings for more than 80% of the one and two syllable high frequency items, they read only at about 60% of the low frequency words correctly. Since reading accuracy for the three syllable words already decreased considerably for the high frequency items, no frequency effect could be observed. The missing frequency effect for the long words probably has to be explained by the fact that due to restrictions in item selection word frequency of the three syllable high frequency words was lower than for the one and two syllable items.

Effects of Lexicality

Figure 2 presents the percentages of correct readings for words (high and low frequency combined) and nonwords for the three word lengths (max=32).

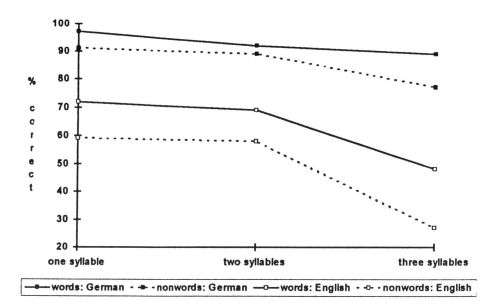

Figure 2. Percentage of correct readings for words and nonwords.

From Figure 2, it is evident that lexicality has a much stronger effect on English than on German children's reading accuracy. While the German dyslexics read the one and two syllable nonwords almost perfectly and could still read 89% of the three syllable items correctly, the distortion of the word spellings into nonwords had a much more detrimental effect on English dyslexics' performance. Only 60% of the one and two syllable and just 27% of the three syllable nonwords could be read correctly. This poor perfomance on the nonwords is surprising if we take into consideration that the one and two syllable nonwords were constructed in such a way that they allowed reading by analogy with onset and rime units of existing words. Reading by analogy was not possible for the three syllable items which may be one of the reasons why children's performance was especially poor.

Effects of Word Length

For the high frequency words item length is confounded with frequency (frequency for the three syllable words is lower than for the one and two syllable words) so that the effects of item length cannot be interpreted. Therefore, we compared English and German children's performance on the low frequency words and the nonwords that were derived from the low frequency words (max=16). Figure 3 presents the mean percentages of correct readings for these items.

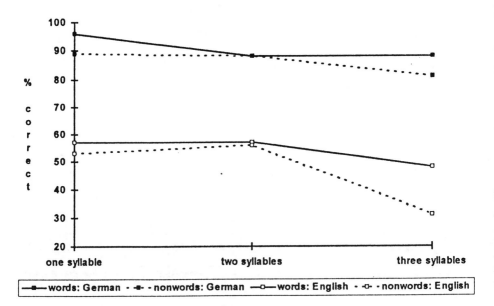

Figure 3. Percentage of correct readings for low frequency words and derived nonwords.

Once again the high reading accuracy of the German dyslexics becomes evident from Figure 3. There is hardly any decrease in the percentage of correct responses from one to three syllable items. For the English dyslexics the length effect is mainly evident for the three syllable items. For the words the decrease from short to long items is 11%, for the nonwords the decrease is considerably larger with 26%.

Reading Speed

Because of space limitations the effects on children's reading speed will not be discussed in detail. Figure 4, which presents the mean reaction times for correctly read words (irrespective of word frequency) and nonwords separately for one, two and three syllable items, shows two things. First, the ease of the German and the difficulty of the English dyslexics in reading the presented items is not only evident from their reading accuracy but also from their reading speed. Thus, German dyslexics' high reading accuracy cannot be explained by an accuracy-speed trade-off. Second, it is evident that for the one syllable words English dyslexics' reading speed was nearly as high as that of the German dyslexics. In Figure 4, reaction times for the high frequency words are not distinguished from those for low frequency words. Interestingly, there was no difference at all between the two orthography groups in reading speed for the one syllable high frequency words. In all other conditions, however, English dyslexics' reading speed is considerably lower than that of the German children. Obviously, the effects of word frequency, lexicality and item length are more detrimental for English than for German dyslexics, especially if these effects occur in combination.

Analysis of Reading Errors

A further question is, if the two orthography groups differ only in the number of errors or if there are also differences in the kind of reading errors they make. A first observation is that there is no difference between English and German dyslexics with respect to the percentage of errors that result in word and nonword pronunciations. More than half of the incorrect responses for the word items of both English and German dyslexics resulted in nonword pronunciations (56 and 62%, respectively) although the children were informed that the presented items were existing words. For the nonwords the percentage of reading errors that resulted in existing words was even lower. Sixteen percent and 18% respectively of English and German children's errors for the one and two syllable nonwords were of this error type. For the three syllable items, only 4% of the English children's errors and none of the German children's errors resulted in existing words. This is not surprising since the children were informed that "strange words" would be presented which "didn't have a meaning". However, that the majority of errors resulted in nonwords is evidence that the English as well as the German children tried to assemble prununciations via grapheme-phoneme translation.

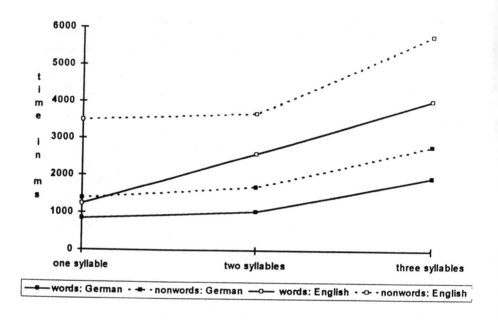

Figure 4. Mean reaction times for words and nonwords.

Here, an interesting length effect could be observed for the German dyslexics' errors for word items. While the percentage of errors that resulted in nonword pronunciations was more or less the same for the three word lengths for the English children, the German dyslexics showed a decrease of this error type with increasing word length. For the one syllable words German dyslexics committed only 13 errors altogether, however, 12 of these

13 errors resulted in existing words (e.g., "Bild" for *blind*, "Jagd" for *Jacht* or "Hund" for *rund*). But of the 59 errors that the children committed for the three syllable items only 15% resulted in existing words. Most of these word pronunciations were morphological derivations of the presented word (e.g., "elektronisch" for *elektrisch* or "garantiert" for *Garantie*). However, the majority of the 59 errors for three syllable words were omissions, substitutions or additions of a single phoneme which resulted in nonword pronunciations (e.g., /postif/ for *positiv*, /elektroti∫/ for *elektronisch* or /ataraktif/ for *attraktiv*). It seems that the German children rely so heavily on their decoding strategy that they do not even try to complement their bottom up grapheme-phoneme translation by top down activation of a word that sounds similar.

Another indication of a grapheme-phoneme translation strategy are regularisation errors. However, this error type can only occur for English children because in German the regular pronunciation of a grapheme sequence is always the correct one. Thirty percent of the English children's incorrect responses for the one and two syllable words were regularisations (e.g., /jat∫/ or /jæt∫/ for *yacht*; /komb/ for *comb*; /balət/ or /bælət/ for *ballet*; "beer" for *bear*). These errors show that children try to read unknown words by assembling a pronunciation via phonological coding. However, because of the inconsistency of English orthography this phonological coding process was not always successful but resulted in regularisation errors instead. But the fact that regularisations occurred in only 30% of the errrors for the one and two syllable words shows that English dyslexics' phonological coding abilities are not very well developed anyway.

A striking difference between English and German dyslexics is the ability to decode long grapheme sequences. While the German dyslexics read both three syllable words and nonwords very accurately, English dyslexics' performance was poor, especially for the nonwords. The high complexity of the grapheme sequences of the three syllable words is probably responsible for the fact that the English dyslexics were not able to assemble a pronunciation starting with a systematic grapheme-phoneme translation. Their strategy to read these long words seems to be to find a word which includes as many phonemes as possible which are represented by graphemes in the presented word. Quite often, the correct sequence of the graphemes is ignored. Of course, this partial grapheme-phoneme translation leads to a high number of errors like "guardian" or "great tree" for *guarantee*, "calculator" for *catalogue* or "permit" for *peppermint*. An impressive example of a partial grapheme-phoneme translation which resulted in a word that included nearly all graphemes but in a completely different order is "dreamed" for *modern*. Here, only the grapheme *n* was not translated and the phoneme /d/ occurred twice in the child's response.

If no word can be accessed which fits the partial grapheme-phoneme translation then a nonword pronunciation is assembled which once again includes many phonemes of the presented item. Sometimes, these nonwords are quite close to the target word (e.g., /kokont/ for *coconut* or /disakaʃən/ for *discussion*). But sometimes only the graphemes at the beginning of the word are translated correctly, otherwise, there is little resemblance between presented word and the child's response (e.g., diskariʃənt/ for *discussion* or /eksəlot/ for *exotic*).

When a nonword was presented, children were not searching for a word that fit best their grapheme-phoneme translation. But while the German dyslexics simply produced the result of their translation process which most of the time was correct anyway, English dyslexics' strategy was different. They too translated the graphemes of the presented nonwords into phonemes and then they generated a plausible pronunciation which included these phonemes. However, since the exact sequence of graphemes was widely ignored, there were many ways to combine the translated phonemes. To illustrate, Table 2 presents all reading errors for the nonword *atledent* which looked exactly the same in English and in German. The reading errors for this item demonstrate impressively how many pronunciations can be assembled with the phonemes of the presented nonword.

Table 2. Reading Errors for the Nonword *atledent*

---

atledent (Engl.) /lætədent/, /ətlænti/, /ledenten/, /ætlendit/, /ælædent/, /atelt/, /əlautment/, /eledent/, /ætləndent/, /edəment/, /entlident/, /ætond/, /ətlendent/, /altident/, /atlement/

atledent (Germ.) Athleten (Engl.: athletes), /atleden/, /atlendet/, /atlete:n/, /atlendent/

It is obvious that German dyslexics' erroneous responses are clearly closer to the target item than English dyslexics'. In their reading errors, the four graphemes at the beginning of the word are always pronounced correctly, only in the second part of the item the bottom up grapheme-phoneme translation goes wrong. The English dyslexics, on the other hand, seem to combine the translated phonemes to any plausible pronunciation that comes to their mind. They use both bottom up and top down processes to assemble a plausible pronunciation. Sometimes, they supply their grapheme-phoneme translation by phonemes that are not included in the presented item. A typical example is /flænd/ instead of *fand* which occurred four times. Instead of the simple onset /f/ the more complex onset cluster /fl/ is activated which includes the represented phoneme /f/, but it also includes an additional phoneme which is not represented by a grapheme.

Comparison of Dyslexics with Normal Readers

Both English and German dyslexic children were compared with reading level (RL) controls. The mean age of the English RL-controls was 8 years 3 months, the mean age of the German RL-control children was 8 years 8 months. Table 3 presents the mean percentages of correct responses and the mean reaction times in milliseconds for English dyslexics and RL-controls.

Table 3. Mean percentage of correct responses and mean reaction times for English dyslexics and RL-controls (SD in parentheses)

	Reading Accuracy		Reading Speed (ms.)	
	Dyslexics	RL-Controls	Dyslexics	RL-Controls
one syllable words:				
high frequency	88 (11)	95 (9)	1176 (702)	1196 (796)
low frequency	57 (29)	60 (34)	1277 (525)	1561 (1173)
words (combined)	72 (27)	77 (30)	1226 (553)	1379 (908)
nonwords	59 (18)	74 (17)	3495 (1800)	2577 (1552)
two syllables words:				
high frequency	80 (16)	88 (13)	1771 (1023)	1457 (1063)
low frequency	57 (27)	62 (31)	3378 (2124)	2156 (1621)
words (combined)	69 (25)	75 (27)	2574 (1542)	1807 (1333)
nonwords	57 (16)	80 (12)	3656 (1795)	2976 (1664)
three syllables words:				
high frequency	47 (23)	53 (24)	3839 (2356)	2883 (1882)
low frequency	48 (24)	54 (28)	4384 (2443)	3274 (2114)
words (combined)	48 (23)	53 (24)	4009 (2181)	2975 (1830)
nonwords	27 (15)	40 (20)	5762 (2912)	5156 (4070)

While the dyslexics read the words as accurately and with the same speed as the RL-controls, they performed worse on the nonwords. Especially the percentage of correct readings was reliably lower for the dyslexics than for the younger normal readers. But the reaction times for correctly read items tended to be higher for the dyslexics than for the RL-controls. The data will not be discussed in detail here, however, it is obvious that the English dyslexics of the present study show the specific nonword reading deficit which was reported several times for dyslexics acquiring English orthography (Rack et al., 1992).

Table 4 presents the mean percentages of correct responses and the mean reaction times (ms.) for correctly read items for German dyslexics and RL-controls.

Table 4. Mean percentage of correct responses and mean reaction times for German dyslexics and RL-controls (SD in parentheses)

| | Reading Accuracy | | Reading Speed (ms.) | |
	Dyslexics	RL-Controls	Dyslexics	RL-Controls
one syllable words:				
high frequency	97 (4)	98 (3)	696 (303)	770 (328)
low frequency	96 (5)	95 (6)	993 (914)	975 (542)
words (combined)	97 (5)	97 (5)	845 (591)	872 (426)
nonwords	91 (9)	94 (7)	1387 (821)	1205 (709)
two syllables words:				
high frequency	96 (8)	97 (4)	852 (423)	895 (513)
low frequency	88 (13)	94 (10)	1219 (642)	1134 (672)
words (combined)	92 (11)	95 (8)	1035 (518)	1014 (576)
nonwords	89 (9)	92 (9)	1684 (1063)	1366 (787)
three syllables words:				
high frequency	90 (10)	90 (10)	1879 (946)	1685 (797)
low frequency	88 (10)	91 (10)	1994 (956)	1846 (912)
words (combined)	89 (10)	91 (10)	1937 (932)	1765 (845)
nonwords	77 (16)	82 (11)	2779 (1294)	2837 (1017)

German dyslexics' reading performance is similar to that of the younger normal readers, both for words and nonwords. In contrast to the English dyslexics, no specific nonword reading deficit can be observed, neither with respect to reading accuracy nor with respect to reading speed.

Is a Consistent Orthography Helpful?

The present study replicated Wimmer's (1993, 1996) findings that German dyslexics show high reading accuracy for nonwords as well as words. Since in this comparative study German and English dyslexics were presented with similar items, it can be ruled out that specific item or task characteristics are responsible for this difference between the two orthography groups. Wimmer's (1996) finding of a specific deficit in reading speed for nonwords in German dyslexics could not be replicated. The German dyslexics of the present study read the nonwords with the same speed as the reading age controls. A possible explanation for this difference lies in differences between the nonword tasks. Wimmer used a continuous reading task and his reading speed measure was reading time divided by the number of items, irrespective of correctness of the response. In the present study a more specific reaction time measure was used. We measured the reaction time for each item separately and analysed only the reaction times for those items that were read correctly.

In the present study, both orthography groups read the items extremely slowly. Even for the high frequency words their performance was not better than that of normal readers who are at about four years their juniors. Obviously, they are not able to read via fast and direct recognition of orthographic units but have to rely on phonological coding. German dyslexics are quite competent in phonological coding, therefore, they read slowly, but accurately. English dyslexics, on the other hand, do not decode grapheme sequences in a left to right manner. Since a pure bottom up grapheme-phoneme translation is quite often misleading in English orthography they complement this bottom up process by top down lexical processes for assembly of a plausible pronunciation.

This strategy of complementing the bottom up grapheme-phoneme translation by top down lexical processes explains why word frequency and lexicality have such a strong effect on English dyslexics' reading accuracy. If the presented grapheme sequence is a word then the child is able to search his or her mental lexicon for a word pronunciation that fits best. In case of a high frequency word, this searching process will be faster than in case of a low frequency item. For nonwords, the pronunciation cannot be accessed, but must be assembled. For this assembling the dyslexics still use top down information in form of activation of typical phonological segments like onsets, rimes or complete syllables of existing words which are assembled to a nonword pronunciation. Of course, this strategy is more error prone than a pure bottom up decoding strategy.

This strategy also explains the marked length effect in English dyslexics' performance. In their bottom up grapheme-phoneme translation they do not observe the exact sequence of the presented graphemes. If the number of graphemes is low, then there are only few possibilities to combine the translated phonemes and the chance to read an item correctly is high. If the number of graphemes increases, then the number of possible combinations of the translated phonemes increases as well and the chance to read the item correctly is much lower. The incorrect responses for the nonword *atledent* are an impressive illustration of the many possible phoneme combinations for a three syllable nonword.

Finally, we can also explain why English children's reaction times for correctly read items are also considerably higher than those of the German dyslexics. To search the mental lexicon for a word or nonword pronunciation that fits best with the translated grapheme sequence surely takes longer than simply producing the outcome of a decoding process. Especially for low frequency or for longer items the search process can take quite long because every word that comes to mind has to be checked against the presented grapheme sequence. If it does not fit, the search process has to start all over again.

The interesting question is why both English and German dyslexics do not read directly. This became evident from their high reaction times even for short, high frequency words. Obviously, they had not established direct recognition units for these words yet. At least for the German dyslexics it is unlikely that this deficit in direct reading is a consequence of a deficit in phonological coding. Obviously, these children are quite competent in phonological coding, but they still did not develop direct recognition units. An interesting explanation for dyslexics' deficit in direct reading comes from Perfetti's (1992) assumption of phonologically underpinned orthographic representations. Perfetti assumes that direct recognition units are grapheme sequences which correspond to phonological segments like phonemes, syllable onsets and rimes or syllables. Therefore, only children who are able to group the graphemes according to phonological segments will be able to build up such orthographic units. Children with a phonological deficit, however, will not be able to match graphemes with phonological segments and tend to become dyslexic, irrespective of the orthography they acquire.

The major advantage of being dyslexic in a consistent orthography is that even dyslexic children are able to become self-reliant readers. Basically, they understand the idea of an alphabetic script, although they cannot handle it very well. The high complexity of English orthography, however, quite often prevents children from fully understanding the purpose of the alphabet. A quotation of one of the English dyslexics participating in the present study (actually, he was one of the better readers) illustrates this poor understanding of the alphabetic principle. He explained that nonword reading would be much easier than word reading because for a nonword every pronunciation would be correct. We never heard a remark like that from a German dyslexic child.

REFERENCES

Elliot, C.D., Murray, D.J., & Pearson, L.S. (1983). *British ability scales: Word reading*. Windsor, Berkshire: NFER-NELSON Publishing Company Ltd.

Frith, U. (1985). Beneath the surface of developmental dyslexia. In K.E. Patterson, J.C. Marshall, & M. Coltheart (Eds.), *Surface Dyslexia* (pp. 301-330). Hillsdale, NJ: Erlbaum.

Jorm, A.E. & Share, D.L. (1983). Phonological recoding and reading acquisition. *Applied Psycholoinguistics, 4*, 104-147.

Landerl, K., Wimmer, H., & Moser, E. (1996). *Salzburger Lese- und Rechtschreibtest* (Salzburg reading and spelling test). Unpublished manuscript, University of Salzburg

Perfetti, C. (1992). The representation problem in reading acquisition. In P.B. Gough, L.C. Ehri, & R. Treiman (Eds.), *Reading acquisition*, (pp. 145-174). Hillsdale, NJ: Erlbaum.

Rack, J.P., Snowling, M.J., & Olson, R. (1992). The nonword reading deficit in developmental dyslexia: A review. *Reading Research Quarterly, 27*, 29-53.

Raven, J.C. (1987). *Manual for Raven's Progressive Matrices and Vocabulary Scales, Section 3. Standard Progressive Matrices*. London, UK: H.K. Lewis & Co. Ltd.

Stanovich, K.E. (1994). Annotation: Does dyslexia exist? *Journal of Child Psychology and Psychiatry, 35*, 579-595.

Thorndike, E.L. & Lorge, L. (1944). The teacher's word book of 30,000 words. New York: Columbia University Press.

Wimmer, H. (1993). Characteristics of developmental dyslexia in a regular writing system. *Applied Psycholinguistics, 14*, 1-33.

Wimmer, H. (1996). The nonword reading deficit in developmental dyslexia: Evidence from children learning to read German. *Journal of Experimental Child Psychology, 61*, 80-90.

Wimmer, H., & Goswami, U. (1994). The influence of orthographic consistency on reading development: Word recognition in English and German children. *Cognition, 51*, 91-103.

THE EARLY PREDICTION OF READING AND SPELLING: EVIDENCE FROM THE MUNICH LONGITUDINAL STUDY ON THE GENESIS OF INDIVIDUAL COMPETENCIES

WOLFGANG SCHNEIDER AND JAN CAROL NÄSLUND
Department of Psychology   College of Education
University of Würzburg   University of New Mexico
D-97074 Würzburg   Albuquerque, N.M. 87131
Germany   U.S.A.

Abstract. In this chapter, we present findings from the Munich Longitudinal Study on the Genesis of Individual Competencies (LOGIC) concerning the early prediction of reading and spelling in school. About 210 children participated in the study. The various predictor variables were assessed during the last year of kindergarten and represented four different domains (i.e., IQ, phonological awareness, memory capacity, and early literacy). The criterion measures were assessed from Grade two on and tapped various aspects of reading (i.e., decoding speed and reading comprehension) and spelling. As a main result, the data indicate that all four predictor domains had a significant impact on the acquisition of reading and spelling skills in school. However, the relative contribution of the domains varied as a function of the criterion under study and the measurement point considered. Although the data confirmed the importance of phonological awareness in the process of learning to read and to spell, they also highlight the relevance of early letter knowledge for subsequent literacy. Contrary to expectations, sex differences and individual differences in quality of instruction did not have a major impact on results. Taken together, our findings confirm the results of major Anglo-American and Scandinavian studies, indicating that the importance of predictor domains such as phonological awareness, memory capacity, and early literacy generalizes across several languages.

Longitudinal research on the preschool prediction of reading and spelling has accumulated over the last three decades. Although results of longitudinal studies caught considerable attention in the scientific literature from the very beginning on, there were at least two general problems with most of the earlier studies: (1) The choice of predictor measures was not guided by theoretical considerations concerning reading and spelling processes and possible precursors. A vast array of mostly psychometric measures were used that, in most cases, were not proximal to reading and spelling (e.g., motor skills, general cognitive ability, behavioral-emotional functioning; for reviews, see Horn & Packard, 1985; Tramontana, Hooper, & Selzer, 1988). Interestingly, many of these measures predicted later reading and spelling performance rather well, particularly when the focus was on univariate prediction.

C.K. Leong and R.M. Joshi (Eds.), Cross-Language Studies of Learning to Read and Spell, 139–159.

(2)   Another, related problem concerned the fact that discriminant validity of predictor variables was either not assessed at all or found to be low. In the latter case, measures important for the prediction of reading and spelling were almost equally powerful in predicting achievement in unrelated areas like math.

Fortunately, these problems were overcome in more recent longitudinal studies that derived predictor measures from theoretical assumptions concerning possible prerequisites of reading and spelling (e.g., Bradley & Bryant, 1985; Juel, 1988; Lundberg, Frost, & Petersen, 1988, Skowronek & Marx, 1989; Stanovich, Cunningham & Feeman, 1984).   In all of these studies, it was shown that phonological awareness (the ability to detect and differentiate phonemic units in speech) was a very good predictor of children's later reading and spelling performance (see also Tunmer & Nesdale, 1985; Wagner & Torgesen, 1987).   Further, several studies demonstrated that indicators of memory capacity and information processing speed were additionally related to reading ability (e.g., Daneman & Blennerhassett, 1984; Ellis & Large, 1987; Perfetti & Lesgold, 1978; Skowronek & Marx, 1989), and that the presence or absence of preschool letter knowledge or early literacy turned out to be an issue strongly related to predicting early reading skills (cf. Bradley & Bryant, 1985; Lundberg et al., 1988).

Although these studies greatly enhanced our knowledge regarding the important roles of factors such as phonological awareness, memory capacity, and early literacy for the acquisition of reading and spelling, they still left us with a few open questions.   For instance, one controversial issue concerned the impact of letter knowledge on the development of phonological awareness.   Whereas one group of researchers (Bradley & Bryant, 1985; Lundberg et al., 1988) demonstrated phonological awareness in preschool children who did not know about phoneme-grapheme correspondence rules, another group (Morais, Cary, Alegria, & Bertelson, 1979; Read, Zhang, Nie, & Ding, 1986) claimed that phonological awareness associated with reading and spelling cannot develop in the absence of grapheme-phoneme knowledge.

Furthermore, a problem experienced with many of these longitudinal studies was that the range of predictor variables included in the analyses was restricted. Typically, studies focusing on the role of phonological awareness did not include indicators of working memory or early literacy, and vice versa.   As a consequence, we do not know much about the *relative* contribution of these theoretically relevant measures to the prediction of reading and spelling when *simultaneously* considered in multivariate analyses. In this regard, an interesting question concerns the fact whether the relative contribution of predictor measures varies as a function of the criterion under study (i.e., reading vs. spelling).

Another issue of current debate is whether models of reading acquisition developed in the English-speaking countries tranfer to other languages as well. In the case of German children, research by Wimmer and colleagues (e.g., Wimmer, Hartl, & Moser, 1990) has demonstrated that this assumption may not be valid because the two orthographies vary in difficulty (regularity). Accordingly, predictor variables important for the explanation of reading and spelling processes in German children may differ from those relevant for British or American children.

A final neglected issue concerns the role of educational processes, in particular, differences in the quality of classroom instruction and in students' motivation and attentional processes on the acquisition of reading and spelling. Theoretically, the importance of preschool and kindergarten predictors of reading and spelling should be highest for the early school years because the impact of individual differences in quality of classroom instruction may be slowly developing and thus less important for beginners. However, there is plenty of evidence that individual differences in the quality of classroom instruction influence academic achievement during the later school years (cf. Weinert & Helmke, 1988). Related to this, an issue frequently raised in the German-speaking literature is whether sex differences in reading and spelling are due to girls' superior language skills or to advantages in learning motivation and school adjustment.

The design of our LOGIC study seemed suited to explore these issues. The study started when children were about four years of age, and it included numerous measures of children's early cognitive abilities assessed during the first two years of kindergarten. Thus we decided to carry out a prospective study of prerequisites of reading and spelling, starting with the third (and last) year of kindergarten. We assessed a variety of cognitive measures (to be described below) tapping skills that, according to the literature, seemed suited to predict reading and spelling in elementary school.

Major Goals of the Study

Our study focussed on the following problems (for details, see Näslund, 1990; Näslund & Schneider, 1991, 1993; Schneider & Näslund, 1992, 1993):

(1) We were interested in exploring the interplay among IQ, phonological awareness, memory capacity, and early literacy in predicting reading ability (i.e., decoding speed and reading comprehension) and spelling. Regarding phonological processing, a distinction was made

between phonological awareness in the broad and narrow sense (cf. Skowronek & Marx, 1989). Whereas the earlier refers to the ability to segment the stream of speech sounds into larger units like syllables and rhyme words, the latter requires children to segment speech into the abstract linguistic units of phonemes. Combining indicators of phonological awareness in the broad and narrow sense in one single predictor set enabled us to judge the relative importance of both phonological awareness components for the acquisition of reading and spelling. Furthermore, the inclusion of memory variables and indicators of early literacy should give information on the relative importance of all these variables as a function of the criterion under study (i.e., reading vs. spelling) and measurement point (i.e., early vs late elementary school period).

(2) Another related focus concerned the relative influence of early literacy as compared with phonological awareness in the broad and narrow sense on later reading and spelling performance. As noted above, this issue has been discussed controversially in the literature for quite a while (cf. Bradley & Bryant, 1985; Morais, 1991; Morais et al., 1979, Read et al., 1986). The major issue is whether phonological awareness can be acquired without knowledge about the alphabet. In our view, one source of confusion was that Bradley and Bryant referred to phonological awareness in the broad sense, whereas Morais and colleagues focused on phonological awareness in the narrow sense. As German kindergarten children unlike American or British children do not learn to read before elementary school, their knowledge of the alphabet and phoneme-grapheme correspondences is usually very poor. Thus our study seemed suited to explore the issue whether phonological awareness does have an effect on later reading independent of letter knowledge.

(3) A third goal of the study was to explore the issue of sex differences in reading and spelling. Most German studies on dyslexia have found that the number of boys considerably exceeded that of girls in their samples of dyslexic children. We do not know for sure, however, whether boys generally perform worse than girls, or whether this is only true for the lowest quartile of the distribution. Furthermore, it remains unclear from the available literature whether gender differences are observable from the very beginning of reading instruction on, or whether these differences develop later during the school career. Our longitudinal data base covers the period from second to fifth grade, and thus seems suited to deal with this issue.

(4) A last major issue of interest concerned the effect of individual differences in the quality of classroom instruction on reading and spelling. For about half of our LOGIC subjects, detailed reports on their classroom behavior and information on the quality of instruction were available from grade one on. We were interested in learning whether these variables make a

difference when it comes to the prediction of reading and spelling in elementary school.

Description of Sample and Test Instruments

SUBJECTS

A total of 210 children were initially recruited for the study. Twenty-two children were not promoted to elementary school together with the rest of the sample but stayed in kindergarten for one more year. Reading and spelling data for these subjects are not considered in our analyses. Complete data sets from 163 children were available for the analyses dealing with spelling performance across the first five school years. Due to organizational problems, not all of the children participated in the decoding and reading comprehension tests. Thus the analyses focusing on these variables were based on only 121 subjects. Additional data on classroom behavior and quality of classroom instruction were available for a subsample of 120 children.

Our children began kindergarten at about age four. On average, they were almost six years old when provided with the phonological processing, memory capacity, and IQ tasks during the last year of kindergarten. Reading comprehension, decoding speed, and spelling skill were assessed both at the beginning and at the end of second grade. Additional spelling tests were given in third, fourth, and fifth grade.

Predictor tasks. The following tasks were presented during the last year of kindergarten: (1) The *Bielefeld screening test* consisting of eight different tasks which according to the authors taps children's phonological awareness, their attention and memory performance (cf. Jansen, Knorn, Mannhaupt, Marx, Beck, & Skowronek, 1986; Marx, 1992; Skowronek & Marx, 1989); (2) a *sound categorization task* developed by Bradley and Bryant (1985) tapping children's phonological awareness in the broad sense (rhyming); (3) *verbal memory capacity* assessed by a word span task (Case, Kurland, & Goldberg, 1982), and a listening span (sentence span) task developed by Daneman and Blennerhassett (1984); (4) *early literacy* assessed by children's letter knowledge, name writing, and sign knowledge, and (5) *verbal and nonverbal intelligence*, indicated by children's performance on the Hannover Wechsler Intelligence Test for Preschool Children (HAWIVA; Eggert 1978), and the Columbia Mental Maturity Scale (Burgemeister, Blum, & Lorge, 1972).

Four subtests of the Bielefeld screening instrument assessed components of phonological awareness. The *rhyming task* consisted of 10 word pairs, half of which did rhyme. Children had to indicate which word pairs did rhyme and which did not. In the *syllable segmentation task*, 10 words were presented via audio tape. The children's task was to segment each word into its syllables, thereby clapping their hands for each syllable. In the *sound-to-word-matching task*, children were presented with a number of 10 audio-taped words. After having repeated each word, children had to indicate whether a specific sound pattern (e.g., an "au") could be identified in the test word (e.g., "Auge"). Finally, the *sound blending task* tapped children's awareness of isolated sounds. The words presented were segmented into their constituent sounds, and the children's task was to identify the words.

The remaining four subtests of the Bielefeld screening instrument tapped memory and attentional processes. The *visual word matching test* required children to identify the "twin" (identical word) of a target word out of a number of four alternatives. The target word was always given in the upper row of a card, and three distractor items and the target word were depicted in a second row below. The number of correct solutions (max = 12) was taken as the dependent variable. In the *repetition of nonsense words* subtest, children were asked to listen carefully to a series of pseudowords ("Zippelzak", "Binne-basselbus") that they should repeat as accurately as possible. The number of pseudowords correctly repeated was used as the dependent variable. Finally, two different *rapid naming tasks* were given because there is evidence in the literature that poor readers cannot access information in semantic or lexical memory as quickly as normal and good readers (cf. Blachman, 1984; Denckla & Rudel, 1976). The first task required rapid naming of the colours of objects from uncoloured line drawings. Here, the children's task was to indicate the correct colors as quickly as possible. The second task was structurally similar and required rapid naming of the correct colours of objects with incongruent colours (e.g., a blue lemon). This task differs from the first in that the child has to cope with interference and distraction problems. In both tasks, the number of mistakes and the time needed to complete the trials was used as the dependent variable.

The *sound categorization task (phonological oddity measure)* developed by Bradley and Bryant (1985) consisted of three different components. In the first subtest (*first sound oddity*), series of four one-syllable words were given. Children's task was to identify the word with a different first sound (example: Fest, Feld, Fels, Helm). The number of correct solution (max = 9) was used as the dependent variable. The two remaining subtests were similar in nature. In the *middle sound oddity* task, children had to find out which of four words did not share the same middle sound (example: Hahn, Sohn, Lohn, Mohn). In the *end sound oddity* task, the same experimental structure was used. This time, the children's task was to identify the word that had a different end sound as the other three (e.g., Speck, Dreck, Stern, Fleck).

To assess *verbal memory capacity*, two different tasks were used. The *word span task* developed by Case, Kurland, and Goldberg (1982) consisted of 10 sets of one-syllable words. The set sizes varied between three and seven items. Beginning with sets of three words, two trials were given for each set size. Children were instructed to first listen to the entire set, then repeat the words they heard. Children's word span was defined as the maximum number of words that could be repeated in the correct order.

In addition, the *sentence span/listening span task* adapted from Daneman and Blennerhassett was used to tap memory capacity. Seventy-five sentences (at maximum), ranging in length from three to seven words, were read to each child. Sentences were grouped in five sets each of one, two, three, four, and five sentences. Children were asked to repeat the sentences in each set verbatim. Testing terminated when the child failed to recall all five sentences at a particular level. The total number of sentences (or words) recalled correctly was chosen as the dependent variable.

Three different tasks assessed *early literacy* and concepts about print in our kindergarten children. A *letter naming task* assessed children's knowledge about phoneme-grapheme correspondences. The number of letters correctly identified was used as dependent variable. The second task (*sign knowledge or Logo task*) was originally developed by Brügelmann (1986) and later modified by the Bielefeld group (Skowronek & Marx, 1989). The Logo task tapped children's knowledge of letters and words that are hidden in familar settings. Typical examples are traffic signs (e.g., the STOP sign) and trade marks. In some trials, only the original letters were given without any graphic context. In others, only the graphic context was given and the letters omitted. The dependent variable in the present analysis was the number of correct responses in trials focusing on the letters. Finally, *name writing* was chosen as another variable tapping early literacy. Children were asked to write down as many words as they already knew. The number of words correctly spelled was used as the dependent variable.

Tests of *verbal and nonverbal intelligence* were given to assess the importance of unspecific predictors of reading and spelling. *General verbal ability* was measured by the verbal section of the Hannover-Wechsler Intelligence Test (HAWIVA) for preschoolers. This section includes vocabulary and verbal comprehension items. The Columbia Mental Maturity Scale (CMMS) developed by Burgemeister, Blum, and Lorge (1972) was considered an appropriate test to assess children's *nonverbal intellectual ability*. This test taps general reasoning ability of children aged 3 years 6 months through 9 years 11 months. Depending on the subjects' age level, between 52 and 65 pictorial and figural classification items were administered. For each item, children were asked to look at the pictures on a card (varying between 3 to 5), and to select the one that was different from or unrelated to the others. The number of correct solutions was taken as the dependent variable.

Criterion Tasks Assessed in Elementary School.

The task assessing *word and nonword decoding speed* was adapted from Rott and Zielinski (1984). The items (four-letter words and pseudowords) were presented on a computer screen. An internal timing device measured children's responses from the moment of presentations on the screen. A total of 30 words and 30 nonwords were provided. Mean decoding speed was calculated separately for both types of words. The decoding speed tasks were first given at the beginning of second grade and repeated at the end of the school year.

A thirty-item test developed by Näslund (1988) was used to measure *reading comprehension* and *word knowledge* within the context of single sentences and longer texts (short stories). A total of 18 multiple-choice items tapped word knowledge. They included finding synonyms and antonyms within the context of a sentence. The text comprehension part consisted of five short stories followed by two or three multiple-choice questions. This task was designed to test children's understanding of the text, deducing answers from inferences based only on information in the stories.

Finally, the first two *spelling tests* (word dictations) consisted of two partially overlapping versions, the first presented at the beginning of second grade and the other shortly before the end of second grade. Each test included about twenty target words which were taken from different sources and seemed particularly suited to assess spelling competence in second grade. The spelling tests provided in grades three, four, and five were more comprehensive (60 words, 81 words, and 88 words in the third, fourth, and fifth grade, respectively), and were given as sentence dictations. About two-thirds of the materials consisted of familiar words taken from the official list of vocabulary for third and fourth graders distributed by the Bavarian Ministry of Education. The remaining items were less familiar and irregular words. For all spelling measures, the number of correctly written words was chosen as the dependent variable.

Results

Table 1 gives the means, standard deviations, and the ranges for the various predictor variables used in the present analyses. As can be seen from Table 1, children performed very well on most subtests of the Bielefeld screening test. This finding is in accord with the principles of test construction used by the Bielefeld research group. That is, only those subtests were included in the final version of the screening test that particularly discriminated in the lower third of the distribution.   A comparison of the Bielefeld rhyming test and Bradley and Bryant's sound categorisation task shows pronounced differences in task difficulty: On average, about 80 percent of the children succeeded on the Bielefeld rhyming test, whereas less than 50 percent of the responses to the first sound oddity task were correct.

Table 1. Means, standard deviations, and range for the predictor variables included in the study.

Variable	M	SD	Min	Max
Nonverbal IQ	109.51	11.70	79	137
Word span	3.48	0.97	1	6
Sentence span	14.04	6.64	2	38
Sign knowledge	0.94	1.45	0	5
Letter knowledge	6.75	7.44	0	26
Names written	2.06	1.93	0	12
First sound oddity	4.21	2.07	1	9
Middle sound oddity	7.03	2.22	2	9
End sound oddity	6.62	2.31	2	9
Bielefeld screening				
Rhyming task	8.12	1.39	3	10
Syllable segmentation	8.41	1.79	3	10
Sound-to-word matching	6.83	2.20	0	10
Sound blending	6.98	1.95	0	10
Visual word matching	10.13	2.11	0	12
Repetition of nonsense words	7.21	2.04	0	11
Rapid naming (time)	65.47	18.73	27	149

Compared to the Bielefeld screening subtests, the various tasks concerning early literacy turned out to be rather difficult.   In particular, the findings regarding letter knowledge showed that most German kindergarten children do not know much about grapheme-phoneme correspondences. Almost 50% of the children did not know more than two letters or less; only a minority of children (about 9%) knew between 22 and 26 letters and thus could be considered familiar with the alphabet.   This finding certainly differs from those typically reported for six-year-olds from Great Britain or the United States.

The means and standard deviations of the various criterion measures are given in Table 2. Although both word decoding accuracy and word decoding speed were assessed in Grade two, only the speed measure was used in the present analyses. It turned out that most children were already very accurate readers at the beginning of grade two, leaving us with a ceiling effect for the accuracy variable. On average, subjects also performed rather well on the reading comprehension and spelling tests. However, ceiling effects were not observed for these measures.

Table 2. Means, standard deviations, and range for the criterion variables included in the analyses.

Variable	M	SD	Min	Max
Word decoding (Grade 2/1)	1.85	0.57	0.9	3.2
Word decoding (Grade 2/2)	1.68	0.62	0.8	3.3
Read. comprehens. (Grade 2/1)	22.17	6.45	7	28
Read. comprehens. (Grade 2/2)	25.98	4.19	8	29
Spelling (Grade 2/1)	10.22	2.18	4	17
Spelling (Grade 2/2)	11.04	3.97	5	18
Spelling (Grade 3)	31.07	5.92	8	40
Spelling (Grade 4)	51.69	6.30	25	60
Spelling (Grade 5)	76.41	9.81	39	88

Relative Importance of the Various Predictor Variables for Subsequent Reading and Spelling

Multiple stepwise regression analyses were performed to determine the relative influence of the various predictor variables on reading related and spelling skills in elementary school. The dependent measures were word decoding speed, reading comprehension, and spelling. We adopted the procedure used by Bradley and Bryant (1985) in that (nonverbal) IQ was always the first variable to enter the regression equation, followed by those other predictor variables that additionally explained significant proportions of the variance in the respective criterion variable. Although such a procedure probably overestimates the influence of intelligence on the reading and spelling variables, it seems appropriate for our purposes because it ensures that the impact of the remaining predictors on the criterion variables is unconfounded with IQ. Contrary to expectations, the nonverbal IQ variable was generally more predictive of later reading and spelling than its verbal counterpart. Thus only nonverbal IQ was considered in the following analyses.

The results concerning *word decoding speed* showed that different patterns of results emerged for the two testing occasions. IQ and letter knowledge accounted for most of the variance in decoding speed measured at the beginning of second grade, whereas memory capacity (listening span), attentional features (word matching), phonological awareness in the narrow sense (phoneme-word matching), and information processing speed (rapid naming) all made a significant but numerically small contribution. In comparison, only phonological awareness in the broad sense (end sound oddity task) and information processing speed contributed substantially to the prediction of word decoding speed assessed at the end of second grade. Regardless of measurement point, the total amount of variance explained in word decoding speed was only modest (28% vs. 27% for the first and second measurement point, respectively).

The findings concerning *reading comprehension* were somewhat different. Nonverbal IQ explained a considerable proportion of the variance in reading comprehension for both measurement points. Three indicators of phonological awareness (i.e., first sound oddity, middle sound oddity, and phoneme blending) accounted for the rest of the variance in reading comprehension assessed at the beginning of grade two. While IQ explained about 15 percent of the variance in reading comprehension, the combined additional contribution of the phonological awareness variables was even more substantial (about 20% of the variance was explained by these variables).

The findings for the second measurement point differed from those obtained for the first in that the impact of phonological awareness (middle sound oddity, syllable segmenting) was comparably low, and that IQ turns out to be by far most influential predictor. Only 27 percent of the variance in reading comprehension assessed at the end of second grade was explained by the four predictors included in the regression equation.

As the findings for *spelling* assessed in second grade were very similar on both occasions, only the results for the second measurement point (i.e., end of second grade) are given here. In addition to IQ, information processing speed (rapid naming) and letter knowledge made a substantial impact, followed by two phonological awareness variables (sound-to-word matching, sound blending). The impact of the remaining predictor variables (sign knowledge, listening span, and name writing) was comparably small. Overall, about 36 percent of the total variance in spelling assessed at the end of second grade was explained by the various kindergarten predictors.

Interestingly enough, the predictor quality of the kindergarten variables seemed to improve over time. When spelling in Grade three was chosen as the dependent variable, almost 50 percent of the variance in spelling could be accounted for by eight predictor variables. Again, IQ and letter knowledge made the comparably strongest impact, explaining a little more than 30 percent of the variance. In addition, listening span and sound categorisation (middle sound oddity, end sound oddity) contributed significantly to the prediction of spelling skills at the end of third grade. The fact that the kindergarten predictor measures explained more variance in third grade spelling, as compared to spelling in grade two, may be due to the larger variance in performance obtained for the later spelling tests. Results of the regression analyses performed for spelling at the end of fourth and fifth grade were similar to those performed for third grade spelling and will not be discussed in detail because of space restrictions.

The Interplay of Phonological Awareness and Early Literacy in Predicting Reading and Writing in Elementary School

As noted above, the causal status of phononogical awareness in the process of learning to read has been discussed controversely in the literature. For some researchers, the emergence of phonological awareness is simply a by-product of learning to read (e.g., Morais, 1991; Morais, Bertelson, Cary, & Alegria, 1986). For others, it is just the other way around in that the ability to segment the speech stream into units of phoneme size makes children understand the alphabetical principle (cf. Bradley & Bryant, 1985; Lundberg et al., 1988). A third alternative is reciprocal causation, that is, a causal connection running in both directions (cf. Perfetti, Beck, Bell, & Hughes, 1987).

Although our data are correlational in nature which prevents us from causal inferences, they allow us to test the assumption that phonological awareness (in the broad and narrow sense) can be found among nonreaders. Those 58 children in our sample who did not identify more than 2 letters obviously did not understand the alphabetic principle. When comparing this subgroup with the rest of the sample, we found that, on average, these children scored significantly lower than the others on most tests of phonological awareness. However, performance was significantly above chance level even for this subgroup. These findings nicely replicate those reported by Lundberg and Hoien (1991) for Danish and Swedish children.

A second question of interest concerned the status of IQ, phonological awareness, and memory capacity as predictors of reading and spelling for the subgroup of children with minimal letter knowledge. In particular, we explored the question as to whether indicators of phonological awareness developed without insight into the alphabetic principle can predict reading and spelling in elementary school.

Multiple stepwise regression analyses carried out for this subgroup clearly confirmed this assumption.   As can be seen from Table 3, three phonological awareness measures (first sound oddity, end sound odddity, phoneme blending task) accounted for about 37 percent of the variance in the word decoding speed measure. The results were similar when reading comprehension was used as the dependent variable: The ability to categorise sounds (first sound oddity, end sound oddity) and to segment syllables explained most of the variance in the dependent variable (about 44%). Similar results were obtained for the various spelling measures.

Table 3. Results of the stepwise regression analysis using word decoding speed and reading comprehension in grade 2 as the criterion variables (subgroup with minimal letter knowledge; N=57).

Predictors	R-Square	R-Square change
(1) Word decoding speed		
Nonverbal IQ	.15	
First sound oddity	.31	.16
Sound blending	.44	.13
End sound oddity	.52	.08
Rapid naming	.58	.06
Nonword repetition	.64	.06
(2) Reading comprehension		
Nonverbal IQ	.12	
First sound oddity	.32	.20
Rapid naming	.43	.11
Syllable segmentation	.57	.14
End sound oddity	.67	.10

From these findings, we can conclude that it is possible to develop phonological awareness in the narrow sense despite a very limited knowledge of the alphabet, and that phonological awareness in the broad sense developed without insight into the alphabetic principle predicts subsequent reading and spelling. On the other hand, it seems important to note that letter knowledge was positively related to phonological awareness. At the end of kindergarten, those children who seemed to understand the alphabetic principle were better than the children with low letter knowledge on most metalinguistic tasks. Moreover, this early advantage persisted over the elementary school years: on average, children who acquired the alphabetical principle before school turned out to be the better readers and spellers in elementary school.

The Role of Sex Differences

The hypothesis that girls score higher than boys on tests of metalinguistic ability was only partially confirmed for our sample. We found no sex differences for the subtests of the Bradley and Bryant sound categorization task. Similarly, boys and girls did not differ on most of the Bielefeld screening tasks. There were a few exceptions. Girls outperformed boys on the word comparison task (10.27 vs. 9.51; $p < .05$). Furthermore, girls were faster than boys on the two rapid naming tasks. As the rapid naming measures are supposed to assess children's ability to quickly approach their semantic lexicon, the girls' advantage on these task may indicate somewhat superior language skills. However, we do not have any direct evidence for this. Although girls tended to be better on some of the Bielefeld screening subtests, the overall "risk score" (computed by summing up the "risk points" for each task) did not differ between boys and girls.

The findings concerning early literacy were also mixed. Girls and boys did not differ with regard to their letter knowledge. Also, no sex differences concerning sign knowledge were found. However, girls were able to write down more names than boys (3.5 vs 2.3, $p < .05$). Taken together, these findings indicate that although slight differences in favor of girls were occasionally observed, precursors of reading and spelling assessed during the last year of kindergarten did not differ much as a function of gender.

Did the situation change across the school years? We could not detect any sex differences for the word decoding speed and reading comprehension measures administered in Grade two. The analysis conducted for the spelling tests obtained for grades two to five shows a somewhat different picture. Table 4 gives the means and standard deviations for these tests as a function of gender. The mean number of words spelled correctly at the two testing points in Grade two did not differ as a function of gender, although girls tended to be better at the end of the school year ($t=1.77$, $p < .10$). More pronounced performance differences between girls and boys were observed for the tests in Grades three and four. On each occasion, girls were significantly better (t's =2.18 and 2.17 for Grades three and four, respectively, all p's <.05). Although these differences were reliable, they did not indicate substantial effects. Girls also outperformed boys in Grade five. Due to ceiling effects, however, these differences did not reach statistical significance.

Table 4. Number of correct words in the various spelling tests, as a function of gender.

Grade	M	SD	Min	Max
2 (beginning)				
Boys	10.31	2.16	4	16
Girls	10.06	2.26	5	17
2 (end)				
Boys	10.71	4.25	2	18
Girls	11.72	3.70	3	18
3				
Boys	27.93	8.29	7	40
Girls	30.27	6.55	13	39
4				
Boys	48.56	9.02	17	60
Girls	51.10	7.08	23	60
5				
Boys	75.92	10.60	39	88
Girls	77.51	8.10	56	88

All in all, our findings support the view that performance differences between boys and girls increase with age and amount of schooling. On the other hand, they also confirm the finding reported in earlier studies (e.g., Vellutino et al., 1992) that considerably more boys than girls belong to the lowest quartile of the performance distribution from the very beginning on. Stability of individual differences in spelling performance over time was found to be high from the end of Grade two on, regardless of gender (cf. Table 5). Interestingly, the correlations were also very high for the time between Grades two and three, despite the fact that new teachers had taken over the classrooms by the beginning of Grade three.

The Impact of Individual Differences in Quality of Classroom Instruction on the Development of Spelling

Observational measures of classroom attentional behavior and ratings of the quality of instructions assessed in the SCHOLASTIC project (School learning and socialization of talents, interests, and individual competencies;

see Helmke, Schneider, & Weinert, 1986) were used to assess the impact of classroom differences on the development of reading and spelling. Overall, regression analyses using word decoding speed, reading comprehension, and spelling as criterion variables and IQ, gender, SES, attentional behavior and quality of instruction as predictor variables showed that the classroom predictor variables did not account for much of the variance in the various criterion variables. Their contribution did not prove to be significant, regardless of the criterion variable under consideration.

Table 5. Intercorrelations among the various spelling tests of the LOGIC study as a function of gender (coefficients for boys are depicted above the diagonal, those for girls below the diagonal).

	(1)	(2)	(3)	(4)	(5)
(1) Test Grade 2/1	—	.60	.52	.49	.46
(2) Test Grade 2/2	.42	---	.84	.77	.59
(3) Test Grade 3	.55	.85	---	.86	.79
(4) Test Grade 4	.51	.70	.87	---	.81
(5) Test Grade 5	.46	.60	.78	.86	—

In a second step, a repeated measurement MANOVA using the words provided in Grades 3, 4, and 5 as the dependent factor and sex, SES, IQ, and the two classroom variables as independent factors were carried out. The main effect of IQ just failed to be significant ($p<.06$). There were no other between subjects effects. While spelling performance improved over time, $F(2,254)=69.08$, $p<.01$, there were no significant interactions. Accordingly, changes in spelling performance over time were not related to the independent variables used in the analysis.

Of course, our findings do not rule out the possibility that certain classroom variables may be suited to account for individual differences in reading and spelling. They simply indicate that the classroom measures included in the present analysis were not suited to reveal such an impact - in case it really exists.

Conclusions

The longitudinal analysis of the LOGIC data provided valuable information on the relative impact of phonological awareness, memory capacity, early literacy, and intelligence on the development of reading and spelling in German school children. It seems important to note that all four predictor domains assessed during the last year of kindergarten had a significant impact on the acquisition of reading and spelling skills in elementary school. The results further show that their impact differed as a function of both the dependent measure under study and the measurement point considered. Individual differences in word decoding speed assessed in Grade two were only partially explained by the kindergarten predictor variables.   The quality of prediction was better for the reading comprehension criterion measures obtained at about the same time, and was best for the spelling measures in Grades three and four.

Regarding word decoding speed, children's letter knowledge and IQ turned out to be the best predictors for the first assessment (i.e., the beginning of Grade two), whereas indicators of phonological awareness and information processing speed were considerably more important at the end of Grade two. IQ was also a significant predictor of children's reading comprehension. However, indicators of phonological awareness in the broad sense (i.e., subtests of the sound categorization task) proved even more important for the prediction of individual differences in this criterion variable. As indicated by the regression analyses for the various spelling measures, the overall impact of the four predictor domains seemed to increase with time.   Altogether, they accounted for almost 50% of the variance in spelling assessed at the end of Grade three.   Given that the type of stepwise regression analysis chosen generally overestimated the impact of IQ, the results indicate that indicators of early literacy (i.e., letter knowledge, name writing, sign knowledge) had the comparably strongest impact, followed by measures of memory capacity, phonological awareness in the narrow sense, and information processing speed.

Our findings concerning the "causal" status of phonological awareness in the process of learning to read and spell confirm those obtained in the British and Scandinavian longitudinal studies (e.g., Bradley & Bryant, 1985; Lundberg et al., 1988).   They indicate that phonological awareness both in the broad and in the narrow sense predict later reading and spelling even in those children who did not learn to break the alphabetic code before the end of kindergarten. The fact that a few children in this subgroup performed very well in the sound-blending and sound-to-word matching tasks contradicts the position that letter knowledge is a necessary condition for phonological awareness in the narrow sense (e.g., Morais, 1991). However, it should be noted that phonological awareness in the subgroup with minimal letter knowledge was generally lower than that observed for the rest of the sample. Thus letter knowledge in kindergarten clearly makes a difference with regard to phonological processing skills.   Children who already detected the alphabetical principle in kindergarten performed better on most reading and spelling tests administered in elementary school.   This indicates that early differences in letter knowledge seem to have long-lasting effects.

Overall, sex differences did not play a major role. We found only a few performance differences in favor of girls on the various kindergarten measures of metalinguistic abilities and memory capacity. Similarly, boys and girls did not differ on our measures of decoding speed, reading comprehension, and spelling assessed in Grade two. The fact that girls outperformed boys in spelling tests administered later in time suggests that non-cognitive factors such as attentional behavior, learning motivation and attitude towards school may cause gender differences in spelling frequently observed during the late school years.

Taken together, our findings show that phonological awareness, early literacy, and memory capacity do qualify as important predictors of reading and spelling. These variables proved to be specific predictors of the acquisition of literacy in that they did not relate to other subjects such as math. Our findings thus confirm the results of major Anglo-American and Scandinavian longitudinal studies, indicating that the importance of these predictor domains generalizes across several languages. They go beyond those obtained in most other longitudinal studies in that the relative impact of the various predictor domains was found to vary as a function of the criterion measure under study. For instance, indicators of phonological awareness in the broad sense such as rhyming turned out to be important for the prediction of decoding speed and reading comprehension in Grade two. However, they seem to be less relevant than letter knowledge or memory span in predicting spelling performance in subsequent school years. Finally, the approach chosen in this study clearly shows that the role of IQ in predicting reading and spelling was overrated in earlier longitudinal studies. The predictive power of general cognitive abilities is greatly reduced when measures more specifically related to processes of reading and spelling are simultaneously considered.

REFERENCES

Blachman, B.A. (1984). Relationship of rapid naming ability and language analysis skills to kindergarten and first-grade reading achievement. *Journal of Educational Psychology, 76*, 610-622.

Bradley, L., & Bryant, P. (1985). *Rhyme and reason in reading and spelling*. Ann Arbor: The University of Michigan Press.

Brügelmann, H. (1986). *Lese- und Schreibaufgaben für Schulanfänger* [Reading and spelling tasks designed for first-grade children]. Universität Bremen: Studiengang

Primarstufe.

Burgemeister, B., Blum, L., & Lorge, J. (1972). *Columbia Mental Maturity Scale.* New York: Harcourt Brace.

Case, R., Kurland, D.M., & Goldberg, J. (1982). Operational efficiency and the growth of short-term memory span. *Journal of Experimental Child Psychology, 33,* 386-404.

Daneman, M., & Blennerhassett, A. (1984). How to assess the listening comprehension skills of prereaders. *Journal of Educational Psychology, 76,* 1372-1381.

Denckla, M.B., & Rudel, R.G. (1976). Rapid 'automatized' naming (R.A.N.): Dyslexia differentiated from other learning disabilities. *Neuropsychologia, 14,* 471-479.

Eggert, D. (1978). *Hannover-Wechsler-Intelligenztest für Kinder* [Hannover-Wechsler intelligence test for children]. Bern, Switzerland: Huber-Verlag.

Ellis, N., & Large, B. (1987). The development of reading: As you seek so shall you find. *British Journal of Psychology, 78,* 1-28.

Helmke, A., Schneider, W., & Weinert, F.E. (1986). Quality of instruction and classroom learning outcomes: The German contribution to the IEA Classroom Environment Study. *Teaching and Teacher Education, 2,* 1-18.

Horn, W.F., & Packard, T. (1985). Early identification of learning problems: A meta-analysis. *Journal of Educational Psychology, 77,* 597-607.

Jansen, H., Knorn, P., Mannhaupt, G., Marx, H., Beck, M., & Skowronek, H. (1986). *Bielefelder Screening zur Vorhersage von Lese- und Rechtschreibschwierigkeiten.* Universität Bielefeld, SFB 227.

Juel, C. (1988). Learning to read and write: A longitudinal study of 54 children from frist through fourth grades. *Journal of Educational Psychology, 80,* 437-447.

Lundberg, I., Frost, J., & Petersen, O.P. (1988). Effects of an extensive program for stimulating phonological awareness in preschool children. *Reading Research Quarterly, 23,* 261-284.

Lundberg, I., & Hoien, T. (1991). Initial enabling knowledge and skills in reading acquisition: Print awareness and phonological segmentation. In D.J. Sawyer & B.J. Fox (Eds.), *Phonological awareness in reading - The evolution of current perspectives* (pp. 73-96). New York: Springer Verlag.

Marx, H. (1992). *Vorhersage von Rechtschreibschwierigkeiten in Theorie und Anwendung* [The prediction of reading and spelling problems in theory and practice]. Unpublished manuscript, University of Bielefeld.

Morais, J. (1991). Constraints on the development of phonemic awareness. In S.A. Brady, & D.P. Shankweiler (Eds.), *Phonological processes in literacy -A tribute to Isabelle Y. Liberman* (pp. 5-27). Hillsdale, New Jersey: Erlbaum.

Morais, J., Bertelson, P., Cary, L., & Alegria, J. (1986). Literacy training and speech segmentation. *Cognition, 24,* 45-64.

Morais, J., Cary, L., Alegria, J., & Bertelson, P. (1979). Does awareness of speech as a sequence of phones arise spontaneously? *Cognition, 7,* 323-331.

Näslund, J.C. (1990). The interrelationships among preschool predictors of reading acquisition for German children. *Reading & Writing: An Interdisciplinary Journal, 2,* 327-380.

Näslund, J.C., & Schneider, W. (1991). Longitudinal effects of verbal ability, memory capacity, and phonological awareness on reading performance. *European Journal of Psychology of Education, 6,* 375-392.

Näslund, J.C., & Schneider, W. (1993). Emerging literacy from kindergarten to second grade: Evidence from the Munich Longitudinal Study on the Genesis of Individual Competencies. In H. Grimm & H. Skowronek (Eds.), *Language acquisition problems and reading disorders: Aspects of diagnosis and intervention* (pp. 295-318). New York: de Gruyter.

Perfetti, C.A., Beck, I., Bell, L.C., & Hughes, C. (1987). Phonemic knowledge and learning to read are reciprocal: A longitudinal study of first grade children. *Merrill-Palmer Quarterly, 33,* 255-281.

Perfetti, C.A., & Lesgold, A.M. (1978). Coding and comprehension in skilled reading and instruction. In L.B. Resnick & P.A. Weaver (Eds.), *Theory and practice of early reading,* (Vol. 1, pp.57-84). Hillsdale, NJ: Erlbaum.

Read, C., Zhang, Y., Nie, H., & Ding, B. (1986). The ability to manipulate speech sounds depends on knowing alphabetic writing. *Cognition, 24,* 31-45.

Rott, C., & Zielinski, W. (1986). Entwicklung der Lesefertigkeit in der Grundschule [The development of reading skills in elementary school]. *Zeitschrift für Entwicklungspsychologie und Pädagogische Psychologie, 18,* 165-175.

Schneider, W., & Näslund, J.C. (1992). Cognitive prerequisites of reading and spelling: A longitudinal approach. In A. Demetriou, M. Shayer, & A. Efklides (Eds.), *Neo-Piagetian theories of cognitive development: Implications and applications for education* (pp. 256-274). London: Routledge.

Schneider, W., & Näslund, J.C. (1993). The impact of early meta-linguistic competencies and memory capacity on reading and spelling in elementary school: Results of the Munich Longitudinal Study on the Genesis of Individual Competencies (LOGIC). *European Journal of Psychology of Education, 8,* 273-287.

Schneider, W., & Treiber, B. (1984). Classroom differences in the determination of achievement changes. *American Educational Research Journal, 21,* 195-211.

Skowronek, H., & Marx, H. (1989). The Bielefeld longitudinal study on early identification of risks in learning to write and read: Theoretical background and first results. In M. Brambring, F. Lösel, & H. Skowronek (Eds.), *Children at risk: Assessment, longitudinal research, and intervention* (pp. 268-294). New York: De Gruyter.

Stanovich, K., Cunningham, A.E., & Feeman, D.J. (1984). Intelligence, cognitive skills, and early reading progress. *Reading Research Quarterly, 19,* 278-303.

Tramontana, M.G., Hooper, S.R., & Selzer, S.C. (1988).   Research on the preschool prediction of later academic achievement: A review. *Developmental Review, 8*, 89-146.

Tunmer, W.E., & Nesdale, A.R. (1985).   Phonemic segmentation skill and beginning reading. *Journal of Educational Psychology, 77*, 417-427.

Vellutino, F.R., et al. (1992).   *Gender differences in early reading, language and arithmetic abilities in kindergarten children.* Paper presented at AERA Annual Meeting, San Francisco.

Wagner, R., & Torgesen, J. (1987).   The nature of phonological processing and its causal role in the acquisition of reading skills. *Psychological Bulletin, 101*, 192-212.

Weinert, F.E., & Helmke, A. (1988).   Individual differences in cognitive development: Does instruction make a difference? In E.M. Hetherington & R.M. Lerner (Eds.), *Child development in life-span perspective* (pp. 219-239).   Hillsdale, NJ: Erlbaum.

Wimmer, H., Hartl, M., & Moser, E. (1990).   Passen "englische" Modelle des Schriftspracherwerbs auf "deutsche" Kinder? Zweifel an der Bedeutsamkeit der logographischen Stufe [Do "English" models of reading acquisition apply to German children? Doubts concerning the significance of the logo-graphic stage]. *Zeitschrift für Entwicklungspsychologie und Pädagogische Psychologie, 22*, 136-154.

CULTURAL INFLUENCES ON LITERACY DEVELOPMENT

GERD MANNHAUPT, HEINER JANSEN, and HARALD MARX
Department of Psychology
University of Bielefeld
D-33501 Bielefeld
Germany

ABSTRACT. The impact of cultural differences on cognitive processes is hard to detect, especially when scientific results and models are adopted from another culture. This phenomenon can be observed when models of reading and spelling development in English-speaking children are used by German-speaking investigators without empirical examination. In a longitudinal study of the development of reading and spelling from preschool age up to the end of 4th grade, empirical data are assessed that are useful for the examination of the stage models of literacy. Ten weeks after beginning school, the reading behavior of 153 German first graders were assessed when reading familiar words and pseudowords consisting of either familiar letters or with at least one unfamiliar letter. The behavior is analyzed to detect and discriminate different basal reading strategies (i.e., logographic or cue vs. alphabetic or cipher reading). The results show that two months after beginning institutional reading acquisition there are nearly no logographic reading children. In connection with other German-speaking studies about preschool and early school literacy development, the reported results suggest that for German-speaking children the existence of a common reading strategy before alphabetic reading is to be questioned. Above that, taking over results and models of early literacy or literacy prediction from another written language culture must very carefully be considered.

For decades, psychological research in Europe has been influenced substantially by Anglo-American research. Many current psychological models and trends, such as the theory of achievement motivation (Weiner, 1980) and phonological awareness (Skowronek & Marx, 1989) stem from the Anglo-American language area. It is hardly ever asked whether models transferred in this way take culture and society-specific conditions into account, and whether a direct transfer actually serves any useful purpose.

For developmental models of literacy, too, it is necessary to consider the central question of their culture and language dependence. Although developed within and for the English-language area (Frith, 1985; Marsh, Friedman, Welch, & Desberg, 1980, 1981), they are transferred to German conditions without changing their core assumptions (see Günther, 1986, 1987).

C.K. Leong and R.M. Joshi (Eds.), Cross-Language Studies of Learning to Read and Spell, 161–173.
© 1997 *Kluwer Academic Publishers. Printed in the Netherlands.*

Since the beginning of the 1980s, stage models of literacy development have been proposed (Frith, 1985, 1986; Marsh, Friedman, Welch, & Desberg, 1980, 1981), although the idea that literacy development proceeds in stages or waves is not new (see Chall, 1983, p. 130-141). The advantage of these models lies in the possibility of assigning various reading and spelling strategies to one developmental stage and, in addition, conceptualizing specific disturbances of the acquisition process as transfer problems from one stage to the next (Frith, 1985; Snowling, Stackhouse, & Rack, 1986).

Among these models, Frith's (1985) contribution has been to integrate both reading and spelling development into one single model. The model postulates three developmental stages for both reading and spelling: the logographic, the alphabetic, and the orthographic stage.

Within the logographic stage, the reading strategy is characterized by relating the meaning of a written word to its visual representation. Within the alphabetic stage, children increasingly master sound analysis and synthesis skills (word attack skills, Fox & Routh, 1976). During the orthographic stage, children overcome the shortcomings of the alphabetic strategy. They are increasingly able to take orthographic rules into account and to operate with higher-order units (letter groups).

Besides this, it is assumed that the alphabetic strategy in reading is prepared by spelling (Bryant & Bradley, 1980; Frith, 1985). Spelling is thought to start within the logographic stage, but that it soon leaves this stage because this is required by writing the written fixation of each letter. Then, as it is assumed, the alphabetic strategy is longer kept in spelling than in ·reading because the orthographic rules are easier learned by reading and therefore orthographic reading prepares orthographic spelling.

The Frith (1985) model, developed for English-speaking children, has not stayed unchallenged. Particular doubt has been cast on the postulate of an initial logographic stage (Ehri, 1987, 1989; Ehri & Wilce, 1985; Scott & Ehri, 1990; Stuart, 1990; Stuart & Coltheart, 1988).

Findings from these studies indicate that Anglo-American children do not necessarily start instructed literacy acquisition in school with a logographic reading strategy. Instead, the appearance of this strategy is related to prior knowledge when beginning school and to the way reading and writing is taught.

Günther's Transferal and Adaptation of the Stage Model for the German-Language Area

The stage model Frith (1985) has been discussed within the German-language area in various contexts. While some colleagues attach heuristic value to the model and assume that literacy development can but does not have to proceed in this way (see Scheerer-Neumann, Kretschmann, & Brügelmann, 1986), Günther (1986, 1987, 1989) considers that running through all the stages is a "condition *sine qua non* of the development to a competent availability of the written language" (Günther, 1989, p. 14, translated). Günther's model (Günther, 1986) not only incorporates the stages proposed by Frith (1985), but also extends them: first, by a preliterate-symbolic (pre-)stage, and, second, by an integrative-automatic stage following the orthographic stage. Furthermore, each stage is further differentiated, and additional interaction relations between reading and spelling development are postulated.

According to Wimmer, Landerl, Linortner, and Hummer (1991), the logographic stage has been supported solely by results on literacy acquisition in English and by theoretical arguments. Because in the German-language area, however, literacy instruction is conducted with analytic-synthetic primers, a logographic strategy only seems to be probable if one assumes that "instead of all segmenting, analyzing, and synthesizing practice, the much easier and more economic logographic strategy is winning through by all children" (Günther, 1986, p. 46, translated). Another problem arises out of the fact that, in contrast to the German language, the English language is much more inconsistent in its phoneme-grapheme correspondences (Nyikos, 1990; Venezky, 1972). Because of this, German children should acquire and use decoding strategies much more easily and quickly than English children (Nyikos, 1990).

Günther's (1986) reanalysis of a study of Dehn (1984) also indicates that German children begin literacy instruction logographically. This analysis showed that the proportion of logographic reading children after 18 and 36 weeks of instruction was 62% and 83% respectively. It must be kept in mind, that the definition of logographic reading as "immediate, correct reading without articulatory interruption and without comprehension impairment" (Günther, 1986, p. 47, translated) does not differentiate between logographic and automatized orthographic reading. In contrast, after eight months of instruction, Wimmer et al. (1991) found that a sample of normal reading Austrian first graders were able to read two-thirds of the offered pseudowords, and only one-fifth of their errors were logographic ones. After eight months of schooling, the logographic reading strategy seems to have lost its importance.

Jansen (1992) tested whether a logographic stage could be detected earlier in the 1st grade. After 10 weeks of instruction, 53.8% of the sample were not able to read at least one of the unknown words. In terms of overt reading behavior (senseless misreading, prior reading trials for one word, stretched reading) only 21.5% of the children could be labeled potentially logographic readers. After 19 weeks of instruction, all children exhibited alphabetic reading behavior. Only five out of 65 children were not able to read at least one unknown word.

Jansen's (1992) findings show that even at an earlier time than that chosen by Wimmer et al. (1991), a logographic reading strategy for all children is unlikely. But it is still not clear whether the children who were named as potential logographic readers actually use more logographic reading strategies while reading known words. If this were the case, these children should read unknown words or pseudowords with a strong visual similarity to the known primer words by answering with a known primer word or with "don't know."

If the proportion of meaningful misreadings were not higher in the logographic than in the alphabetic group, and if, additionally, a high proportion of "don't know" answers could be observed in the former group, then this result would allow two interpretations:

First, it could be assumed that logographic readers visually analyze the pseudowords very exactly and that they answer with a primer word only when all relevant features are realized. Because highly similar pseudowords per definition correspond only partly to the primer words, a small proportion of meaningful misreadings connected with a high proportion of "don't know" answers could be interpreted as a highly controlled logographic strategy.

Second, poor performance in reading primer words connected with a low proportion of meaningful misreadings and a high proportion of "don't know" answers when reading the pseudowords would support the assumption that the so-called logographic group actually does not consist of logographic reading children but of poor, alphabetic readers.

The present study tried to answer the following questions:

1. What proportions of children (a) already read unknown pseudowords after 14 weeks of instruction and can therefore be classified as alphabetic readers; (b) cannot read pseudowords, but show first signs of alphabetic reading behavior (i.e., more than one reading trial or syllabic and/or phonemic subdividing of the word); and (c) can neither read pseudowords

nor exhibit alphabetic reading behavior and should therefore be classified as at least potentially logographic readers?

2. Which of the above-mentioned reading behavior patterns corresponds to the reading behavior of the potentially logographic reading group? Can they be said to read highly visually analytically logographically or purely alphabetically?

Sample

As part of the Bielefeld Longitudinal Study (Marx, Jansen, Mannhaupt, & Skowronek, 1983), 187 children (87 girls, 100 boys; age in months: Mean = 83.18; S.D. = 3.64) from 53 elementary schools in Bielefeld, Germany were given various instruments to assess the development of early literacy acquisition after 14 weeks of schooling (see Jansen, Mannhaupt, Marx, & Skowronek, 1987).   The children's classes used nine different reading primers that followed a synthetic-analytic approach to reading instruction.

Tasks

Subjects were given a 24-item reading task that they had to read aloud. This word list contained three different sets of eight items that were presented to the children in a random order. The three sets were:

1. *Known primer words.* We ascertained the actual page that each class had reached in its primer and developed specific test materials for each class consisting of three and four letter words taken from their primer.   This ensured that all primer words were comparable in terms of the students' knowledge level.

2. *Primer words with one unknown letter (pseudowords).* These were constructed by swapping one letter in each word for an unknown one (e.g., *Foto-Foty or Ina -Iva*).

3. *Transfer pseudowords.* A set of eight pseudowords was constructed from letters that had already been learned in school (e.g., *mato, lita, lom*).

The experimenter protocolled reading behavior online in writing. Each of the children's utterances was protocolled, so that not only the reading outcome but also the way of reading (i.e., in syllables or phoneme by phoneme) and each missed reading trial were recorded.

Division into Reading Groups

The sample was divided into three reading strategy groups on the basis of their performance and their behavior when reading the transfer pseudoword:

1. *Alphabetic readers.* Children who correctly read at least one transfer pseudoword.

2. *In transition (to alphabetic reading).* Children who could not read one transfer pseudoword correctly, but showed signs of alphabetic reading behavior (prior reading attempts, syllabic or phonematic subdividing of a word).

3. *Logographic readers.* Children who read no transfer pseudoword correctly and showed no signs of alphabetic reading.

Results

The 187 children in the sample distributed among the three groups as follows: 160 (85.6%) belonged to the alphabetic, 17 (9.1%) to the transition, and 10 (5.3%) to the logographic reading group. This made clear that, after 14 weeks of school instruction, only a very small portion of the children could be classified as logographic readers. Because of the large difference in the sizes of the three groups, we were unable to apply direct inference statistics to test the group differences in reading behavior and performance. To permit such an analysis, we selected a random sample of 17 children from the 160 subjects within the alphabetic group. The following analyses were based on this sample.

To assess reading behavior and performance independently from the measure that was used for the classification (reading of transfer pseudowords), the observed reading performance and behavior when reading pseudowords were used for the following analyses.

Jonckheere's (1954) trend test was used to construct an ascending rank order of reading performance across the three groups (see Table 1). It was assumed that no differences would appear for the primer words, because logographic children should also recognize the known words without problems. On the other hand, it was assumed that the pseudowords could only be read by alphabetic readers.

Table 1. Means (standard deviations) of reading performance on known and pseudowords in the three reading groups

| | Reading Group | | |
	Alphabetic	In transition	Logographic
Known words	6.42 (1.87)	3.65 (2.23)	3.10 (2.03)
Pseudowords	2.59 (2.52)	0.29 (0.59)	0.30 (0.68)

Reading performance for known words was significant ($S = 438$, $p < .05$), that is, both the logographic and transition group performed significantly worse than the alphabetic group. On the other hand, differences in reading pseudowords were not significant ($S = 348$, $p > .05$). The logographic and transition groups performed slightly less well than the alphabetic group, but this difference failed to reach significance. A Wilcoxon Rank-Sum Test was used to analyze whether pseudowords were read worse than known words. This difference was significant ($z = -5.71$, $p < .05$). In all three groups, pseudowords were read less well than known words.

If a logographic reader is confronted with unknown words, the typical response should be either not to read them (i.e., "don't know" answers) or to misread them as meaningful words. Therefore, the logographic group should exhibit a much higher proportion of these behaviors than the other two groups.

Table 2. Means (standard deviations) of the number of semantic misreadings and "don't know" answers in the three reading groups

| | Reading Group | | |
	Alphabetic	In transition	Logographic
Number of semantic misreadings	0.41 (0.80)	0.59 (1.06)	0.30 (0.68)
Number of "don't know" answers	0.42 (1.33)	1.24 (1.52)	5.30 (3.20)

Table 2 reports the proportion of semantically meaningful misreadings and "don't know" answers when reading pseudowords. Jonckheere's (1954) trend test failed to confirm the assumption that the logographic group would exhibit the most and the alphabetic reading group the fewest meaningful misreadings ($S = 135$, $p > .05$). Meaningful misreadings were exhibited to the same extent in all three reading groups. The logographic group did not exhibit an overproportional amount of such reading behavior, and meaningful misreading could also be observed within the alphabetic reading group.

The number of "don't know" answers resulted in an ascending rank order from the alphabetic to the logographic group ($S = 413$, $p < .05$).

Discussion

Fourteen weeks after beginning literacy instruction in school, only 5.3% of the analyzed sample are unable to read any pseudoword and do not show any signs of alphabetic reading behavior, whereas 94.7% either show first attempts at alphabetic reading or they are able to read unknown pseudowords. The latter can only succeed if alphabetical reading strategies are used. Our findings correspond to the results of Jansen (1992) and support Wimmer et al.'s (1991) claim that an initial logographic stage of literacy does not exist. These converging findings lead us to assume that Günther (1986) has presumptions in interpreting the immediate readings of the children as logographic in his reanalysis. Spontaneous and correct readings by children who have attended school for 18 or 36 weeks do not have to be based on logographic reading strategies. Rather, it seems highly probable that such readings are based on already developed and well-practised alphabetic reading strategies.

Although our findings clearly show that all German children do not use a logographic reading strategy, the 5.3% who were classified as potentially logographic readers may well have really used logographic reading strategies. The present results again contradict such an assumption. Groups were divided on the basis of the reading of transfer pseudowords. Taking the reading behavior of the pseudowords into account, the group of potential logographic reading children would have been decreased by two more children. This shows, on the one hand, that the classification into reading groups depends on the reading material that is used. On the other hand, it reveals that the number of logographic reading children is probably even lower than the actual classification would suggest.

Looking at the reading behavior of the logographic group, the proportion of "don't know" answers is much higher than in the alphabetic group. This supports the assumption that children with a logographic reading strategy cannot tackle an unknown word in any way. But they do not answer with a wrong word, but a similar known word. Moreover, it has to be said that such a behavior can be seen in all three groups to about the same extent, although the pseudowords were constructed to be visually very similar to the primer words in order to force meaningful misreadings. Obviously, these pseudowords are analyzed very exactly, and children prefer to say nothing rather than answer with similar known words.

At the same time, the primer word reading analysis shows that children who do not read one transfer pseudoword also read the primer words substantially worse than alphabetic readers. Fourteen weeks after beginning literacy instruction with a very small primer reading vocabulary, this finding would be astonishing if logographic reading really dominates, and it is assumed that children are able to build up a sight-word vocabulary of about 100 words without much effort (Günther, 1986). Besides, it is clearly shown that children within the logographic group obviously face problems with the alphabetic strategy.

In sum, the result reveals the unlikeliness of visually logographic reading even among the children in the potentially logographic reading group. The assumption that these children are still unable to manage the alphabetic reading strategy seems much more plausible.

Conclusions

The development of literacy during school age in German-speaking children cannot be described adequately by either the model of Frith (1985) or its extended version of Günther (1986). Only a very few children in our study show no alphabetic reading behavior; following the stage models, they are classified as logographic readers. The analysis of their reading behavior reveals that they do not behave in the way that the models would assume. They can neither manage the reading of a known word nor guess when reading visually similar, but unknown pseudowords. Instead, their reactions support the notion that they are not able to read properly yet. So, this group does not consist of logographic readers but of poor readers. This empirically reputes the basis for the assumption of a logographic reading stage in German children.

One possible objection is that our design cannot detect the logographic strategy in German children because this reading strategy takes place before children attend school. Two points can be raised against this argument: First, results from case studies of preschoolers reported by Günther (1986) himself speak against this assumption. Second, in 182 first graders who were assessed during the first weeks of the school year, Rathenow and Vöge (1982) found no notable number of children who were able to read sight words out of their daily environments while not mastering the synthesis, one alphabetic reading strategy. The reported as well the referred studies show that an initial logographic reading stage cannot be observed in German-speaking children. This stresses the need to test the empirical validity of this model when transferring it to other cultures.

Although it is tempting to transfer models from other cultures and differentiate them, more research should be focused on checking the cultural validity of the transferred models in the target culture. Figure 1 shows how difficult this project can be. In replicating a study by Hakes (1980) Hoepner-Stamos and Olschewski (1991) found, for example, that the phoneme segmentation task (Liberman, Shankweiler, Fischer, & Carter, 1974) very sensitively reflects the differences between US-American and German children's development in the transition from kindergarten to school. While at the age of 4 and 5 years, no differences can be observed, within the period between 5 and 7 years, performances differ widely. It is only, when entering Grade 2, between 7 and 8 years, that both samples fully master this task. One consequence to be drawn from this is that one should very carefully compare and check findings, studies, and models on literacy development from the other culture when the empirical work addresses children between kindergarten and 2nd grade.

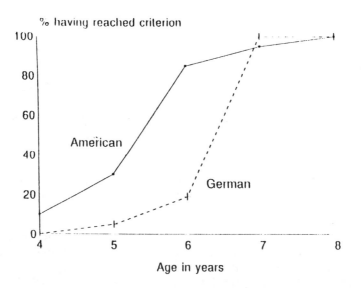

Figure 1. Phoneme segmentation of American and German children (Hakes, 1980, compared to Hoepner-Stamos, & Olschweski, 1991).

The general conclusion is that one should not think of cultural differences in only static concepts such as speech - written language relations, but also in dynamic ways. That is, that differences between two cultures may be important during specific age periods, but unimportant during others. Especially within literacy research, these problems must be tackled very carefully to ensure that, when an international perspective is involved, we do not make global assumptions about literacy development and difficulties, when very fine-grained descriptions and explanations in terms of culture and age are needed.

REFERENCES

Bryant, P.E., & Bradley, L. (1980). Why children sometimes write words which they do not read. In U. Frith (Ed.), *Cognitive processes in spelling* (pp. 355-370). London: Academic Press.

Chall, J.S. (1983). *Stages of reading development*. New York: McGraw-Hill.

Dehn, M. (1984). Lernschwierigkeiten beim Schriftspracherwerb. (Learning difficulties in literacy). *Zeitschrift für Pädagogik, (Journal of Education), 30*, 93-114.

Ehri, L.C. (1987). Learning to read and spell words. *Journal of Reading Behavior, 24*, 5-31.

Ehri, L.C. (1989). The development of spelling knowledge and its role in reading acquisition and reading disability. *Journal of Learning Disabilities, 22*, 356-365.

Ehri, L.C., & Wilce, L.S. (1985). Movement into reading: Is the first stage of printed word learning visual or phonetic? *Reading Research Quarterly, 20*, 163-179.

Fox, B., & Routh, D.K. (1976). Phonemic analysis and synthesis as word-attack skills. *Journal of Educational Psychology, 68*, 70-74.

Frith, U. (1985). Beneath the surface of developmental dyslexia. Are comparisons between developmental and acquired disorders meaningful? In K. E. Patterson, J. C. Marshall, & M. Coltheart (Eds.), *Surface dyslexia* (pp. 301-330). London: Erlbaum.

Frith, U. (1986). Psychologische Aspekte des Orthographischen Wissens: Entwicklung und Entwicklungsstörung (Psychological aspects of orthographic knowledge: Development and developmental disturbance). In G. Augst (Ed.), *New trends in graphemics and orthography* (pp. 218-233). Berlin: de Gruyter.

Günther, K.B. (1986). Ein Stufenmodell der Entwicklung kindlicher Lese- und Schreibstrategien (A stage model of the development of children's reading and spelling strategies). In H. Brügelmann (Ed.), *ABC und Schriftsprache: Rätsel für Kinder, Lehrer und Forscher* (ABC and literacy: Riddles for children, teachers, and researchers). (pp. 32-54). Konstanz: Faude.

Günther, K.B. (1987). Schriftspracherwerb: Modellhafte und individuelle Entwicklung (Literacy acquisition: Developments conform to models and individuals).

In H. Balhorn, & H. Brügelmann (Eds.), *Welten der Schrift in der Erfahrung der Kinder* (Worlds of literacy in children's experiences). (pp. 103-109). Konstanz: Faude.

Günther, K.B. (1989). Ontogenese, Entwicklungsprozeß und Störungen beim Schriftspracherwerb unter besonderer Berücksichtigung der Schwierigkeiten von lern- und sprachbehinderten Kindern (Ontogenesis, developmental process and disturbances in literacy acquisition under special respect of the difficulties of learning and speech disabled children). In K.-B. Günther (Ed.), *Ontogenese, Entwicklungsprozeß und Störungen beim Schriftspracherwerb* (Ontogenesis, developmental process and disturbances in literacy acquisition). (pp. 12-33). Heidelberg: Schindele.

Hakes, D.T. (1980). *The development of metalinguistic abilities in children.* Berlin: Springer.

Hoepner-Stamos, F., & Olschewski, P. (1991). *Zum Zusammenhang zwischen metalinguistischen und kognitiven Leistungen bei Kindern. Replikation einer amerikanischen Studie an Kindern im Alter zwischen vier und acht Jahren* (On the relationship between metalinguistic and cognitive abilities. Replication of an American study with children between the ages of four and eight years). Unpublished master's thesis, Universität Bielefeld, Bielefeld.

Jansen, H. (1992). *Untersuchungen zur Entwicklung lautsynthetischer Verarbeitungsprozesse im Vorschul- und frühen Grundschulalter* (Studies on the development of sound synthesis processes in preschool and early elementary school age). Egelsbach: Hänsel-Hohenhausen.

Jansen, H., Mannhaupt, G., Marx, H., & Skowronek, H. (1987). *Materialien der ersten Grundschuluntersuchung (T3) 14 Wochen nach Einschulung* (Materials of the first elementary school assessment (T3) 14 weeks after attending school). Unpublished manuscript, Universität Bielefeld.

Jonckheere, A.R. (1954). A distribution-free k-sample test against ordered alternatives. *Biometrika, 41,* 133-145.

Liberman, I.Y., Shankweiler, D., Fischer, W., & Carter, B. (1974). Explicit syllable and phoneme segmentation in the young child. *Journal of Child Psychology, 18,* 201-212.

Marsh, G., Friedman, M., Welch, V., & Desberg, P. (1980). The development of strategies in spelling. In U. Frith (Ed.), *Cognitive processes in spelling* (pp. 339-353). London: Academic Press.

Marsh, G., Friedman, M. Welch, V., & Desberg, P. (1981). A cognitive-developmental theory of reading acquisition. In T. Waller, & G. MacKinnon (Eds.), *Reading research: Advances in theory and practice* (pp. 199-201). New York: Academic Press.

Marx, H., Jansen, H., Mannhaupt, G., & Skowronek, H. (1993). Prediction of difficulties in reading and spelling on the basis of the Bielefeld Screening. In H. Grimm, & H. Skowronek (Eds.), *Language acquisition problems and reading disorders: Aspects of diagnosis and intervention* (pp. 219-242). Berlin: de Gruyter.

Nyikos, K. (1990). Comparative task difficulty in initial reading: German versus English. In F. Biglmaier (Ed.), *Reading at the crossroads* (pp. 72-81). Berlin: Zentrale Universitätsdruckerei der Freien Universität Berlin (West).

Rathenow, P., & Vöge, J. (1982). *Erkennen und Fördern von Schülern mit Lese-Rechtschreibschwierigkeiten* (Diagnosis and remediation of students with reading and writing disabilities). Braunschweig: Westermann.

Scheerer-Neumann, G., Kretschmann, R., & Brügelmann, H. (1986). Andrea, Ben und Jana: Selbstgewählte Wege zum Lesen und Schreiben (Andrea, Ben, and Jana: Self elected ways to reading and spelling). In H. Brügelmann (Ed.), *ABC und Schriftsprache: Rätsel für Kinder, Lehrer und Forscher* (ABC and literacy: Riddles for children, teachers, and researchers). (pp. 55-96). Konstanz: Faude.

Scott, J. A., & Ehri, L. C. (1990). Sight word reading in prereaders: Use of logographic vs. alphabetic access routes. *Journal of Reading Behavior, 22*, 149 - 166.

Skowronek, H., & Marx, H. (1989). Die Bielefelder Längsschnittstudie zur Früherkennung der Lese-Rechtschreibschwäche: Theoretischer Hintergrund und erste Befunde (The Bielefeld longitudinal study on the prediction of reading and writing disabilities: Theoretical background and first results). *Heilpädagogische Forschung, 15*, 38-49.

Snowling, M., Stackhouse, J., & Rack, J. (1986). Phonological dyslexia and dysgraphia - a developmental analysis. *Cognitive Neuropsychology, 3*, 309-339.

Stuart, M. (1990). Processing strategies in a phoneme deletion task. *The Quarterly Journal of Experimental Psychology, 42A*, 305-327.

Stuart, M., & Coltheart, M. (1988). Does reading develop in a sequence of stages? *Cognition, 30*, 139-181.

Venezky, R. (1972). *Language and cognition in reading*. Tech. Rep. No. 188, Madison : Wisconsin Research and Developmental Center for Cognitive Learning. ERIC Document Reproduction Service Nr. ED 067 646.

Weiner, B. (1980). *Human motivation*. New York: Holt, Rinehart & Winston.

Wimmer, H., Landerl, K., Linortner, R., & Hummer, P. (1991). The relationship of phonemic awareness to reading acquisition: More consequence than precondition but still important. *Cognition, 40*, 219-249.

STRATEGIES OF SPELLING AND READING OF YOUNG CHILDREN LEARNING GERMAN ORTHOGRAPHY

RENATE VALTIN
Humboldt Universität Berlin
Institut für Schulpädagogik
Unter den Linden 6
10099 Berlin
Germany

ABSTRACT. Recent research in the field of written language acquisition has led to the realization that children develop strategies to deal with and communicate in print, which follows a developmental sequence as a result of an interaction between the child's emerging process abilities and the structure of orthography. Similar sequential patterns for the English orthography were identified. Referring to German studies, the sequential patterns of spelling and reading strategies which have been found with young children learning the German orthography are outlined. The data show that the acquisition of written language may be characterized as a sequence of dominant strategies. It is argued that these dominant strategies reflect important insights into the nature of written language, such as the concept of the word and the word boundary, the awareness of phonemes and of the principles of orthography. In comparison with learners of English orthography, a long logographic phase seems not to be typical for German children. Only poor readers and spellers who have not yet grasped the alphabetic principle have been observed to use this strategy. The possible difference between English and German speaking children may be explained by two factors: The complexity of orthography, and the effect of school instruction. The rather regular grapheme-phoneme-correspondence of German orthography may facilitate the early development of an alphabetic strategy as a "rational" choice. In classroom instruction both in Austria and Germany teachers place heavy emphasis on phonics. Furthermore, in the first weeks or months of instruction many teachers or primers present only words that are rather regular and have consistent and one-to-one grapheme-phoneme-correspondence. The sequential model offering a new framework for dyslexia is discussed.

Recent research in the field of written language acquisition has led to the realization that learning to read and spell is an active process in which children build theories by forming, testing and modifying hypotheses about the function and features of written language (Downing & Valtin 1984) and develop strategies to deal and communicate with print. These strategies are not haphazard but follow a developmental sequence which is the result of an interaction between the child's emerging process abilities and the structure of orthography. Similar sequential patterns for the English orthography were identified by Henderson and Beers (1980), Gentry (1981), Temple, Nathan and Burris (1982), and Frith (1985), all showing that children develop from prealphabetic (when spelling new words) or logographic (when spelling

C.K. Leong and R.M. Joshi (Eds.), Cross-Language Studies of Learning to Read and Spell, 175–193.
© 1997 *Kluwer Academic Publishers. Printed in the Netherlands.*

familiar words) to alphabetic and orthographic strategies. For reading, similar strategies are postulated by Frith (1985).

It is of interest to examine whether learners of other orthographies will develop the same strategies. One might hypothesize that - given the highly irregular English orthography - logographic strategies will play a more prominent part in learning to read and write than in more phonetically regular scripts. German orthography is more regular in comparison with English so it would be a "rational" choice to use an alphabetic strategy in early phases of learning written language. Another factor influencing these strategies may be different instructional methods. The "look-and-say" method in English and American schools - apart from being better suited for a highly irregular orthography - may foster logographic strategies. In German speaking countries class room instruction places heavy weight on phonemic segmentation and blending while reading and spelling are integrated.

Since the middle 1980s there are a number of observational studies in Germany trying to describe the development of reading and spelling competence in young children. Referring to these studies, the sequential patterns of spelling and reading strategies, which have been found with young children learning the German orthography, will be outlined. For a better understanding a short description of German orthography is presented.

Some Remarks on German Orthography

In German, the grapheme-phoneme relations are rather regular when compared to English. About 40 phonemes (including 16 vowels and 3 digraphs) are represented by 85 graphemes each consisting of one, two or three letters. The German alphabet has 30 letters, including ä, ö, ü und ß. Estimates of the amount of words that can be written phonologically vary from 50 to 75 per cent of the total number of words (Thomé, 1987), foreign loan words presenting the most number of irregularities.

While the main principle that governs German orthography is phonological, there are some exceptions due to other principles, such as morphological: morphemes are spelled the same way even if pronounced differently in various contexts, e.g. Hand - Hände; logical: homonyms are written differently, e.g. Ferse - Verse; esthetical: a word is spelled in such a way that it looks "good", e.g., "ck" for "kk", "sp" for "schp"; grammatical: nouns are written with initial capital letter (for more details, see Valtin, 1989a).

Since the letter-sound correspondence rules are rather consistent, a "sounding-out" strategy leads to an articulatory code that is rather similar to the real word. Thus reading does not present as many problems as writing because the sound-letter-correspondence is less predictable. Main difficulties are the following:

- at word final position the voiced consonants <d>, <b>, and <g> are pronounced /t/,/p/ and /k/.

- graphic markers for long and short vowels: Long vowel sounds may be represented by the doubling of the vowel or by adding an -h, such as <aa> and <ah> for /a:/. Short vowel sounds may be marked by the following of double consonants.

- the phoneme /s/ may be represented by <s>, <ss>, <ß> or <c>

- German is the only orthography in which nouns are written with capital letters, but there are many exceptions, and nearly nobody masters the 78 corresponding rules.

Analysis of spelling errors of adults and of older pupils show that the last three of these difficulties contribute to about two-third of all spelling errors (Thomé, 1987).

The existing spelling system goes back to 1902 and is described in the "Duden", a book that has been edited and revised 20 times since then (for the last version, see Dudenredaktion, 1991). Over the years various reform movements have been trying to simplify the spelling system and to abolish the capitalization of nouns. Very recently, representatives of all German speaking countries (Germany, Switzerland and Austria) made a proposal for a spelling reform that seemed to have good chances for realization because it contained only moderate alterations (and sticking to the capitalized nouns). But the initiative has been stopped recently by Bavarian politicians who fear a decline of civilization. Chances for a spelling reform are now quite low since all 16 states of the Federal Republic of Germany are educationally autonomous and have to agree to a reform.

Despite these orthographic difficulties and irregularities, for a beginning learner it seems quite a safe and rational strategy to use phonemic spellings because the probability of correct spelling is quite high as can be seen in Table 1. Thomé (1989) has computed on the basis of 10000 phonemes the percentage of graphemes written either phonemically or according to orthographic rules.

Table 1. Percentage of phonemes with phonemic or orthographic spelling in German orthography.

Phoneme	Grapheme phonemic spelling		Grapheme orthographic spelling						
/ɑ:/	\<a\>	89,8 %	\<ah\>	8,9 %	\<aa\>	1,3 %		
/e:/	\<e\>	90,7 %	\<eh\>	8,3 %	\<ee\>	1,0 %		
/i:/	\<ie\>	82,6 %	\<ih\>	13,9 %	\<i\>	3,2 %	\<ieh\>	0,3 %
/o:/	\<o\>	87,8 %	\<oh\>	11,2 %	\<oo\>	1,0 %		
/u:/	\<u\>	90,5 %	\<uh\>	9,5 %				
/ɛ:/	\<ä\>	61,5 %	\<äh\>	38,5 %				
/ø:/	\<ö\>	50,0 %	\<öh\>	50,0 %				
/y:/	\<ü\>	86,0 %	\<üh\>	14,0 %				
/a/	\<a\>	100 %						
/ə/	\<e\>	100 %						
/ɪ/	\<i\>	98,5 %	\<ie\>	1,5 %				
/ɔ/	\<o\>	100 %						
/U/	\<u\>	100 %						
/ɛ/	\<e\>	89,2%	\<ä\>	10,8%				
/oe/	\<ö\>	100 %						
/Y/	\<ü\>	100 %						
/al/	\<ei\>	100 %						
/aɔ/	\<au\>	99,3 %	\<auh\>	0,7 %				
/ɔy/	\<eu\>	72,7 %	\<äu\>	23,7 %				
/p/	\<p\>	58,3 %	\<b\>	38,9 %	\<pp\>	2,8 %	\<dt\>	0,5 %
/t/	\<t\>	73,6 %	\<d\>	19,8 %	\<tt\>	6,0 %		
/k/	\<k\>	67,2 %	\<g\>	22,4 %	\<ck\>	10,3 %		
/s/	\<s\>	80,6 %	\<ß\>	15,3 %	\<ss\>	4,1 %		
/f/	\<f\>	67,4 %	\<v\>	30,3 %	\<ff\>	2,3 %		
/b/	\<b\>	100 %						
/d/	\<d\>	100 %						
/g/	\<g\>	100 %						
/z/	\<s\>	100 %						
/v/	\<w\>	99,1 %	\<v\>	0,9 %				
/r/	\<r\>	99,5 %	\<rr\>	0,5 %				
/l/	\<l\>	88,8 %	\<ll\>	11,2 %				
/m/	\<m\>	88,2 %	\<mm\>	11,8 %				
/n/	\<n\>	94,3 %	\<nn\>	5,7 %				
/h/	\<h\>	100 %						
/j/	\<j\>	100 %						
/ks/	\<chs\>	100 %						
/kv/	\<qu\>	100 %						
/ts/	\<z\>	87,1 %	\<tz\>	12,9 %				
/ʃ/	\<sch\>	53,8 %	\<s\> (vor t od. p) 46,2 %					
/x/	\<ch\>	92,9 %	\<g\> (nach i) 7,1 % (z. B. „freudig")					
/ŋ/	\<ng\>	73,1 %	\<n\> (vor k) 26,9 %					

Strategies of learning to spell

While in the 1970s most of the German researchers in the domain of written language investigated problem children and tried to identify cognitive deficits of dyslexic children or partial processes in which children with dyslexia are deficient, in the 1980s their focus switched to "normal" readers and spellers, especially to beginning learners. Researchers in the field of education and psychology reported, on the basis of natural observation in the classroom (or of their own children), developmental data, mainly on children learning to spell unfamiliar words.

Spitta (1986/1993) referring to Gentry (1982) differentiated six phases of the development of writing: (1) precommunicative abilities: scribbling, (2) prephonetic (3) semiphonetic, (4) phonetic phase, (5) phonetic spelling with integration of orthographic regularities and (6) developed spelling competence.

Dehn (1987/1994) investigated 66 first graders and their spellings of unfamiliar words, dictated to them at different times of the school year. She observed the following strategies:
- diffuse spellings: no correspondence between letters and sounds,
- rudimentary spellings: some sound aspects are represented,
- spellings that represent irrelevant phonetic elements,
- phonemic spellings,
- use of orthographic elements, and
- morphemic spellings.

Scheerer-Neumann (1989/1993), on the basis of case studies, described also six strategies that resemble those outlined by Dehn and Spitta. She made an important distinction between two components of spelling: spelling of learned words (or sight-words) and of new words. Learned words are stored in memory and can be recalled. Unfamiliar words have to be constructed by means of strategies the child develops gradually and which deal with phoneme-grapheme-correspondences and orthographic and morphemic regularities. Children initially learn some words by heart (e.g., their own name, favorite words or some words from their primers) which are internally represented as memory images. Their written vocabulary remains limited, however; only when they have recognized the function of letters and have learned the specific connections between letters and sounds children do begin to acquire more and more learned words.

The developmental models by Dehn, Spitta and Scheerer-Neumann refer to single word spelling. The model that will be described below also takes account of the very early writings of the child and the spelling of entire sentences or texts.

The examples are taken from longitudinal studies in four class rooms in Berlin (one preschool class of five year olds, three first grades). In these studies 96 pupils were observed in their spontaneous writings (words, sentences, "letters" to absent friends) and their writings after dictation (for further results of one part of the study see, Valtin, 1989a, 1989b; Valtin & Naegele, 1986/1993). Our stage model covers six phases of the development of spelling strategies. Each phase may be characterized by a *dominant* strategy. This means that strategies are not substituted by a following one, but that children acquire more strategies and use them in a flexible way. Note that these strategies refer primarily to the spelling of unfamiliar words and sentences.

I = Figurative strategies

Here the focus of the child is on perceptually discriminable features: either imitating the writing behavior of adults (scribbling) or representing features of the object (drawing). At this phase, as well as at the next, children as yet have no concepts of words as linguistic units and no awareness of phonemes. When scribbling, most children show that they have grasped some important and most remarkable figurative aspects of print: linearity, boundaries, irregularities in graphic structures (Example 1).

Some children, when "writing" draw pictures seemingly thinking that the message is in the pictures they draw (see example 2, a letter written by Charly to his friend Martin). Charly when asked to read his letter aloud commented on the pictures as follows: "Martin is big. Martin is in the bathtub. The sun is going down".

Already at the age of three, some children begin imitating the writing of adults. For them, writing means mimicking the hand movements of writing and making marks on paper, generally without realizing that these marks have a communicative significance. Some very young children also engage in copying written words or sentences without knowledge of the content. That this copying is a highly active reconstruction process and not mirroring is shown by the next example of a little boy (3:6 years): He copies one sentence and writes backwards when he reaches the end of the line. This "furrow" solution could also be observed in other German children (Scheerer-Neumann, Kretschmann, & Brügelmann, 1986) and was also found in ancient Greek writings.

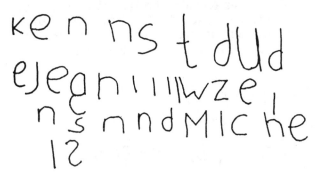

Kennst du die Zwillinge Jens und Michel? (Do you know the twins Jens and Michel?)

Figurative strategies may mainly be observed in young preschool children who are not yet able to write their own name.

II = Logographic strategy: drawing arbitrary sequences of letters or letterlike forms, ("pseudowords")

In this phase children have gained more figurative knowledge of letters. When asked to write a certain utterance they produce strings of idiosyncratic characters or conventional letters phonetically unrelated to the utterance. For example: After three months of instruction children transformed the spoken sentence "Ich bin ein Junge/Mädchen (I am a boy/a girl)" into written form as follows:

Daniel L.

MRO ZL

Carsten

iFEϒ

Nadine

ORAƷt ʰm

Very rarely children mark word boundaries like Melanie who commented, "I make a line where it stops." This indicated that she was beginning to grasp the fact that sentences are segmented, though she divided this sentence into only three units probably because she did not count the article ("ein") and the function word ("und"). Moreover, there is no correspondence between the length of oral and written sentences (the second sentence with the same amount of words is written much longer).

ditｕatﬀUa

Ich bin ein Mädchen (I am a girl)

uAfteℓtamiuⅠkutfeꞵ

Oma und Opa lesen (Grandma and Grandpa are reading)

With regard to word boundaries, it is interesting to note that in ancient Greek and Latin writings, words were written continuously without space. The first word boundary marks were little dots. In our sample also a few children used dots or - in the case of Melanie - vertical lines.

Learned words: At this stage children are able to write some words learned by rote memory. Since a word for them is an assembly of letters they have difficulties in reproducing the right shape and the order of the letter. Very frequent are letter omissions, reversals of single letters or errors in the sequence.

III = Beginning phonetic strategy: rudimentary or skeleton writings

Here, the very first signs of alphabetic writing become recognizable. With growing awareness of the sound structure of words children begin to represent phonetic elements. However, the representation of spoken in written language remains rudimentary and children only represent some phonetic cues. Some children only write down the first letter, others represent only the most important and articulatory salient sounds. Frequently, every syllable is indicated at least by one letter, e.g., in the case of Daniela who knows her name as a sight-word.

EHSDANIELA (Ich heiße Daniela).

Some children when representing syllables of CV-structure use the letter name for representing the sound (HS instead of "heiße"). Regarding the representation of words, the children in our sample reproduced almost all the words in the sentences, with the exception of functors (Example 6). Only a very few children left gaps, either in a word or between the words.

DIM OIS SAFE

HOS AN

Die Mäuse schlafen (in den) Häusern: The mice sleep (in the) houses.

At this stage, the size of the *learned vocabulary* is still very limited. But the knowledge of some letter-sound-correspondences helps the child when recalling a word (mainly at the beginning of a word).

IV = Phonetic-articulatory strategy

Children have now grasped the principle of the alphabetic code and know most of the letters. Observations show that children, when analyzing the sound structure, orient themselves primarily to articulatory cues, saying the words slowly out loud and trying to "catch" all sounds of their pronunciation, for instance, "*aien" or "*aein" for "ein", and "*ont" for "und".

Esch Ben A ie n MeTscht iF

Ich bin ein Mädchen (I am a girl)

The slow articulation as well as dialects result in quite artificially different sounds as well: "*esch" for "ich", "*ben" instead of "bin", "*leshn" instead of "lesen". Some children miss sounds that have no clear salient articulatory base like nasals (*"ut" instead of "und") or stop consonants followed by a continuant.

In transcribing the sentence "Oma und Opa lesen" some children put the word Grandpa before Grandma, another indication that they refer to their own speech, because in German, males always have the first position reflecting the hierarchical gender order.

Learned words: At phase 3 it can be observed that irregular sight-words are sometimes spelled phonemically ("*Rola" instead of "Roller", "*Metchen" instead of "Mädchen", "*Berk" instead of "Berg").

V = Phonemic strategy with first use of orthographic patterns

At this phase children begin to segment phonemically. Children who learn the cipher must develop a new classification system for the sound structure since phonemes in some part are artificial and arbitrary categories of speech sounds: for instance in Japan there is a no phonemic difference between /l/ and /r/. German children when detecting the alphabetic principle develop the rule: "Spell as you speak", and start with an analysis of their articulatory cues, often distorted by dialect. Mainly under the influence of print, children develop the phonemic classification system (for a more detailed analysis, see Valtin, 1984) and detect also inconsistencies between sound and orthographic patterns of a word. In their spelling they now begin to use orthographic regularities. For example: The phonetically written "*unt" becomes a correct "und", and "*lesn" becomes "lesen".

On this level, many mistakes arise from the fact that the children wrongly apply specific orthographic regularities where they are not needed.   Some examples of such overgeneralizations that also may affect sight-words are: "*mier" instead of "mir"; "*Oper" instead of "Opa".   Other examples of overgeneralization of specific orthographic rules are visible in the next letter written by Katarina (6:8 years).

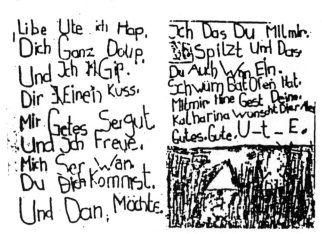

In her "love letter" Katarina shows evidence of "private" rules such as: Every word starts with a capital letter, and every line ends by a punctuation mark.   Katarina's word segmentation follows the intonation pattern, so two word expressions are sometimes written without space: "mitmir" (with me), "sergut" (very good). These examples show that, similar as in oral language learning, children form specific rules regarding the relationship between oral and written language.

VI = Complete phonemic strategy, influenced by orthographic and morphemic information of words

At this phase the children have learned important orthographic and morphemic knowledge and apply it rather consistently to unfamiliar words. Since children now possess a big vocabulary of learned words which they can spell automatically the necessity of constructing words is low.

In presenting this model it has already been pointed out that characteristic errors in the sight-words of children refer to specific strategies.   Thus, we have the paradoxical situation that the occurrence of errors in already learned sight-words may indicate a development of spelling competence!

Regarding the time of acquisition of various strategies, it can be observed (Valtin & Naegele, 1986/1993) that some German children may use very early, from about their fourth month in school, orthographic elements in their spellings. After half a year in school the majority of children have acquired the phonetic-articulatory strategy and develop orthographic and morphemic strategies. However, particularly under stress (time or achievement pressure, when writing long or difficult words) or when their concentration began to flag toward the end of a text children were frequently observed to regress to a simpler strategy.

May (1990) reports data on spelling errors from a longitudinal study of more than 400 first graders followed up until grade 4. Children were classified according their spelling competence in grade 4 into groups of different levels. Table 2 shows the typical spellings of three different groups (good spellers: above PR 25, average spellers: around PR 50, and poor spellers: below PR 5) of the word "Blätter" (leaves), disregarding the initial capital letter.

Table 2. How children spell the word "Blätter" at different grade levels (according to May, 1990, p. 248).

| | Groups of spellers | | |
Grade levels	Good	Average	poor
Grade 1 middle	blet-a- blet-er	pl-t-a	-----
Grade 1 end	blet-er blät-er	blet-a- blet-er	---t--- pl-t---
Grade 2 middle	blät-er	blet-er	plet-a- blet-a-
Grade 2 end	blätter	blet-er blät-er	blet-a-
Grade 3 middle		blätter	blet-er
Grade 4 middle			blet-er blät-er
Grade 4 end			blät-er blätter

The spellings demonstrate that good spellers already apply orthographic strategies after six months of school while very poor spellers use rudimentary spellings up to the end of grade one and are far behind their average classmates.

Strategies of Learning to Read

Concerning the strategies in reading, up to now we do not have large scale empirical evidence in Germany.   The model outlined here derives from observations by Scheerer-Neumann (1987) and myself (Valtin 1993). Scheerer-Neumann (1987) has pointed out, "In the course of learning to read, children's preferred reading strategies change.   Despite individual variation, a certain general, systematic order can be discerned in this development. However, this does not imply that all children follow the same course of development, let alone keeping in perfect step" (Scheerer-Neumann, 1987, p. 221).

As in the case of spelling, six strategies may be outlined referring to the reading of unfamiliar words or texts:

I = "Pretend reading"

In this phase, children as early as three years of age may imitate the overt behavior of practiced readers and pretend to read.   They hold a book (sometimes upside down) in front of their nose, mumble to themselves, repeat stories they have heard or invent new ones, and speak with an unnatural intonation.

II = "Naive-holistic" reading

Still lacking insight into the relationship between letters and sounds, children guess at words, orienting themselves at the context and figurative cues, e.g., individual letters and occasionally certain details of these letters. When one asks children at this phase how they have recognized a certain word, one might get very strange answers.   Jochen recognized his own handwritten name "by the worm", that is, by the curlicue at the bottom of the letter J. Ute recognized the word "Maus" (mouse) by the "mouse ears" of the capital M.

III = Beginning alphabetic strategy (phonetic cue reading)

With the beginning insight into letter-sound-relationships children guess words while they rely on the context and mainly use the beginning lettersound and/or other salient letters.

IV = Sounding-out-strategy (reading letter by letter)

By this time the child has learned most of the letters and their sounds, and now attempts to read each word letter by letter, purely synthetically. Some children have difficulties in getting the correct phonetic form and the meaning of the word. When reading words in context children are more successful than with single words.

V = Alphabetic reading with use of chunks

Children gradually learn to use alphabetic units that are larger than letters, such as syllables, frequently occurring letter groups, and also morphemes. Since reading out a word still requires a great deal of concentration, they often have no reserve attention available to form hypotheses, that is, to anticipate the meaning of a word from the context of the sentence.

VI = Automatized word recognition

"With time the translation of letters (or larger units) requires less and less concentration - the process becomes increasingly 'automatic'. As this part of the task becomes easier, the child can concentrate more on meaning and, with its aid, form expectations about the probable course of the sentence. Their 'reaction potential' to words that 'fit' in terms of grammar and meaning increases, i.e., the speed at which they can read out individual words accelerates" (Scheerer-Neumann, 1987, p. 223).

The model outlined above refers to the observation of children in natural settings, either at home or in the classroom. Thus the data do not answer the question as to whether the strategies of German children fit the model of Frith regarding a long stage of logographic reading. Case studies seem to indicate that the strategy of "naive-holistic reading" can mainly be observed at the preschool level. German children enter school at about six years old and after only a few weeks in school normally show phonetic cue reading.

The question whether a long logographic phase is characteristic for German speaking children has been further investigated in Austria. Wimmer, Hartl, and Moser (1990) demonstrated that German speaking children after eight months of school were able to read pseudowords and showed alphabetic strategies when reading single words. They cast doubt on the transferability of "English" models to German orthography. However, their study might not have been a suitable test because of the relatively long time the children had stayed in school already. In a longitudinal study of first graders, Klicpera and Gasteiger-Klicpera (1993) administered the first tests nine weeks after the beginning of reading instruction (a synthetic approach) and observed that average children were already able to read new words and pseudowords. They conclude that children very early in first grade use two strategies: a logographic strategy with familiar words (children showed no evidence of sounding out and very often substituted these words for other words of their primer - irrespective of graphemic similarities) and a phonological recoding strategy with new or pseudowords (children used stressed pronunciation). In a further analysis children were differentiated into three groups according to their reading ability at the end of first grade: Good readers, poor readers at the beginning who improved in the course of the school year, and persistent poor readers. Good readers showed during their first months in school no evidence of logographic reading (errors in familiar words showed high graphic similarity and no word substitution occurred). Initially poor readers show the two different reading strategies outlined above: Logographic strategies with familiar words and alphabetic strategies with new and pseudowords. The persistent poor readers start with logographic strategies and show no evidence of phonological recoding before the middle of the school year. Compared to the other groups these children had more difficulties in naming letters and associating graphemes and phonemes.

Discussion

Most researchers whose models have been presented here see the acquisition of written language from the standpoint of cognitive psychology. In this framework the learner's contribution to actively structuring and reconstructing the object of learning is heavily emphasized. In analogy to the way they learn to speak, children when learning to read and spell develop hypotheses and set up rules concerning written language - hypotheses and rules which may or may not be adequate to the learning object. The mode of development is the activity of the child who builds hypotheses, tries to assimilate new information and - when he or she experiences the inadequacies of their solutions and a cognitive conflict - may transform or develop new hypotheses which fit better.

Each stage by which the child develops towards spelling and reading competence may be characterized by a dominant strategy which reflect important insights into the nature of written language, such as the following:

- the recognition of the communicative function of written language: that the squiggles on the page represent language;

- the concept of the word and the word boundary, i.e., that a written sentence contains all parts of speech, and that gaps are left between the words. As many studies have shown preschool children and first graders have not yet developed the concept of a word as a linguistic unit (Downing, 1984; Valtin, 1984), and believe that only certain words, such as nouns or verbs, are visually represented in written language. The average pre-schooler seems to think that articles and other function words are not represented in a written sentence (Ferreiro, 1978; Valtin, 1989b);

- an awareness of phonemes, i.e., that words can be divided into sound segments, and that certain letters can be associated with these sound segments. That these phonological abilities are crucial for learning to read and write has been demonstrated in a variety of studies (Downing & Valtin, 1984);

-an awareness of the principles of orthography (e.g., phonemic, orthographic, morphemic or grammatical).

Comparing the sequential patterns of spelling and reading, we find a striking similarity. However, it is doubtful whether there is indeed a strict parallel in the development of reading and spelling strategies. As case studies show (Scheerer-Neumann, et al., 1986) some children learn the phonetic strategy when spelling but are not yet able to read what they had spelled. Other children learn to sound out words before being able to segment words into phonemes. In older dyslexic children a disparity between the relatively good reading competence and the poor spelling achievement is very characteristic (Valtin 1989a).

The long logographic phase that has been proclaimed by Frith for English speaking children seems not to be typical for German children. Only poor readers and spellers who have not yet grasped the alphabetic principle have been observed to use this strategy. Klicpera, and Gasteiger-Klicpera (1993), who have done the most extensive studies in this domain with Austrian children, explain the possible difference between English and German speaking children with reference to two factors: The complexity of the orthography and the effect of school instruction. The rather regular grapheme-phoneme-correspondence of German orthography may facilitate the early development of an alphabetic strategy. In class room instruction both in Austria and in Germany teachers place heavy emphasis on phonics. Furthermore, in the first weeks or months of instruction many teachers or primers present only words that are rather regular and have consistent and one-to-one grapheme-phoneme-correspondences.

The sequential strategies outlined above are of relevance for reading instructors and, insofar as they provide a tool for diagnosing the strengths and weaknesses of the learner, yield hints as to the zone of proximal development. These models also offer a new framework for dyslexia and are useful for the description, diagnosis and remediation of dyslexic children. It can be shown that dyslexics need more time than their classmates at lower phases. In a study comparing good and poor spellers (Valtin 1989a), poor spellers in third, fourth and six grade preferred a phonetic strategy and had developed inadequate orthographic rules and ineffective learning strategies. Being at a lower stage leads to a growing gap between the strategies of a child and the learning demands in the classroom. This mismatch prevents the child to profit from general instruction. The resulting experiences of failure may lead to emotional problems and a low self-concept, thus starting a vicious circle. The above outlined models, however, only allow a description of spelling and reading problems and have no explanatory power. The question is: Why do some pupils stay longer at lower stages, especially those with "skeleton" writings and a phonetic-articulatory strategy? It seems plausible that dyslexic children have to overcome bigger hurdles because of a variety of cognitive, language, emotional and motivational factors. Further research is needed concerning the question as to how these factors impede the progress in acquiring more advanced strategies of reading and spelling.

REFERENCES

Dehn, M. (1987/1994). Wie Kinder Schriftsprache erlernen [How children learn written language]. In I. Naegele, & R. Valtin (Eds.), *Rechtschreibunterricht in den Klassen 1 - 6* [Spelling instruction in grades 1 to 6], (3rd. ed.) (pp. 28-37). Frankfurt: Arbeitskreis Grundschule.

Dudenredaktion (Ed.), (1991). Duden Rechtschreibung [Duden spelling]. Mannheim. 20th revised ed.

Downing, J. (1984). Task awareness in the development of reading skill. In J. Downing, & R. Valtin (Eds.), *Language awareness and learning to read* (pp. 27-56). New York: Springer.

Downing, J., & Valtin, R. (1984) (Eds.), *Language awareness and learning to read.* New York: Springer.

Ferreiro, E. (1978). What is written in a written sentence: A developmental answer. *Journal of Education, 160*, 25-39.

Frith, U. (1985). Beneath the surface of developmental dyslexia. In K. E. Patterson, J. C. Marshall, & M. Coltheart (Eds.), *Surface dyslexia: Neurological and cognitive studies of phonological reading* (pp. 301-330). Hillsdale, NJ: Erlbaum.

Gentry, J.R. (1981). Learning to spell developmentally. *The Reading Teacher*, 34, 378-381.

Gentry, J. R. (1982). An analysis of developmental spelling in GNYS AT WRK. *The Reading Teacher* , 36, 192 - 199.

Henderson, E.H., & Beers, J.W. (Eds.). (1980). *Developmental and cognitive aspects of learning to spell.* Newark, DE: International Reading Association.

Klicpera, Ch., & Gasteiger-Klicpera, B. (1993). *Lesen und Schreiben. Entwicklung und Schwierigkeiten* [Reading and writing: Development and difficulties]. Bern:Hans Huber.

May, P. (1990). Kinder lernen rechtschreiben. Gemeinsamkeiten und Unterschiede guter und schwacher Lerner [Children learn to spell. Similarities and differences of good and poor learners]. In H. Brügelmann, & H. Balhorn. (Eds.), *Das Gehirn, sein Alfabet und andere Geschichten* [The brain, its alphabet and other stories] (pp. 245-253). Konstanz: Faude.

Scheerer-Neumann, G. (1987). Wortspezifisch: JA - Wortbild: NEIN [Wordspecific: yes. Word engrams: no] In H. Balhorn & H. Brügelmann (Eds.), *ABC und Schriftspracherwerb* [ABC and written language acquisition] (pp. 171-186). Konstanz: Faude.

Scheerer-Neumann, G. (1989/1993). Rechtschreibschwäche im Kontext der Entwicklung [Difficulties of spelling seen in the context of development]. In I. Naegele, & R. Valtin (Eds.), *LRS in den Klassen 1-10. Handbuch der Lese-Rechtschreibschwierigkeiten* [Dyslexia in grades 1 to 10. Handbook of reading and spelling difficulties] (3rd ed.) (pp. 25-35). Weinheim: Beltz.

Scheerer-Neumann, G., Kretschmann, R.,& Brügelmann, H. (1986). Andrea, Ben und Jana: Selbstgewählte Wege zum Lesen und Schreiben [Andrea, Ben, and Jana: Their different ways to learn reading and writing]. In H. Brügelmann (Ed.), *ABC und Schriftsprache: Rätsel für Kinder, Lehrer und Forscher* [ABC and written language: A riddle for children, teachers and researchers] (2nd ed.) (pp. 55 - 96). Konstanz: Faude.

Spitta, G. (1986/1993). Kinder entdecken die Schriftsprache [Children detect written language]. In R. Valtin, & I. Naegele (Eds.), *"Schreiben ist wichtig!" Grundlagen und Beispiele für kommunikatives Schreiben(lernen)* [Writing is important: Foundations and examples for (learning) communicative writing] (3rd ed.) (pp. 67-83). Frankfurt: Arbeitskreis Grundschule.

Temple, C.A., Nathan, R.G., & Burris, N.A. (1982). *The beginning of writing*. Boston, MA: Allyn & Bacon.

Thomé, G. (1987). *Rechtschreibfehler türkischer und deutscher Schüler* [Spelling errors of German and Turkish pupils]. Heidelberg: Groos.

Thomé, G. (1989). Rechtschreibfehler und Orthographie [Spelling errors and orthography] *Der Deutschunterricht, 41 (6)*, 29 - 38.

Valtin, R. (1984). Awareness of features and functions of language. In J. Downing, & R. Valtin (Eds.), *Language awareness and learning to read* (pp. 227-260). New York: Springer-Verlag.

Valtin, R. (1989a). Dyslexia in the German Language. In P.G. Aaron, & R.M. Joshi (Eds.), *Reading and writing disorders in different orthographic systems* (pp. 119-135). Boston/London: Kluwer Academic Publishers.

Valtin, R. (1989b). Prediction of writing and reading achievement - some findings from a pilot study. In Brambring et al. (Eds.), *Children at risk: Assessment, longitudinal research, and intervention* (pp. 245-267). Berlin, New York: Walter de Gruyter.

Valtin, R. (1993). Stufen des Lese- und Schreibenlernens [Stages of learning to read and write]. In D. Haarmann (Ed.), *Handbuch Grundschule* [Handbook on primary school]. (Vol. 2, pp. 68-80). Weinheim: Beltz.

Valtin, R.,& Naegele, I. (Eds.) (1986/1993). *"Schreiben ist wichtig!" Grundlagen und Beispiele für kommunikatives Schreiben(lernen)* [Writing is important. Foundations and examples for (learning) communicative writing]. (3rd ed.). Frankfurt: Arbeitskreis Grundschule.

Wimmer, H., Hartl, M., & Moser, E. (1990). Passen "englische" Modelle des Schriftspracherwerbs auf "deutsche" Kinder? Zweifel an der Bedeutsamkeit der logographischen Stufe [Do "English" models fit "German" children? Doubts about the relevance of the logographic stage]. *Zeitschrift für Entwicklungspsychologie und Pädagogische Psychologie, 22*, 136 - 154.

READING DEVELOPMENT IN ELEMENTARY SCHOOL: DO SYLLABLES PLAY A ROLE IN PHONOLOGICAL DECODING?

HANNEKE W.M.J. WENTINK, WIM H.J. VAN BON, AND ROBERT SCHREUDER
Department of Special Education and Interfaculty Research Unit for Language and Speech
University of Nijmegen
PO Box 9104, 6500 HE Nijmegen
The Netherlands

ABSTRACT. The present study assessed the relation between the development of reading skills and syllable-bound progress in naming latency of grades 1 to 6 children for monosyllabic pseudowords of three orthographic structures: CVC, CCVC/CVCC and CCVCC. The naming task was a modified replication of van den Bosch (1991), in which poor readers were trained in reading aloud monosyllabic words and pseudowords. Based on the results of van den Bosch, parallel progress in naming latency over adjacent reading levels was expected between these three orthographic structures. However, the results of the present study replicated the findings of van den Bosch only partially. In the development of phonological decoding skills, beginning readers seem to use grapheme-phoneme conversions while processes at the syllabic level appear to play a role in phonological decoding when children become more competent readers. These findings are discussed in relation to current theories about the development of phonological decoding in normal readers.

There is ample evidence that phonological decoding skills play a crucial role in the development of reading ability. Good decoding skills enable the reader to identify words accurately, automatically and rapidly (Ehri, 1987). This facilitates comprehension of text and the acquisition of word specific orthographic knowledge.

Reading Development in Normal Readers

Two basic mechanisms can be used to recognize words (see Coltheart's dual-route model, 1978). The first mechanism involves the use of phonological information. This is generally described as the phonological (indirect, nonlexical) route. The reader uses knowledge of grapheme-phoneme correspondences (GPC) to translate the printed word form into an internal phonological representation, which is then used to retrieve the meaning of the word. This process of converting letters into sounds is assumed to operate in a left-to-right manner and is therefore referred to as sequential decoding. The second mechanism, generally described as the visual (direct, lexical) route, allows a direct mapping from the visual word form onto word meaning.

C.K. Leong and R.M. Joshi (Eds.), Cross-Language Studies of Learning to Read and Spell, 195–212.
© *1997 Kluwer Academic Publishers. Printed in the Netherlands.*

When children start learning to read, they acquire knowledge of letter-sound relationships that can be used to identify words. By systematically analyzing a letter string into its constituent graphemes (*graphemic parsing*) and converting graphemes into their phonemic counterparts (*phonemic assignment*), a phonological representation of a regularly spelled word can be generated. Subsequently, this representation can be used to gain access to the mental lexicon and retrieve the meaning of the word and other word-specific information like the pronunciation. When children become more competent readers as a result of reading practice, they improve their decoding skills, which leads to an increase in accuracy and speed of visual word recognition. As a result of accurate and fast decoding, the phonological representation of a word becomes directly associated with its orthographic form (Adams, 1990; Ehri, 1987; Jorm & Share, 1983). Skilled readers are assumed to use whole-word orthographic representations for the recognition of familiar, high-frequency words, whereas low-frequency words are recognized on the basis of phonological information. Children need to develop direct word recognition strategies in order to achieve fast reading for meaning (Wimmer & Goswami, 1994).

Reading Problems of Poor Readers

Although acquiring competence in reading proves to be easy for most children, some children have serious problems with it. There is substantial evidence that poor readers' problems with word recognition are primarily associated with a deficiency in phonological decoding (Beech & Harding, 1984; Bradley & Bryant, 1983; Bryant & Bradley, 1985; Rack, Snowling, & Olson, 1992; Wagner & Torgesen, 1987). For instance, Beech and Harding found support for the hypothesis of a developmental lag in phonemic processes in poor readers. Poor readers show a slower progress in phonemic processing abilities, compared to their good reading peers. They are, therefore, less effective in using grapheme-phoneme correspondence information for word recognition (Backman, Bruck, Hebert, & Seidenberg, 1984; Bruck, 1988). This results in a (partial) failure to build up word-specific associations between phonological and orthographic word form representations and, subsequently, in poor text comprehension.

Training of Decoding Skills

Since there is substantial evidence that training in phonological decoding affects children's phonological skills (e.g., Wagner & Torgesen, 1987), the remediation of reading difficulties should provide extensive practice in phonological decoding. In order to achieve improvement in phonological decoding skills in poor readers, van den Bosch (1991; also described in van den Bosch, van Bon, & Schreuder, 1995) trained 8- to 13-year-old Dutch children from schools for special education in reading aloud monosyllabic words and pseudowords. A pseudoword is a letter string that, in view of its orthographic and phonological structure, might have been a real word but does not actually exist in the language (i.e., Dutch). Pseudowords are often used as stimuli, because, in contrast to real words, they can only be decoded nonlexically. Since pseudowords do not have a stored representation in the mental lexicon, they can only be named by using a nonlexical route. Naming a pseudoword can, for instance, be accomplished by decoding each grapheme into its phonemic counterpart.

The participants in the van den Bosch study were rated as 'poor readers' by their teachers. Their reading level was comparable to the reading level of normal readers in grade two. The poor readers were able to decode short pseudowords accurately, but their decoding rate was very slow. The main goal of the training was to speed up the decoding processes during reading. To accomplish this, a flash card method was used. In this method, words are presented very briefly. This, supposedly, stimulates children to process words in units beyond the graphemic level. In the van den Bosch study, the exposure duration was determined on-line, for each child individually. It varied as a function of the child's accuracy. The accuracy rate was maintained at a constant level of approximately 67%.

During the training, naming latencies became shorter for both words and pseudowords. All the words and most of the pseudowords were presented only once. Thus, the improvement in naming latency was not the result of increased familiarity with the set of words and pseudowords. An overall length effect was found, demonstrating that it took children longer to name a long (pseudo-)word than a short (pseudo-)word. This is in agreement with the traditional dual-route model of reading aloud (Coltheart, 1978; Coltheart, Curtis, Atkins, & Haller, 1993). Since for beginning readers grapheme-phoneme conversions are assumed to operate in a left-to-right manner, decoding long (pseudo-)words takes longer than decoding short (pseudo-)words for which fewer graphemes have to be converted. A puzzling result, however, was that the progress in naming latency was equal for short and for long (pseudo-)words (see also van Bon, van Kessel, & Kortenhorst, 1987). This parallel progress seems to be in conflict with the dual-route theory. If decoding takes place at the level of individual graphemes and phonemes only and operates in a left-to-right manner, then improvement in naming latency should be larger for long than for short (pseudo-)words, because reading long (pseudo-)words requires more grapheme-phoneme conversions (van den Bosch, 1991).

PROCESSING UNITS IN DECODING

Two explanations were proposed for these results. First, progress might be the result of improved articulatory programming rather than improved decoding. Second, decoding processes might operate on units beyond the level of individual graphemes. For instance, Treiman and her colleagues (e.g., Treiman & Chafetz, 1987; Treiman & Zukowski, 1988; Wise, Olson, & Treiman, 1990) proposed that beginning and skilled readers process words and pseudowords in onset and rime units. The onset of a syllable is defined as the initial consonant or consonant cluster. The rime is the part of the syllable that begins with a vowel (the nucleus) and any consonants coming after it (the coda).

However, another study of van den Bosch (1991) obtained no support for either of these explanations. No evidence was found for the idea that progress in naming latency is the result of improved articulatory programming. The time to transform an abstract phonological code into an articulatory motor program was not affected by the number of phonemes. The second account was also not supported by the data. The significance of onsets and rimes in reading demonstrated by Treiman and Chafetz (1987) was not found in the van den Bosch study. The absence of onset-rime effects in the study of van den Bosch might be related to a different relation between orthography and phonology in Dutch, in comparison with English. English has a relatively opaque orthography in contrast with Dutch, which has a highly transparent orthography.

SYLLABLE-BOUND PROCESSING

An alternative explanation for the parallel progress in naming latency, proposed by van den Bosch is that the syllable is involved in phonological decoding. Since all the words and pseudowords that were used in van den Bosch's training were monosyllabic, the training might have affected the efficiency of decoding processes at the syllabic level.

There is ample evidence that the information about a word's syllabic structure is stored in the mental lexicon and retrieved during the process of lexical access (Levelt, 1989; Levelt & Wheeldon, 1994; Zwitserlood, Schriefers, Lahiri, & van Donselaar, 1993). Some evidence is found for syllable-bound segmentation strategies during comprehension of spoken sentences in Dutch. Cutler (1986) showed that Dutch listeners are clearly sensitive to the syllabic structure of spoken words. This in contrast to speakers of English who are more sensitive to stress. Also very young English-speakers are more sensitive to prosodic information (e.g., to stress) in the speech signal than to syllabic information (Gerken, 1994). A plausible conclusion is that different processing routines are used for different languages, depending on their phonological structure.

Indications for syllabic involvement during phonological decoding of printed words were obtained in a visual word naming study of Klapp,

Anderson and Berrian (1973). They investigated the effect of number of syllables (with equal number of letters) on naming latency (e.g., *clock* vs. *camel*). One-syllable words were named significantly faster than two-syllable words. This syllable effect was a real phonological decoding effect and not an articulatory programming effect. The results of Klapp et al. indicate that syllable-bound processes play a role during the process of converting an orthographic representation into its phonological counterpart. In addition, Mason (1978) found a syllable effect that was larger for poor than for good readers and larger for pseudowords than for words. This can also be taken as support for the position that the syllable effect emerges in the construction of a phonological code. This chapter reports the results of a first study in a series of studies that aims at testing the possible involvement of syllable-bound decoding processes in word reading and the way these might affect reading skills.

The Role of the Syllable in Normal Reading

The central question of this first study was whether parallel progress in naming latency for monosyllabic (pseudo-)words of different orthographic structure is a result of a specific training (van den Bosch, 1991; van den Bosch et al., 1995), or whether it represents a general phenomenon in reading development. A modified replication of van den Bosch was conducted in elementary schools (grade 1 to 6). Naming latencies and accuracy were measured for monosyllabic pseudowords of three orthographic structures: CVC, CCVC/CVCC and CCVCC (CCVC and CVCC pseudowords were taken together, since in van den Bosch's study accuracy and latency of naming CVCC- and CCVC-pseudowords were similar). In the present study, participants were required to read aloud a visually presented pseudoword as fast and as accurately as possible. If parallel progress in naming latency represents a general phenomenon in reading development, we expect to find an equally large progress in naming latency over reading levels for these three orthographic structures. Otherwise, the conclusion should be that the results of van den Bosch were a consequence of the relatively short but intensive training of phonological decoding skills. This would indicate that the poor readers in the van den Bosch study had acquired other decoding strategies (e.g., improved at another decoding level) than children normally develop during the acquisition of reading skill.

Method

PARTICIPANTS

Children from two elementary schools in the southern part of the Netherlands participated in this experiment (N=128; 70 girls). An equal number of children was selected from each grade (grade 1 to 6). Their ages ranged from 7 to 13 years. All children were native speakers of Dutch and were rated as 'normal readers' by their teachers. The reading methods used by the schools were primarily based upon a phonics approach of reading instruction.

A pseudoword reading test was constructed in order to test whether the children were able to read the orthographic structures that were selected for the experiment. The pseudoword reading test consisted of 10 CCVCC-pseudowords (see Appendix A). Children were instructed to read the pseudowords as accurately as possible. Only if a child had read 7 pseudowords of the list correctly, he/she was selected for the experiment.

The ability to read isolated real words was measured by a standardized reading test (the 'Drie-Minuten-Toets' (DMT) [Three-Minutes-Test]; Verhoeven, 1992). The DMT consists of three cards containing several columns of words. The reading materials on the cards are of increasing difficulty. The instruction is to read the words aloud as quickly and accurately as possible in one minute per card. Errors are recorded. The number of correctly produced words is used as a measure, with the maximum number being 150 (card 1 and card 2) or 120 (card 3). Based on the scores on this test, the children were divided into five reading levels (see Table 1). The distribution of children over the five groups was done in a way that the mean score differences between reading levels was equal.

Table 1. The distribution of participants over five reading levels, based on the mean score on the 'Drie-Minuten-Toets' [Three-Minutes-Test] (DMT; SD in parentheses)

RL	n=127	Mean age (in months)		Mean score DMT	
1	17	89.71	(6.71)	25.71	(6.64)
2	22	97.86	(10.63)	46.44	(6.83)
3	32	114.44	(16.98)	67.64	(5.91)
4	35	125.14	(12.62)	85.46	(6.15)
5	21	138.62	(9.63)	108.48	(4.86)

RL = Reading Level

MATERIALS

The monosyllabic pseudowords were randomly selected from the van den Bosch pseudoword materials and were made up of the following three orthographic structures: CVC, CCVC/CVCC and CCVCC. For each orthographic structure 30 pseudowords were selected: 15 pseudowords with a monograph vowel and 15 pseudowords with a digraph vowel. Pseudowords with two equal liquids (e.g., 'gleulp' or 'kreir') were eliminated, because they might pose difficulties for pronunciation.   The complete list of pseudowords can be found in Appendix B.

APPARATUS

A Macintosh Plus ED was used in this experiment.   Pseudowords were presented in black, lower case letters on a white background in the center of the screen. A six-letter string measured roughly 3 by 0.6 cm. Children were seated approximately 60-80 centimeters from the screen. A letter font used in many educational text books was chosen. Naming latencies were measured accurately to the millisecond by a voice-activated relay attached to the computer. Verbal responses were coded as correct or incorrect by the experimenter by means of a buttonbox that was connected to the computer.

PROCEDURE

The ninety monosyllabic pseudowords were presented in a random order. The children were instructed to name the presented pseudoword as quickly and accurately as possible.   Five hundred milliseconds before stimulus presentation an acoustic signal was given via headphones, followed by an asterisk in the center of the screen. This served as a fixation point and remained on the screen for 500 ms. The target stimulus appeared 500 ms after the asterisk at the same location.   The presentation duration was determined by the naming response of the child (with a maximum of 6500 ms).   The stimulus disappeared 1 second after triggering of the voice-activated relay. The response latency was determined for each trial. Latency is defined as the time between the onset of word presentation and the onset of the verbal response of the individual. By pushing buttons on a buttonbox the experimenter recorded whether the stimulus was identified correctly and whether the voice-activated relay was triggered by the verbal response of the child. The participants received no feedback about their performance. The child was familiarized with the task format by 10 practice trials.

Results

Naming latencies and the number of pseudowords named correctly were determined for each child for all experimental conditions.   Data were analyzed separately for latency and accuracy.   Latencies of incorrect responses (9.4%) were not used. Data of one participant were lost due to a disk-crash.

LATENCY

Trials on which the response was correct but did not stop the timer, or on which the timer was stopped by a sound other than the name of the stimulus, were eliminated. For each child the median naming latency (instead of the mean) was computed to reduce the effect of outliers. This was done for each orthographic structure separately. The subject median naming latencies were based on at least 10 observations per orthographic structure (33% correct). These data were used for analyzing the course of naming latency over the adjacent reading levels.

Figure 1 displays naming latency per reading level and per orthographic structure (see also Appendix C for the mean latencies). In order to investigate the relation between reading level and naming latency, the pseudoword naming latencies were submitted to a repeated measures analysis of variance, with Orthographic Structure (CVC, CCVC/CVCC and CCVCC) as the within-subjects factor and Reading Level (1 to 5) as the between-subjects factor.

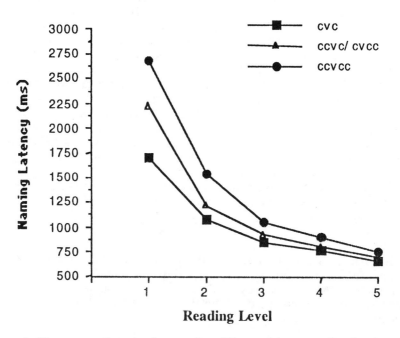

Figure 1. The course of naming latency (in milliseconds) over reading levels, split by orthographic structure.

An overall main effect of Reading Level was found (F(4, 122) = 51.06, MSe = 415457.10, $p<.001$), which indicates that naming latency increased with improvement of reading competence[1]. Significant effects of Reading Level were also obtained in the two relevant planned comparisons of CVC- versus CCVC/CVCC-pseudowords and CCVC/CVCC- versus CCVCC-pseudowords (F(4, 122) = 47.98, MSe = 213652.17, $p<.001$, and F(4, 122) = 52.52, MSe = 360215.76, $p<.001$, respectively).

Naming latency varied between the orthographic structures, indicated by a main effect of Orthographic Structure (F(2, 244) = 118.10, MSe = 36560.14, $p<.001$). The two planned comparisons of CVC- versus CCVC/CVCC-pseudowords and CCVC/CVCC- versus CCVCC-pseudowords also revealed significant effects for Orthographic Structure (F(1, 122) = 94.95, MSe = 16661.26, $p<.001$, and F(1, 122) = 97.45, MSe = 28657.86, $p<.001$, respectively). Short pseudowords were named faster than long pseudowords.

Most importantly, the interaction between Reading Level and Orthographic Structure was significant (F(8, 244) = 18.54, $p<.001$). The planned comparisons of CVCs versus CCVC/CVCCs and CCVC/CVCCs versus CCVCCs also yielded significant interactions between Reading Level and Orthographic Structure (F(4, 122) = 23.60, $p<.001$, and F(4, 122) = 10.96, $p<.001$, respectively). The significant interaction between Orthographic Structure and Reading Level resulted from decreasing differences in naming latency between orthographic structures over the reading levels. That is, the higher the reading level, the smaller the differences in naming latency between the three orthographic structures (see Figure 1).

Inspection of Figure 1 suggested that the interaction between Orthographic Structure and Reading Level was mainly due to the first three reading levels. Separate analyses were therefore done for reading levels 1 to 3 and for reading levels 3 to 5. The analysis over reading levels 1 to 3 yielded a significant interaction between Orthographic Structure and Reading Level (F(4, 136) = 15.41, MSe = 55343.07, $p<.001$). In contrast, in the analysis over reading levels 3 to 5, no interaction was obtained (F(4, 170) = 2.25, MSe = 11056.01, $p<.10$), indicating a parallel progress in naming latency over the latter two reading levels.

ACCURACY

The number of pseudowords named correctly per orthographic structure was calculated for each respondent. Figure 2 displays the number of correct responses per reading level and orthographic structure (see also Appendix D for the mean numbers of correct responses).

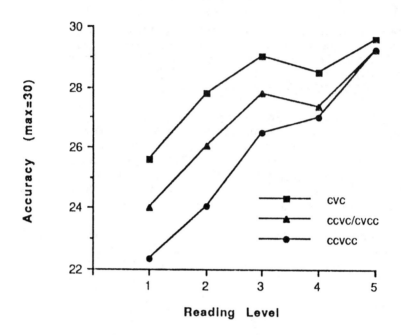

Figure 2. Accuracy over reading levels, split by orthographic structure.

In order to test whether accuracy improves over reading levels, the number of pseudowords named correctly per orthographic structure were submitted to a repeated measures analysis of variance. Orthographic Structure served as the within-subjects factor and Reading Level as the between-subjects factor.

Accuracy increased over reading levels, indicated by a significant main effect of Reading Level $(F(4,122) = 12.55$, MSe $= 19.44$, $p<.001)^2$. Significant effects of Reading Level were also obtained in the two relevant planned comparisons CVC- versus CCVC/CVCC-pseudowords and CCVC/CVCC- versus CCVCC-pseudowords $(F(4, 122) = 10.45$, MSe $= 11.39$, $p<.001$, and $F(4, 122) = 12.17$, MSe $= 17.28$, $p <.001$, respectively.)

Accuracy varied between the orthographic structures, as indicated by a main effect of Orthographic Structure $(F(2, 244) = 56.53$, MSe $= 2.74$, $p<.001$). Planned comparisons of CVC- versus CCVC/CVCC-pseudowords and CCVC/CVCC- versus CCVCC-pseudowords showed that orthographic structures differed with respect to accuracy $(F(1, 122) = 36.97$, MSe $= 2.38$,

$p<.001$, and F(1, 122) = 27.25, MSe = 2.46, $p<.001$, respectively). Accuracy was larger for CVC- than for CCVC/CVCC-pseudowords, while CCVC/CVCC-pseudowords were read more often correctly than CCVCC-pseudowords. The interaction between Reading Level and Orthographic Structure was significant (F(8, 244) = 3.86, $p<.001$). The planned comparison of CVCs versus CCVC/CVCCs showed no interaction (F(4, 122) = 1.26, $p = .289$), in contrast with the planned comparison of CCVC/CVCCs versus CCVCCs (F(4, 122) = 3.40, $p<.05$). A significant interaction between Orthographic Structure and Reading Level resulted from decreasing differences in accuracy between CVC- and CCVC/CVCC-pseudowords over adjacent reading levels. The improvement in accuracy between CCVC/CVCC- and CCVCC-pseudowords was equally large over the reading levels.

Correlations between naming latency and accuracy were significant at the .01 level for the three orthographic structures (for CVC: r = -.33, for CCVC/CVCC: r = -.39, and for CCVCC: r = -.45). A decrease of naming latencies went together with an increase of accuracy. Hence it appears that children improved both naming latency and accuracy over adjacent reading levels.

Discussion

The central question of this study was whether parallel progress in naming latency for monosyllabic (pseudo-)words of different orthographic structure is a result of a specific training (van den Bosch, 1991), or whether it represents a general phenomenon in reading development. Van den Bosch trained poor readers in decoding monosyllabic words and pseudowords by using a flash card method. He found an overall length effect, which was demonstrated by the fact that short monosyllabic (pseudo-)words were named faster than long monosyllabic (pseudo-)words. However, the improvement in naming latency during the training was equally large for the different orthographic structures. A possible explanation for this parallel progress in naming latency is that the syllable is involved in phonological decoding (van den Bosch, 1991). Rather than converting individual graphemes into their phonemic counterparts, syllables might be the units of conversion.

The present study investigated whether this parallel progress in naming latency can also be observed in normal reading development. Latencies of monosyllabic pseudowords with different numbers of graphemes revealed a progress in naming latency and accuracy over the successive reading levels. However, the overall progress in naming latency converged. The differences in naming latency between the orthographic structures diminished with increased reading competence. Development under a training condition thus seem to differ from normal reading development.

The results of additional analyses, however, suggest that beginning and more competent readers use different decoding strategies. Beginning readers (in this study roughly reading levels 1 to 3) seem to decode pseudowords by using grapheme-phoneme conversion rules, as indicated by a convergent progress over the reading levels 1 to 3. These findings are in agreement with the dual-route theory, which predicts a larger improvement in naming latency for long than for short words, as children become faster in grapheme-phoneme conversions with increased reading practice. In contrast, for the more competent readers in this study (roughly reading levels 4 and 5) a parallel progress in naming latency was found. This result is compatible with the claim that decoding processes at the syllabic level play a role as children become more literate[3].

There is some evidence that as children become more familiar with spelling patterns, their ability to syllabify printed words increases (Adams, 1990). According to Friedrich, Schadler and Juola (1979), the use of syllabic units in printed words is a late-emerging skill among normal readers. They found that children do not use syllabic units until they are in the fourth grade. This finding fits fairly well with the results of the present study.

The parallel progress in decoding skills for the more competent readers in this study is in agreement with the results of van den Bosch, indicating that the advanced readers in the present study and the poor readers in the van den Bosch study used the same decoding strategies. However, the poor readers in the van den Bosch study were much slower in naming pseudowords than the advanced readers in the present study, suggesting that the two groups differed in the efficiency of using decoding strategies at the syllabic level. The reading competence of the poor readers in the van den Bosch study, as established by a standardized reading test, was comparable to that of the children at reading level 2 in the present study. According to this global measure, the reading competence of the poor readers in the van den Bosch study was thus at the same level as the reading skills of the beginning readers in the present study. However, the decoding strategy used by the poor readers during the flash card training seems to be more comparable to the strategy used by the advanced readers in the present study, as is suggested by the parallel progress in naming latency for both groups of readers.

This leaves the question as to why the poor readers in the van den Bosch study seem to use decoding strategies that are not observed in normal readers at the same global level of reading competence. At least two factors might have been responsible for this counterintuitive finding. The first relates to the remedial teaching of reading in the Netherlands. The second factor is related to attentional effects of the flash card method.

In the Netherlands, poor readers receive ample special reading remediation at special schools for children with learning problems. Due to the ample training, they will have had more experience in reading words (certainly in reading multisyllabic words) than children of the same reading level at normal schools. It is possible that as a result of this ample remediation, the poor readers in the van den Bosch study had already acquired the principles of syllable-bound processing before receiving the flash card training, in contrast to the beginning readers in the present study.

The second factor has to do with some specifics of the flash card training. Poor readers probably acquire a syllable-bound decoding strategy (as indicated by the parallel progress in naming latency throughout the whole flash card training), but do not necessarily or usually use this strategy during normal reading. The flash card method may have forced the poor readers to decode the words more quickly than they usually do. Given the limited amount of time that the orthographic information is available, a grapheme-phoneme conversion strategy might not be very successful. As a result, children might be inclined to adopt a different decoding strategy (cf. LaBerge & Samuels, 1974).

If this account of the difference between the results in the van den Bosch study and the present study is correct, it suggests that poor readers have acquired the appropriate representations for the application of decoding strategies beyond the graphemic level, but very often do not allocate their attention to this higher level. It seems that poor readers stick to the codes that are laid down first, and have problems shifting to higher levels or organization, even when the relevant knowledge is acquired. The flash card method, however, stimulates readers to pay attention to higher levels of representation, such as the syllable. It therefore may induce processing at levels beyond the individual graphemes and phonemes.

In summary, beginning readers seem to rely on grapheme-phoneme conversion rules, while advanced normal readers appear to use syllable-bound strategies in phonological decoding. These findings provide some evidence that processes at the syllabic level play a role in the development of phonological decoding skills. The fact that advanced normal readers and poor readers during a specific training seem to use comparable decoding strategies, can be explained by assuming that a flash card method stimulates poor readers to process pseudowords more rapidly, using syllable-bound processes in phonological decoding. Perhaps the poor readers' problem is not a lack of syllable-bound processing strategies, but a failure to use them. The results of the present study, in combination with results found in a flash card training, indicate that poor readers acquire normal reading strategies beyond the grapheme-phoneme level. Poor readers, however, do not use these strategies efficiently during reading. Remediation therefore should aim at reinforcing poor readers to use syllable-bound processing strategies. For this purpose, a specific flash card method might be a promising remediation tool.

REFERENCES

Adams, M.J. (1990). *Beginning to read: Thinking and learning about print.* Cambridge, MA: MIT Press.

Backman, J., Bruck, M., Hebert, M., & Seidenberg, M.S. (1984). Acquisition and use of spelling-sound correspondences in reading. *Journal of Experimental Child Psychology, 38,* 114-133.

Beech, J.R., & Harding, L.M. (1984). Phonemic processing and the poor reader from a developmental lag viewpoint. *Reading Research Quarterly, 19,* 357-366.

Bradley, L., & Bryant, P.E. (1983). Categorizing sounds and learning to read: A causal connection. *Nature, 301,* 419-421.

Bruck, M. (1988). The word recognition and spelling of dyslexic children. *Reading Research Quarterly, 23,* 51-69.

Bryant, P.E., & Bradley, L. (1985). *Children's reading problems.* Oxford: Basil Blackwell.

Coltheart, M. (1978). Lexical access in simple reading tasks. In G. Underwood (Ed.), *Strategies in Information Processing.* (pp. 151-216). London: Academic Press.

Coltheart, M., Curtis, B., Atkins, P., & Haller, M. (1993). Models of reading aloud: Dual-route and parallel-distributed-processing approaches. *Psychological Review, 100,* 589-608.

Cutler, A. (1986). Phonological structure in speech recognition. *Phonology Yearbook, 3,* 161-178.

Ehri, L.C. (1987). Learning to read and spell words. *Journal of Reading Behavior, 19,* 5-31.

Friedrich, F.J., Schadler, M., & Juola, J.F. (1979). Developmental changes in units of processing in reading. *Journal of Experimental Child Psychology, 28,* 344-358.

Gerken, L. (1994). Young children's representation of prosodic phonology: Evidence from English-speakers' weak syllable productions. *Journal of Memory and Language, 33,* 19-38.

Jorm, A.F., & Share, D.L. (1983). Phonological recoding and reading acquisition. *Applied Psycholinguistics, 4,* 103-147.

Klapp, S.T., Anderson, W. G., & Berrian, R. W. (1973). Implicit speech in reading, reconsidered. *Journal of Experimental Psychology, 100,* 368-374.

LaBerge, D., & Samuels, S.J. (1974). Toward a theory of automatic information processing in reading. *Cognitive Psychology, 6,* 293-323.

Levelt, W.J.M. (1989). Speaking: From intention to articulation. Cambridge, MA: MIT Press.

Levelt, W.J.M., & Wheeldon, L. (1994). Do speakers have access to a mental syllabary? *Cognition, 50,* 239-269.

Mason, M. (1978). From print to sound in mature readers as a function of reader ability and two forms of orthographic regularity. *Memory & Cognition, 6,* 568-581.

Rack, J.P., Snowling, M.J., & Olson, R.K. (1992). The nonword reading deficit in developmental dyslexia: A review. *Reading Research Quarterly, 27,* 29-53.

Treiman, R., & Chafetz, J. (1987). Are there onset- and rime-like units in printed words? In M. Coltheart (Ed.), *Attention and Performance, XII* (pp. 281-298). Hillsdale, NJ:Lawrence Erlbaum Associates.

Treiman, R., & Zukowski, A. (1988). Units in reading and spelling. *Journal of Memory and Language, 27,* 466-477.

van Bon, W.H.J., van Kessel, A.E.G., & Kortenhorst, E.P.M. (1987). Beïnvloeding van woordherkenningssnelheid door middel van flash cards [Affecting word identification speed by flash cards]. In J. Hamers, & A. van der Leij (Eds.), *Dyslexie 87.* (pp. 87-94). Lisse: Swets & Zeitlinger.

van den Bosch, K. (1991). *Poor readers' decoding skills: Effects of training, task, and word characteristics.* Unpublished doctoral dissertation, University of Nijmegen.

van den Bosch, K., van Bon, W.H.J., & Schreuder, R. (1995). Poor readers' decoding skills: Effects of training with limited exposure duration. *Reading Research Quarterly, 30,* 110-125.

Verhoeven, L. (1992). *Drie-Minuten-Toets, vorm A* [Three-Minutes-Test, form A]. Arnhem: Cito.

Wagner, R.K., & Torgesen, J.K. (1987). The nature of phonological processing and its causal role in the acquisition of reading skills. *Psychological Bulletin, 101,* 192-212.

Wentink, H.W.M.J., van Bon, W.H.J., & Schreuder, R. (in preparation). *Phonological decoding in reading development: An indication for syllable-bound decoding processes in word naming.*

Wimmer, H., & Goswami, U. (1994). The influence of orthographic consistency on reading development: word recognition in English and German children. *Cognition, 51,* 91-103.

Wise, B.W., Olson, R.K., & Treiman, R. (1990). Subsyllabic units in computerized reading instruction: onset and rime vs postvowel segmentation. *Journal of Experimental Child Psychology, 49,* 1-19.

Zwitserlood, P., Schriefers, H., Lahiri, A., & van Donselaar, W. (1993). The role of syllables in the perception of spoken Dutch. *Journal of Experimental Psychology: Learning, Memory, and Cognition, 19,* 260-271.

APPENDIX A. THE PSEUDOWORD READING TEST USED IN THE SELECTION PROCEDURE

The pseudoword reading test consisted of the following ten CCVCC-pseudowords:

dwarg
brouft
klemp
snors
twuuts
praast
krunt
smierk
knoelf
flins

APPENDIX B. MONOSYLLABIC PSEUDOWORDS PRESENTED IN THE NAMING TASK

CVC

bog	len	sut	boop	koef	veek
dap	mil	tan	doom	lijg	vuun
ges	ner	vik	geik	muin	weel
huk	pir	wan	haaf	neul	wies
kof	rut	zas	jaat	toup	zeet

CCVC/CVCC

brel	trup	klaaf	hilm	vost	miets
grop	vluk	kreen	kemt	wark	paant
knep	zwar	smuuk	lump	beems	roeks
plis	blijt	stuim	naks	kuust	soont
slam	droek	vroog	rets	leust	tuilt

CCVCC

brens	klats	spilk	briers	preets	stuunt
dwirs	kront	spuns	griens	sloort	traast
flots	kwort	stark	kraaft	speens	twuurp
flurp	pluts	stimp	kweurs	spoert	vleums
glens	prant	zwert	ploost	stuilf	vruilp

APPENDIX C. NAMING LATENCIES OF CVC-, CCVC/CVCC- AND CCVCC-
PSEUDOWORDS PER READING LEVEL (SD IN PARENTHESES)

RL	n	Naming latency (ms)					
		CVC		CCVC/CVCC		CCVCC	
1	17	1699.03	(736.30)	2220.35	(812.08)	2683.06	(975.33)
2	22	1075.18	(303.85)	1212.55	(378.93)	1550.59	(670.86)
3	32	840.05	(148.25)	928.00	(181.82)	1053.47	(266.76)
4	35	758.17	(130.24)	798.40	(136.90)	896.63	(291.36)
5	21	656.88	(121.00)	688.45	(187.82)	751.45	(295.37)

RL = Reading Level

APPENDIX D. NUMBER OF CORRECT RESPONSES PER READING LEVEL
AND PER ORTHOGRAPHIC STRUCTURE (SD IN PARENTHESES)

RL	n	Number correct (max = 30)					
		CVC		CCVC/CVCC		CCVCC	
1	17	25.59	(3.00)	24.00	(3.34)	22.35	(4.17)
2	22	27.82	(2.84)	26.05	(3.29)	24.05	(4.36)
3	32	29.03	(1.20)	27.81	(1.66)	26.50	(2.49)
4	35	28.51	(2.79)	27.37	(4.00)	27.00	(3.69)
5	21	29.62	(0.59)	29.24	(0.89)	29.24	(1.18)

RL = Reading Level

Author Notes. The present study, which was part of the dissertation research project of the first author, was supported by the Netherlands Organization for Scientific Research (NWO). We gratefully acknowledge the assistance of Astrid Struik, Inge UitdeHaag, Gertie van Vorst and Esther Wittenburg in the data collection. We are most grateful to the staff and the pupils of 'De Bolster' and the 'Nicolaasschool', both in Oss, for their co-operation.

Footnotes

[1] Kruskal-Wallis one-way analysis of variance was additionally used to test the effect of Reading Level ($\chi2(4, n = 127) = 76.40$, $p<.001$), because the five reading levels did not meet the requirement of homogeneity of variance. Since the patterns of significance were the same for both procedures, the results from the repeated measures analysis of variance are reported in the text.

[2] Since the patterns of significance were the same for the Kruskal-Wallis one-way analysis of variance ($\chi2(4, n = 127) = 45.69$, $p<.001$) and the repeated measures analysis of variance, the results from the last procedure are reported in the text (see also note 1).

[3] These results were replicated by Wentink, van Bon and Schreuder (in preparation). They also found indications for syllable-bound processing in advanced readers in naming multisyllabic pseudowords.

HOW TO GET FRIENDS IN BEGINNING WORD RECOGNITION

PIETER REITSMA
Paedologisch Instituut - Vrije Universiteit Amsterdam,
PO Box 303, 1115 ZG Duivendrecht
The Netherlands

ABSTRACT. This chapter addresses the issue of whether development of reading skill entails the acquisition of multiletter recognition units that can be used to decode new printed words more efficiently. As an alternative, the possibility is raised that reading acquisition involves gradually learning more about orthgraphic representations of words and also increasing the number of orthographic lexical entries. Through lexical analogies, a new word having many orthographic neighbors in the mental lexicon (so-called friends) may then be easier to read than one with a few friends. In an experimental training study, beginning readers with about seven months of formal training in reading practised a varying number of times the reading of short lists of unfamiliar words that differ in only one or two initial letters. They also practised reading lists of dissimilar words. In a pretest and posttest the practised words, untrained analogous transfer words and the common letter clusters were separately tested with appropriate controls. The results showed that the gain in naming times for the transfer words was affected by the frequency of having practised similar words, but the efficiency of reading the common rime units was not affected at all. It is concluded that an account in terms of familiar sublexical grapheme clusters is probably not correct. Instead a mental analogy process is suggested to be the basis for transfer effects.

Imagine a young child who recognizes just two printed words, his own name and the name of mom. Assume that these two printed words happen to be Jan and Henny. He can read no other words, but seems to enjoy life very much. One day in kindergarten this child discovers at the back of a seat in classroom another name which strongly resembles his own, Janny, the name of an adorable girl in his group. Will he be able to see the new combination of his own name and a substring of his mom's name? Is he able to recognize his own name as the initial part of this new word and to segment the orthographic pattern of his mom's name and the new word to see that they end similarly? If so, is he then able to reconstruct the name on the basis of these familiar parts? Of course, he already knows the name of this girl in spoken form. But the issue is now how he learns to read this new word. The more general question to be asked is whether this procedure of comparing and contrasting is the way young readers generally learn to read new words. Or is it "Look at the word and remember it"? Or is the alternative "Sound the letters and blend them into a word" a more general and adequate description?

The processes of reading acquisition are currently by no means entirely understood. It is known that fluent reading comprises a great number of

C.K. Leong and R.M. Joshi (Eds.), Cross-Language Studies of Learning to Read and Spell, 213–233.
© 1997 *Kluwer Academic Publishers. Printed in the Netherlands.*

different sub processes and that becoming a skilled reader must therefore entail a variety of distinct types of learning for each of the individual subskills. The most prominent of these subskills is of course printed word identification. There seems to be a growing consensus among researchers on reading that the ability to pronounce single words is probably one of the most important skills that has to be acquired by a child in the process of learning to read. But further questions can then be raised: What strategy does the beginning reader employ in identifying printed words? And also, how does printed word reading change with increasing reading skill and experience? Do beginners read letter by letter, or do they recognize whole words from the start?

The visual units that are used in word recognition is a topic which over decades has been studied in a large number of experiments. In 1886, Cattell presented the results of his tachistoscopic presentations of letters and words. He found that skilled readers could recognize only three or four unrelated letters, or two unconnected words, or four contextually related words within an exposure of 10 milliseconds. He concluded that words are read as wholes, and not letter by letter. This conclusion was not accepted without discussion. For example, Zeitler (1900) concluded instead that letter processing was basic and that the belief that one was reading in whole words was a deception resulting from familiarity with print. Huey (1908/1968, p.81) commented " ...the more unfamiliar a sequence of letters may be, the more the perception of it proceeds by letters. With increase of familiarity, fewer and fewer clues suffice to touch off the recognition of the word or phrase, the tendency being toward reading in word wholes. So reading is now by letters, now by groups of letters or by syllables, now by word wholes, all in the same sentence sometimes, or even in the same word, as the reader may most quickly attain his purpose."

Some of the big questions are the old ones rephrased. In what follows, I will confine myself to the issues of whether beginning readers can infer the pronunciation of a new word from the pronunciation of a known word with a similar spelling pattern and whether the development of reading entails the acquisition of multiletter recognition units. Some recent views on the reading acquisition process are briefly discussed. Then the results are presented of an experiment that has been carried out in our own department. On the basis of the results it will be argued that for the understanding of learning to read processes the role of accumulating word-specific orthographic knowledge is crucial and should be fully accounted for.

Beginning Reading Development

Novice readers who are usually already quite fluent in the use of spoken language encounter many words that are visually unfamiliar to them. In order to be able to identify these unknown words by themselves, the beginning reader must at some point acquire knowledge of the alphabetic principle, i.e. of the spelling-to-sound mappings. Of course, initially a few words may be learned by simple rote associations and/or linguistic guessing. Printed words that are frequently seen in their environment, for example, the child's own name or a label on a cereal box, may be recognized on the basis of some arbitrary and salient characteristic, such as the first letter or the overall outline of the word. When an unfamiliar word is encountered, the child will often guess at a likely word using the context as a guide. In this phase 'reading behaviour' can be described as essentially a linguistic guessing strategy (Marsh, Friedman, Welch & Desberg, 1981; Frith, 1985). When more words are learned by rote associations, the guesses tend to be based on additional visual letter cues (word length, final letter, etc.) as well as linguistic context. The graphemic cues are, however, only processed to the extent that they are necessary to discriminate one word from another. One could well ask whether word identification processes at this stage constitutes or resemble real reading processes.

The important initial phase in real reading development, however, is characterised by the use of sequential decoding in a letter-by-letter and phoneme-by-phoneme fashion. One may refer to this stage as one in which alphabetic strategies are employed. For the young reader, the printed form of only a few words is familiar, while most words are relatively unknown and there is thus no direct visual recognition route available. A coding process in which a familiar phonological representation is constructed permits the reader to obtain access to the meaning of the word. According to Jorm & Share (1983), children who have knowledge of phonics can decode an unfamiliar word. Therefore, beginning reading instruction should incorporate some form of phonics instruction explicitly. For a decoding reading strategy both phoneme awareness and knowledge about letter-sound correspondences are needed (Byrne & Fielding-Barnsley, 1989).

There is often quite a sharp transition from earlier phases to the alphabetic phase, at least in The Netherlands. Most of the time children seem to enter this stage of reading development as soon as explicit instruction in the use of letter-sound correspondence rules is given. In the Netherlands decoding skills are taught intensively from the very beginning. After only a few weeks of instruction most beginning readers are quite rigidly following the strategy of decoding. The adoption of an alphabetic strategy may be considered as a major breakthrough in reading development. Basically, this strategy enables readers to pronounce (not necessarily correctly) novel and nonsense words all by themselves. The strategy also allows them to no longer be (exclusively) dependent on context or other persons in their environment to identify a printed word.

The child needs to learn the grapheme-phoneme correspondences and the manner in which they vary in different letter combinations and word contexts. With practice the beginning reader usually develops considerable skill in generating phonological approximations on the basis of letter-sound correspondences. In order to identify a written word the beginning reader might use his knowledge about the correspondence between letters or groups of letters and sounds. If he succeeds in combining the individual phonemes or phoneme patterns into units appropriate for speech, then there should be no serious problem with regular words and pronounceable non-words. As in English the correspondences in Dutch orthography are not always simple and straightforward. Perfectly predictable correspondence may often not be required though, because in most circumstances the conversion of letters to sounds only yields a rough schema for pronunciation (most of the letters should be accounted for phonologically). The child may use this approximation to guess at similar-sounding words that are in his vocabulary. Even though the conversion rules are not perfect in specifying a pronunciation uniquely, they are usually good enough, possibly with some help of context.

However, sometimes one must know or be able to determine which word is being represented in order to know what phonological values are to be assigned to the graphemes, for the relationship of letters to phonemes is neither one-to-one nor invariant. The use of correspondence rules does not by itself guarantee competent reading behaviour. Decoding procedures need to become sensitive to the other letters surrounding the letter being pronounced. The alphabetic skill of simply translating letters to sound must be replaced by orthographic skills, i.e. attempts to decipher words have to be assisted by knowledge of the orthography. Thus, after the alphabetic phase a final stage in reading development should follow in which the reading processes begins to resemble the reading behaviour of the fluent reader. This phase may be called the orthographic stage (Marsh et al., 1981; Frith, 1985). Decoding in this stage becomes hierarchical, i.e., the interpretation of each grapheme and the selection of the appropriate phonemes becomes dependent on the letter context.

Friends Can Help to Decode New Words

As argued recently by Share (1995), the procedure of phonological recoding enables the beginning reader to acquire an autonomous orthographic lexicon. Children who have knowledge of phonics can decode unfamiliar words. By attending to the letters of a word and sounding out its components children gradually become acquainted with the word-specific orthographic pattern. The repetition of decoding activity on a particular word leads to the possibility of directly recognising the orthographic image, without sounding it out anymore. After sufficient repetitions, children directly recognize the graphemic structure of the printed word. Knowledge about the orthographic characteristics of words can gradually accumulate through extended reading activities and this knowledge allows the experienced reader to recognize known words visually, as familiar letter strings. There is substantial evidence for word-specific learning of orthographic patterns in beginning readers (e.g., Brooks, 1977; Ehri, 1994;

Ehri & Saltmarsh, 1995; Ehri & Wilce, 1979; Manis, 1985; Reitsma, 1983a, 1983b, 1989).

Reading acquisition then involves gradually learning more about orthographic representations of words and also increasing the number of lexical entries. At some point in development, but surely at the stage of the proficient and experienced reader, this body of knowledge about print-sound connections may serve to read new words or non-words (e.g. Seidenberg & McClelland, 1989). According to lexical analogy theory, various orthographic segments of the presented letter string are activating corresponding phonological segments by analogy to the stored spelling-sound patterns in lexical memory. All orthographic neighbours or friends, i.e., known words in which letter clusters are pronounced in the same way, are being used to assign the most plausible pronunciation to the new letter sequence. A new word having many friends in the orthographic neighbourhood may be easier to read and can more readily be incorporated in the existing lexical memory. Laxon, Smith and Masterson (1995) have presented results which appear to be consistent with these suggestions. They found that young readers assigned more correct pronunciations to non-words with many orthographic neighbours than to those which had few.

Another important component of reading acquisition may be the development of recognizing sublexical orthographic patterns. Through reading experience frequently occurring letter clusters, such as spelling patterns, may be learned as perceptual units. Instead of processing the letters in a word serially and one-by-one, orthographic knowledge may allow the reader to directly perceive and process certain letter clusters as a unit. There are some regularities within the array of graphemes which may be of considerable help to the developing reader. Gibson, Pick, Osser and Hammond (1962) advanced the idea of a spelling pattern, a cluster of letters that consistently corresponds to a pattern of phonemes. While individual letters in English do not have invariant phonetic interpretations, certain arrangements of letters do, particularly, when their locations within the words are taken into account.

The idea that the development of efficient word recognition can be characterised as involving increasingly larger units has been advocated by LaBerge and Samuels (1974). They argued that the size of the visual unit of processing, (i.e., whether it is a distinctive feature, letter, spelling pattern, or word) depends upon several factors, such as the reader's skills and familiarity with the word. In the early stages of reading development the distinctive features of letters are important, but with practice the distinctive features are supposed to become unitized into a letter code. Also, with sufficient practice and exposure to certain recurrent letter combinations, the developing reader begins to see them as spelling patterns. These recurrent patterns of letters would not be processed as separate letters but as single visual units. Frith (1985) also suggested that larger graphemic units or orthographic chunks may come to influence reading performance during development. The recognition units may be an important tool to increase the skill of reading new words. Instead of analogies at the lexical level, the link between analogous words in terms of processing may be that they share a grapheme cluster which is identified as one unit. Seymour (1987) suggested that especially word endings would play a role.

Evidence that young readers are able to use analogies comes also from research by Goswami (1986, 1988, 1993). For example, she showed young children a word which they could not read (such as *beak*), pronounced it for them, and then asked then to read other words. Some of these words shared the same spelling patterns and had a sound in common with the original word (*bean, peak*), while others did not. Goswami (1986) found that beginning readers were able to work out the analogical relationship for themselves. The results of Goswami showed that especially the analogies between the spelling patterns at the end of words, such as *beak - peak*, were easier for the children, and emerged first developmentally.

Why is the word ending so important? Research has provided evidence that the initial consonant or consonant cluster (onset) and the vowel plus any following consonants (rime) are natural parsing units in spoken monosyllabic words (Treiman, 1985; Treiman & Zukowski, 1988). Treiman argued further that for two reasons these units are also dominant in reading and spelling. First, these units correspond to the natural phonological subdivisions of a syllable. Second, readers may use vowel-final consonant units because they know that, in English, the consonant that follows a vowel may systematically affect the pronunciation or spelling of that vowel (e.g. *can, car*), whereas the consonant that precedes a vowel rarely does (except *bad* vs. *wad*). Because young children appear to be aware of onset and rime units they might profit in pronouncing unfamiliar words for example from knowing words that have a similar vowel-final consonant pattern. The findings of the research of Goswami (1993) seem to corroborate this hypothesis of Treiman. She demonstrated in a series of experiments that in deciphering new words children often make use of similarities to the rime part of known words. The effects of analogy have basically been confirmed by Bruck and Treiman (1992), but they pointed to an important constraint. While their subjects indeed could use analogies, and children who were taught to use the shared rime units did learn new words fastest, on a generalization test the analogy trained groups did perform less well than a group who received training in the correspondences between vowel graphemes and sounds. They concluded that although beginners can sometimes profitably use analogies, the most important and crucial component for decoding new words is using the correspondences between individual graphemes and phonemes (see also, Ehri & Robbins, 1992).

With respect to the first argument of Treiman (1985) for the saliency of onset rime units, there is no reason to believe that the onset-rime distinction is less natural for Dutch children than for English speakers. The second argument, however, is not valid for Dutch because in Dutch orthography such contextual and directional dependencies between the pronunciation of the vowel and the following consonant(s) can be observed only sporadically (that is within monosyllabic words). Findings with Dutch beginning readers do not imply such position specific effects (see for a review, Reitsma, 1990, and also Van Daal, Reitsma & Van der Leij, 1994). Hence, the fact that the ends of words (rimes) seem to be more important for word naming in English may be a specific effect of the properties of English orthography: the pronunciation of vowels are more influenced by the following letters than by the preceding letters.

An Experimental Study Measuring the Effects of Practice and Transfer

The issue of whether multiletter units play a role in analogical transfer effects was investigated in a experiment with so-called 'structured word lists' or word families. This is a format of reading practice in which short series of words are read that differ in only one or a few letters. Alterations can occur either at the beginning, the middle, or at the end of the words (e.g., *hand, sand, band, land* or *cat, cap, can, cab*). The grapheme-phoneme correspondences are always regular in these lists (in Dutch this is much easier to accomplish than in English) and most of the time monosyllabic words are used. Although these lists are widely used in Dutch initial reading instruction, it is not precisely known what the functional effects of these lists in reading practice are. The lists may provide an attractive context for practising blending skills. It has also been suggested that practice with structured word lists has the effect of alerting or sensitising the young reader to relatively small differences among words and of stimulating the reader to closely attend to the orthographic resemblances and differences among the words that are being practised.

An alternative view is that practice with these lists can lead to establishing recognition units for the letter clusters that remain unaltered in such word lists. Extended practice with various words that all have an identical letter cluster in common may promote a direct recognition of the particular combination of letters and may eventually facilitate the reading of new words which also contain this cluster. With regard to theories about printed word representation in which subword letter clusters may receive a special status (e.g., Perfetti, 1992) it is important to ask whether it is knowledge about the graphemic cluster itself or the familiarity with a certain exemplar word that serves as a basis for transfer.

A group of beginning readers received practice in reading structured word lists and as a control they also practised reading words in lists that did not have a common letter cluster (mixed lists). Because some previous studies (Reitsma,

1990; Van Daal, Reitsma, & Van der Leij, 1994) did not reveal a difference between initial and final alterations, for this experiment it was decided to use only initial alterations. The word families employed in this experiment thus had all a common rime spelling pattern. According to the research findings of Treiman and Goswami (e.g., Goswami, 1986, 1988, 1993; Treiman, 1985, 1992; Treiman, Goswami, & Bruck, 1990; Treiman & Zukowski, 1988;) one would expect this condition would be most favourable for transfer effects concerning common sublexical units.

During practice all words were repeated a varying number of times (4, 8 or 16). Practising with either structured or mixed word lists would of course foster the fluency of identifying the practised words. The extent to which this affected reading performance was tested by comparing performance in a pre-test and post-test. The main question for this experiment is whether accumulated knowledge of the practised words would influence the reading of analogous words. Therefore, in the pre-test and post-test we also included words that were not practised. Some of them had the same common unit as being used in the structured word lists. If, in terms of the analogy model described earlier, the practice can lead to availability of useful friends for reading a new word with the same sublexical units, then one would expect a significant gain between the pre-test and the post-test in reading the unfamiliar words. If the common letter clusters become unitized during practice and form one unit of recognition, then one would expect that reading these clusters separately would also significantly improve.

SUBJECTS

The experiment was conducted with a sample of 25 beginning readers. Ten boys and 15 girls (mean age 7 years) from two different schools participated. These first graders had about 7 months of formal reading instruction at the time the experiment started. The same reading method was followed at each school (VLL, Ceasar). This reading method can be described as an indirect phonics approach and is used in about 80 percent of the elementary schools in The Netherlands. All subjects were quite able to use the decoding strategy (although they were certainly not yet fluent), they knew all the regular grapheme-phoneme correspondences and were relatively skilled in blending procedures. On a standardized reading test in which subjects are asked to read aloud a graded list of word within one minute as fast and accurately as possible they scored on average 14.5 (s.d. 4.0; individual scores ranged from 10 to 23).

MATERIALS AND PROCEDURE

Because the subjects already had about seven months of training in reading, it was thought to be appropriate not to include the simpler cvc-words (because of possible ceiling effects), but instead focus on more difficult words.

Therefore, a set of 48 regular CCVC or CVCC words was selected. The selected words were assumed to be relatively unfamiliar because they did not or very infrequently appear in the materials that are in use at school or in children's books of that reading level. The words were unfamiliar in print, but an independent group of teachers judged that at least 70% of the words were well known by subjects of this age in spoken form. All spellings were regular or transparent to the sound structure of the words so that the subjects would not have specific difficulty in decoding the words.

The set of 48 words allowed us to construct 12 lists of 4 similar words; lists of the first three words were used in the practice sessions, the final word was reserved for testing transfer. Within each list of words initial alterations of the consonant or of the consonant cluster were employed. Thus the rime component of all the words within a list was preserved. Each subject received 3 lists as a word family, while the other 9 lists were used to construct the mixed lists. In practice the subjects thus received a specific word either in the structured or in the mixed condition. For each next subject the designation of words to structured or mixed lists was changed so that over subjects all lists and words appeared in each condition (almost) equally often (12 subjects were needed to complete this scheme of changing designations, so subject #13 had the same words in each condition as subject #1, etc.). Because the assignment of word material to practice conditions was varied systematically between subjects, the words appeared in all conditions about an equal number of times when considered over subjects. In this way possible confounding of word-specific effects on differences in conditions was minimized as much as possible.

Table 1. Examples of practice materials.

structured lists		mixed lists	
gast	vloek	rand	plank
mast	broek	blok	merk
kast	kloek	waard	blauw

In Table 1 some examples are given of lists that were practised. Note that in the structured list only the initial consonant or consonant cluster differed among the words. The words in the structured list did not resemble the words in the mixed lists and the latter were also dissimilar with respect to multiletter rime units. Corresponding transfer words for the lists in the Table were for example *wast, snoek,* and *zand, kerk.*

The subjects practised in reading the lists of three words during four sessions at consecutive days. Each day 14 lists were practised and the materials were so organized that over sessions the 3 word family lists were practised either 4, 8, or 16 times, and the same applied to three mixed lists.

The words were presented on a computer screen in lists of three words, i.e., they were vertically aligned and the second word was added as soon as the first word has been read, the third appeared after the second had been pronounced. The words were shown at the screen in a lower-case type that closely resembled the type the children were used to in the materials at school. During practice the subjects were asked to read aloud each word presented and received sustaining feedback by a research assistant when they had difficulties or made errors.

During a pre-test and the post-test all the 18 words used during practice were presented one by one. Also, the generalization or transfer word belonging to each of the practised lists (12 in total) and the separate final letter clusters that could serve as the basis of analogies (all of the -VC or -VCC type, e.g., *oek*, or *ast*) were included in the tests. Finally, some control words and letter clusters that had not been trained nor had any similarity to the practice words were also included. During the pre-test and the post-test the various types of words were presented in random order with the restriction that at least two other words were read between a practised word and a corresponding transfer word. No feedback or help was provided during testing, except that the instruction to read as accurately as possible was repeated once in a while. For each item in the pre-test and post-test the accuracy and the naming times were registered.

One second before a word was presented in the pre-test or post-test an alert sound was given together with a large empty fixation box in the centre of the screen. As soon as the item was presented on the screen a timing routine was started. The experimenter stopped the timing by pushing the space button on the keyboard at the moment the subject had pronounced the whole word. Naming latencies were registered in tenth's of a second (e.g., 4.3 sec). Previous experimentation with a voice-key procedure in which a timer is stopped by the first sound spoken by the child appeared to be quite unreliable and clumsy. Children often started with the first part (the consonant) of the word, then hesitated or repeated this first part, and finally said the word completely. A voice-key response for the initial burst of sound would be an incorrect indication of reading proficiency. Therefore, it was decided to use human timing of word decoding speed. After stopping the clock by pushing the space key, other keys were used to classify the accuracy of the response. The experimenter was quite experienced in timing the responses and for reliability checks all sessions were tape-recorded. Independent control of naming times during 14 sessions (9 pre-test and 5 post-test sessions) out of the total of 50 sessions showed an averaged inter observer reliability of .88.

RESULTS

In Table 2, the averaged naming times (in seconds) and percentage of errors for all the different types of stimulus items are presented as a function of testing moment (pre-test versus post-test). In order to allow for comparisons and statistical analyses the average naming latencies are based on responses that were correct in both pre-test and post-test only.

Reading errors were most often an assignment of a incorrect phoneme to a letter, the deletion or addition of a single phoneme. Almost all errors (87 per cent) were a CCVC or CVCC word. It is worth mentioning that both in the pre-test and the post-test about 35 per cent of the errors constituted of substitutions, i.e., the errors were actually words that were either presented in the tests or served only as practice words. This relatively high proportion of substitutions was no surprise, because all the words were chosen to be familiar in spoken form and young readers often try to make sense of their reading attempts. The results showed that the error rate decreased significantly ($p < .05$) from pre-test (mean 8.2%) to post-test (4.1%). But this proportional decrease of 50 percent appeared to be roughly similar for all conditions; no significant interactions with regard to the error rate were found and the proportion of substitutions did not change significantly either.

Naming times appeared to be significantly affected by the practice conditions. The averaged naming time for all the words that have been practised was in the pre-test 4.25 sec and in the post-test 2.88 sec and this decrease in naming times was significant ($F (1,24) = 79.58, p < .001$). The last column of Table 2 shows the difference in naming time between the pre-test and the post-test. The reduction in naming times interacted with the frequency of training ($F (1,24) = 2.99, p < .05$), the reduction being much larger when the words were practised more frequently. The data in Table 2 clearly show that for the practised words the difference in naming times is larger when words are practised more frequently both for words in structured and in mixed lists (no significant interaction effect with type of list was obtained). In Figure 1, the gain in naming speed is displayed as a function of type of list in which words were trained and the total frequency. On the left, the results for the practised words are drawn and these bars clearly show that the total number of times a word has been practised consistently had an effect on the gain in naming speed.

For the transfer words the naming times during the post-test were also significantly shorter than during the pre-test ($F(1,24) = 21.95, p < .01$). The averaged decrease in naming time was 0.55 sec, from 4.03 to 3.48 sec. Overall the reduction in naming times for the transfer words was, however, much less than for the words that have been practised ($F(1,24) = 37.79, p < .01$): for example, after 4 times practising words a reduction in naming times of about 1.15 sec was obtained whereas the reduction for the corresponding transfer words was 0.35 sec. The latter reduction of naming times was not significant, i.e. the transfer words corresponding to similar words that have been practised 4 times were not read faster in the post-test than in the pre-test.

Table 2. Mean naming times and proportion of errors and the difference in naming time between pre-test and post-test.

	pre-test time	%error	post-test time	%error	difference in naming time
practised words					
structured list - frequency					
4 times	4.34	10.6	3.24	5.3	1.10
8 times	4.37	4.0	2.99	5.3	1.38
16 times	4.31	8.0	2.70	2.6	1.61
mixed list - frequency					
4 times	4.17	4.0	2.98	2.6	1.19
8 times	4.16	9.3	2.75	2.6	1.42
16 times	4.11	9.3	2.62	2.6	1.49
transfer words					
structured list - frequency					
4 times	4.08	1.3	3.70	2.6	0.38
8 times	3.96	1.3	3.34	1.3	0.62
16 times	4.16	6.7	3.18	0.0	0.98
mixed list - frequency					
4 times	3.97	9.3	3.64	5.3	0.33
8 times	4.08	13.3	3.56	8.0	0.52
16 times	3.91	8.0	3.35	6.7	0.56
rime-units					
structured list - frequency					
4 times	2.80	1.3	2.33	0.0	0.47
8 times	2.78	1.3	2.52	1.3	0.26
16 times	3.01	2.6	2.46	0.0	0.55
mixed list - frequency					
4 times	2.92	4.0	2.47	4.0	0.45
8 times	3.05	6.7	2.58	5.3	0.47
16 times	2.83	5.3	2.46	2.6	0.37
nonpractised items					
words	4.12	13.3	3.81	10.7	0.31
clusters	2.63	12.0	2.15	0.0	0.48

As in the practised words, an effect of practice frequency on the decrease of naming times in the transfer words was found ($F(2,23) = 5.31$, $p<.01$). It is clear from Figure 1 that the gain in naming times of the transfer words indeed is larger when the words that are similar to transfer words have been practised more often. The difference in naming times for transfer words in the pre-test and in the post-test were significant when they correspond to similar words that have been trained 8 or 16 times. Thus, although the specific transfer words were of course not practised, they apparently were read more easily when similar words with identical rime units were practised a large number of times. One could argue that the transfer words were at least read once before, i.e., during the pre-test, and that although a second presentation in the post-test occurred five days later this repeated presentation already causes gains in reading proficiency. But this explanation is not sufficient to explain the effect of frequency of practising similar base words on the transfer words, because then the increase in naming speed for transfer words would be almost equal for the different frequency conditions. Whereas an effect of repeated presentations of the transfer words in pre-test and post-test on the naming times cannot be excluded, it is clear that the effects of frequency of practice are superimposed on such possible word-specific repetition effects by testing.

Furthermore, a significant effect of the interaction between frequency and type of training list on the naming times of transfer words was revealed in the analyses. The most important finding for the present issue is that after practising a structured list 16 times the reading of words that could have been included in this list (i.e. the transfer words) is facilitated more than the words that correspond to words in a mixed list that are trained equally frequent ($F(2,23) = 3.84$, $p=.03$). No significant interactions were obtained for the conditions of 4 and 8 repetitions. As can be seen in both Table 2 and Figure 1, the gain in naming times for transfer words was almost twice as large for the words corresponding to words that are trained with 16 repetitions in structured lists (.98 sec) than for words that are equally often trained in mixed lists (.56 sec). It should be noted that the control words, which were only presented in the tests and had no resemblance to the practised words, also were read more fluently in the post-test than in the pre-test: a non significant ($F (1,24) = 2.76$, n.s.) gain of .31 sec was found. Except for the transfer words that were similar to words that have been practised in structured lists 16 times, the increase in reading speed of the other transfer words did not differ significantly from the increase in speed of reading the control words.

Analyses of the data on the separate grapheme clusters (rime units) derived from the practised words did not show any of these effects. Although the post-test times (2.49 sec) were generally shorter than the pre-test naming times (2.91 sec) and significantly so ($F (1,24) = 34.5$, $p <.01$), no effect of practice condition could be found. Also the reading of control clusters improved from pre-test to

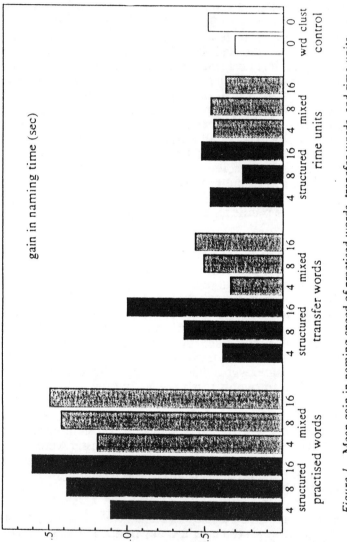

Figure 1. Mean gain in naming speed of practised words, transfer words. and rime-units after practising words in structured or mixed lists as a function of type of list, frequency and tested word.

post-test with a gain of .48 sec (F (1,24) = 21.92, $p<.01$), and this too was not significantly different from the improvement in reading the rime units. Thus, no difference was found between gains in reading the grapheme clusters that were part of the practised words and the control clusters that were not seen at all during practice.

Discussion of Results

The results of this experiment do again clearly demonstrate that practice in reading words gradually increases familiarity with these words. Irrespective of the practice condition (structured list or unrelated random list), there is a strong effect of the number of repetitions on the gain in reading speed for practised words. Because word-specific orthographic information seems to be acquired relatively rapidly (Brooks, 1977; Manis, 1985; Reitsma, 1983a, 1983b, 1990), in the present study the increase in reading speed may indicate that through repeated readings a gradually more detailed memory of the unique letter sequence of the words is established. The storage of orthographic information is functional in that it facilitates and assists decoding processes of the same items on subsequent readings. The findings therefore are corroborating the view that a substantial component of reading acquisition is based on acquiring word-specific orthographic representations. It is probably not the mere repeated exposure to the words that causes increases in reading proficiency. Simply seeing the words without some analytic processing with regard to the grapheme-phoneme correspondences is likely not to be sufficient. Instead, initial decoding processes are crucial and may serve as a kind of self-teaching mechanism. Only by independent and successful decoding the words progressively is a complete and detailed representation of the words established in lexical memory (Ehri & Saltmarsh, 1995; Share, 1995; Reitsma, 1983a, 1990).

The present study tested whether practice in reading a set of specific words would have transfer effects to the reading of similar words. Also, it was asked whether transfer effects are affected by the way the base words were practised. The results clearly show that reading progress for the untrained analogy or generalization words is affected by the number of repetitions, but this effect was only significant for the words that are analogous to the words trained in structure lists. No such effect is found for analogy words of the words trained within unrelated random lists. Thus transfer effects or practice were clearly obtained, but only for specific training conditions. The question then is what could be considered the basis for this transfer effects. Why is there a significant fluency gain in reading the words similar to the practised words? Two optional explanations are possible and need to be discussed.

A first possible account of the transfer effects is that by the repeated practice in reading words with a common rime unit this sublexical string of letters has become a familiar unit. After considerable practice in decoding words with this same letter cluster the unit is recognized at once and can be translated into a corresponding phonological segment without resort to single grapheme-phoneme correspondences. The multiletter units that remain unchanged in the structured lists are repeated 48 times during practice. During practice the unit can gradually come to function as a recognition unit. When after extended practice a word is encountered in the post-test that contains this known letter cluster, the reading of that word may be facilitated, because part of the word is recognized immediately. In fact, for the same reason one would expect that the practise words in the structured lists would also progress in naming proficiency. However, one limitation of this account is that the words practised in the mixed list did increase in naming speed almost as much as the words with the common units.

If the common unit account would be correct than there should be a substantial difference in progress between the words practised in structured list and the words practised in mixed list. This was not found in the present results though. But more important in this respect is another finding. No significant effects were obtained for the separate letter clusters. Thus, whereas naming times for new words analogous to the words practised in structure lists are faster than for new words that have a multiletter unit in common with words trained in random lists, no differences in naming times were observed when the (non-word) units were separately presented for naming. When a common grapheme unit which has been repeated 48 times within the practice words is presented in isolation (e.g. *oek*, or *ast*, see Table 1) then no significant difference with other control units in the gain of naming speed between pre-test and post-test is found. If the hypothesis concerning a familiar recognition unit would hold, then there would be a predicted effect on the separate reading of the grapheme cluster. Because no effects were obtained, we cannot escape the conclusion that the account in terms of a familiar sub lexical grapheme cluster as a basis for the present transfer effects is not correct.

An alternative explanation for the present transfer effect is that the process of reading the transfer words during the post-test is facilitated by knowledge about the very similar practised words. Through practice in reading close connections between orthographic and phonological representations have been established for these words in the mental lexicon. Because the reader has during the experimental training learned about the bonds between the pattern of letters and the sound structure for several highly similar words, he or she can draw upon this knowledge in processing the transfer words. Instead of a recognition of common sublexical multiletter units, a mental analogy process in lexical memory is suggested to be the basis for the transfer effects. The basic difference is that instead of claiming a separate memory storage or representation of multiletter units the obtained transfer effects are exclusively based on increasingly detailed and well specified representations at a lexical level.

It is important to note that in the present experiment for each transfer word with a specific rime unit there were three other words that were practised and containing the same unit. Thus, in the condition where the transfer effects were significant, for each specific transfer word three different analogous words were extensively trained: each analogous word was read 16 times in total during practice. The averaged gain for these three words did not differ significantly from the averaged gain for the dissimilar words trained in the mixed lists. Word-specific improvements in reading speed was by and large in both conditions the same, and only the effects on transfer words were different. Therefore, it is difficult to refute the conjecture that the difference in number of practised words between the two conditions is crucial. In terms of the orthographic neighbourhood model discussed earlier, there probably are up to three friends available in lexical memory to assist in reading the relatively unfamiliar transfer words. For the transfer words corresponding to the words trained in mixed lists only one friend was available. Apparently, in the specific conditions of the present experiment one friendly neighbour is not sufficient for facilitation effects to take place.

Is it possible to specify the mechanisms by which the transfer effects are produced? Of course, the present experiment was not designed to answer questions with respect to the processes responsible for this facilitation effects. It could be that after the training the practised words were known to the young readers in sufficient detail to allow them during the post-test to mentally compare and contrast the specific transfer word with these three words stored in memory. However, a description in terms of comparing and contrasting seems to implicate deliberative and intentional processes, which are likely to be quite time-consuming. The naming times for the transfer words in the post-test appeared to be a little more than 3 sec on average and included the time to articulate the words. One can dispute whether or not within these time constraints reflexive processes are left sufficient time to successfully reach a decision. Alternatively, one might conjecture that the analogy relationships are evoked quite automatically and unintentionally.

The processes involved in memorising details of spelling-sound mappings for words and the effects of this knowledge both on the same word and on reading unfamiliar similar words are not yet fully understood. But a reasonable assumption is that it is extremely difficult to consciously access and verbally comment on these connections. In fact, learning to read may have strong similarities to transitions from novice to expert in other areas of skill acquisition. For example, master chess players seem to recognize in a single glance a complex board position pattern without being able to acknowledge how they do this, whereas beginners soon lose track in reproducing even a simple pattern. The experts probably never explicitly set out to develop this memory for chess patterns; they rather acquire an extended domain-specific base of knowledge by actually playing chess and studying other games. They acquire this knowledge quite incidentally and their knowledge-base, while very functional, is difficult to report on. Similarly, a skilled typist (using all their fingers to play the keyboard) has often a hard time to name which finger is used for a given key, without imagining themselves hitting the key. Novices can frequently report the finger accurately. So, we need not expect that beginning readers as they increase in reading proficiency are able to phrase *why* they are increasing in ability. In the present experiment verbal reports nor other observations provided a clue to how the transfer effects were produced. Further experiments are needed to uncover the mechanisms through which the facilitation of existing lexical knowledge on the reading of relatively unknown words operates.

An important and remaining question is why there is no transfer to the reading of the separate rime-units? If some printed words with an identical subword letter sequence have become familiar, why then is there no significant improvement in reading this particular unit separately? One possibility could be that the effects of similarity in orthographic structure only operate within certain constraints of word length or orthographic structure. Lexical analogy effects are most likely to occur between words with (almost) the same number of letters. Also, some resemblance in the graphemic structure in terms of the pattern of consonants and vowels is probably required. If these conditions are indeed important then it is no surprise that the rime-units are not affected by knowledge of the practised words. The rime-units have less letters (one or two less than the practised words) and they all start with a vowel in stead of a consonant or consonant cluster. And, of course, the fact that all rime-units were non-words may also have contributed to the absence of facilitation effects.

Finally, the present finding of an effect of three friendly words on the reading of an unfamiliar word is no firm basis for general statements about the required number for analogy effects. It is, for example, unknown whether only one very well known word would also suffice. Previous research suggests, however, that having practised three friendly neighbour words does facilitate the reading of a new and similar word considerably more than having practised only one word even four times as frequently (Reitsma, 1990, p.58). Also, it has yet to be determined whether a larger number of words could have even more effect on reading a new word or whether there is some limit after which additions of more familiar words do not have any further effects. Probably, it also depends on the stage of reading development and the total number of different printed words known or the degree in which they are familiar. More research is necessary to unravel the intricate developmental relationships between various stages of word-specific knowledge, number of printed words stored in lexical memory, the degree of similarity between known words and an unfamiliar target word, and the resulting facilitative, or perhaps sometimes also inhibitory, effects.

Conclusion

Only a few successful attempts to fully decode a word may be sufficient to store knowledge about the word-specific relationship between spelling and sound, which is functional to later reading the same word again. But this knowledge is not readily sufficient to serve as an analogy in reading similar words. For effective analogising a number of similar word must be firmly stored and detailed knowledge of the connection between the orthographic pattern and pronunciation must be available.

The results of the study reported here are clearly incompatible with a view on learning to read in which a gradually expanding set of multiletter units is acquired as an intermediary between letter and entire word recognition. In order to explain the positive transfer effect on the words analogous to the words practised one may instead suggest that lexical orthographic knowledge is pivotal for transfer of learning. Although it is difficult to specify how analogy information is extracted or compiled, word-specific orthographic knowledge may serve as an indispensable basis for making analogies between a new word and familiar words sharing a similar spelling pattern.

The development of orthographic knowledge of specific words and knowing several words that are similar in spelling appears to have an impact on lexical processes of analogy. It is probably not the ability to make analogies that develops (very young readers can already do this, as have been demonstrated by Goswami, 1986), but the number of printed words in a child's mental lexicon from which analogies can be made. The present results showing that the familiarity of the clue word plays an important role in determining transfer effects to new words corroborate the conjecture that it may well be that before knowledge of letter clusters can fruitfully be used for other new words, beginning readers need to be familiar with quite a few exemplar words in which these clusters are represented. The present findings on the influence of friendly words on the reading of new words fit well with the results of a study of Juel and Roper/Schneider (1985). They found that the types of words which appear in beginning reading texts may well exert a powerful influence in shaping children's word identification strategies. A gradually expanding and improving memory for printed words may be an essential dimension of developmental change in reading skill. In fact, in line with Ehri (1994), Perfetti (1992), and Share (1995), the hypothesis might be advanced that, after and beyond initial learning of letter-sounds correspondences and blending procedures, it is the most important change that the child goes through in learning to read.

REFERENCES

Brooks, L. (1977). Visual pattern in fluent word identification. In A.S. Reber & D.L. Scarborough (Eds.), *Toward a psychology of reading* (pp. 143-181). Hillsdale: Lawrence Erlbaum.

Bruck, M., & Treiman, R. (1992). Learning to pronounce words: The limitations of analogies. *Reading Research Quarterly*, *27*, 374-388.

Byrne, B., & Fielding-Barnsley, R. (1989. Phonemic awareness and letter knowledge in the child's acquisition of the alphabetic principle. *Journal of Educational Psychology*, *81*, 313-321.

Cattell, J.M. (1886). The time taken up by cerebral operations. *Mind, 11*, 220-242, 377-392, & 524-538.

Ehri, L.C. (1994). Development of the ability to read words: Update. In: R. Ruddell, M. Ruddell & H. Singer (Eds.), *Theoretical models and processes of reading*, (4th ed.) (pp. 323-358). Newark, DE: International Reading Association.

Ehri, L.C., & Wilce, L.S. (1979). Does word training increase or decrease interference in a Stroop Task? *Journal of Experimental Child Psychology*, *27*, 352-364.

Ehri, L.C., & Robbins, C. (1992). Beginners need some decoding skill to read words by analogy. *Reading Research Quarterly*, *27*, 13-26.

Ehri, L.C., & Saltmarsh, J. (1995). Beginning readers outperform older disabled readers in learning to read words by sight. *Reading and Writing: An Interdisciplinary Journal*, *7*, 295-326.

Frith, U. (1985). Beneath the surface of developmental dyslexia. In K.E. Patterson, J.C. Marshall, & M. Coltheart (Eds.), *Surface dyslexia* (pp. 301-330). London: Lawrence Erlbaum.

Gibson, E.J., Pick, A.D., Osser, H., & Hammond, M. (1962). The role of grapheme-phoneme correspondence in the perception of words. *American Journal of Psychology*, *75*, 554-570.

Goswami, U. (1986). Children's use of analogy on learning to read: A developmental study. *Journal of Experimental Child Psychology*, *42*, 73-83.

Goswami, U. (1988). Orthographic analogies and reading development. *Quarterly Journal of Experimental Psychology*, *40A*, 239-268.

Goswami, U. (1993). Toward an interactive analogy model of reading development: Decoding vowel graphemes in beginning reading. *Journal of Experimental Child Psychology*, *56*, 443-475.

Huey, E.B. (1908). *The psychology and pedagogy of reading*. Cambridge, MA.: MIT Press (1968 reprinted).

Jorm, A.F., & Share, D.L. (1983). Phonological recoding and reading acquisition. *Applied Psycholinguistics*, *4*, 103-147.

Juel, C., & Roper/Schneider, D. (1985). The influence of basal readers on first grade reading. *Reading Research Quarterly*, *20*, 134-152.

LaBerge, D., & Samuels, S.J. (1974). Toward a theory of automatic information processing in reading. *Cognitive Psychology*, *6*, 293-323.

Laxon, V., Smith, B., & Masterson, J. (1995). Children's nonword reading: Pseudohomophones, neighbourhood size, and priming effects. *Reading Research Quarterly, 30,* 126-144.

Manis, F.R. (1985). Acquisition of word identification skills in normal and disabled readers. *Journal of Educational Psychology, 77,* 78-90.

Marsh, G., Friedman, M., Welch, V., & Desberg, P. (1981). A cognitive developmental theory of reading acquisition. In G.E. MacKinnon & T.G. Waller, *Reading research: Advances in theory and practice, (Vol. 3.)* (pp. 199-221). New York: Academic Press.

Perfetti, C.A. (1992). The representation problem in reading acquisition. In P.B.Gough, L.C. Ehri, & R. Treiman (Eds.), *Reading acquisition* (pp. 145-174). Hillsdale: Lawrence Erlbaum.

Reitsma, P. (1983a). Word-specific knowledge in beginning reading. *Journal of Research in Reading, 6,* 41-56.

Reitsma, P. (1983b). Printed word learning in beginning readers. *Journal of Experimental Child Psychology, 36,* 321-339.

Reitsma, P. (1989). Orthographic memory and learning to read. In P.G.Aaron & R.M.Joshi (Eds.), *Reading and writing disorders in different orthographic systems* (pp. 51-73). Dordrecht: Kluwer.

Reitsma, P. (1990). Development of orthographic knowledge. In P. Reitsma & L. Verhoeven (Eds). *Acquisition of reading in Dutch* (pp. 43-64). Dordrecht: Foris Publications.

Seidenberg, M.S., & McClelland, J.L. (1989). A distributed, developmental model of word recognition and naming. *Psychological Review, 96,* 523-568.

Seymour, P.H.K. (1987). Developmental dyslexia: A cognitive experimental analysis. In M. Coltheart, R. Job, & G. Sartori (Eds.), *The cognitive neuropsychology of language* (pp. 351-395). Hillsdale, NJ: Lawrence Erlbaum.

Share, D.L. (1995). Phonological recoding and self-teaching: Sine qua non of reading acquisition. *Cognition, 55,* 151-218.

Treiman, R. (1985). Onsets and rimes as units of spoken syllables: Evidence from children. *Journal of Experimental Child Psychology, 39,* 161-181.

Treiman, R., & Zukowski, A. (1988). Units in reading and spelling. *Journal of Memory and Language, 27,* 466-477.

Treiman, R. (1992). The role of intrasyllabic units in learning to read and spell. In P.B.Gough, L.C.Ehri, & R. Treiman (Eds.), *Reading acquisition* (pp. 65-106). Hillsdale: Lawrence Erlbaum.

Treiman, R. Goswami, U., & Bruck, M. (1990). Not all nonwords are alike: Implications for reading development and theory. *Memory and Cognition, 18,* 559-567.

Van Daal, V.H.P., Reitsma, P., & Van der Leij, A. (1994). Processing units in word reading by disabled readers. *Journal of Experimental Child Psychology, 57,* 180-210.

VISUAL PROCESSES IN WORD RECOGNITION BY POOR READERS: RELATIVE USE OF VISUAL, PHONOLOGICAL AND ORTHOGRAPHIC CUES

EGBERT M.H. ASSINK
Department of Psychology
University of Utrecht
Heidelberglaan 2
3584 CS Utrecht, The Netherlands

ABSTRACT. In two reading level design studies, poor and normal readers, matched for reading age, were presented visual matching tasks on a computer screen. In Experiment 1, letter symbols were used. The strings consisted of uppercase--lowercase congruent letters (e.g., o/O) or uppercase--lowercase incongruent letters (e.g. a/A). Real words and pseudowords were used. Poor readers needed significantly more time to match uppercase--lowercase incongruent pairs, especially when the pairs consisted of pseudowords. Experiment 2 examined if phonological, orthographic, or visual mechanisms were responsible for this effect. Strings of letters, digit strings and abstract figure symbols were used. Letter strings included words, pseudowords or nonwords. Poor readers needed more time to match incongruent letter case pairs, consistent with Experiment 1. Poor readers were slower on letter and digit string matching, but not on the figure symbol matching task. No evidence was found for differential use of orthographic (multiletter) constraints. The combined data on the letter, digit and graphic symbol matching experiments point to inadequate access to grapheme--phoneme associations as the underlying factor accounting for the effects found in Experiment 1. Evidence for poor visual processing as an independent factor accounting for ability differences in reading could not be established.

Reading disability has been associated with visual deficiencies ever since the work of Orton (1925). In the last two decades, the perceptual deficiency hypothesis has declined in popularity. The alternative that reading disability is basically associated with poor verbal processing became widely accepted (Morrison & Manis 1982; Vellutino, 1980, 1987; Vellutino & Scanlon, 1982). In this conception, dyslexia and poor reading are supposed to be the consequence of limited facility in using language codes. Referring to an extensive body of research, Vellutino (1980, 1987) has claimed that dyslexia is a subtle language deficiency, rooted in phonological--coding deficits, poor vocabulary and syntactic skills. This theoretical position is still dominant.

The role of visual factors in poor reading has become recently a topic of renewed interest. The publication of *Visual Processes in Reading and Reading Disabilities* (Willows, Kruk & Corcos, 1993) illustrates this. The

C.K. Leong and R.M. Joshi (Eds.), Cross-Language Studies of Learning to Read and Spell, 235–248.
© 1997 *Kluwer Academic Publishers. Printed in the Netherlands.*

revival of interest for visual factors in reading disability motivated us to conduct a series of experiments focussing on the visual aspects of letter processing and reading disability.

There is ample evidence that intra word alternations of letter case negatively affect word recognition in skilled readers. There is not yet conclusive evidence which permits us to conclude that poor readers are especially susceptible to lettercase manipulations. The question if poor readers are differentially affected by letter alternations in printed words stimulated us to design the present experiments. In a well known study by Pollatsek, Well and Schindler (1975), students were used as subjects. Pollatsek et al. manipulated letter case in words and nonwords using a same-different task. They found shorter response latencies for words than for nonwords, even for pairs of letter strings that differed only in case [e.g., *clape-CLAPE* (nonword) versus *site-SITE* (word)]. They also found that visual properties of words, as defined by case alterations, contribute to this effect. Experiment 1 assessed differences in letter processing by comparing poor readers with reading level matched controls in their capacity to automatically process letter features in words and pseudowords.

Experiment 1

METHOD

Subjects. Two groups of normal and poor readers (n=21 each) matched on reading level participated in the experiment. The poor readers attended a school for children with learning problems to improve their reading skills. Poor readers were defined as subjects scoring at least 2 years below the age norm, as measured by a standard Dutch reading ability test (Brus & Voeten, 1972). Poor readers (12.7 yrs) were matched on this test with a group of normal readers (9.4 yrs). There were no significant IQ differences on the WISC, Dutch version. (Verbal IQ, Normal Readers: 102.8, SD=8.6; Poor readers: 98.4, SD=10.1; Full Scale IQ, Normal Readers: 102.2, SD=7.4; Poor readers: 100.1, SD=10.3.)

Materials. The experimental task consisted of comparing the identity of two strings of letters presented on a computer screen. The elements of an item were either real words or pseudowords. The other manipulated factor was the shape, or more precisely the uppercase/lowercase congruence, of the individual letters of the presented strings. Letters were divided in uppercase/lowercase congruent (e.g. the letters o/O, s/S, p/P, etc.) or incongruent (e.g. a/A, b/B, r/R, etc.). Specimen pairs presented are: koop - KOOP and BEER - beer (words, congruent and incongruent case, respectively) versus JOUK - jouk and frad - FRAD (pseudo words, congruent and incongruent case, respectively). In addition to identical strings ("yes" items), there was an equal number of controls ("no" items). These items contained a letter string in which the first and the last letter were transposed (e.g. luik - KUIL (congruent case, control item) and BRET - treb (incongruent case, control item).

Procedure and design. An IBM Personal Computer with a monochrome cathode-ray tube (CRT) display with a 60 Hz refresh rate and a 9x14 letter raster was used. Subjects were instructed by the experimenter. After finishing instruction the subjects could ask for additional explanation, and then they were presented five practice items. Subjects responded by pushing one of two buttons, a green one for 'yes' (same) and a red one for 'no' responses. Response registration was effected by the computer program. Stimulus presentation order was fully randomized across sessions and subjects, using the Micro Experimental Laboratory (MEL) program (Schneider, 1988). A specially designed screen synchronization program enabled registration of reaction times (RT) with a precision of 1 ms. A 2 (groups) x 2 (string types) x 2 (congruence) mixed factorial repeated measures design was used.

RESULTS

An analysis of variance of the reaction times for correct decisions showed three main effects: one for group, $F(1,40)=7.01$, $p<0.012$, one for Congruence $F(1,40)=18.60$, $p<.001$, and one for String Type $F(1,40)=106.01$, $p<.001$. There were first order interactions of Group by Congruence $F(1,40)=11.27$, $p<.002$. Finally, there was a second order interaction of Group by Congruence by String Type $F(1,40)=7.38$, $p<.01$. This interaction is graphically presented in Figure 1.

Poor readers overall needed more decision time in this experiment. As expected, evaluating pseudoword letter strings took more decision time than real words. The overall picture arising from the data is that uppercase/lowercase letter congruence appears to influence word recognition speed. Poor readers proved to be extra vulnerable for incongruent uppercase/lowercase shifts, in particular when pseudowords, meaningless word-like letter strings, were involved.

An additional analysis of the results on the control items ("no" - decisions) showed a main effect of Group $F(1,40)=6.31$, $p<0.016$, and a first order Congruence by String Type interaction, $F(1,40)=9.96$, $p<0.003$. Poor readers had more difficulty in identifying differences between the two elements of an item. This problem manifested itself in particular when pseudowords were involved. This pattern of results is complementary with the results on the experimental items ("yes" - decisions).

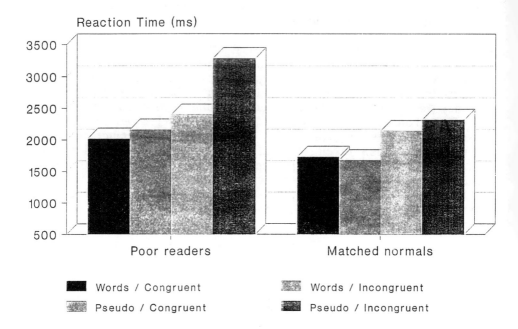

Figure 1. Letter congruence in words and pseudowords, Experiment 1.

DISCUSSION

The emerging picture from this pattern of results is that there may be nothing intrinsically wrong with poor readers' letter identification abilities, but when orthographic and/or phonological complexity are added, there is a strain on their processing system.   This experiment demonstrated that normal and poor readers who are beyond the stage of initial reading markedly differ in their capacity to automatically process abstract letter features.   Poor readers' word identification strategies are characterized by their inflexibility in dealing with abstract letter features.   This basic problem appears to dominate their access speed to printed words.

Word identification cannot be regarded as an "all-or-nothing" mechanism but as a compound and complex process in which phonological and visual-perceptual submechanisms interact.   Our data suggest that poor readers not only have more difficulty in phonological processing, but also in processing at the graphemic level. This is in accordance with recent research evidence on reading ability and print exposure (Stanovich & Cunningham, 1992). Explicit and implicit knowledge and use of orthographic structure enables the reader to accelerate his reading speed.

In normal reading, letter case appears to be largely irrelevant to the perception of words. This has led to the widespread acceptance that word identification proceeds largely through case- and font-independent abstract letter identities (Besner, Coltheart & Davelaar, 1984). Our results demonstrate that poor and normal readers differ as to their capacity to automatically process letter features. Experiments AlTeRnAtInG uPpErCaSe AnD LoWeRcAsE letters within word pairs simultaneously will shed further light on this issue. The role of phonemic factors should explicitly be included in these studies. Experiment 2 addressed these questions.

Experiment 2

The poor readers participating in Experiment 1 proved to have extra problems with matching words and pseudowords in incongruent letter case. However, the crucial question remains to what extent this effect can be interpreted as really visual. This need not necessarily be the case. An alternative possibility is that phonological processing factors might as well be the source of the effect. This would be consistent with Vellutino's (1987) point of view.

Of special importance in the reopened discussion on visual processes and reading disability is a series of experiments conducted by Vellutino and his colleagues aimed at assessing visual memory differences between normal and disabled readers (See Vellutino, 1979 for details). These studies involved having children view difficult-to-label visual stimuli, and then after the stimili had been removed, "copy" them from memory or to recognize them from a list. No between group differences were found. Many researchers have considered these studies as conclusive evidence for the verbal processing hypothesis. However, these experiments have been criticized on methodological and statistical grounds. In their review of the research, Willows et al. (1993) suggest "... the conclusion by some theorists that disabled readers have no visual processing difficulties appears to be premature" (p.281).

We designed a series of follow-up experiments (labeled 2-a to 2-d further on in this text) in order to contribute to this discussion. The logic we used was to present matching tasks comparable to the task used in Experiment 1 and to vary it with different types of visual stimuli. In addition to matching pairs containing letter stimuli, we also presented digit symbols and unfamiliar visual shapes. The follow--up letter matching experiments also used unpronouceable nonword pairs. Another addition was the manipulation of uppercase-lowercase alternation at the SiNgLe SyMbOl LeVeL. As an alternative for the letter congruence manipulation we manipulated *symbol size* in the digit and figure experiments. All experiments were run with the same two groups of reading level matched normal and poor readers, comparable to the subjects participating in the first study.

Letter case alternation at the single symbol level is expected to further boost the previously found effects. If orthographic (multiletter) processing was the critical factor in Experiment 1, the group interaction effects found in the pseudoword condition should disappear when nonwords are used. On the other hand, if visual processing accounts for the effects in Experiment 1 similar response patterns for pseudowords and nonwords should be obtained.

As to the experiments using digits and visual shape symbols, we expect a differential pattern of results. Unlike hard-to-label visual shapes, strings of digits can effectively be matched using phonological codes. Thus, if verbal coding factors explain the effects found in Experiment 1, we expect to find on the digit string matching tasks response patterns that are comparable to the patterns found previously in the letter matching. Moreover, alternation effect at the single symbol level will be comparable to the effects predicted in the experiment using letter strings described earlier.

With regard to the visual shape matching task we expect that if visual processing accounts for the results found previously in Experiment 1, the response patterns on figure matching will be comparable to the results found in the pseudoword condition in Experiment 1. Size alternation at the single symbol level will affect comparable to the effect of size alternation with digit symbols. If poor verbal, or more precisely: poor orthographic processing is the underlying factor in Experiment 1, the effects found in the letter and digit string matching task will not be found for figure matching.

METHOD

Subjects. Two groups of normal and poor readers participated in the experiment. The poor readers were recruited from the same school for learning disabled children as used in Experiment 1. Since Experiment 2 was conducted one year later, the same age category could be used. Reader groups were defined in the same way as in Experiment 1. Poor readers (n=19; mean age 12.6 yrs) were matched on reading level (Brus & Voeten, 1972) with normal readers (n=19; mean age 9.4 yrs). There were no significant IQ differences on the WISC, Dutch version. (Verbal IQ, Normal Readers: 101.8, SD=9.6; Poor readers: 99.5, SD=11.2; Full Scale IQ, Normal Readers: 103.2, SD=8.4; Poor readers: 101.1, SD=10.3).

Materials. The task consisted of matching two strings of letters, digits or figures presented on a computer screen. Four experiments with the following stimulus materials were designed:

Experiment 2-a replicated the first study, adding one critical letter condition. In addition to words and pseudowords, nonwords (unpronounceable strings of letters) were used. Examples of positive pairs are: skpz - SKPZ (nonword, case congruent) and bqrg - BQRG (nonword, case incongruent).

Experiment 2-b presents uppercase/lowercase alternations at the intra word level, using words, pseudowords and nonwords. Sample items in this experiment are presented in Table 1:

Table 1. Sample items used in Experiment 2-b (within string alternation).

yes (same) items	no (different) items	
KoUs - kOuS	kOuS - KoOs	(words, case congruent)
BeEr - bEeR	BeEr - rEeB	(words, case incongruent)
sUuP - SuUp	SuUp - SwUp	(pseudo words, case congruent)
mEg - MeG	MeG - mEf	(pseudo words, case incongruent)
XcZs - xCzS	XcZs - xCpS	(nonwords, case congruent)
mGb - MgB	mGb - MgF	(nonwords, case incongruent)

Experiment 2-c presents the alternations at the string and intra string level, using digit symbols. Specimen items are presented in Table 2:

Table 2. Sample items used in Experiment 2-c.

4 8 3 9 - **4 8 3 9**		(between string, yes-item)
4 8 3 9 - **4 8 6 9**		(within string, no-item)

Experiment 2-d presents the alternations at the string and the single symbol level using figure symbols. Specimen items are presented in Table 3:

Table 3. Sample items used in Experiment 2-d

Procedure and design. An IBM Personal Computer with a monochrome cathode-ray tube (CRT) display with a 60 Hz refresh rate and a 9x14 letter raster was used. Subjects were instructed by the experimenter. After finishing instruction, the subjects could ask for additional explanation, and then they were presented with five practice items. Subjects responded by pushing one of two buttons, a green button for 'yes' (same) and a red button for 'no' (different) responses. Response registration was affected by the computer program. A specially designed screen synchronization program enabled registration of reaction times (RT) with a precision of one millisecond. As in Experiment 1, stimulus presentation order was fully randomized across sessions and subjects, using the Micro Experimental Laboratory (MEL) program (Schneider, 1988). All subjects participated in Experiments 2-a through 2-d. The experiments were run in two days. On the first day, subjects did one letter experiment (2-a or 2-b) and one non-letter experiment (2-c or 2-d), and on the second day they participated in the other two remaining experiments. Participation order of subjects in the experiments was randomized.

RESULTS

The data were analysed using analysis of variance. Dependent measures were accuracy and reaction time for correct responses. The data sets collected in Experiments 2-a through 2-d were combined for statistical analysis. Four analyses were conducted, one over-all analysis for a comparison of letters, digits and figures and three additional analyses focusing on the three stimulus types separately. For the overall RT analysis, a 2 (reading group) x 2 (alternation type) x 3 (stimulus type) ANOVA was computed with alternation and stimulus type as repeated measures within-subjects factors and reading group as a between-subjects factor.

REACTION TIME DATA

Overall analysis. Table 4 shows mean RT scores for both reading groups for all conditions. The overall 2 (reading group) x 2 (alternation type) x 3 (stimulus type) ANOVA showed main effects for group, stimulus type and for alternation. Poor readers were slower overall (M=2507 ms) than control readers (M=2401 ms), $F(1,36)=21.46$, $p<.001$. Mean RT for matching letters was 2181 ms. For digits and figures these values were 2415 ms and 2844 ms, respectively $F(2,72)=296.8$, $p<.001$. Within string alternation trials took mean RTs of 2661 ms versus 2255 ms for between string trials. There was a group by stimulus interaction, $F(1,36)=7.42$, $p<.001$. Poor readers were slower on the letter and digit matching tasks, whereas they did not differ on the figure string matching task that was presented in Experiment 2-d. This interaction effect is graphically represented in Figure 2. Interestingly, there were no other interaction effects, implying that there was no differential effect of the within-between alternantion manipulation for the various stimulus types used in Experiment 2.

Table 4. Mean reaction times[a] of poor readers and controls for letter, digit, and figure matching tasks, Experiment 2.

	Poor Readers	Matched Controls
Letters	2227 (992)	2137 (928)
Digits	2526 (888)	2305 (836)
Figures	2848 (914)	2840 (832)

[a]RT in milliseconds, standard deviations in parentheses

Letter experiments (Experiments 2-a and 2-b). The data sets of Experiments 2-a and 2-b were joined and analyzed using a 2 (reading group) x 2 (congruence type) x 2 (alternation) x 3 (word, pseudo, nonword) ANOVA with repeated measures on congruence, alternantion and word type. Poor readers were slower than normal controls (2507 ms vs. 2401 ms). Table 5 shows mean RT scores for both reading groups for the three letter conditions.

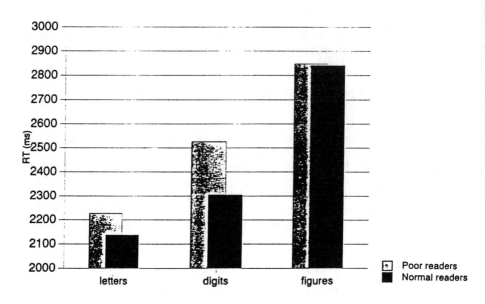

Figure 2. Stimulus by group interaction, Experiment 2.

Table 5. Mean reaction times[a] of poor readers and controls on letter matching tasks, Experiments 2-a and 2-b

	Poor Readers	Matched Controls
Between string alternation (Experiment 2-a)		
Words	1549 (624)	1561 (633)
PseudoWords	1839 (753)	1751 (655)
Nonwords	2872 (981)	2610 (924)
Within string alternation (Experiment 2-b)		
Words	1991 (814)	2015 (820)
PseudoWords	2444 (948)	2235 (917)
Nonwords	3200 (1065)	2975 (963)

[a]RT in milliseconds, standard deviations in parentheses

There were main effects for group, F(1,36)=14.39, word type, F(2,72)=401.05, alternantion, F(1,36)=184.25 and for congruence, F(1,36)=136.68. Poor readers were overall slower (M=1995 ms vs. 1917 ms). Words were processed faster than pseudowords (1729 ms vs. 2018 ms), whereas nonwords took the longest RTs (2817 ms). Items alternating at the within string level took 2615 ms vs. 2210 ms for between string items. Mean RT for matching uppercase-lowercase congruent items was 1994 versus 2292 ms for incongruent items. There were three first order interactions, one for group by word type, F(2,72)=5.35, p<.005, showing that poor readers were slower on pseudoword and nonword trials, but not on trials using real words. There was a group by congruence effect, F(2,72)=8.76, p<.001, showing that poor readers were extra slow in matching incongruent items. Finally, there was a word type by congruence effect, showing that the effect of congruence was specifically large in nonword trials (575 ms difference vs. 250 ms and 271 ms for words and pseudo words). Finally, and most interestingly, the group by alternation interaction effect turned out to be nonsignificant F(1,36)= .14, p<.71.

DIGIT AND FIGURE EXPERIMENTS (EXPERIMENTS 2-C AND 2-D).

The data of the digit experiment (2-c) were analyzed using a 2 (group) x 2 (alternation) design with repeated measures on the alternation factor. There were main effects of group, F(1,36)=33.34, p<.000 and for alternation, F(1,36)= 96.98, p<.000. Overall poor readers were slower (see Table 4). Digit trials presenting within string alternation elicited RTs of 2607 ms versus 2231 ms for between string alternation. The group by alternation interaction was not significant, F(1,36)=.59, p<.442.

For the figure matching data (2-d), an analogous 2 (group) x 2 (alternation) design with repeated measures on the alternation was used. This analysis showed a main effect of alternation, F(1,36)= 87.05, p<.000. Within string alternation trials took 3035 ms, versus 2663 ms for between string alternation. There was no main effect for group, F(1,36)=.00, p<.97. The group by alternation effect was significant, F(1,36)=7.35, p<.007. Normal controls were 100 ms faster on between string trials (2610 ms vs. 2719 ms), and for within string items the reverse was true.

ACCURACY DATA

Table 6 shows mean accuracy scores for both reading groups for all conditions. A 2 (reading group) x 2 (alternation) x 3 (stimulus type) ANOVA showed main effects for stimulus type, F(2,72)=70.68, p<.000 and for alternation, F(1,36)=7.28. Both effects paralleled the Reaction Time data. There were no overall accuracy differences between both groups, but there was a first order group by stimulus type interaction, F(2,72)=4.65. As

Table 6. Accuracy data (Percent errors) on letter, digit, and figure matching,
       Experiment 2.

	Poor Readers	Matched Controls
Between string alternation		
Letters	11.7	8.0
Digits	2.7	2.7
Figures	2.7	3.5
Within string alternation		
Letters	12.7	10.8
Digits	4.1	4.5
Figures	3.5	5.5

can be seen in Table 6 poor readers made more errors when matching letter strings, but they did better on figure string matching. The most striking difference in comparison with the latency data is that the error scores on digit matching do not differentiate between groups.

General Discussion

Comparison and combination of the results found in Experiments 1 suggest a reasonable consistent picture with regard to our initial question addressing the issue of visual and phonological processing in normal and poor readers. This picture may be summarized in the following points. Letters, digits and figure matching tasks intrinsically differed in difficulty. Most likely these differences in accessibility are dependent on potential coding options they contain. Letter matching presents at least possibilities for graphemic and phonemic processing and, if real words are involved, semantic cues may also be accessed. Digit string matching may also be performed successfully using the phonological information available. The figure strings used in Experiment 2-d, undoubtedly, were most difficult to access for matching.

A major conclusion that can be drawn from Experiment 2 is that the group by congruence interaction effects found in Experiment 1 should be interpreted as reflecting a basically phonologically driven process. There are two complementary indications in our data which provide evidence for this. First, poor readers performed worse on letter and digit matching, whereas they did not differ on figure matching. They proved to have more difficulty in accessing phonological cues available. This finding is consistent with a large body of earlier research (Brady & Shankweiler, 1991)

There is a second source of evidence in our data which supports the hypothesis that the differences between our poor readers and reading matched controls were essentially based on a deficiency in fully developed, automatized access to grapheme-phoneme associations. This complementary source of evidence is the finding that poor readers were not differently affected by the manipulation of alternation. There were no group by alternation interactions, neither in the comprehensive over all analysis, nor in the separately conducted analyses. The finding that in the analysis of the letter experiments group interacted with letter case congruence, but not with alternation most clearly illustrates this.

Manipulation of alternation specifically affects the process of visual scanning. An interesting finding in relation with this is the fact that the overall analysis made clear that the effect of alternation was largest in the letter experiments. This is probably due to the fact that in these experiments there were two independently operating factors, congruence and alternation, affecting the visual processing mechanism. Our data suggest that the poor readers participating in our studies were not handicapped by poorly developed visual scanning mechanisms. An unsolved question so far is why in Experiment 2 the group differences on the digit matching task were only found at the latency level. Our knowledge of speed-accuracy trade offs in this type of experiment is too limited to transcend the domain of sheer speculation.

Another interesting point which needs discussion here is that in the letter experiments nonwords turned out to produce the largest between group differences. We interpret this outcome as evidence for the hypothesis that differences between normal and poor readers are not primarily to be located at the orthographic (multiletter) level. If poor orthographic processing or differential use of orthographic constraints would have been a critical factor, the differences found in the pseudoword condition should have disappeared on the nonwords. Our results point in the opposite direction. On the other hand, the present experiments are not conclusive on differential use of multiletter units. Future research exploring the effects of lettercase alternation at the multiletter level should shed further light on this most interesting issue.

Author Note: The results of Experiment 1 were presented at the annual meeting of the American Educational Research Association in New Orleans, April 1994. The author would like to thank pupils and teaching staff of the Utrechtse Heuvelrug School for Special Education in Zeist (Utrecht, NL) and the Kohnstamm School for Primary Education in Utrecht (Utrecht, NL) for their cooperation in the experiments reported in this paper.

REFERENCES

Besner, D., Coltheart, M., & Davelaar, E. (1984). Basic processes in reading: computation of abstract letter identities. *Canadian Journal of Psychology, 38*, 126-134.

Brady, S.A. & Shankweiler, D.P. (1991). *Phonological processes in literacy. A tribute to Isabelle Y. Liberman.* Hillsdale, NJ: Lawrence Erlbaum.

Brus, B.Th. & Voeten, M. (1972). *Eén minuut test* [One-minute test]. Nijmegen: Berkhout.

Morrison, F.J. & Manis, F.R. (1982). Cognitive Processes and Reading Disability: A Critique and Proposal. In C.J. Brainerd & M. Pressley (Eds.), *Verbal processes in children: Progress in cognitive development research* (pp. 59-93). New York: Springer.

Orton, S.T. (1925). Word-blindness in school children. *Archives of Neurology and Psychiatry, 14*, 581-615.

Pollatsek, A., Well, A.D., & Schindler, R.M. (1975). Familiarity affects visual processing of words. *Journal of Experimental Psychology: Human Perception and Performance, 1*, 328-338.

Schneider, W. (1988). Micro experimental laboratory: An integrated system for IBM PC compatibles. *Behavior Research Methods, Instruments, and Computers, 20*, 206-217.

Stanovich, K.E. & Cunningham, A.E. (1992). Studying the consequences of literacy within a literate society: The cognitive correlates of print exposure. *Memory and Cognition, 20*, 51-68.

Vellutino, F.R. (1980). Dyslexia. Perceptual deficiency or perceptual inefficiency. In J.F. Kavanagh & R.L. Venezky (Eds), *Orthography, reading and dyslexia* (pp. 251-271). Baltimore,MD: University Park Press.

Vellutino, F.R. (1987). Dyslexia. *Scientific American, 256 (3)*, 20-28.

Vellutino, F.R. & Scanlon, D.M. (1982). Verbal Processing in Poor and Normal Readers. In C.J.Brainerd & M.Pressley (Eds.), *Verbal Processes in children: Progress in cognitive development research.* (pp. 189-264). New York: Springer.

Willows, D., Kruk, R. & Corcos, E. (1993). Are there differences between disabled and normal readers in their processing of visual information? In D.Willows, R.Kruk & E.Corcos (Eds.), *Visual processes in reading and reading disabilities* (pp. 265-285). Hillsdale, NJ: Erlbaum.

READING AND SPELLING IN DUTCH FIRST AND SECOND GRADERS: DO THEY USE AN ORTHOGRAPHIC STRATEGY?

M.J.W.L. COENEN   W.H.J. VAN BON   AND   R. SCHREUDER
Department of Special Education and Interfaculty Research Unit for Language and Speech
University of Nijmegen
P.O. Box 9104
6500 HE Nijmegen
The Netherlands

ABSTRACT. The present experiment investigates whether Dutch first and second graders use an orthographic strategy to read and spell words, and whether the strategy is used in reading before it is used in spelling (Frith, 1985). Thirty-seven first graders (mean age 7-0 years) and 34 second graders (mean age 8-0 years) participated in the experiment. They were required to read aloud words, pseudohomophones, and pseudowords that were presented one by one on a computer screen, and to write words that were presented to them orally. The naming time data provide evidence that Dutch beginning readers use lexical information - both stored phonological representations and stored orthographic representations - in reading words aloud. The spelling data provide evidence that Dutch children first use a nonlexical phonological strategy. Already in an early stage of the development of spelling skill knowledge of word-specific orthographic patterns is used. No evidence was found that an orthographic strategy is used in reading before it is used in spelling.

Reading and spelling are two related skills. In reading, printed words are converted into sound; in spelling, spoken words are converted into written form. Reading skill and spelling skill may, however, not develop in parallel (Mommers, 1987). Frith (1985) proposes a theory of literacy acquisition in which it is suggested that reading and spelling development proceed out of step. She suggests that children use their knowledge of Phoneme-to-Grapheme correspondence (PGC) rules in spelling before they use Grapheme-to-Phoneme correspondence (GPC) rules in reading, and that word-specific orthographic knowledge is used in reading before it is used in spelling. In the present experiment we investigated whether Dutch children who have had four to fifteen months of formal reading and spelling instruction use an orthographic strategy to read and spell words, and whether that strategy is used in reading before it is used in spelling. If the latter is the case, then at some stage of literacy acquisition children will use a phonological spelling strategy and an orthographic reading strategy.

First, we will discuss the two routes of lexical access as proposed by dual-route models of word recognition, and the two analogous routes of spelling

C.K. Leong and R.M. Joshi (Eds.), Cross-Language Studies of Learning to Read and Spell, 249-269.
© 1997 *Kluwer Academic Publishers. Printed in the Netherlands.*

production. Next, Frith's theory of reading and spelling acquisition will be discussed.

Dual-Route Models of Word Recognition

Dual-route models of word recognition distinguish two routes from a printed word to its entry in the mental lexicon, a 'direct' route and an 'indirect', phonological route. If the reader is familiar with the orthographic pattern of a word, the letter pattern can be used to access the orthographic representation for that word in the mental lexicon. This whole word orthographic representation can then be used to access the word's semantic representation or its phonological representation, which can be used to pronounce the word. This mechanism of lexical access is generally referred to as the 'direct' or visual route (Coltheart, 1978). The other mechanism involves 'phonological decoding'. The letter string is first segmented into its constituent graphemes. A phonological representation is then constructed by applying GPC rules. A match between the generated phonological representation and the stored phonological representation gives access to the semantic representation of that word in the lexicon. This mechanism of lexical access is generally referred to as the 'indirect' or phonological route (Coltheart, 1978). There is substantial evidence that the indirect route characterizes beginning reading (Stuart & Coltheart, 1988; Wimmer & Hummer, 1990). Advanced reading - dual-route models of word recognition suggest - is characterized by the direct route (Doctor & Coltheart, 1980). Reitsma (1983) provided evidence that already after a few months of training in reading Dutch children use their knowledge of word-specific orthographic patterns to pronounce printed words. Since we will use the same methodology, this study will be discussed in some detail.

Reitsma (1983) examined whether Dutch first graders and second graders use an orthographic strategy in reading words aloud, by comparing the naming times of words and their corresponding pseudohomophones. A pseudohomophone is a string of letters that do not form a word, but that sound as if they do. (A Dutch example is 'fein' which sounds the same as 'fijn' (fine), because the graphemes 'ei' and 'ij' both represent the phoneme /ɛi/; another example is 'tauw' which sounds the same as 'touw' (rope), because the graphemes 'au' and 'ou' both represent the phoneme /ɑu/.) If children construct a phonological code - in preparing to pronounce a printed word - only by application of GPC rules, there should be no difference in the naming times of words and their corresponding pseudohomophones. If children use their knowledge of word-specific orthographic patterns to access the phonological code stored in the mental lexicon, words should be read faster than their pseudohomophones, since the phonological code for a pseudohomophone can only be generated along the presumably slower, 'indirect' route.

Dual-Route Models of Spelling Production

Analogously to dual-route models of word recognition, it has been suggested that a 'direct' or lexical route and an 'indirect' or phonological route can be used in spelling (Valle-Arroyo, 1990; Bosman & Van Leerdam, 1993). If the speller is familiar with the orthographic pattern of a word, the correct spelling can simply be read out from the mental lexicon. Pseudowords and words which are unfamiliar in printed form can only be spelled by means of 'phonological recoding'. It is assumed that the spelling process of beginning spellers is characterized by sequential recoding of phonemes into the corresponding graphemes, whereas the spelling process of advanced spellers is mainly characterized by reading out the orthographic representation from the mental lexicon. Bosman and Van Leerdam (1993) provided evidence that Dutch beginning spellers predominantly use a phonological strategy.

Frith's Theory of Reading and Spelling Acquisition

Frith (1985) proposes a theory of literacy acquisition that is compatible with the dual-route models of word recognition and spelling production, in the sense that it is assumed that in normal reading and spelling development children switch from a phonological strategy to an orthographic strategy. The orthographic representations that children construct from their experience with written language will at first not be precise enough to be useful for spelling, but may be sufficient to be used in recognising written words. Therefore, Frith suggests, the orthographic strategy is first adopted for reading and only later for spelling.

THE PRESENT EXPERIMENT

In the present experiment we investigated whether children who have had four to fifteen months of formal reading and spelling instruction use an orthographic strategy to read and spell words, and whether this strategy is used in reading before it is used in spelling.

We examined whether children in the first grade and second grade use their knowledge of word-specific orthographic patterns in *reading* words aloud by comparing the naming times of words containing one of the graphemes 'ij', 'ei' (both representing the phoneme /ɛi/), 'ou' or 'au' (both representing the phoneme /ɑu/), the corresponding pseudohomophones, and pseudowords containing one of the graphemes 'ij', 'ei', 'ou' or 'au'. All words occur frequently in Dutch children's books, and can therefore be assumed to be familiar in printed form. If children construct a phonological code - in preparing to pronounce a printed word - only by application of GPC rules, there should be no difference in the naming times of the words, their pseudohomophones, and the other pseudowords. If children use their knowledge of word-specific orthographic patterns to access the phonological code stored in the mental lexicon directly, words should be read faster than their pseudohomophones and faster than the other pseudowords, since the phonological code for a pseudoword can only be generated along the presumably slower, 'indirect' route.

In Dutch the phoneme /ɛi/ is usually represented by the grapheme 'ij' and the phoneme /ɑu/ is usually represented by the grapheme 'ou'. This asymmetry in use of the graphemes 'ij' and 'ei' to represent the phoneme /ɛi/, and in use of the graphemes 'ou' and 'au' to represent the phoneme /ɑu/ is reflected in the words selected for this experiment. As a consequence of frequency criteria that had to be met, almost all words selected were spelled with 'ij' or 'ou' and consequently almost all pseudohomophones were spelled with 'ei' or 'au'. Therefore an explanation of an advantage of words over pseudohomophones would be that the children are more familiar with the graphemes 'ij' and 'ou' and therefore recognize these graphemes faster than the graphemes 'ei' and 'au' when reading by application of GPC rules. The possibility of this alternative interpretation of the results was investigated by comparing the naming times of pseudowords that were created from the words and thus almost all were spelled with 'ij' or 'ou' and pseudowords that were created from the pseudohomophones and thus almost all were spelled with 'ei' or 'au'.

We examined whether children in the first grade and second grade use their knowledge of word-specific orthographic patterns in *spelling* by comparing the number of correct spellings and the number of incorrect but phonologically correct spellings of words containing one of the ambiguous phonemes /ɛi/ or /ɑu/. Phonologically incorrect spellings were left out of consideration as the spelling errors cannot be attributed unequivocally to a single cause. The child may have misidentified the word, applied an incorrect PGC rule, or made an error reading out the orthographic representation from the mental lexicon. Phonologically correct spelling errors point towards a phonological spelling strategy. When spelling the words containing one of the ambiguous phonemes /ɛi/ or /ɑu/ by application of PGC rules, the child must choose between the two graphemes that can be used to represent the ambiguous phoneme. A phonologically correct spelling error results when the incorrect grapheme is chosen. The correct spelling can be produced by fortuitously selecting the correct grapheme to represent the ambiguous phoneme or by reading out the word from the mental lexicon. If a phonological spelling strategy is used, sometimes the correct spelling will be produced and sometimes an incorrect but phonologically correct spelling will be produced. When children gain knowledge of the spelling pattern of words and use this knowledge in spelling, more correct spellings will be produced. If the number of correct spellings exceeds the number of incorrect but phonologically correct spellings, this would be an indication that knowledge of word-specific orthographic patterns is used.

In the words selected for this experiment, the phoneme /ɛi/ is almost always represented by the grapheme 'ij' and the phoneme /ɑu/ is almost always represented by the grapheme 'ou'. When the children are biased to selecting these graphemes to represent the ambiguous phonemes, the probability of producing the correct spelling is increased considerably. Therefore, we investigated whether children show such a tendency.

The acquisition of word-specific orthographic knowledge depends on good phonological decoding skills. As a result of fast and accurate decoding, the orthographic representation of a word becomes associated with the phonological representation of the word (Adams, 1990). This suggests that good readers have more and better knowledge of the spelling pattern of words than less skilled readers and therefore will spell correctly more words containing one of the phonemes /ɛi/ or /ɑu/. The proportion of correct spellings of the total number of phonologically correct spellings provides a measure of the presence and use of word-specific orthographic knowledge. On the basis of the above line of argument, we would expect this proportion to increase with increasing reading level.

The children were also required to read and write high-frequency and low-frequency words of CCVC and CVCC structure. If they use a nonlexical phonological reading strategy, there should be no effect of word frequency on naming times. If they use a lexical, orthographic reading strategy, high-frequency words should be named faster than low-frequency words. If they use a phonological spelling strategy, there should be no effect of word frequency on percentages correct. If they use an orthographic strategy, high-frequency words should be spelled correctly more often than low-frequency words.

Method

SUBJECTS

Subjects were 37 first graders (15 male and 22 female; mean age 7-0 years) and 34 second graders (15 male and 19 female; mean age 8-0 years) who were randomly selected from two primary schools in two villages in the Netherlands. All subjects were native speakers of Dutch. The reading and spelling data of one subject were excluded from the analyses because, due to illness no data were available on him on the standardized reading achievement test. On one subject no data were available on the spelling test.

APPARATUS

An Apple Macintosh Plus ED computer was used. The words, pseudohomophones and pseudowords were presented in black, lower case letters on a white background in the center of the screen. A letter font (Helvetica) used in many educational text books was chosen. A three-letter string was approximately 0.8 - 1.0 inches wide; a four-letter string approximately 1.0 - 1.4 inches. The letter strings were approximately 0.4 - 0.6 inches high. After every item a mask (%#&+) was presented. The mask was approximately 1.8 by 0.5 inches.

The children were seated approximately 20 inches from the screen. Naming times were measured accurately to the millisecond by a voice-activated relay attached to the computer. The relay was connected to the microphone of a headset.

MATERIALS

All words were selected from Staphorsius, Krom, and De Geus (1988). This is a frequency count of printed words in Dutch books and textbooks for children from 7 to 13 years old. The corpus contains 202,526 words. The selected words are familiar in meaning to first and second graders.

(Pseudo)words containing /ɛi/ or /ɑu/. Twenty-one high-frequency words (printed frequency count of more than 14) spelled with 'ij', 'ei', 'ou' or 'au' were selected. The words were of simple orthographic structures (CVC, CV or VC). In most words the phoneme /ɛi/ is represented by the grapheme 'ij', and the phoneme /ɑu/ by the grapheme 'ou'. The corresponding homophonic pseudowords (pseudohomophones) were created by replacing 'ij' with 'ei' or 'ei' with 'ij', and 'ou' with 'au' or 'au' with 'ou'. Forty-two pseudowords were created by changing or deleting the final consonant of the words and pseudohomophones, or by adding one when the word and pseudohomophone were of CV structure. The same change was made in a word and its corresponding pseudohomophone. Therefore the two resulting pseudowords were homophonic.

Filler items: (pseudo)words. Twenty-one high-frequency words (printed frequency count of more than 14) spelled with 'v' or 'z' at word-initial position or with 'g', 'd' or 't' at word-final position were selected. The words were of simple orthographic structures (CVC or CV). "Homophonic" pseudowords were created by replacing 'v' with 'f', 'z' with 's', 'g' with 'ch', 'd' with 't', and 't' with 'd'. Forty-two pseudowords were created by changing the vowel of the words and the corresponding "homophonic" pseudowords. These words and pseudowords were included in the item set to distract the subjects' attention from the (pseudo)words containing /ɛi/ or /ɑu/.

Words containing a consonant cluster. Thirty-six high-frequency words (printed frequency count of more than 14) and 38 low-frequency words (printed frequency count of less than 6) were selected. Half of the high-frequency words and about half of the low-frequency words were of CCVC structure; the other words were of CVCC structure. The high-frequency words and low-frequency words for the most part contained the same consonant clusters. All words were regular words; their orthographic structure directly reflects their surface phonology and can be derived through the application of PGC rules.

In the reading test all words, pseudohomophones, and pseudowords were presented to the children. In the spelling test only the real words were presented. In order to prevent misspellings due to misidentifications of the spoken words, sentence contexts were constructed for each of the 116 real words. All the words used in these sentence contexts are regarded as familiar in meaning to six-year-old children by at least 75 percent of Dutch teachers in kindergarten and first grade (Kohnstamm, Schaerlaekens, De Vries, Akkerhuis, & Froninckxs, 1981).

DESIGN

Reading test. The reading test was split up into two or three sessions. The high-frequency and low-frequency words containing a consonant cluster were divided evenly over the sessions, as well as the words spelled with 'ij', 'ei', 'ou', or 'au', the pseudohomophones, and the pseudowords. A word and its pseudohomophone were not presented in the same session. Homophonic pseudowords were not presented in the same session either. All item types were mixed on presentation. The order of presentation of the words, pseudohomophones and pseudowords within each session was random, and different for each subject.

Spelling test. The 116 words were divided over five sessions. In each session minimally three and maximally five words from each word category (high-frequency CCVC words, high-frequency CVCC words, low-frequency CCVC words, low-frequency CVCC words, words containing /ɛi/ or /ɑu/) were presented. Words from the same category were never presented directly after one another. The order of presentation of words from the five categories was different in each session. The order of presentation was the same for all children.

PROCEDURE

The experiment was conducted in a three-week period starting at the beginning of January on one school and in a six-week period starting at the beginning of February on the other school. The children in the first grade then had four to five months of formal reading and writing instruction. In the first week of this period the spelling test was conducted. In the next week the reading test started.

After the reading test, a *standardized reading achievement test*, the 'Drie-Minuten-Toets' [Three-Minutes-Test] (Verhoeven, 1992) was administered to determine the reading level of the subjects. This test consists of three lists of isolated words of increasing difficulty. The first list is made up of monosyllabic words of simple orthographic structure (CVC, CV or VC). The second list is made up of monosyllabic words containing one or two consonant clusters. The third list is made up of words of two, three or four syllables. The task is to read the words as fast and accurately as possible. For each list the number of words read correctly in one minute is counted.

The five sessions of the *spelling test* were scheduled on five consecutive days. On each trial the experimenter read the sentence aloud once, and then pronounced the target word separately. The children were then given as much time as they needed to write down the word. They were given the opportunity to correct their spellings when they themselves thought they had made an error. The procedure was practised three times prior to the first dictation. Each session lasted approximately 30 minutes.

In the *reading test*, the words, pseudohomophones and pseudowords were presented on a computer screen. Presentation of each item was preceded by the presentation of an asterisk (500 msec) in the center of the screen. At the same time an attention signal was given. After 500 msec, the item appeared on the screen. Maximum presentation time was 6500 msec. As soon as the voice-activated relay was triggered by a sound, the item disappeared again and the mask appeared where the item was before. The mask was on the screen for 1000 msec. By pushing a button on a button box the experimenter indicated whether the item was read correctly and whether the clock was stopped by the verbal response of the subject.

The experimental reading test was split into three sessions of approximately 20 to 30 minutes for the children of the first grade, and it was split into two sessions of approximately 30 minutes for the children of the second grade. The two or three sessions were scheduled on different days. At least six practice items were given at the beginning of each session. The children were given the opportunity to have a break whenever they wanted.

The reading tests were administered individually in a quiet room in the school. The spelling test was administered collectively in the classroom.

Results[1]

The children were divided into four groups of about equal size on the basis of their scores on the Three-Minutes-Test [3 to 44: Reading Level 1 (18 subjects); 45 to 88: Reading Level 2 (17 subjects); 89 to 175: Reading Level 3 (18 subjects); 176 to 260: Reading Level 4 (17 subjects)].

READING TASK

Naming times for words, pseudohomophones, and pseudowords that were read incorrectly and times recorded when the clock had not been stopped by the verbal response of the subject but by another sound, were discarded. Because of a large number of missing values in the naming time data of the children of Reading Level 1 (48%), these data were left out of the analyses. Median naming times were calculated across items. The data were analyzed using subjects as a random factor. Median naming times were used, because the median is a better characterization of central tendency than the mean for a set of naming times (Noordman-Vonk, 1979, pp. 10-14).

(Pseudo)words spelled with 'ij', 'ei', 'ou', or 'au'. Median naming times were calculated for the words, for the pseudohomophones, for the pseudowords that had been created from the words, and for the pseudowords that had been created from the pseudohomophones. Table 1 presents the mean difference of the median naming times for the words and the pseudohomophones (P.H. - W.), for the words and the pseudowords that had been created from the words (P.W.(w) - W.), for the pseudohomophones and the pseudowords that had been created from them (P.W.(ph) - P.H.), and for the pseudowords that had been created from the words and the pseudowords that had been created from the pseudohomophones (P.W.(ph) - P.W.(w)). For each Reading Level (RL) analyses of variance were performed with each of the four types of difference scores as the dependent variable. It was tested whether the difference scores differed significantly from zero.

At each Reading Level, words were named faster than their pseudohomophones (P.H. - W.: RL 2 $F (1, 14) = 35.48$, $p < .001$; RL 3 $F (1, 17) = 18.29$, $p < .01$; RL 4 $F (1, 16) = 9.80$, $p < .01$) and words were named faster than the pseudowords that had been created from them (P.W.(w) - W.: RL 2 $F (1, 13) = 62.66$, $p < .001$; RL 3 $F (1, 14) = 15.44$, $p < .01$; RL 4 $F (1, 16) = 19.84$, $p < .001$). Also, at each Reading Level, the pseudowords that had been created from the words and thus almost all were spelled with 'ij' or 'ou' and the pseudowords that had been created from the pseudohomophones and thus almost all were spelled with 'ei' or 'au' were named approximately equally fast (P.W.(ph) - P.W.(w): RL 2 $F (1, 7) < 1$; RL 3 $F (1, 13) < 1$; RL 4 $F (1, 16) < 1$).

Table 1. Mean differences of median naming times for the words, pseudohomophones, and pseudowords in milliseconds (standard deviations in parentheses).

Reading Level	P.H. - W. *fein*	*fijn (fine)*	n	P.W.(ph) - P.W.(w) *feip*	*fijp*	n
2	356	(231)	15	47	(466)	8
3	132	(131)	18	37	(175)	14
4	40	(53)	17	18	(79)	17

Reading Level	P.W.(w) - W. *fijp*	*fijn (fine)*	n	P.W.(ph) - P.H. *feip*	*fein*	n
2	771	(364)	14	551	(353)	9
3	236	(233)	15	156	(225)	15
4	92	(85)	17	70	(103)	17

Note. Abbreviations are explained in the text.
Examples of the words, pseudohomophones, and pseudowords are presented in italics in the headings of the table.

Another interesting finding was that the pseudohomophones were named faster than the pseudowords that had been created from them (P.W.(ph) - P.H.: RL 2 $F (1, 8) = 21.83, p < .01$; RL 3 $F (1, 14) = 7.19, p < .05$; RL 4 $F (1, 16) = 7.92, p < .05$). Across Reading Levels the effect of lexicality (P.W.(w) - W.) was larger than the effect of phonological lexicality (P.W.(ph) - P.H.) alone ($F(1, 36) = 5.55, p < .05$).

Words containing a consonant cluster. Median naming times were calculated for the high-frequency words and for the low-frequency words. Table 2 presents the mean of the median naming times for the high-frequency and low-frequency words containing a consonant cluster. For each Reading Level, an analysis of variance was performed with median naming times as the dependent variable and Frequency (high-frequency vs. low-frequency) as a within-subjects variable.

Table 2. Mean of median naming times for high-frequency and low-frequency words in milliseconds (standard deviations in parentheses)

Reading Level	n	High-frequency		Low-frequency	
2	13	2173	(563)	2421	(599)
3	17	966	(276)	1060	(340)
4	17	685	(81)	713	(95)

At each Reading Level high-frequency words were named faster than low-frequency words (RL 2: F (1, 12) = 19.06, $p < .01$; RL 3: F (1, 16) = 14.15, $p < .01$; RL 4: F (1, 16) = 12.67, $p < .01$).

SPELLING TASK

Words containing /ɛi/ or /ɑu/. We first investigated whether the children know which graphemes can be used to represent the phonemes /ɛi/ and /ɑu/. When the chosen grapheme does not represent the intended phoneme, a phonologically incorrect error is made. For each subject, the number of phonologically incorrect misspellings of the phonemes /ɛi/ and /ɑu/ was counted. Table 3 presents mean percentages of phonologically incorrect errors.

Table 3. Mean percentages of phonologically incorrect misspellings of the phonemes /ɛi/ and /ɑu/ (standard deviations in parentheses)

Reading Level	n	Phonologically incorrect errors	
1	18	22.3	(25.9)
2	17	3.1	(5.6)
3	18	4.0	(9.4)
4	16	1.8	(4.2)

Planned comparisons of the number of *phonologically incorrect spelling errors* showed that error percentages were higher at RL 1 than at RL 2 (F (1, 33) = 8.95, p < .05), but that error percentages did not differ significantly at RL 2 and RL 3 (F (1, 33) < 1) and at RL 3 and RL 4 (F (1, 32) < 1).

Next, we investigated whether the children show a tendency to use the grapheme 'ij' instead of 'ei' to represent the phoneme /ɛi/ and to use the grapheme 'ou' instead of 'au' to represent the phoneme /ɑu/. Such a bias would be demonstrated when the grapheme 'ij' is used to represent the phoneme /ɛi/ more often than required in the selected set of words and when the grapheme 'ou' is used to represent the phoneme /ɑu/ more often than required in the selected set of words.

The ratio of 'ij' to 'ei' is 10 to 1 and the ratio of 'ou' to 'au' is 9 to 1. Expected frequencies of 'ij' and 'ei', and of 'ou' and 'au' were calculated for each Reading Level using these ratios. For each Reading Level the number of times the grapheme 'ij' was used to represent the phoneme /ɛi/ (observed frequency) and the number of times the grapheme 'ei' was used to represent this phoneme (observed frequency) was counted. The sum of these frequencies was computed and multiplied by 10/11-producing the expected frequency for 'ij'-and multiplied by 1/11-producing the expected frequency for 'ei'. The same procedure was used to calculate expected frequency for 'ou' and 'au' - multiplying the sum of the observed frequencies by 9/10 and 1/10, respectively. Table 4 presents observed and expected frequencies of 'ij' and 'ei' and of 'ou' and 'au'.

Table 4. Observed (O) and Expected (E) Frequencies of 'ij' and 'ei' and of 'ou' and 'au'.

	RL 1 (n = 18)		RL 2 (n = 17)		RL 3 (n = 18)		RL 4 (n = 16)	
Grapheme	O	E	O	E	O	E	O	E
ij	156	157	161	169	173	177	153	158
ei	17	16	25	17	22	18	21	16
ou	118	107	149	144	150	151	146	140
au	1	12	11	16	18	17	10	16

For each Reading Level a Chi-Square test was performed to compare the observed frequencies of 'ij' and 'ei' with the expected frequencies. No significant differences were found at RL 1 ($\chi2 = 0.11$, $p = .74$), RL 3 ($\chi^2 = 1.13$, $p = .29$), and RL 4 ($\chi^2 = 1.87$, $p = .17$). At RL 2 the frequency of occurrence of 'ei' was higher than expected ($\chi^2 = 4.26$, $p < .05$).

For each Reading Level a Chi-Square test was performed to compare the observed frequencies of 'ou' and 'au' with the expected frequencies. No significant differences were found at RL 2 ($\chi^2 = 1.74$, $p = .19$), RL 3 ($\chi^2 = 0.10$, $p = .76$), and RL 4 ($\chi^2 = 2.23$, $p = .14$). At RL 1 the frequency of occurrence of 'au' was lower than expected ($\chi^2 = 11.09$, $p < .01$). These results show that the children at Reading Level 1 are biased to selecting the grapheme 'ou' to represent the phoneme /ɑu/.

The spelling of a word was classified as either correct or incorrect, and secondly as either phonologically correct or phonologically incorrect. Different types of phonologically correct spelling errors can be made in spelling the words containing the phoneme /ɛi/ or /ɑu/. (a) The children must choose between the two graphemes that can be used to represent the ambiguous phoneme. A phonologically correct error results when the incorrect one is chosen. (b) The phoneme /ɛi/ is sometimes analyzed as a sequence of two phonemes: /ɛi/ and /j/. When 'j' is inserted in the spelling after the grapheme 'ij' or 'ei', this is considered a phonologically correct error. Neither 'ijj' nor 'eij' are legal spelling patterns in Dutch, however. (c) The phoneme /ɑu/ is sometimes analyzed as a sequence of two phonemes: /ɑu/ and /w/. In some Dutch words the grapheme 'ou' or 'au' is indeed followed by 'w'. Leaving out 'w' in spelling these words, or inappropriately inserting 'w' after the grapheme 'ou' or 'au' is considered a phonologically correct error. Whether or not to insert 'w' constitutes word-specific orthographic knowledge.

Some of the selected words necessitate another choice which may result in a phonologically correct spelling error. (d) In standard Dutch the graphemes 's' and 'z' represent, respectively, the voiceless and voiced alveolar fricatives; the graphemes 'f' and 'v' represent the voiceless and voiced labio-dental fricatives. The distinction has disappeared, however, in many Dutch dialects, and therefore now constitutes word-specific orthographic knowledge. Replacing 's' in word-initial position with 'z' or 'z' with 's', or replacing 'f' in word-initial position with 'v' or 'v' with 'f' are considered phonologically correct errors. (e) Two of the selected words end in 't' and four of the selected words end in 'd'. The consonant 'd' is voiced, but when at the final position of a word it indicates the corresponding voiceless sound normally represented by the consonant 't'. The grapheme 'd' is preserved in the orthography because of morphographemic considerations. When 't' in final position is replaced by 'd' or 'd' in final position is replaced by 't', this is considered a phonologically correct error. A word is spelled phonologically correct when the spelling errors, if any-can all be considered to be phonologically correct.

The appendix contains a list of the selected words and all incorrect but phonologically correct spellings of these words. Not all spellings are equally probable. Neither 'ijj' nor 'eij' are legal spelling patterns in Dutch. The children have never encountered them, and therefore are not very likely to produce them. Furthermore, the children at Reading Level 1 are clearly biased toward selecting the grapheme 'ou' instead of 'au' to represent the phoneme /ɑu/. This bias may also be present to some extent at the higher reading levels. When spelling by application of PGC rules limited by the above biases, the probability of producing the correct spellings for the words is $(21-1) / (120-32-28) = .33.$ [2] Some bias may be assumed toward selecting the grapheme 'ij' instead of 'ei' to represent the phoneme /ɛi/. This bias and a plausible, small tendency to leave out 'w' in spelling words containing the phoneme /ɑu/, suggest that the probability of producing the correct spellings will be somewhat higher. We estimate it at .50. Therefore equal numbers of correct spellings and incorrect but phonologically correct spellings are expected, when children use a phonological spelling strategy. If the number of correct spellings exceeds the number of incorrect but phonologically correct spellings this would be an indication that an orthographic spelling strategy is used.

For each subject the number of correct spellings and the number of phonologically correct spellings of the words containing one of the phonemes /ɛi/ or /ɑu/ was counted. The number of incorrect but phonologically correct spellings of these words was calculated by subtracting the number of correct spellings from the number of phonologically correct spellings. Percentages of the total number of spellings were calculated. Table 5 presents mean percentages of phonologically correct spellings, correct spellings and incorrect but phonologically correct spellings.

An analysis of variance was performed with percentages spelled phonologically correct as the dependent variable and Accuracy (correct vs. incorrect) as a within-subjects variable and Reading Level (1, 2, 3, 4) as a between-subjects variable. A main effect of Accuracy was found [$F (1, 66) = 206.75, p < .01$]. The number of correct spellings exceeded the number of incorrect, but phonologically correct, spellings. The number of phonologically correct spellings increased with reading level. The increase showed a linear trend [$F (1, 66) = 21.22, p < .01$] and a quadratic trend [$F (1, 66) = 7.61, p < .01$]. Inspection of the data showed that the increase was large between Reading Level 1 and Reading Level 2, and very small or absent between Reading Levels 2, 3, and 4. The interaction between Accuracy and the linear component of the Reading Level factor was significant [F (1, 66) = 100.80, p < .01]; the interaction between Accuracy and the quadratic component of the Reading Level factor was not significant [F (1, 66) = 2.23, p = .14].

Table 5. Mean Percentages of Phonologically Correct Spellings, Correct Spellings, and Incorrect but Phonologically Correct Spellings of the Words Containing one of the Phonemes /ɛi/ or /ɑu/ (standard deviations in parentheses)

			Phonologically correct			
Reading Level	n	Phonologically correct	Orthographically correct		Orthographically incorrect	
1	18	72.2 (26.8)	38.6	(16.2)	33.6	(15.3)
2	17	95.5 (5.9)	59.4	(10.7)	36.1	(8.6)
3	18	95.0 (9.9)	68.0	(11.8)	27.0	(13.8)
4	16	97.9 (4.9)	86.0	(12.2)	11.9	(11.9)

To examine the source of the interaction between Accuracy and Reading Level, for each Reading Level, an analysis of variance was performed with percentages spelled phonologically correct as the dependent variable and Accuracy (correct vs. incorrect) as a within-subjects variable. At RL 1 approximately equal numbers of correct and incorrect but phonologically correct spellings were produced (F (1, 17) = 1.64, p = .22). At RL 2, RL 3, and RL 4 the number of correct spellings exceeded the number of incorrect but phonologically correct spellings (RL 2: F_1(1, 16) = 27.04, p < .01; RL 3: F (1, 17) = 54.25, p < .01; RL 4: F (1, 15) = 157.12, p < .01).

To investigate whether an orthographic spelling strategy becomes more important at higher reading levels the proportion of correct spellings of the total number of phonologically correct spellings was calculated, and an analysis of variance was performed with proportions correct as the dependent variable and Reading Level (1, 2, 3, 4) as a between-subjects variable. The proportion correct increased with Reading Level as is shown in Table 6. The increase showed a linear trend (F (1, 66) = 76.08, p < .01), but no quadratic trend (F (1, 66) = 1.39, p = .24).

Table 6. Mean Proportions of Correct Spellings of the Total Number of
Phonologically Correct Spellings of the Words Containing one of the
Phonemes /ɛi/ or /ɑu/ (standard deviations in parentheses)

Reading Level	n	Proportions	
1	18	0.53	(0.13)
2	17	0.62	(0.10)
3	18	0.72	(0.13)
4	16	0.88	(0.12)

Words containing a consonant cluster. Percentages spelled correctly
were calculated for the high-frequency words and for the low-frequency
words. Table 7 presents mean percentages correct for the high-frequency
and low-frequency words containing a consonant cluster. An analysis of
variance was performed with percentages correct as the dependent variable,
Frequency (high-frequency vs. low-frequency) as a within-subjects variable,
and Reading Level as a between-subjects variable (1, 2, 3, 4).

Table 7. Mean percentages correct for high-frequency and low-frequency words (standard
deviations in parentheses)

Reading Level	n	High-frequency		Low-frequency	
1	18	58.8	(28.6)	58.8	(29.6)
2	17	87.3	(9.2)	86.8	(7.0)
3	18	94.6	(4.1)	92.8	(4.2)
4	16	98.3	(1.7)	96.9	(2.8)

The frequency effect approached significance [F (1, 66) = 3.29, p = .07].
The number of words spelled correctly increased with Reading Level. The
increase showed a linear trend [F (1, 66) = 52.93, p < .01), and a quadratic
trend [F (1, 66) = 10.70, p < .01].   The interaction between

Frequency and the linear component of the Reading Level factor, and between Frequency and the quadratic component of the Reading Level factor were both not significant (F (1, 66) = 1.58, p = .21; F (1, 66) < 1).

DISCUSSION

In the present experiment, we investigated whether Dutch first and second graders use word-specific orthographic knowledge to read and spell familiar words, and whether an orthographic strategy is used in reading before it is used in spelling (Frith, 1985).

The naming time data provide evidence that Dutch beginning readers (Reading Levels 2, 3, and 4) use lexical information in reading words aloud. (a) An effect of word frequency was found: high-frequency words were named faster than low-frequency words. (b) Words (e.g., 'fijn') were named faster than their pseudohomophones (e.g., 'fein') and faster than the pseudowords that had been created from them (e.g., 'fijp'). The advantage of words over pseudohomophones cannot be explained by assuming that the children are more familiar with the graphemes 'ij' and 'ou' and therefore recognize these graphemes faster than the graphemes 'ei' and 'au' when reading by application of GPC rules. The pseudowords that had been created from the words (e.g., 'fijp') and thus almost all were spelled with 'ij' or 'ou' and the pseudowords that had been created from the pseudohomophones (e.g., 'feip') and thus almost all were spelled with 'ei' or 'au' were named equally fast.

Dual-route models of word recognition assume that word-specific *orthographic* knowledge is used in reading familiar words. Our data suggest that other types of lexical representation may also be involved. Pseudohomophones (e.g., 'fein') were named faster than the pseudowords that had been created from them (e.g., 'feip'). Since pseudohomophones do not have an orthographic representation in the mental lexicon, an orthographic reading strategy cannot be used. Their phonological code, as of other pseudowords, has to be constructed by application of GPC rules. How then must the advantage of pseudohomophones over other pseudowords be interpreted? The phonological code of a word and its pseudohomophone are the same. A match between the generated phonological representation of the pseudohomophone and the stored phonological representation of the word may have given access to the articulatory code associated with it, and by that have speeded pronunciation of the pseudohomophone. An alternative interpretation of the advantage of words over pseudowords might therefore be that generated phonological representations are used to access stored phonological representations and associated articulatory codes. However, the advantage of words over pseudohomophones cannot be explained in this way. Also, a beneficial effect of orthographic lexicality over phonological lexicality was found. This indicates that the children also use their knowledge of word-specific orthographic patterns in pronouncing printed words. We conclude that beginning readers use both stored phonological representations and stored orthographic representations in reading aloud familiar words.

The spelling data provide evidence that Dutch beginning spellers use lexical information in spelling familiar words. (a) The frequency effect approached significance and was in the right direction at Reading Levels 2, 3, and 4. (b) Also, at Reading Levels 2, 3, and 4 the number of correct spellings of the words containing one of the ambiguous phonemes /ɛi/ or /ɑu/ exceeded the number of incorrect but phonologically correct spellings. The proportion of correct spellings of the total number of phonologically correct spellings increased with reading level, indicating that knowledge of word-specific orthographic patterns is used in spelling to a larger extent by good readers than by less skilled readers.

As is demonstrated by the presence of phonologically correct errors in the spellings of the words, a phonological spelling strategy is used in addition to an orthographic strategy. Words are spelled by sequentially recoding the phonemes into the corresponding graphemes, when word-specific orthographic knowledge is lacking. The phonological spelling strategy becomes less important with increasing reading level.

Although the words containing one of the phonemes /ɛi/ or /ɑu/ were of simple orthographic structures (CVC, CV, VC), the children at Reading Level 1 produced only 72.2% phonologically correct spellings of these words. This appears to suggest that the children do not have good command of the phonological spelling strategy. However, we observed that the children at Reading Level 1 produced 22.3% phonologically incorrect misspellings of the phonemes /ɛi/ and /ɑu/, and that the increase in the number of phonologically correct spellings between Reading Level 1 and Reading Level 2 was accompanied by a decrease in the number of phonologically incorrect misspellings of the ambiguous phonemes by about the same amount. These results suggest that the children at Reading Level 1 spell by application of PGC rules, but that they do not know very well which graphemes can be used to represent the phonemes /ɛi/ and /ɑu/.

We found evidence that Dutch children use stored orthographic representations in reading and spelling already in an early stage of literacy acquisition. This is more remarkable since Dutch has a phonologically rather transparant orthography. Most words can be read successfully by application of GPC rules, and many words can be spelled correctly by application of PGC rules. Perhaps this transparancy allows them to build up orthographic representations quickly. No evidence was found that an orthographic strategy is used in reading before it is used in spelling. Word-specific orthographic knowledge is used at Reading Levels 2, 3, and 4 both in reading and spelling.

---

1.   The data were analysed using MANOVA (Multivariate ANalysis Of VAriance). However, the four Reading Levels did not meet the requirement of homogeneity of variance.   Therefore, the effect of the between-subjects factor Reading Level and interactions with this factor were also tested using the nonparametric Kruskal-Wallis one-way analysis of variance. Since the patterns of significance were the same for both procedures, only the MANOVA results are presented in the text.

2.   Twenty-one words containing one of the phonemes /ɛi/ or /ɑu/ had to be spelled. As can be seen in the appendix, 120 phonologically correct spellings of these words are possible.   Thirty-two of these spellings are highly unlikely, since they contain either 'ijj' or 'eij'.   Twenty-eight more spellings are not very likely, since they contain the grapheme 'au'.   Of the remaining 60 spellings, which are likely to be produced when spelling by application of PGC rules, 21 minus 1 ('gauw') are correct ones.

APPENDIX A.   SELECTED WORDS AND THEIR INCORRECT BUT
PHONOLOGICALLY CORRECT SPELLINGS

geit	gijt, geijt, gijjt, geid, gijd, geijd, gijjd
zijn	zein, zijjn, zeijn, sijn, sein, sijjn, seijn
bij	bei, bijj, beij
mijn	mein, mijjn, meijn
jij	jei, jijj, jeij
fijn	fein, fijjn, feijn, vijn, vein, vijjn, veijn
vijf	veif, vijjf, veijf, fijf, feif, fijjf, feijf
pijn	pein, pijjn, peijn
rij	rei, rijj, reij
lijn	lein, lijjn, leijn
tijd	teid, tijjd, teijd, tijt, teit, tijjt, teijt
gauw	gouw, gau, gou
nou	nau, nouw, nauw
hout	haut, houwt, hauwt, houd, haud, houwd, hauwd
jou	jau, jouw, jauw
jouw	jauw, jou, jau
touw	tauw, tou, tau
kou	kau, kouw, kauw
oud	aud, ouwd, auwd, out, aut, ouwt, auwt
koud	kaud, kouwd, kauwd, kout, kaut, kouwt, kauwt
goud	gaud, gouwd, gauwd, gout, gaut, gouwt, gauwt

REFERENCES

Adams, M.J. (1990). *Beginning to read: Thinking and learning about print.* Cambridge, MA: MIT Press.

Bosman, A.M.T., & Van Leerdam, M. (1993). Aanvankelijk spellen: De dominantie van de verklankende spelwijze en de geringe effectiviteit van lezen als spellinginstructie-methode [Beginning spelling: Prevalence of the phonologic strategy in spelling and the limited effect of reading as a spelling-instruction method]. *Pedagogische Studiën, 70,* 28-45.

Coltheart, M. (1978). Lexical access in simple reading tasks. In G. Underwood (Ed.), *Strategies of information processing* (pp. 151-216). London: Academic Press Inc.

Doctor, E.A., & Coltheart, M. (1980). Children's use of phonological encoding when reading for meaning. *Memory & Cognition, 8,* 195-209.

Frith, U. (1985). Beneath the surface of developmental dyslexia. In K. Patterson, M. Coltheart, & J. Marshall (Eds.), *Surface dyslexia* (pp. 301-330). London: Lawrence Erlbaum.

Kohnstamm, G.A., Schaerlaekens, A.M., De Vries, A.K., Akkerhuis, G.W., & Frooninckxs, M. (1981). *Nieuwe streeflijst woordenschat voor 6-jarigen* [The new vocabulary target list for six-year-olds]. Lisse: Swets & Zeitlinger.

Mommers, M.J.C. (1987). An investigation into the relation between word recognition skills, reading comprehension, and spelling skills in the first two years of primary school. *Journal of Research in Reading, 10,* 122-143.

Noordman-Vonk, W. (1979). *Retrieval from semantic memory.* New York: Springer Verlag.

Reitsma, P. (1983). *Phonemic and graphemic codes in learning to read.* Unpublished Doctoral dissertation, Vrije Universiteit, Amsterdam.

Staphorsius, G., Krom, R.S.H., & De Geus, K. (1988). *Frequenties van woordvormen en letterposities in jeugdlectuur* [Word frequencies and frequencies of letter positions in reading matter for the youth]. Arnhem: CITO.

Stuart, M., & Coltheart, M. (1988). Does reading develop in a sequence of stages? *Cognition, 30,* 139-181.

Valle-Arroyo, F. (1990). Spelling errors in Spanish. *Reading and Writing, 2,* 83-98.

Verhoeven, L. (1992). *Drie-Minuten-Toets* [Three-Minutes-Test]. Arnhem: CITO.

Wimmer, H., & Hummer, P. (1990). How German-speaking first graders read and spell? Doubts on the importance of the logographic stage. *Applied Psycholinguistics, 11,* 349-368.

MEASURING WORD IDENTIFICATION SKILLS AND RELATED VARIABLES IN DUTCH CHILDREN

KEES P. VAN DEN BOS   HENK C.L. SPELBERG
Department of Special Education
Rijksuniversiteit Groningen
Grote Rozenstraat 38
9712 TJ Groningen
The Netherlands

ABSTRACT.   In this chapter a simple definition of dyslexia is adopted: Word identification ability below a certain performance criterion on a suitable word identification test. In Study 1, the research focus is on two word identification tests, a real-word test (RWT) and a pseudoword test (PWT). The question is: Are these tests differentially sensitive to phonological and lexical 'routes' or subcomponents of word identification ability?   Beginning readers are supposed to use the phonological word identification component in both tests, whereas more experienced readers make use of the lexical component while reading the RWT words.   Because the PWT words - except parts of them - are new, the lexical component cannot (fully) be used in the PWT. If the two subcomponents exist, a decreasing correlation between RWT and PWT scores is expected with increasing reading performance age. The results of the Study 1 show little evidence in favor of this prediction. Correlations between RWT and PWT scores remain high at elementary grade levels. It is suggested that the Dutch RWT and PWT are not differentially sensitive to different word identification component skills. In Study 2, two recently proposed aspects of underlying reading processes were investigated: Sensitivity at the level of phonological cluster discrimination, and naming speed of symbols. The results of stepwise regression analyses clearly support the predictions that beginning readers and dyslexic readers show the same predictive structure. Naming speed was the only significant predictor of word identification. On the other hand, in more experienced readers the phonological sensitivity was the main predictor variable. Therefore, it was concluded that the reading performance of dyslexic children is mainly limited by mental speed capacity, as it is the case in normal beginning readers.

Recent conceptual analyses and empirical research have shown that the nature of word identification problems in variously defined reading disability groups is highly similar (Siegel, 1989; Stanovich, 1994; Toth & Siegel, 1994).   Thus, it seems inappropriate to extend the definition of dyslexia beyond the variable of word identification ability.

A straightforward consequence of this 'simple definition' of dyslexia is that - in order to identify or select dyslexic readers - one only needs tests that reliably measure the ability of word identification, and a performance criterion below which the performance is called dyslexic. The question that guided our research is: Which tests do we need? Do we actually need more

C.K. Leong and R.M. Joshi (Eds.), Cross-Language Studies of Learning to Read and Spell, 271–287.
© 1997 *Kluwer Academic Publishers. Printed in the Netherlands.*

than one test? Reading theory such as that of (Coltheart, 1978) proposes that word identification can be achieved via the phonological route, in which spelling-sound correspondence rules are applied, and the 'direct'/lexical/orthographic route, in which relatively large chunks of graphic codes are compared with orthographic chunks in the mental lexicon. Therefore, we were interested in word identification tests that might be differentially 'sensitive' to these two subcomponents.

The first test that we employ is a word identification test that is widely used in The Netherlands, viz., Brus and Voeten's (1973) One-minute Test. This context-free reading test consists of *real* words. Individuals are required to read aloud as many words - in one minute - as they can from a card containing four columns of, in total, 116 real words. The raw score is the number of words read correctly within the time limit. In the remainder of this paper the one-minute test will be referred to as the Real Word Test (RWT). For this test we provided updated norms (van den Bos & Spelberg, 1994) for 7 to 13-year-old children. This age range spans six grade levels in regular elementary Dutch schools and the first grade level of secondary education. Moreover, we decided to adopt the Wechsler measurement scale as the scaling type of standard scores; in this scale standard scores range from 1 to 19; mean = 10; standard deviation = 3.

With regard to the two subcomponents of word identification the following developmental course of reading *real* words was sketched (van den Bos & Spelberg, 1994): In The Netherlands, the large majority of children learn to read by methods which stress phonological decoding principles (Reitsma, 1990). Therefore, it is assumed that young readers with little experience with written words, will decode words by applying knowledge about grapheme-phoneme correspondance rules. Gradually, however, the child is increasingly exposed to printed language and reading experience accumulates. Word identification becomes more 'lexical' in the sense that relative large chunks of word-specific/orthographic information mediate the reading process, although there remains occasionally room for the phonological route, especially when words are infrequent or if they contain 'difficult' orthographic structures. Normal word identification development, then, means that the lexical route gradually acquires 'dominance' over the phonological route.

With regard to dyslexia an influential hypothesis (Stanovich, 1988; 1994) is that many dyslexics have a deficit in phonological language skills, although they "may ultimately acquire word-specific knowledge" (Rack, Snowling & Olson, 1992, p. 29). This means that with words which allow the use of 'direct' or lexical procedures, reading performance might be better than with words in which these procedures cannot be applied. In order to test this hypothesis researchers have widely used pronounceable nonwords (*pseudowords*). By definition, these words are nonlexical, and tasks with pseudowords are therefore regarded as 'cleaner' indices for phonological reading skills than real words.

This motivated us to construct and standardize a second word identification test. Our pseudoword reading test - in the remainder of this paper to be referred to as the Pseudoword Test (PWT) - was essentially derived from the items in the real-word test (RWT). Apart from different time limits (the PWT has a standard time limit of two minutes) both tests were standardized with the same samples of subjects, and the administration procedure and scaling type of standard scores (Wechsler measurement scale) is identical.

Also with regard to pseudowords, it is possible to provide a (developmental) outline of involvement of the subcomponents of word identification: Beginning readers apply phonological decoding principles just as with real words. However, in contrast with real words, pseudowords will 'maintain a preference' for the phonological route, even at higher age or reading experience levels. Also here, however, this does not mean that pseudowords are never processed through the 'other' route (i.e., the lexicon). Sometimes pseudowords, or parts thereof, can be read by analogy to real words. Therefore, also in this case we preferred to speak of 'dominance' instead of completely excluding the 'other' route (van den Bos & Spelberg, 1994).

The present chapter contains two studies. Study 1 re-examines the central prediction in our previous study (van den Bos & Spelberg, 1994) about decreasing correlations, with age, between RWT and PWT scores. As will be shown, reconsideration of the RWT-PWT correlation coefficients and the discrepancy data indicate less support for the prediction than previously suggested. Several questions, however, can be raised. How can the high correlations be interpreted? Is it still useful to distinguish subcomponents of word identification in the sense of different *routes*? How do recent reading theories specify underlying processes and how can their relationship with word identification ability developmentally be specified?

Study 2, in fact, will take up these questions and considers recent theoretical proposals of Wimmer (1993) and Wimmer and Goswami (1994). Their theory offers some new accounts of underlying reading processes and their development in languages with consistent orthographies. Two aspects will be considered, viz., phonological sensitivity at the onset-rhyme discrimination level, and naming speed of symbols. The first objective of Study 2 is, then, to test predictions about relationships between these variables and several word/pseudoword identification measures at various grade levels in a regular elementary school population.

The second objective of Study 2 is to investigate the nature of these relationships in dyslexic children, that is, a sample of children with very poor word identification skills. These children were selected from special schools for children with learning disabilities (LD). Performance profiles will be compared with those of the regular school population.

Study I

A Re-Examination of the Relationship between RWT and PWT Reading Performance

As stated in the introductory section of this paper, children's reading performance on real-word and pseudoword tests can be assumed to depend on two knowledge sources/procedures: spelling-sound correspondence rules (phonological route) and lexical, word-specific information (direct or orthographic route). Further, a 'developmental switch' of usage of these procedures was assumed for real words, whereas pseudowords would maintain a preference for the phonological route. One of our major predictions was that, if this were true, there should be a decrease in correlations between the RWT and PWT data as a function of increased reading experience or age.

Van den Bos and Spelberg (1994) interpreted the neatly descending coefficients in the standardization samples (see Table 1; especially A-form data) as support for the prediction. However, it is clear from Table 1 that if the correlation coefficients are corrected for attenuation, support for the prediction becomes less strong.

The second issue that was addressed in the van den Bos and Spelberg (1994) research concerned discrepancy profiles. Assuming that, in general, both phonological route and orthographic route abilities are necessary for word identification, we predicted a high prevalence rate of so-called balanced profiles (i.e., no RWT-PWT score discrepancies; NONDIS) across grade and ability levels. However, since it was also assumed that - beyond beginning reading - pseudoword and real-word reading are increasingly mediated by different routes, one would also expect a decreasing frequency of balanced profiles with grade levels. Furthermore, consistent with the dual-route model, two types of discrepancies were expected: a DIS profile where the RWT score would significantly exceed the PWT score (this would be interpreted as a *relatively* better direct route ability), and a 'reversed' discrepancy profile (DISrev) in which the PWT score would significantly exceed the RWT (this would be interpreted as a relatively better phonological route ability).

Table 1. Correlations (r) and their attenuation corrections (ac), per grade level, between raw scores of corresponding test forms of RWT and PWT in standardization samples (data based on van den Bos & Spelberg, 1994).

Grade	A-forms			B-forms		
	r	a c	N	r	a c	N
1	.91	.97	161	.88	.94	220
2	.89	.95	98	.84	.89	96
3	.84	.91	110	.78	.84	95
4	.83	.90	99	.85	.92	97
5	.81	.91	123	.74	.83	136
6	.76	.91	106	.81	.97	109
7	.69	.78	202	.66	.74	194

In van den Bos and Spelberg (1994), three levels of word identification proficiency were described at which balanced and discrepant profiles can occur. So, a total of nine profiles was distinguished. However, a more fine-grained classification system is possible. Figure 1 contains a 5 x 5 matrix of combinations of RWT and PWT standard score levels. The x-axis contains, from left to right, the RWT levels '4' (standard scores 1 through 5), '7' (standard scores 6 through 8), '10' (9 through 11), '13' (12 through 14), and '16' (15 through 19). The y-axis (top to bottom) contains these levels for the PWT. Each cell contains histograms of case percentages for the group of 155 10- to 12-year-old dyslexic students from special schools for learning disabilities (LD), and for the grade levels 1 through 7 of the standardization samples; see Table 1 for n's. The 'diagonal' cells of the matrix contain the percentages of the NONDIS score combinations, whereas the cells towards the upper right and lower left corners of the matrix contain increasingly discrepant profiles. The triangle left to the diagonal contains DISrev profiles (higher PWT scores than RWT scores) whereas the triangle right to the diagonal contains DIS profiles (higher RWT scores than PWT scores).

Figure 1 shows that for the standardization samples and the LD group, the large majority of cases concerns nondiscrepant or balanced RWT-PWT profiles. If the percentages across the diagonal are summed per grade level, the following totals are obtained for the LD group and the grade levels 1 through 7, respectively: 66%, 66%, 60%, 62%, 64%, 68%, 57%, and 50%.

Although a decrease of percentages seems apparent at grades 6 and 7, a χ^2 test (df = 6) indicated no significant difference between the 7 percentages ($\chi2$= 4.043, p>.05). Hence, the prediction of a decreasing frequency of balanced profiles with grade levels is not confirmed.

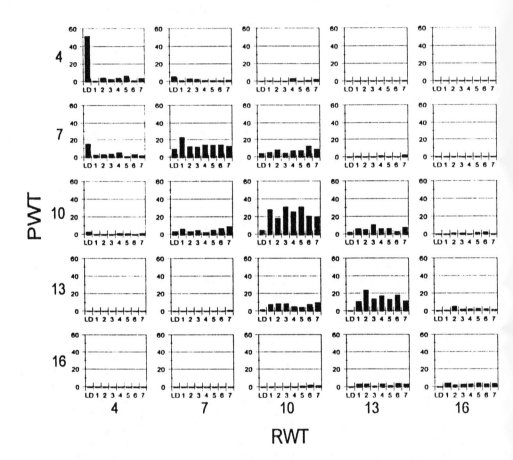

Figure 1. Five by five matrix of combinations of RWT and PWT standard score levels. Level 4 means a score in the range of standard scores 1 through 5, level 7 = 6 through 8, level 10 = 9 through 11, level 13 = 12 through 14, level 16 = 15 through 19. The first bar in each cell represents 10-12 year-old students from special schools for learning disabilities (LD). The next bars (from left to right) represent grade levels 1 through 6 in regular elementary schools, and grade level 1 (here indicated as 7) of regular secondary schools.

Conclusion and discussion

On the basis of the assumption that, in general, both phonological and lexical (direct-route) processes are *necessary* for word identification, high correlations between the RWT and PWT were expected, and found. However, it was also expected - due to an assumed developmental switch in the relative application of routes/procedures in the two word types - that there would be a decrease in correlational strength with age; and for this prediction the present analyses do not offer much support. Correlations between real-word and pseudoword reading performance *remain* high, at least at elementary grade levels.

The tentative conclusion, then, is that the RWT and the PWT basically measure the same 'things' - at least *per* grade level - and that they are *not differentially sensitive* to qualitatively different routes or procedures. Although it is still possible that there are inter-individual and intra-individual differences in the proficiency with which different procedures of word identification are applied, it seems not very likely that these procedures are *differently* applied - *within* grade levels - in the different word sets of the RWT and the PWT.

The suggestion that the RWT and PWT measure the same 'things' does not necessarily mean that these 'things' are the same or that they have the same 'weight' *with age or grade levels.* For example, the high correlation in grade 1 might be interpreted as reflecting that ability X mediates both the RWT and the PWT, whereas in grade 6 the high correlation between the RWT and the PWT could mean that both tests are mediated by abilities X + Y.

The basic questions that arise again are: Which are these abilities? What is the developmental pattern of their relationships with word identification skill? How do these patterns compare with performance profiles in dyslexics?

In summary, this discussion suggests that the Dutch RWT and PWT are not differentially sensitive to different 'route' skills. The evidence, however, remained indirect because no independent operationalizations of 'routes' or other underlying processes were used in our previous research (van den Bos & Spelberg, 1994).

Study II

Introduction

With regard to the question as to which relevant underlying abilities or subcomponents of word identification can be distinguished, recent models no longer seem to favor the idea of *independent* routes and switches therein (Rack et al., 1992). Instead, researchers (Bosman, 1994; Ehri, 1992; Juel, 1994; Rack et al., 1992; van den Broeck, 1993; Wimmer & Goswami, 1994) seem to agree that an increase in word identification skill is better interpreted as increasing mastery along a phonological-linguistic *continuum* with differently sized recognition units, than as a switch between two qualitatively different procedures (phonological route and direct route) - especially in orthographically consistent languages like German and Dutch (Wimmer & Goswami, 1994).

What is the nature of this phonological-linguistic continuum? Similar to characterizations of beginning reading in Dutch (Reitsma, 1990; van Bon, Schreuder, Duighuisen & Kerstholt, 1994; van den Bos & Spelberg, 1994), Wimmer and Goswami (1994) propose that *beginning* German readers rely on grapheme-phoneme conversions (GPC) and that the reading process consists of assembling pronunciations from letter sounds. However, it is obvious that more experienced readers do not continue with the phonemic assembly approach. Along with traditional models, Wimmer and Goswami (1994) propose that, in order to become *faster* readers, it is necessary that higher-order 'recognition' units are established. However, according to Wimmer and Goswami - and this contrasts with traditional dual-route assumptions - these units are not acquired on the basis of visual properties of letter groups or spelling patterns, but again on a phonological basis, viz., at the subsyllabic level of onsets and rimes.

Apart from the representational aspect of phonological-linguistic variables, the recent literature also mentions the aspect of *speed* of verbal-symbolic encoding or retrieval. Although some researchers explicitly go 'beyond the phonological module' (see, e.g., Share, 1994) and consider processing speed in relation to concepts such as automatization of complex skills (Nicolson & Fawcett, 1990) and temporal-order integration (Share, 1994), we first want to establish the relationship with word identification performance. Wimmer's (1993) observation of the impact of continuous-naming speed deficits in poor readers seems especially relevant. According to Wimmer (1993, p. 30), "It is the consistency of the German writing system that makes word decoding rather easy, so that even children with initial decoding difficulties do not give up decoding, using visual word identification and context-dependent guessing instead. However,...the difficulties with reading persist...The affected children suffer from slow, laborious word decoding....." Because of the strong association with speed impairments on rapid naming tasks (especially numerals), Wimmer (1993) speaks of 'speed dyslexia'.

Having chosen two word identification related variables, we want to evaluate whether they are differentially related to the RWT and the PWT. If these tests measure the same things, then there should be no differential relationships with these variables. However, this does not mean that there are no 'developmental' differences (i.e., differences between grade levels) in the relationships with underlying variables.

From the assumption that in German and Dutch populations of readers the relationship between onset-rime based recognition units and word identification ability emerges later than the GPC-reading relationship, it can be predicted that correlations between word identification skill (measured, in the present study, by the RWT and PWT) and a test that measures phonological sensitivity at an onset-rime level, should be higher in later grades than in grade one. In addition, a prediction about the relationship between the other variable, viz., naming speed and developing word/pseudoword identification can be formulated. More specifically, the task that will be employed is Wimmer and Goswami's (1994) numeral naming task. Although numerals are not graphemes, we interpret their processing as similar to GPC processes. If GPC processes are the dominant skill in beginning reading then numeral naming speed should show a higher correlation with RWT and PWT performance in first graders than in later grades.

Finally, performance profiles of older dyslexic children (10-12 year-olds) will be compared with those of grades 1 through 4 in the regular school population.

Method

SUBJECTS

Subjects were children at the grade levels 1 through 4 of a regular elementary school in a northern Dutch town. The n's at these grade levels were 27, 31, 17, and 26 subjects, respectively. The mean ages of the children at these grade levels were 7, 8, 9, and 10 years.

The second subject sample was drawn from 10- to 12-year-olds in two special schools for learning disabilities in the town of Groningen. The decision criterion for dyslexia is a score below the first standard deviation (standard score below 7) on either the RWT or the PWT, or on both tests. As was expected, the large majority (45 children) of the screened subjects (65 children) could be classified as dyslexic. In the remainder of this study, this sample of 45 children will be referred to as learning disabled (LD).

Word identification tests. Within individual test sessions, the RWT and PWT (A-forms) were consecutively administered. RWT-PWT administration procedures were modified in the sense that the children were required to read the first 87 items of both the RWT and the PWT. This was done in order to obtain separate reading time and error data for each of the two tests. During administration, the test assistant marked on her scoring form the word read, each time that one minute had passed. Hence, the raw scores and standard scores which belong to the standard procedure of RWT and PWT administrations (one minute for the RWT and two minutes for the PWT) could also be computed. Thus, there were eight variables: **RWTr** (=raw score RWT; number of correctly read words in the first minute), **RWTs** (= raw score converted into standard score), **RWTt** (= average reading time per item in the fixed set of 87 words), **RWTe** (number of incorrectly read words - errors - in the fixed set of 87 words), **PWTr** (= raw score PWT; number of correctly read words in the first two minutes), **PWTs, PWTt,** and **PWTe**.

Phonology: Rhyme-and-alliteration (R&A) task. The R&A task was administered in groups of about 10 students. The test consists of seven practice trials and 28 experimental items, which were derived from a larger set constructed by Brons (1990), who in turn had based her work on Bradley and Bryant (1983). An item consists of four real words. The set of 28 items consists of four instances - with varying correct-rejection positions - of seven linguistic categories each. The categories are: Rhyme (three words of an item rhyme, and one does not; example of item: *mes, was, bes, les*), Starting Cluster (in all words but one the onset is the same; there are 3 subcategories: the number of letters in the starting clusters can be 1, 2, or 3; example of item from first subcategory: *keer, zaag, koop, kiem*), and End Cluster (in all words but one the end cluster is the same; there are three subcategories: the number of letters in the end clusters can be 1, 2, or 3; example of item from second subcategory: *bank, zink, melk, lonk*).

Items are audiotaped and presented to the children via a tape recorder. After having listened to an item twice, the child's task is to check-mark on a sheet - with four empty blocks for each item - which word "does not belong to the set on the basis of its sound". The test's score is the number of correct responses. The variable is called rhyme and alliteration (**R&A**).

Speed: Continuous naming of numerals. Individual children were administered three continuous reading tasks derived from Wimmer and Goswami (1994): A numeral reading task, a number word reading task, and a pseudo number-word reading task (PNU). In this chapter we will only address the numeral reading task. Two lists of 18 items were presented (each list on a separate page). The lists were created by including each of the numerals 2, 3, 4, 5, 6, 7, 9, 10, and 12 twice in each list (Wimmer & Goswami, 1994). The child's task was to read out loud the rows of numerals as fast and errorlessly as he/she could, and the child's performance was timed per page. All other procedural details (practice session, ordering constraints of numbers in the lists, lay-out of materials, counterbalancing of six task orders per grade level, etc.) mentioned in Wimmer and Goswami (1994) were replicated in this study. The avarage reading speed per item, and the overall number of reading errors were computed. Two variables will be considered: **NMLt** (= average reading time per item in the numeral reading task), **NMLe** (= number of errors in the numeral reading task).

Results

Means and standard deviations of all variables are presented in Table 2.

Table 2. Means and standard deviations of word reading test performance and related variables for children at grade levels 1 through 4 (age: 7-10 year-olds) in a regular elementary school, and for 10-12 year-old children from special schools for learning disabilities (LD).

variables	Grade 1 (n=27)	Grade 2 (n=31)	Grade 3 (n=17)	Grade 4 (n=26)	LD (n=45)
Real word Test - number of words read in one minute minus words read incorrectly (raw score = RWTr)					
RWTr	23.3 (19.6)	54.8 (19.1)	65.5 (13.8)	68.7 (12.1)	35.4 (14.7)
Pseudoword Test - number of words read in two minutes minus words read incorrectly (raw score = PWTr)					
PWTr	21.6 (15.1)	49.5 (21.4)	51.7 (15.65)	60.7 (15.7)	25.8 (13.1)
Real Word Test - standard score (RWTs)					
RWTs	9.3 (4.1)	11.5 (3.8)	11.0 (2.8)	10.7 (2.9)	2.5 (2.0)
Pseudoword Test - standard score (PWTs)					
PWTs	9.8 (3.6)	13.3 (4.0)	10.3 (2.6)	10.1 (2.9)	3.6 (2.6)
Real Word Test - mean reading time (secs) per item in fixed set of 87 words (RWTt)					
RWTt	- -	1.7 (1.1)	1.0 (0.4)	0.9 (.0.2)	2.5 (1.4)
Pseudoword Test - mean reading time (secs) per item in fixed set of 87 words (PWTt)					
PWTt	- -	2.7 (2.3)	1.9 (0.7)	1.6 (0.5)	3.3 (1.8)
Real Word Test - number of misread words (errors) in fixed set of 87 words (RWTe)					
RWTe	- -	9.1 (15.3)	7.1 (9.5)	3.1 (4.2)	19.9 (11.7)
Pseudoword Test - number of misread words (errors) in fixed set of 87 words (PWTe)					
PWTe	- -	18.9 (14.6)	18.1 (14.7)	12.7 (10.1)	44.1 (16.6)
Numeral-reading task - mean reading time (secs) per item (NMLt)					
NMLt	1.02 (0.40)	0.58 (0.11)	0.51 (0.06)	0.49 (0.06)	0.60 (0.13)
Numeral-reading task - errors (max = 36) NMLe					
NMLe	0.6 (2.0)	0.2 (0.5)	0.0 (0.0)	0.0 (0.0)	0.1 (0.3)
Rhyme and alliteration task - raw score (max = 28) (R&A)					
R & A	11.1 (3.9)	17.0 (5.1)	17.2 (5.1)	20.8 (4.1)	14.1 (5.1)

RWTt/e and PWTt/e data for Grade one students are missing, because the task of reading the fixed lists of 2 x 87 (pseudo)words appeared too taxing for a substantial number of students. However, the time limits of one minute and two minutes for the RWT and PWT, respectively, did not create problems. Hence, standard scores could be computed for both the RWT and the PWT. A further remark concerns the error data of the numeral reading task. As is clear from Table 2, very few errors were made in this task. Therefore, the variable NMLe will not be further considered.

Regular elementary-school sample. First, we will focus on the regular school sample, grades 1 through 4. The correlations between the RWT and PWT standard scores at the grade levels 1 through 4 were .93, .80, .84 and .80, respectively. These findings are similar to the raw score correlations at these grade levels in our previous study (cf. Table 1). Also of interest were the correlations between the reading related variables of phonological ability (rhyme and alliteration) and continuous symbol naming speed. For grade levels 1 through 4 these correlations had the nonsignificant values of -.25, -.28, -.13, and -.11.

Of central interest are the analyses concerning the questions whether there would be differential relationships between reading related variables and RWT and PWT scores, and whether there would be developmental differences (i.e., differences between grade levels) in the relationships with underlying variables. The latter question is answered by the results in Table 3.

Table 3. Correlations per grade level between RWT and PWT standard scores (RWTs and PWTs), numeral-reading time per item (NMLt), and Rhyme-and-alliteration task score (R&A).

Grade	RWTs		PWTs	
	NMLt	R&A	NMLt	R&A
1 (n = 27)	-.58*	.30	-.60*	.10
2 (n = 31)	-.36*	.47*	-.28	.34
3 (n = 17)	-.37	.61*	-.45	.47
4 (n = 26)	-.18	.54*	-.16	.72**

* $p < .05$
** $p < .01$

Table 3 indicates two trends: whereas the correlations between RWTs/PWTs and NMLt decrease with grade, there is an increase with grade of the correlations between RWTs/PWTs and R&A.   This supports two predictions.   First, it was predicted that the correlation between word identification skill and scores on a test for phonological sensitivity at an onset-rime level, should be higher in later grades than in grade 1.   Second, interpreting numeral naming speed as similar to GPC processes, it was predicted that in beginning readers (grade 1 children) numeral naming speed should correlate higher with RWT and PWT performance than in later grades.

Finally, our first question (Are there differential relationships between the reading related variables and the RWT and PWT scores?) was considered.   It is obvious from Table 3 that, for first graders, the answer is negative.   In beginning readers only naming speed correlates with reading, and the relationship is equally strong for both the RWT and the PWT.   As was already suggested by the very high correlation between the two tests at this grade level, the RWT and the PWT seem to measure the same things.

On data of children from grade levels higher than grade 1, six stepwise regression analyses were conducted.   In all analyses the predictor variables were numeral naming speed (NMLt) and R&A task performance.   In the first three analyses, RWTs (RWT standard score) and RWTt (average reading time per item in the fixed set of 87 words) and RWTe (number of misread words in the fixed set of 87 words) were the criterion variables.   In the last three analyses the criterion variables were PWTs, PWTt, and PWTe.   Further, it should be noted that the variables RWTt/e and PWTt/e were first regressed on grade before the predictors NMLt and R&A were evaluated.   Results are presented in the left panel of Table 4.

With regard to RWT and PWT standard scores, and RWT and PWT error scores on the sets of 87 pseudowords, it seems that predictive profiles are parallel to each other.   However, with respect to reading times correspondence is less close.   Here, the variable RWTt is more strongly related to the variable R&A, whereas the PWTt is only related to naming speed.   A tentative explanation for this diversity in results is that, for most children, the set of pseudowords read is much larger in the RWTt/PWTt conditions than in the RWTs/PWTs conditions which are based on one-minute and two-minute time limits, respectively.   Moreover, not only are the RWTt/PWTt lists longer, they contain - on the average - longer and more difficult words as well.   It is possible that especially the pseudowords were 'closely' inspected, and that small-scale reading operations - even at the GPC level - were necessary.   This would explain why in these difficult circumstances a variable similar to GPC (i.e., numeral naming speed) again emerged as a predictor.   Interestingly, however, this does not apply to the error variables RWTe and PWTe. Here, the variable R&A is the 'only' significant predictor.

Table 4. Significant predictors according to stepwise regression analysis on RWT and PWT data of combined grade levels 2 through 4 (regular elementary school) and dyslexic children from special schools for learning disabilities (LD).

			Grades 2-4 (n=74)				LD (10-12 year-olds; n=45)			
Analysis	Criterion variable	Step	Pred.	R^2	F-ch	Sig. ch	Pred.	R^2	F-ch	Sig. ch
1	RWTs	1	R&A	.21	16.42	.000	NMLt	.11	5.11	.029
		2	-	-	-	-	-	-	-	-
2	RWTt	1	R&A	.16	11.57	.001	NMLt	.41	29.84	.000
		2	NMLt	.21	4.24	.044	R&A	.49	5.39	.025
3	RWTe	1	R&A	.08	5.44	.023	R&A	.20	10.43	.002
		2	-	-	-	-	NMLt	.38	12.78	.001
4	PWTs	1	R&A	.10	7.12	.010	NMLt	.17	8.28	.006
		2	-	-	-	-	R&A	.29	6.98	.012
5	PWTt	1	NMLt	.08	5.52	.022	NMLt	.35	22.39	.000
		2	-	-	-	-	-	-	-	-
6	PWTe	1	R&A	.21	16.42	.000	NMLt	.13	6.00	.019
		2	-	-	-	-	-	-	-	-

Note: In the grade 2-4 sample, the RWTt, RWTe, PWTt, and PWTe scores were regressed on grade.

Dyslexic children. Table 2 indicates that the mean RWT and PWT standard scores of this group of 10-12 year-old children are very low. The means are below the -2SD cut-off line of the Wechsler scale (mean = 10; SD = 3). The severity of the reading disturbance can also be judged from the raw scores on the RWT and PWT and the time and error scores on the 87 item-lists: in all cases the LD group's means fall below the second graders' means. Also on the reading-related variables (numeral naming speed NML and phonological sensitivity R&A) the LD group performs at the level of children who are two to three years younger. The LD group's R&A mean score is significantly higher than the first graders' mean but significantly lower (t = 2.44, p < .02) than in second graders and beyond. The LD group's NMLt mean score is not significantly different from the mean of second graders, but significantly different from third graders (t = -2.74, p < .01) and beyond.

In order to investigate the predictive structure of the reading-related variables, the same analyses as described in the previous section were conducted on the LD group's data. The results are presented in the right panel of Table 4. From this table it is clear that in five out of six analyses the speed variable (NMLt) is the primary predictor of reading performance. It seems, therefore, that in this dyslexic group both RWT and PWT performances are restricted by the same variable. In only one analysis the R&A variable is a primary predictor, and in two analyses this variable is a secondary predictor. This contrasts with the results of the combined grade 2-4 group of regular elementary school children in which the R&A variable was the best predictor of reading performance in five out of six analyses.

Conclusions

Our first conclusion is that the real-word test (RWT) and the pseudoword test (PWT) can be considered as largely measuring the same things, and that they cannot be considered as operationalizations of different word identification 'routes' or procedures. This is most obvious for first graders. Here, the RWT-PWT correlations were extremely high. Moreover, the correlational strength with a GPC-like process (numeral naming speed) was identical for both the RWT and the PWT.

Also beyond grade 1, correlations between the RWT and the PWT remained high across the range of elementary-school ages (Study 1 and Study 2). It was predicted, however, that correlations with reading-*related* variables might change during reading development, and the question was whether differential relationships with the RWT and the PWT would emerge. The results supported a theoretical framework which conceptualizes reading development as an increasing establishment of 'phonologically underpinned recognition units' (Wimmer & Goswami, 1994). For second graders and beyond, the relationship between word identification ability and the sensitivity for rhyme and alliteration units in spoken language appeared substantial as compared to first graders. However, these relationships were not differential for the RWT and PWT.

Our second conclusion pertains to the results of the dyslexic children. In general, we believe that Wimmer's (1993) characterization of dyslexia as 'speed dyslexia' is largely correct. The finding that the 10-12 year-old LD children's reading performance is best predicted (and restricted!) by the speed variable (NMLt) is reminiscent to the much younger seven year-olds' data (grade 1) which indicated the same trend.

ACKOWLEDGEMENTS. We are indebted to Marlies Jansen for letting us use her numeral-naming task data which she collected at the R.K. Jenaplanschool St. Lukas in Drachten. We thank this school and its principal W.T.J. Kruiper for their generous cooperation in Study 2 of this report. We also would like to thank the following schools - in the town of Groningen - for children with learning disabilities: the 'Kimkiel', the 'Pestalozzischool', and the 'Trampolien'. Furthermore, we would like to thank the following students for assistance: Renate Mulder, Wijjanda Bootsma, Myra de Jong, and Claudine Kempa. Finally, we are indebted to the Netherlands Organization for Scientific Research (NWO) for grant R59-326 awarded to the first author.

REFERENCES

Bosman, A.M.T. (1994). *Reading and spelling in children and adults: Evidence for a single-route model.* Unpublished doctoral dissertation, University of Amsterdam.

Bradley, L., & Bryant, P. (1983). *Rhyme and reason in reading and spelling.* Ann Arbor, MI: The University of Michigan Press.

Brons, I. (1990). *De constructie van een meetinstrument voor fonologisch bewustzijn* (The construction of a measurement instrument on phonological awareness, Internal report on project 'Language acquisition and reading strategies in deaf children'. Groningen: University of Groningen.

Brus, B. Th., & Voeten, M.J.M. (1973). *Eén minuut test* (One-minute test). Nijmegen: Berkhout.

Coltheart, M. (1978). Lexical access in simple reading tasks. In G. Underwood (Ed.), *Strategies of information processing* (pp. 151-216). London: Academic Press.

Ehri, L.C. (1992). Reconceptualizing the development of sight word reading and its relationship to decoding. In P. Gough, L. Ehri, & R. Treiman (Eds.), *Reading acquisition* (pp. 107-143). Hillsdale, NJ: Erlbaum.

Juel, C. (1994). *Learning to read and write in one elementary school.* New-York: Springer-Verlag.

Nicolson, R.I., & Fawcett, A.J. (1990). Automaticity: A new framework for dyslexia research. *Cognition, 35,* 159-182.

Rack, J.P., Snowling, M.J., & Olson, R.K. (1992). The nonword reading deficit in developmental dyslexia: A review. *Reading Research Quarterly, 27,* 29-53.

Reitsma, P. (1990). Development of orthographic knowledge. In P. Reitsma & L. Verhoeven (Eds.), *Acquisition of reading in Dutch* (pp. 43-64). Dordrecht: Foris Publications.

Share, D.L. (1994). Deficient phonological processing in disabled readers implicates processing deficits beyond the phonological module. In K.P. van den Bos, L.S. Siegel, D.J. Bakker & D.L. Share (Eds.), *Current directions in dyslexia research* (pp. 149-167). Lisse: Swets & Zeitlinger.

Siegel, L.S. (1989). IQ is irrelevant to the definition of learning disabilities. *Journal of Learning Disabilities, 22,* 469 - 478.

Stanovich, K.E. (1988). Explaining the differences between the dyslexic and the garden-variety poor reader: The phonological-core variable-difference model. *Journal of Learning Disabilities, 21*, 590 - 604.

Stanovich, K.E. (1994). Are discrepancy-based definitions of dyslexia empirically defensible? In K.P. van den Bos, L.S. Siegel, D.J. Bakker & D.L. Share (Eds.), *Current directions in dyslexia research* (pp. 15-30). Lisse: Swets & Zeitlinger.

Toth, G., & Siegel, L.S. (1994). A critical evaluation of the IQ-achievement discrepancy-based definition of dyslexia. In K.P. van den Bos, L.S. Siegel, D.J. Bakker & D.L. Share (Eds.), *Current directions in dyslexia research* (pp. 45-70). Lisse: Swets & Zeitlinger.

van Bon, W.H.J., Schreuder, R., Duighuisen, H.C.M., & Kersholt, M.T. (1994). Phonemic segmentation: Testing and training. In K.P. van den Bos, L.S. Siegel, D.J. Bakker & D.L. Share (Eds.), *Current directions in dyslexia research* (pp. 169-181). Lisse: Swets & Zeitlinger.

van den Bos, K.P., & Spelberg, H.C.L. (1994). Word identification routes and reading disorders. In K.P.van den Bos, L.S. Siegel, D.J. Bakker & D.L. Share (Eds.), Current directions in dyslexia research (pp. 201-219). Lisse: Swets & Zeitlinger.

van den Broeck, W. (1993). Theorieën van woordherkenning en praktische implicaties (Theories of word recognition and practical implications). *Tijdschrift voor Orthopedagogiek (Journal of Special Education), 32*, 474-488.

Wimmer, H. (1993). Characteristics of developmental dyslexia in a regular writing system. *Applied Psycholinguistics, 14*, 1-33.

Wimmer, H., & Goswami, U. (1994). The influence of orthographic consistency on reading development: Word recognition in English and German children. *Cognition, 51*, 91 - 103.

EARLY LANGUAGE DEVELOPMENT AND KINDERGARTEN PHONOLOGICAL AWARENESS AS PREDICTORS OF READING PROBLEMS: FROM 3 TO 8 YEARS OF AGE

ÅKE OLOFSSON
Dept. of Psychology
Umeå University
Umeå, Sweden

JAN NIEDERSØE
Office of School Psychology
Bornholm
Denmark

ABSTRACT. The predictive relationship between early language development and reading acquisition was assessed in a longitudinal study of 248 Danish children from 3 years of age to grade 2 in school (age 8). At 3 years of age several aspects of language development were measured, i.e., vocabulary, language comprehension, speech production/articulation and sentence production. In kindergarten, at age 6, the children were tested on syntax, phonological production and language awareness as well as verbal class inclusion and working memory. In the latter part of grade 2, the children's word decoding ability was measured. A path analysis revealed significant paths from early phonological, morphological and syntactic variables, through working memory and language awareness in kindergarten, and to word decoding in Grade 2. Language awareness in kindergarten, as assessed with a group test in the present study, contributed uniquely to the prediction of Grade 2 word decoding ability even after controlling for working memory and language abilities in kindergarten. Morphological development measured at age 3 was found to have a unique effect on word decoding in Grade 2, beyond the effect mediated via kindergarten language variables. The interrelationship between various deficits in phonological processing is discussed.

As early as grade 2, some school children have a slower reading development than their peers. Early difficulties in word decoding may be the first signs of long lasting reading problems or dyslexia (Adams, 1990; Stanovich, 1993).

It has been determined from several studies that the strongest predictors of reading development are tasks demanding explicit phonological awareness, such as finding the first sound in a word, blending sounds (phonemes) into a word, or analysing the constituent sounds in a word (see e.g., Brady & Shankweiler, 1991; Joshi & Leong, 1993; Sawyer & Fox, 1991, for recent reviews). There is also intriguing evidence from research on dyslexic children, that phonological deficits may be a core deficit behind dyslexia (See Rack, 1994, for a review of this hypothesis).

C.K. Leong and R.M. Joshi (Eds.), Cross-Language Studies of Learning to Read and Spell, 289–303.

Recently, several studies have demonstrated the causal efficiency of phonemic awareness training in kindergarten on later success in reading acquisition (Ball & Blachman, 1991; Kozminsky & Kozminsky, 1993; Lundberg, Frost & Petersen, 1988; Olofsson, 1993; Schneider, Visé, Reimers & Blaesser, 1994). These findings have clear educational implications but do not answer questions about the origin of individual differences in phonological awareness. Although the obtained training effects indicate that particular environmental manipulations improve phonological awareness, even after such training individual differences still exist. Not all children respond to phonemic awareness training nor can their initial levels of ability be fully explained by early environmental factors. Furthermore, children with normal phonological awareness abilities in kindergarten may still run into reading problems at school (see review in Ball, 1993). The aim of the present longitudinal study was to relate early language development at age 3 to kindergarten phonological abilities and reading acquisition in grade 2.

Scarborough (1990), in a longitudinal study of 32 children from dyslexic families, found significant relationships between reading problems in grade 2 and the children's syntax and phonological production at 2 1/2 years of age. Bryant, Bradley, Maclean, & Crossland (1989) found a strong connection between nursery rhyme knowledge at age 3, development of phonological sensitivity during the pre-school years and success in learning to read. This relationship even prevailed after controlling for differences in intelligence, vocabulary, social background and initial phonological sensitivity.

There is now a growing consensus that the key deficit in dyslexia is located at the level of word recognition and that dyslexic children have difficulties with several related phonological tasks, such as naming, the use of phonological coding in short-term memory, categorical perception and speech production (see Stanovich, 1993). Whether all these phonological deficits reflect a single underlying problem is not clear. The present investigation will, in the kindergarten, include several measures of working memory with high demands on phonological processing ability (Brady, 1991).

Scarborough (1990) and Bryant et al. (1989) found stronger correlations between early language measures and reading than those reported for epidemiological studies (e.g., McGee, Williams & Silva, 1988; Stevenson, 1984; Westerlund, 1994). There are at least two reasons for this. First, the tests used by Scarborough (1990) and Bryant et al. (1989) are generally more elaborate, comprehensive, and detailed than those used for large scale population studies. Second, the dependent variables used by Bryant et al. (1989) contain measures of word recognition, whereas in epidemiological research the distinction between decoding and comprehension is less clear and hence the reading measures used are less sensitive to decoding problems. As to the predictor variables, it is also true that Scarborough's language measurements (at age 2 1/2) were based on elaborate analysis of tape-recorded speech from a 2-hour session with each child. Measures with high reliability is obligatory in order to detect long-term relationships. In addition, the Scarborough study used highly selected subjects, that is children of dyslexic parents, in order to maximise the effect of early language deficits compared to the control groups.

The present study used detailed early language measures that were more easily administered than in the Scarborough study, but the participants were from a normal population of children. The aim was to look at early measures of phonology and other language skills, well before the development of phonological awareness and the start of school, and to relate these early measures to the later development of word decoding ability.

Method

Participants

At the end of grade 2, 465 children on the Danish island Bornholm were screened using group tests for word decoding. For 248 of these children, language and speech data from the speech-therapist's screening at age 3 were available as well as language comprehension and linguistic awareness data from the kindergarten year (age 6).

Analysis of the differences between the sample having all data (N = 249) and the sample having missing data (that is, children having only grade 2 data) revealed no significant difference. The high power of this test (N = 463) meant that between group effects as small as $\eta^2 < .03$ should have been detected.

Procedure

The project is a longitudinal one and the present paper reports measures from four sessions (waves). The first of the sessions was in the children's homes, the second and third in kindergarten, and the last session in the children's schools.

Screening at 3 years of age

The children were tested by a speech therapist who had several years of experience with the testing procedure. Five speech therapists were involved in the testing, which is part of the regular annual procedure in this region. The test was carried out in playful and relaxed conditions and at least one of the parents was present but did not participate in the testing activities. The beginning of the session had two important goals; first, to establish the communication between child and tester and, second, to introduce some of the materials that were going to be used. The testing material and procedure were developed by Niedersøe (1986a, 1986b, 1990). The following tests were used:

Vocabulary. The child was presented with a series of pictures and prompted to respond to questions like *What is that?; What colour is ...?; What is he/she doing?* The number of correctly used words was scored, for the total of 23 items. The reliability of the test was .93 (Cronbach alpha).

Phonology 1. The child's pronunciation of words in other tasks, mainly the vocabulary task, was scored for phonological accuracy. For a total of 22 items, 12 measured the accuracy of single consonants, 3 measured consonants in a special position, and 5 items measured consonant pairs in initial position. Another item consisted of a consonant pair inside a word, and finally, a cluster with three consonants inside a word. The reliability of the test was .90 (Cronbach alpha).

Speech comprehension. The child had to comprehend 11 questions about a picture. (Examples of questions: *What is mummy bringing?*; *What is under the table?*; *How can the boy get his Teddy?*") (Chronbach alpha .96).

Sentence construction. This measure was scored as the sum of two variables. First, sentence length was registered into the categories, less than 4 words, 4 words, and more than 4 words. Second, the speech therapist rated the child's sentence construction, based on the overall impression from the complete testing session, into 3 categories, OK, almost OK, and under age standards.

Morphology. This measure consisted of three parts of which the first two reflected the use of word endings (the child's use of the plural form, 2 items, and the use of the present form of the verb, 3 items). The third was a colour naming task with 4 items. The measures were taken during the vocabulary task (Cronbach alpha .82).

Measures at start of kindergarten (Age 6)

Phonology 2a. The child had to repeat 10 sentences in which the 22 target sounds (items) were embedded. These target sounds consisted of 11 initial consonant pairs, 5 initial clusters of 3 consonants, 3 pairs of consonants within words and 3 single consonants. None of the sentences ended with a target sound, but in one sentence the first sound was the target (Kjær, 1980) (Cronbach alpha .77).

Phonology2b. Another phonology test but with longer words and a picture-naming format was used with 4 items; løbehjul, linial, fodgængerovergang, bagagebærer. (Ege, 1987).

Auditory digit span. This was tested with 3, 4 and 5 digits.

Sentence repetition. The child had to repeat a sentence. Three sentences with 14 syllables each were used.

Sentence completion. The beginning of a sentence was presented and the child had to continue and make a complete sentence. Four sentences were used.

Classification. The child had to name the common category for 4 objects, presented on pictures. Three sets of pictures were used (Ege, 1977).
Class inclusion 1. The child first had to listen to a verbal description of the target, and then to identify the target person or object on a picture. The task demanded cross-classification and class inclusion, and the verbal description interacted with the visual information and spatial layout of the picture in a complicated way. (For example; *Point at the smallest of the white cats,* on a picture with black and white cats of varying size.) The test was initially developed by Rommetveit (1978) and Rommetveit & Rommetveit (1980). Thirty-four of the original 100 items were translated from Norwegian and used in the present investigation (Cronbach alpha .77).

Working memory 1. The child had to listen to a short verbal instruction and then to make a drawing. The instructions were of varying length and referred to everyday objects as well as geometric forms, number, size, relation and direction. The test was first developed by Krogh (1977) and is widely known in Denmark under the name KTI. It is supposed to give a broad measure of language comprehension and of working memory but the two easiest items also tap more general aspects of child development.

Measures at the end of kindergarten (Age 6-7)

Class inclusion 2. The same test as in the beginning of the kindergarten year was used (Cronbach alpha .78).

Working memory 2. The same test as *working memory 1,* was used but was administered 7 month later.

Language Awareness. This measure included 5 subtests, all group tests, using small pictures. Five items required the child to mark the rhyming pair out of 3 given pictures. Four items required the judgement of word length. Six items needed the marking of number of syllables, 5 items the selection of a picture with a specific initial sound, and finally there were 5 items where the child had to mark the number of phonemes in words. The test was adopted from Lundberg et al. (1988).

School measures (Age 8)

Word reading. The test was given in grade 2 as a group test in April. The task was to read a word (silent) and then mark one out of four small pictures that represents the word. The test had 120 words and the time limit was 15 minutes. The scores used in the data analysis were computed from the number of correctly read words if the reader used the entire 15 minutes. If the reader finished before 15 minutes a function of words per minute was added to partly compensate for the time left. The logarithm of the scores was that taken in order to achieve a better approximation to the normal distribution. (In Denmark the test is titled *OS120.*)

Results

The descriptive statistics for the variables are presented in Table 1. The mean number of words read in the grade 2 reading test was 97 (SD 31) and the mean time used was 11 minutes and 20 seconds (SD 3:50). As indicated by the skewness values, there was a ceiling effect for the phonology measure in kindergarten (Phonology 2).

The intercorrelations between the variables (presented in Table 2) were substantial within the group of variables measured at the age of 3 years. High correlations also existed between repeated measures of the same variable (e.g., r=.67 between working memory 1 and 2) and between the two short term memory variables, sentence repetition and auditory digit span (r = .43). For language awareness in kindergarten the highest correlation was with word reading (in grade 2).

The correlation matrix is large and it must be interpreted with some caution considering the correlation coefficient's sensitivity to the distribution form and range of the variables (see Table 1). In order to disentangle the structure of the relationships from language variables at the age of 3 to word reading in grade 2, a multiple regression approach was used. Hence, the linear relationships between word decoding in grade 2 and the pre-school predictor variables was modelled using the method of path analysis (Duncan, 1975; Werts & Linn, 1970). A model was formulated with the variables ordered according to the time of measurement. That is, three waves of independent variables (measured at 3 years, kindergarten Fall and kindergarten Spring) followed by language awareness (kindergarten Spring) and finally the word reading test in grade 2.

All variables were first entered into the regression equations. Then the variables not reaching significance was deleted and thereafter the new restricted set of equations was analysed. This "cleaning" procedure decreases the risk of capitalising on chance and thus substantially reduces the proportion of explained variance in the dependent variable (R^2) as compared to when all independent variables are entered in the equation. During the cleaning steps some problems with multicollinearity were detected but disappeared after the deletion of the variable phonology 2b.

Table 1. Descriptive statistics for the variables.

Variable	Mean	SD	Skewness	Min	Max
Age 3					
Vocabulary	16.98	5.25	-1.58	0	23
Phonology1	18.76	3.52	-1.23	6	22
Speech compreh.	9.35	2.69	-2.15	0	11
Sentence constr.	3.21	1.47	-1.47	0	4
Morphology	3.85	1.95	-.25	0	6
Kindergarten, Fall (Age 6)					
Phonology2	21.55	1.22	-4.44	13	22
Phonology2b	3.29	.90	-1.17	0	4
Aud. digit sp.	1.96	.70	-.17	0	3
Sentence repet.	2.11	.80	-.45	0	3
Sentence complet.	3.10	1.09	-1.10	0	4
Classification	3.24	1.29	-.94	0	6
Class inclusion 1	17.17	4.90	.20	5	31
Working memory 1	3.25	1.01	-.03	1	5
Kindergarten, Spring (Age 6 1/2)					
Class inclusion 2	21.53	5.14	-.34	6	32
Working memory 2	3.77	.91	-.22	2	5
Language awareness	18.00	3.55	-.34	6	25
Grade 2, Spring (Age 8)					
Word reading	.92	.33	-.64	.00	1.48

Note. N = 248.

The parameter estimates of the path coefficients are presented in Figure 1. Variables with no significant contribution are omitted. It can be seen that after entering the age-3 and kindergarten variables into the regression equation the kindergarten language awareness variable does still contribute significantly to the prediction of grade 2 reading. This is not a function of low predictive value for the preceding variables, since they are explaining more than 20% of the variance in word reading. Entering language awareness increased R^2 by only .036, but because of the large sample size this small contribution is significant (F Change $(1, 242) = 11.6$, $p < .001$). To summarise, the results revealed a high predictive capacity for the language and memory variables and a relatively small unique contribution for the language awareness variable. The uniqueness in language awareness is moreover demonstrated in its regression on working memory 2, class inclusion 2 and speech comprehension. This results in $R^2 = .15$, which is much lower than the variance explained in working memory 2 and class inclusion 2 ($R^2 = .25$ and .52 respectively).

Figure 1 also shows a very strong relationship between the test-retest measures of both working memory and class inclusion, which further adds to the picture of an interpretable and clear structure in the data. The only variable among the age-3 tests that had a direct effect on the word decoding variable, not being mediated via the kindergarten variables, was the morphology variable. However, the strength of the morphology variable must be interpreted in the light of the rather high correlation within the group of language variables at age 3 (presented in Table 2), and it should also be noted that the other four age-3 variables are hampered by skewed distributions (see Table 1). Taken together, the results indicate that we have a rather unspecific language factor at age-3, which first affects kindergarten language variables and thereafter affects learning to read. In the middle of this causal chain (in kindergarten) the important variables, in the sense of having direct effects on reading, seem to involve memory.

Finally, there is another reason for being cautious when comparing the relative strengths of the early language variables. A closer inspection of the pre-school data revealed unexpectedly low scores (and lower correlation) by one of the speech-therapists on the age-3 variables vocabulary and phonology. The only explanation for this finding is that the speech therapist **must** have failed (for unknown reasons) in recording the results for the vocabulary tasks. It would be tempting to delete the data collected by this therapist and make a new analysis, which would surely give much stronger relationships between early vocabulary, phonology and grade 2 reading. However, such an analysis would suffer from having an element of ad hoc, thus, we refrain from pursuing this line of extended analysis.

Table 2. Intercorrelations between pre-school language variables and word decoding in grade 2.

Variable	1	2	3	4	5	6	7	8	9	10	11	12	13	14	15	16
1. Vocabulary	1.0															
2. Phonology 1	.32	1.0														
3. Speech compreh.	.64	.28	1.0													
4. Sentence constr.	.33	.59	.42	1.0												
5. Morphology	.72	.45	.38	.45	1.0											
6. Phonology 2	.17	.46	.18	.38	.23	1.0										
7. Phonology 2b	.14	.40	.09	.33	.30	.30	1.0									
8. Aud. digit sp.	.27	.29	.19	.19	.35	.17	.38	1.0								
9. Sentence repet.	.16	.30	.16	.26	.27	.18	.38	.43	1.0							
10. Sentence complet.	.12	.17	.08	.10	.17	.29	.26	.26	.32	1.0						
11. Classification	-.07	.15	.01	.14	.09	.13	.25	.23	.20	.25	1.0					
12. Class inclusion 1	.09	.16	.11	.21	.24	.06	.23	.23	.32	.19	.26	1.0				
13. Working memory 1	.07	.25	.08	.28	.17	.20	.19	.24	.35	.20	.16	.42	1.0			
14. Class inclusion 2	.17	.26	.19	.27	.29	.11	.24	.33	.40	.32	.24	.67	.37	1.0		
15. Working memory 2	.14	.13	.20	.24	.18	.19	.19	.22	.29	.15	.04	.29	.46	.32	1.0	
16. Language awareness	.22	.16	.26	.21	.14	.17	.17	.15	.21	.15	.10	.18	.18	.26	.29	1.0
17. Word reading	.23	.18	.23	.29	.27	.32	.10	.19	.30	.17	.08	.24	.35	.30	.34	.32

Note. All coefficients greater than .10 are significant ($p < .05$) N = 248.

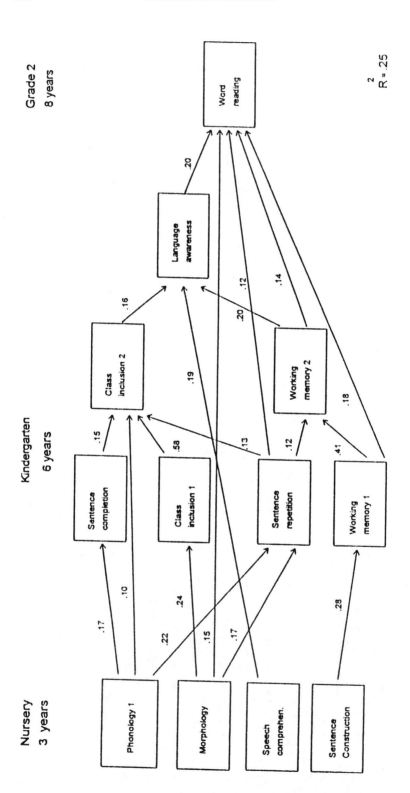

Figure 1. The results of the path analysis with the silent word reading test in Grade 2 (May) as the dependent variable. For each arrow the path coefficient is printed. All path coefficients are significant at *p* < .05. N = 248

To summarise, the results suggest that there is a relationship between early language abilities and learning to read and this relationship extends beyond the proportion mediated by language and language awareness in the late preschool years.

Discussion

The present results show that there is some continuity between early development and learning to read five years later. Phonology as assessed by measures of speech production, working memory, and language awareness, seem to predict later reading skills. The findings in this study extend the results from Scarborough (1990) to a population of normal children. It should further be noted that the present sample does not include children with delayed school start (i.e., children from the original screening at the age of 3, but now in grade 1 instead of grade 2). That is, the correlations reported here are not likely to be inflated by the presence of children with severe language problems (acting more or less like "outliers" in the statistical sense).

The size of the correlation between kindergarten language awareness and reading in grade 2 is lower in the present study than that reported by Lundberg, Olofsson & Wall (1980). This slightly lower correlation could however be expected, since the use of a relatively quick and short group test generally results in lower reliability compared to the carefully individual testing used by Lundberg et al. (1980). Furthermore, the language awareness variable used in the present study is a sum of syllable and phoneme awareness tasks. The strong skewness and the restricted range of the phonemic awareness subtests prevented them from being used separately.

The competent, well planned and strictly administered individual testing implemented in the first part of the present study probably contributed positively to the reported relationships. The relatively small contribution of the kindergarten language variables, which could be a result of their lower reliability, is also in accordance with Scarborough's (1991) suggestion that the measurement of a language ability will give most information if it is conducted during a period when development typically undergoes rapid improvements (see also Elbro, in press).

An interesting finding in the present study is the significant effect of the morphology variable on reading which has a direct effect in addition to the effect mediated by the kindergarten variables. It may be that the early signs of sensitivity to the morphological dimensions of language are related to the child's ability to explore and understand the morpho-phonemic relationships between spoken and written words several years later.

The highly predictive nursery rhyme knowledge variable measured by Bryant et al. (1989) at age 3:4 is an ingeniously simple and robust measurement. Still it may be of less explanatory value since the causality is unclear. Bryant et al. (1989) seem to conclude that nursery rhymes enhance the development of phonological sensitivity (phonological awareness) and may work as an effective cause, executed in an informal and implicit way in mother child interaction and peer groups. However, an equally plausible explanation is that knowledge of nursery rhymes acts as an indicator of the child's basic language development, that is that the child with enough talent for appreciating phonological structures will find it interesting and amusing to engage in nursery rhymes and language play, and thus learn more rhymes. According to this view, the child, or the child's phonological processing system, is picking and creating an environment that will include nursery rhymes. Parents having children interested in rhymes will probably find it more encouraging to do language play with their children than parents whose children do not show any interest in such activities. It may also be that the child's early phonological development is heavily biologically constrained, and that deficits in the phonological system cause deviant and/or delayed development in all related language areas as well as in later reading development. There are ample individual differences in early speech development (e.g., Studdert-Kennedy, 1986) and researchers have not been able to explain these differences by external sources in the children's environment (Vihman, Kay, de Boysson-Bardies, Durand, & Sundberg, 1994).

The present data are congruent with a language deficit hypothesis of dyslexia (Catts, 1989) as well as with the idea of a "phonological core deficit" (Stanovich, 1988; Rack, 1994). However, there is still much research work needed before we can understand the exact nature of the well documented connections between different phonological abilities and reading acquisition (Brady & Shankweiler, 1991; Elbro, (in press); Elbro, Nielsen & Petersen, 1994).

To conclude, the present findings of a significant relationship between early phonological differences and the development of visual word recognition skills are in line with the results of Scarborough (1990, 1991) and Bryant et al. (1989) and lend further support to Fowler's (1991) suggestion that we need to do more research on basic phonological development and its relationship to the ontogenesis of phonological awareness and reading ability. The nature of phonological processing, the structure and interrelationship between various phonological abilities and the causality involved in the relationships between phonological abilities and reading are important domains of which our understanding still needs to be refined (Wagner & Torgesen, 1987).

Author Note: The study was supported in part by grants from the Egmont Foundation to Jan Niedersøe.

REFERENCES

Adams, M.J. (1990). *Beginning to read:Thinking and learning about print.* Cambridge, MA: MIT Press.

Ball, E.W. (1993). Phonological awareness:What's important and to whom? *Reading and Writing*, 5, 141-160.

Ball, E.W., & Blachman, B.A. (1991). Does phoneme segmentation training in kindergarten make a difference in early word recognition and developmental spelling? *Reading Research Quarterly*, 26, 49-66.

Brady, S.A. (1991). The role of working memory in reading disability. In S. A. Brady & D. P. Shankweiler (Eds.), *Phonological processes in literacy* (pp. 129-151). Hillsdale, NJ: Lawrence.

Brady, S.A, & Shankweiler, D.P. (Eds.). (1991). *Phonological processes in literacy.* Hillsdale, NJ: Lawrence.

Bryant, P.E., Bradley, L., Maclean, M., & Crossland, J. (1989). Nursery rhymes, phonological skills and reading. *Journal of Child Language, 16*, 407-428

Catts, H. (1989). Defining dyslexia as a developmental language disorder. *Annals of Dyslexia, 39*, 50-64.

Duncan, O.D. (1975). *Introduction to structural equation models.* New York: Academic Press.

Ege, B. (1987). Sproglig test II (Language test II). Herning, DK: Specialpedagogisk Forlag.

Ege, B. (1977). *Sproglig test III (Language test III).* Herning, DK: Special-pedagogisk Forlag.

Elbro, C. (in press). Early linguistic abilities and reading development: A review and a hypothesis about underlying differences in distinctness of phonological representations of lexical items. *Reading and Writing*.

Elbro, C., Nielsen, I., & Petersen, D.K. (1994). Dyslexia in adults: Evidence for deficits in non-word reading and in the phonological representation of lexical items. *Annals of Dyslexia, 44*, 205-226.

Fowler, A.E. (1991). How early phonological development might set the stage for phonemic awareness. In S. A. Brady & D. P. Shankweiler (Eds.), *Phonological processes in literacy* (pp. 97-118). Hillsdale, NJ: Lawrence Erlbaum.

Joshi, M., & Leong, C.K. (Eds.), (1993). *Reading disabilites: Diagnosis and component processes.* Dordrecht: Kluwer Academic Publishers.

Kjær, B. E. (1980). *Nikolaj [Nikolaj].* Herning, DK: Specialpedagogisk Forlag.

Kozminsky, L. & Kozminsky, E. (1993). *The effects of early phonological awareness training on reading success.* Paper presented at the 5th European Association for Research on Learning and Instruction (EARLI) Conference, Aix-En-Provence, August, 1993.

Krogh, T. (1977). *Kontroleret Tegneiagttagelse.* [Controlled drawing observation]. Søllerød, DK: Pedagogisk Psykologisk Rådgivning.

Lundberg, I., Frost, J., & Petersen, O.-P. (1988). Effects of an extensive program for stimulating phonological awareness in preschool children. *Reading Research Quarterly, 23*, 263-284.

Lundberg, I., Olofsson, Å, & Wall, S. (1980). Reading and spelling skills in the first school years predicted from phonemic awareness skills in kindergarten. *Scandinavian Journal of Psychology, 21*, 159-173.

McGee, R., Williams, S., & Silva, P.A. (1988). Slow starters and long-term backward readers: A replication and extension. *Brittish Journal of Educational Psychology, 58*, 330-337.

Niedersøe, J. (1986a). *Den Bornholmske 3-års screening [The speech screening of 3-year olds at Bornholm]*. Herning, DK: Specialpedagogisk Forlag.

Niedersøe, J. (1986b). *Den Bornholmske 3-års screening [The speech screening of 3-year olds at Bornholm]*. Dansk Audiologopædi. 22, 3. 114-117

Niedersøe, J. (1990). *Den Bornholmske 3-års screening [The speech screening of 3-year olds at Bornholm]*. Dansk Audiologopædi. 26, 2, 55-62

Olofsson, Å. (1993). The relevance of phonological awareness in learning to read: Scandinavian longitudinal and quasi-experimental studies. In R. M. Joshi & C. K. Leong (Eds.), *Reading disabilities:Diagnosis and component processes* (pp. 185-198). Dordrecht: Kluwer.

Rack, J. (1994). Dyslexia: The phonological deficit hypothesis. In A. Fawcett & R. Nicolson (Eds.), *Dyslexia in children: Multidisciplinary perspectives* (pp. 5-37). London: Harvester.

Rommetveit, R. (1978). On Piagetian cognitive operations, semantic competence, and message structure in adult-child communication. In I. Markova (Ed.), *The social context of language* (pp. 113-150). N.Y.: Wiley.

Rommetveit, S. & Rommetveit, R: (1980). *Pek på [Point at]*. Oslo: Tiden.

Sawyer, D. E. & Fox, B. J. (Eds.), (1991). *Phonological awareness in reading: The evolution of current perspectives*. New York: Springer-Verlag.

Scarborough H.S. (1990). Very early language deficits in dyslexic children. *Child Development, 61*, 1728-1743.

Scarborough H.S. (1991). Early syntactic development of dyslexic children. *Annals of Dyslexia, 41*, 207-220.

Schneider, W., Visé, M., Reimers, P. & Blaesser, B. (1994). Auswirkungen eines Trainings der sprachlichen Bewusstheit auf den Schriftspracherwerb in der Schule. [Effects of language awareness training on reading acquisition at school]. *Zeitschrift für Pädagogische Psychologie, 8* (3/4).

Stevenson, J. (1984). Predictive value of speech and language screening. *Developmental Medicine and Child Neurology, 26*, 528-538.

Stanovich, K. E. (1988). Explaining the difference between the dyslexic and garden-variety poor reader: The phonological-core variable-difference model. *Journal of Learning Disabilities, 21*, 590-612.

Stanovich, K. E. (1993). Problems in the differential diagnosis of reading disabilities. In R. M. Joshi & C. K. Leong (Eds.), *Reading disabilities:Diagnosis and component processes* (pp. 3-31). Dordrecht: Kluwer.

Studdert-Kennedy, M. (1986). Sources of variability in early speech development. In J. S. Perkell & D. H. Klatt (Eds.), *Invariance and variability in speech processes* (pp. 58-76). Hillsdale, NJ: Lawrence Erlbaum.

Vihman, M. M., Kay, E., de Boysson-Bardies, B., Durand, C., & Sundberg, U. (1994). External sources of individual differences? A cross-linguistic analysis of the phonetics of mothers' speech to 1-year-old children. *Developmental Psychology, 30*, 651-662.

Wagner, R.K., & Torgesen, J.K. (1987). The nature of phonological processing and its causation, *Psychological Bulletin, 101*, 192-212.

Werts, C. E. & Linn, R. L. (1970). Path analysis: Psychological examples. *Psychological Bulletin, 74*, 193-212.

Westerlund, M. (1994). *Barn med tal- och språkavvikelser. En prospektiv longitudinell epidemiologisk studei av en årskull uppsalabarn vid 4, 7 och 9 års ålder. [Children with speech and language deviations. A prospective longitudinal epidemiological study of a total age cohort at 4, 7, 9 years of age].* Uppsala University, Dissertations in Medicine, 5, Uppsala, Sweden.

SPELLING DEVELOPMENT AND METALINGUISTIC TRAINING BEFORE SCHOOL ENTRANCE: THE EFFECTS OF DIFFERENT METALINGUISTIC TRAINING ON SPELLING DEVELOPMENT IN FIRST GRADE

SOLVEIG-ALMA H. LYSTER
Institute for special education
University of Oslo
Postbox 1140, Blindern
0317 Oslo, Norway

ABSTRACT. This paper presents the long term effects of two different metalinguistic intervention programs in kindergarten on spelling development. Experimental group 1 received a training program with activities that focused the children's attention on the internal sound structure of words. Experimental group 2 received a training program with activities that focused the children's attention on morphological parts of words (e.g., prefixes, suffixes). A control group received no intervention but was regularly visited by the experimenter. Results from different metalinguistic pretests show that children with poorly educated mothers had the lowest scores before entering the experiment. The children received training 25 - 30 minutes weekly for a total period of 17 weeks. At the time of the pretest the age of the children was 5 years 10 months to 6 years 9 months. Both the group receiving metaphonological training and the group receiving metamorphological training benefited in terms of their spelling development. For the school measures, however, significant interactions between group and mother's education suggested that children of poorly educated mothers profited the most from metaphonological training and that children with highly educated mothers profited the most from metamorphological training. Factor analysis of the pre-school measures shows that different linguistic and cognitive measures seems to contribute independently to spelling development. Some of the possible linguistic processes underlying the development of spelling are affected by metalinguistic training while others are not. Implications for teaching and therapy will be discussed.

Recent knowledge about spelling development and spelling failure point to the central role of phonology (Ehri, 1984; Griffith, 1992; Read, 1986; Treiman, 1993). In addition, orthographic knowledge also plays an important role in the development of spelling skills. Until orthographic or word-specific spelling is available the children make use of a phonological spelling strategy. An interplay of the developing phonological and orthographic abilities might be critical to the acquisition of spelling (Snowling 1994). Visual memory impairment might hinder development of lexical knowledge about orthographic structures, but development of phonological skills is more critical to spelling development. Deficits in phonological processing, therefore, have the most devasting effect on spelling development.

C.K. Leong and R.M. Joshi (Eds.), Cross-Language Studies of Learning to Read and Spell, 305–330.
© 1997 *Kluwer Academic Publishers. Printed in the Netherlands.*

Linguistic awareness, phonological processing skills and spelling development

Linguistic awareness is explained by Tunmer and Herriman (1984) as "...the ability to reflect upon and manipulate the structural features of spoken language, treating language itself as an object of thoughts, as opposed to simply using the language system to comprehend and produce sentences" (p.12). When children are linguistically aware they can turn their attention from meaning to form. Phonological awareness refers to the ability to reflect upon the sound structure of words.

It is important to differentiate between different kinds of phonological awareness as shown by Bertelson, Cary, and Alegria (1986) and Morais, Alegria, and Content (1987). Sensitivity to rhyme is one level of phonological skill and awareness of rhyme develops naturally; but awareness of phonemes comes after formal instruction. More difficult phonological tasks such as sound deletion seem to continue to cause children problems up to the age of around nine or ten years (Goswami & Bryant, 1990). Phonemic awareness is a highly specific form of phonological awareness. Both preliterate children and illiterate adults are able to make comparisons of phonological durations, to segment words into syllables, and to appreciate rhyming relationships (Morais, Cary, Alegria & Bertelson, 1979). The acquisition of phonemic awareness, however, seems to develop as a result of reading acquisition (Ehri & Wilce, 1980, 1985; Morais, 1991) and its development requires explicit instruction in the alphabetic code. The acquisition of phonemic awareness and the acquisition of grapheme-phoneme correspondence knowledge are intimately related.

There has been much research into the relationship between phonemic segmentation skills and learning to read and to spell (Blachman, 1991; Bradley & Bryant, 1983; Lundberg Olofsson, & Wall, 1980; Mann, 1991; Olofsson & Lundberg, 1985; Schneider & Näslund, 1993; Stanovich, 1986; Stanovich, Cunningham & Cramer, 1984; Tornéus, 1987; Tunmer, Herriman, & Nesdale, 1988). Phonemic awareness does, however, seem to be more strongly correlated with spelling than with reading (Ellis & Large, 1987; Juel, Griffith & Gough,1986; Snowling & Perin, 1983). There is evidence that the awareness of the phonological structure of spoken words is important in the beginning stages of spelling acquisition (Griffith, 1992; Treiman, 1992).

During the elementary school years children rapidly increase their use of conventional spelling rules. Morphemic spellings, based on the children's knowledge and awareness of the morphemic parts of words, appear later. Thus, as Henry (1993) points out for reading, it is important to consider the additional strategies that older students require for analysing longer words. One such strategy is to be aware of and use morphologic patterns in words.

Morphemes may be entire words and meaningful parts of words such as prefixes and suffixes, and bases or roots. Inflectional morphemes indicate plurality, third person, singular verbs, and verb tense. Derivational morphemes are affixes added to a word to yield different grammatical forms (i.e., to make the noun "singer" from the verb "sing"). Strategies based on morphology and graphemic conventions develop later than the phonemic strategies used for spelling, and learning disabled students do not seem to develop knowledge about the morphemic structure of words by themselves (Elbro, 1990). When they spell words they have problems with morphemic boundaries and lack awareness and knowledge of the morphemic system (Bruck & Waters, 1988; Carlisle, 1987; Henry, 1993; Taft, 1985). Neither the grapheme-phoneme corresponding rules nor the insight into morphological knowledge is automatic (Adams, 1990). Explicit training might be very important for children who have problems developing spelling.

Training Studies

There is rather strong evidence for the fact that training children in phonological skills has a beneficial effect on reading progress (Ball & Blachman, 1988; Bradley and Bryant, 1983, 1985; Cunningham, 1990; Hatcher, Hulme & Ellis, 1994; Lundberg, Frost & Petersen, 1988). In some of these studies it was spelling that seemed to benefit the most from phonological and phonemic awareness training (Bradley & Bryant, 1983; Lundberg et al. , 1988).

Margit Tornéus (1983) found that an experimental group receiving metaphonological training in grade one developed their metaphonological awareness to a significantly higher level than a control group. The experimental group, however, did not develop to a significantly higher level in reading or spelling. Comparisons between the children with the lowest metaphonological performance on the pretest in the experimental and control groups, however, showed that the training had improved the spelling ability, along with the metaphonological ability, in the group of low performing experimental children to a significantly higher level than the low performing control children had reached. Lundberg et al. (1988) showed that children trained in phonological awareness were further ahead in spelling than in reading compared to a control group. The difference in reading between the control group and the experimental group in grade one were only marginal. But the difference between the spelling performances for the two groups were clear and significant at both grade one and grade two levels. Similarly, Olofsson (1989) found that training in the area of phonemic awareness before school entrance had a significant effect on spelling development in school but not on reading development. Olofsson concluded that young children make much more use of phonological processes in spelling than in reading. The effect did not extend to the spelling of irregular words, however. These results show that phonemic awareness training in preschool has an even greater effect on spelling development than on reading development.

In Norway some teachers have used an articulatory component besides a visual and phonological one in teaching children to read and spell. This method, The Articulatory Sequential Analysis, developed by Skjelfjord (1983, 1987), focuses on both phonological sequences and the articulatory sequences in words. It has proved to be effective for reading and spelling development compared to other phonic methods (Lie, 1991). If children who struggle to identify the sound sequences of words are able to identify the articulatory sequences, this might help them in the spelling process.

Treiman (1993) found that first graders did not expect morphemes to be spelled in a consistent fashion. Her study showed that children learn many orthographic constraints implicitly, through experience with print (See also Cunningham & Stanovich, 1990 and Stanovich & West, 1989). Exposure to print, however, is not enough to learn the spellings of different morphemes. Treiman suggests that children should be given extensive instruction to help them to understand the morphological basis of spelling.

There are few experimental studies of morphological awareness training. Notable exception is the work of Henry (1989, 1993) and of Elbro and Arnbak (in press) who report a training study of morphological awareness with dyslexic students. As part of an experimental study, Henry gave 3rd and 5th grade classes five weeks of instruction on language origin and morpheme patterns in the English language. The post-test showed that the students' knowledge of morphological patterns as well as decoding and spelling performance clearly benefited from the training.

Elbro and Arnbak's study (in press) was concerned with teaching morphology to ten- to twelve-year-old dyslexics and with the effects on reading and spelling. The effects of training on reading were quite small and resulted in a more meaning-focused reading strategy for the dyslexic students in the experimental group as compared with the students in the control group. The subjects in the experimental group did not, however, advance more than the controls in word decoding or nonword naming. The gains in spelling were clearly larger in the experimental group than in the control group.

Henry (1993) urges teachers to frequently present used morphemes in their classrooms and Elbro and Arnbak (In press) suggest that an increase in morphological awareness might help dyslexic students to develop alternative strategies which can carry them through reading development despite the difficulty they have with phonology. However, Henry, Elbro and Arnbak have not considered the introduction of morphemes in pre-school or the early grades. We do not know if or in what ways awareness of morphological structures in words will contribute to reading and spelling development in children younger than those participating in Henry's study and to dyslexics younger than the subjects participating in Elbro's study. Neither do we know if morphological awareness training in preschool will promote reading and spelling development.

Present Study

The study presented here is part of a large-scale longitudinal intervention study. One of the questions put forward was whether training in phonological awareness before school entrance affects spelling development in first grade and if all children would benefit from such training. Another question was whether training in phonological awareness was more effective than other types of metalinguistic training, e.g., morphological training. The study also focuses on the predictive validity of different linguistic and cognitive factors.

Method

SUBJECTS

A total of 273 monolingual Norwegian children attending 25 different preschool groups in two different communities outside Oslo participated in the study presented here. The children were first seen ten months before school entrance. Their mean age was then between 5 years 10 months and 6 years 9 months. Norwegian children do not enter school until August the year they reach seven years. No letter instruction and reading or writing instruction is given to children in the ordinary kindergarten system.

Children who were reading at the time of the pretest were excluded from all analyses presented here and this eliminated 16 children identified as readers and 14 identified as beginning readers. The mother's education is used as a central variable in the analyses. Information about the mother's education was not received from 12 of the children and six children moved to other communities before the end of first grade. The analyses presented here were run with the results from the 225 pre-reading children who were still available at the end of first grade and who could be divided into different groups according to their mothers' education. In school the children attended 24 different classes in 18 different schools with a total of 324 children in these classes.

DESIGN

The children were allocated to two experimental groups and one control group. The first experimental group, *The Phonological Group* received training in phonological and phonemic awareness. The training might be viewed as a combination of the training used by Bradley and Bryant (1983, 1985) and Lundberg et al. (1988). The children were exposed to letters corresponding to the sounds they were working/playing with and they were focusing on the articulatory positions for the different sounds and the way the sounds were made. Examples were: The sound /s/ for the letter S was called the snake sound because it sounds similar to the sound some snakes make, and the sound for the letter F was called the rabbit blow because first you look like a rabbit and then you blow to make the /f/. When working/playing with onsets or rimes the children were also exposed to the written words. Their attention was kept on those parts of the words that looked the same and sounded the same, e. g. onsets and rimes.

The second experimental group, *The Morphological Group,* received training in the area of morphemic awareness and morphemic knowledge. They made compound words out of two words, and they found the different words in compound words. They learned about different prefixes and suffixes. The children in this group were also exposed to the written forms of the words they were working/playing with (See appendix 1 for more details).

The *Control Group* children received no training, but were tested and regularly visited by the experimenter. In this way the control group received more attention from people outside the preschool setting than the experimental groups. The pre-school teachers in the experimental groups took care of all the testing and the training with only one or two visits from the experimenter.

Of the 225 pre-readers about whom there was information about the mother's education, 87 were in the Phonological Group, 107 were in the Morphological Group, and 31 were in the Control Group.

The pre-school teachers responsible for the different pre-school groups were taught about reading and spelling development, language development and linguistic awareness the year before they entered the experiment. During the intervention period, the two groups of pre-school teachers had separate lectures and work-shops in which they were given precise instructions about how to carry out the phonological awareness training in one group, and how to carry out the morphological awareness training in the other group. Methodological ideas, however, were suggested by the pre-school teachers themselves. The training period was from

October/November to March/April, the effective amount of training being approximately 25-30 minutes per week for 17 weeks when days off and holidays are accounted for.

No information was given to the teachers in school about the content of the pre-school training until after the children were tested at the end of first grade. The reading and spelling method in all classes was a combination of a whole language approach and phonics. Many teachers in the two communities represented in the study had been for a while to some extent "whole language" oriented, but in the years before the pre-school intervention or at the time of the pre-school intervention, had moved to a more phonic based method.

Measures

PRESCHOOL MEASURES

Pre-tests and post-tests in the area of linguistic knowledge and metalinguistic awareness. All children in the experiment were given the same set of cognitive, linguistic and metalinguistic tasks before the intervention and once more six months later when the intervention ended. These tasks were administered as group tests (Lyster & Tingleff, 1991). The tests were developed to measure different metalinguistic abilities at different levels of development. Measures of the children's vocabulary, naming speed, syntactic knowledge and memory for word sequences were included. Since this study was mainly conducted by one person on a large group of children it was necessary to develop tests that could be presented as group tests (see Lyster, 1995, for a more detailed description of the entire test battery). The following tasks within linguistic and cognitive areas were included in the pre-school battery: *Identification of Word Length, Rhyme Identification, Syllable Identification, Word Onset/Alliteration, Sound Blending, Phoneme Segmentation, Sound Deletion, Knowledge of Compound Words, Word Compounds* (to make compound words out of two presented words), *Analyses of Compound Words, Segmentation of Sentences into Words, Syntactic Awareness, Memory for Word Sequences, Homophones* (naming of two similar sounding nouns/verbs out of four presented pictures), and *Listening Comprehension* (sentences of differing syntactic and morphologic difficulties).

SCHOOL MEASURES

Spelling

All spelling tests were conducted by the experimenter in all 24 classes. If a child was absent the day of testing, spelling data were not collected from this child.

Spelling at school entrance. During the first week in school the children were presented 5 words which they had to write: is (ice-cream), bil (car), kone (wife/lady), fisk (fish), and strømpe (stocking). Each word was first presented to the children embedded in a sentence, then as a single word. The children were told to try to spell the words even if they just knew the first letter, and they could even play-write. The words *is* (ice-cream) and *bil* (car) are words the children probably have seen often in books and on posters in their environment. The most complex word they were presented, *strømpe* (stocking), is a well known word in the children's vocabulary, but it is a word that seldom is seen on posters and in Norwegian books for children. Each correct letter in correct position received a one-point score. A child spelling all words correctly thus received 20 points. Internal reliability (alpha) was found to be 0.95.

Spelling measures at the end of first grade

I. Spelling Regular Words. This spelling test is part of Gjessing's (1958) spelling test. The second part of his test is the next test presented, Spelling Irregular Words. All words were first presented to the children in a sentence, and then alone. The 18 items in the test are presented in Appendix 2. Gjessing's scoring system, one point for each correct word, was used.

II. Spelling Irregular Words. The 18 words in this test are presented in Appendix 2. The test contains words that do not have a one-to-one phoneme-grapheme correspondence. Some of the words contains so called "silent letters", while others have spellings that do not correspond to the pronunciation of the words. The same scoring system is used as for Spelling Regular Words.

III. Spelling Complex Regular Words. In composing this test effort was made to include words with consonant clusters initially (onset clusters) and/or finally (rime clusters). The clusters in the different words are assumed to correspond to phonological structures of varying difficulties. All these words do not occur as frequently in children's books or school books as the regular words from Gjessing's word list above, but were well known to the children. All words were first presented to the children embedded in a sentence in a way that should enlighten the meaning of the word, and then alone. The nine words in the test are presented in Appendix 2. The children's responses are coded in two ways. One of the scoring systems used is to give one point for each correctly spelled word, while another system is to give one point for each sound coded into a correct letter in a correct position. The word "leverpostei" contained an irregular diphthong, but both phonetic spelling and the correct irregular spelling of the diphthong *ei* (/æi/) in "leverpostei" were accepted for the present analyses. Internal reliability (alpha) for this test was found to be. 83 when using the scoring system of one point for each correct word.

IV. Spelling non-words. This test is composed of nine one -, two -, and three syllable non-words. The non-word structures were easy VCV and CVC combinations as well as a more complicated CCCVCC and CVCCC structures (See Appendix 2). The children were told that all the words they would be presented with were non-words. But even if they were given words with no meaning, they should try to spell the non-words as they thought they should be spelled. Each non-word was presented twice before the children wrote it. The results were coded in two ways. One of the scoring systems was to give the children one mark for each correctly spelled non-word. Another system was to give them one mark for each number of correct letters in correct positions (which means that no points are given if a phoneme is correctly analyzed and converted to the corresponding letter if the letter is not presented in its correct position in the letter sequence). Internal reliability (alpha) was found to be. 78 when using the scoring system of one point for each correct word.

Other school measures

Mathematics. The mathematical test used for the project is one developed by Tornes (1968). The reliability, using the Spearman-Brown split-half formula, for the addition part, subtraction part, and practical part (mathematical problems) were 0.98, 0.96, and 0.88 respectively.

IQ-measures. Three sub-tests from Wechsler Intelligence Scale for Children-Revised (WISC-R): Vocabulary, Similarities, and Digit Span, were given to the children 3-4 months after school entrance. The Standard Raven's Progressive Matrices (Raven, 1956) was given to the children at the time of the reading and spelling tests at the end of first grade.

Results

STATISTICAL ISSUES AND EVALUATION OF ASSUMPTIONS

Non-parametric statistics are presented in some of the analyses to be reported if assumptions for analysis of variance and multiple regression were violated. The Mann-Whitney U test was then used to compare the distributions of scores between two independent samples and the Kruskal-Wallis test to compare the distributions of scores for three independent samples.

PRETEST ANALYSES

Mother's education and children's linguistic development

Children with highly educated mothers entered the study with a higher linguistic and cognitive level than children with poorly educated mothers (Lyster, 1995). The mothers were ranked as poorly educated if they had less than 3 years of schooling after the 9 years which are obligatory in Norway to-day.

Analyses of variance and covariance were run for the pre-readers (n=225) (See Lyster, 1995, for presentation of the analyses). The analyses show that children with highly educated mothers (n=108) scored significantly higher than children who had mothers with low education (n=117) on most of the pre-tests. There were also significant differences between the groups on the three sub-tests from WISC-R: Similarities, Vocabulary, and Digit Span, and on Raven's Progressive Matrices. No significant differences were found on Segmentation of Sentences into Words, Phoneme Segmentation, Sound Deletion, and Homophones. Even when controlling for verbal IQ the children of highly educated mothers were ahead of the other children on most linguistic and metalinguistic tests with the exception of *Segmentation of Sentences into Words, Phoneme Segmentation, Sound Deletion*, and *Homophones*. Since these two groups of children differ in their phonological and cognitive abilities, the mother's educational level will be added to some of the analyses presented here as an independent/predictive variable.

The pre-reading children at the highest cognitive and linguistic levels had, however, not developed the ability to manipulate the smallest linguistic units in words, the phonemes or single sounds, and they were not aware of the word units in sentences.

Pre-test comparisons between training groups

Significant differences between the three groups in the experiment were found for the pre-tests Syntactic Awareness, $F(2,211) = 4.85$, $p =.009$ and Phoneme Segmentation, $F(2,203) = 6.82$, $p =.001$. Post hoc Scheffé tests showed that the Phonological Group scored significantly higher than the Morphological Group on both tests. The difference was at the lower end of the scale. More children had a zero score than a one point score in the Morphological Group while the opposite was the reality for the Phonological Group (maximum score=6). Since the differences were found between the Phonological Group and the Morphological Group, they should not create a problem comparing the development in the two experimental groups with the development in the Control Group. The initial differences can also be controlled for in analyses of covariance. No other differences than these two were found between the groups on the pre-test measures.

IQ

There were no differences between the groups on Vocabulary, F(2,221) = 1. 03, p =.36, Similarities, F(2,221) = 1.05, p =.35, Digit Span, F(2, 221) = 2. 81, p =.06, and Raven's Progressive Matrices, F(216)=1. 29, p=.28.

Post-test analyses

Table 1 shows the means and standard deviations for the different post-test measures in the different groups. As can be seen from this Table there were ceiling effects for some of the measures. These ceiling effects are troublesome because they might cover up group differences or training effects. In addition, assumptions for homogeneity of variance in the different groups were not met for all the measures. It is important to be aware of the statistical problems these ceiling effects can create. No significant differences between the groups were found for Homophones, Memory for Word Sequences, Sound Blending, Knowledge of Compound Words, Word Compounds, and Listening Comprehension. Lack of differences for some of these tests may be due to ceiling effects, but could also be explained by the fact that children at this age master some of the abilities tested in these tasks to a certain extent whether they have had metalinguistic training or not. Both the Phonological Group and the Morphological Group, however, had scores significantly higher than the Control Group for Word Length, Rhyme Identification, Syllable Identification, Segmentation of Sentences into Words, and Analyses of Compound Words. In addition, the Phonological Group had a significantly higher score than the Control Group on Word Onset/Alliteration and significantly higher scores than both the Morphological Group and Control Group for Phoneme Segmentation, Phoneme Deletion, and Syntactic Awareness. For Phoneme Segmentation and Syntactic Awareness the differences held also when controlling for the existing pre-test differences.

SPELLING DEVELOPMENT

Table 2 shows the means and standard deviations for the different spelling measures at school entrance and in the end of first grade. The results in mathematics in the end of first grade are also presented. The two experimental groups were ahead of the Control Group on all the spelling measures. The Control Group, however, was ahead of both experimental groups in mathematics.

Table 1. Post-test differences between experiemntal groups and control group.

Measure	Max. Score	Phonological training		Morphological training		Control	
		Mean	S.D.	Mean	S.D.	Mean	S.D.
Identification of word length	6.00	5.48	0.95	5.24	1.28	4.42	1.26
Rhyme identification	9.00	8.49	1.36	8.21	1.45	7.39	1.71
Syllable identification	16.00	13.05	3.38	13.04	3.18	11.19	3.79
Word onset/alliteration	10.00	9.24	1.25	8.84	1.73	8.32	1.96
Sound blending	9.00	7.99	1.54	7.56	1.82	8.10	0.96
Phoneme segmentation	6.00	3.43	1.88	2.58	1.87	2.00	1.41
Sound deletion	9.00	6.77	1.99	5.58	1.96	4.90	1.75
Knowledge of compound words	11.00	9.84	1.38	9.86	1.40	10.10	1.60
Word compounds	7.00	6.18	1.20	5.70	1.68	5.55	1.86
Analyses of compound words	8.00	6.26	1.95	5.62	2.20	3.97	1.49
Segmentation of sentences into words	6.00	3.46	1.85	3.26	1.63	2.21	1.22
Syntactic awareness	10.00	7.90	1.79	6.79	2.49	6.35	2.21
Memory for word sequences	8.00	5.95	2.04	5.95	2.14	5.62	2.18
Homophones	16.00	9.05	4.02	8.32	4.17	8.13	3.52
Listening comprehension	28.00	24.24	2.66	23.08	3.53	22.65	3.86

Table 2. Spelling results and mathematical results differences between experiemntal groups and control group.

Measure	Max. Score	Phonological training		Morphological training		Control	
		Mean	S.D.	Mean	S.D.	Mean	S.D.
Spelling at school entrance	20	10.48	7.40	10.40	7.23	5.39	5.31
Spelling regular words	18	12.91	4.74	13.27	4.66	13.39	3.99
Spelling irregular words	18	8.91	4.92	8.29	4.75	7.16	4.68
Spelling complex regular words	9	5.16	2.76	4.62	2.74	4.39	2.67
Spelling non-words	9	5.47	2.21	5.50	2.41	5.29	2.49
Mathematics	121	62.67	24.96	60.96	25.10	68.73	25.39

Spelling at school entrance

Homogeneity of variance tests showed significant differences between the variances in the different training groups on Spelling at School entrance. Since assumptions for analysis of variance were not met, non-parametric statistics was used to analyze differences between the groups.

Figure 1 shows the results from Spelling at School Entrance. Both groups and mothers' education are graphically presented. As can be seen from the figure, both children with poorly and those with highly educated mothers in the experimental groups were ahead of children in the control group. Thus the two metalinguistic training programs both had an effect on early spelling development both for children of the lowest educated mothers and for children of the highest educated mothers in the two training groups. The Kruskal-Wallis one-way ANOVA showed a significant difference between groups, $\chi^2 = 14.72$, p=. 000. The Phonological Group had the highest mean rank (118. 63) closely followed by the Morphological Group (116. 83). The Control Group had the lowest mean rank (70. 34).

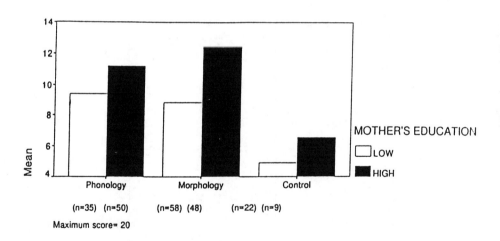

Figure 1. Spelling regular words at school entrance - Differences between training groups.

Spelling measures at the end of first grade

The spelling results in the different groups depends to a certain extent on how the spelling results are coded. Figure 2a shows the result from Spelling Complex Regular Words when the nine items, each word, are coded as correct or incorrect (maximum score = 9). As can be seen from Figure 2a children of poorly educated mothers in The Phonological Group were ahead of children of poorly educated mothers in the other two groups. Children of highly educated mothers in The Morphological Group were ahead of other children with highly educated mothers. Figure 2b shows the results when each correct phoneme -grapheme correspondence receive a one point score (maximum score=68). The differences between the groups and subgroups of children change when more details of children's spellings are coded. The differences between the two sub-groups of children in The Morphological Group and in The Control Group increase when different levels of mastery are taken into account. Children of highly educated mothers seem to be closer to a correct spelling than children of poorly educated mothers even if a word as a whole is not correctly spelled.

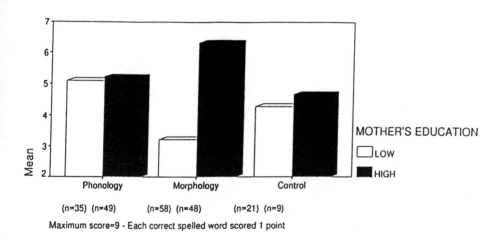

Figure 2a. Spelling complex regular words at the end of first grade - Interactions
            between training groups and mother's education.

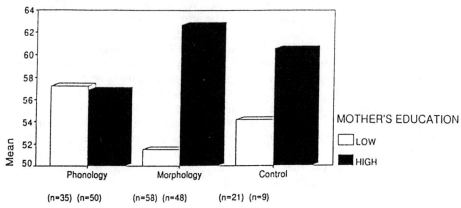

Figure 2b. Spelling complex regular words at the end of first grade - Interactions between training groups and mother's education.

A principal-component solution for the spelling measures yielded one component with eigenvalue greater than 1. The different tests had loadings between .759 and .898 on the unrotated factor matrix. The percent of variance accounted for by the factor was 68.2. The factor scores were used to present the results of the children's spelling development. Figure 3 shows the results of the children's spelling performance at the end of first grade, expressed as factor scores. These results are similar to the results for *Spelling Complex Regular Words*. Children of poorly educated mothers in The Phonological Group were ahead of children of poorly educated mothers in the other groups, and children of highly educated mothers in The Morphological Group were ahead of children of highly educated mothers in the other groups.

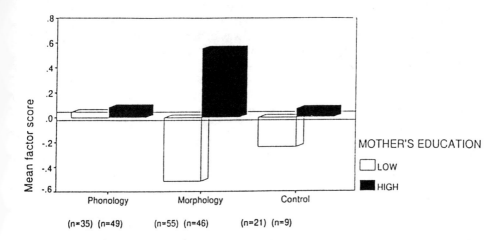

Figure 3. Total spelling scores at the end of first grade - Interactions between training
groups and mother's education.

Regression analyses were used to measure the possible significance of the differences seen in Figure 3. The factor scores for the spelling measures were entered as the dependent variable. Mother's education (ME) and pre-school training were both used as independent variables. For representing the training effect two contrast variables were created to be used as independent variables. One of these variables was Phoncon, which contrasts the results in the Phonological Group (coded 1) with the results in the Control Group (coded-1) (See Cohen & Cohen, 1983 and also Stanovich & Siegel, 1994). The second independent variable for the training groups were Morphcon. It contrasts the results in the Morphological Group (coded 1) with the results in the Control Group (coded -1). The first "main effect" contrast is therefore the result for the Phonological Group versus the Control Group and the second "main effect" is the result for the Morphological Group versus the Control Group. These main effects, however, will be of no interest if there are interactions between training and mother's education. The first interaction contrast in the regression was carried by the product of the first main effect and mother's education, Phoncon X ME. The second interaction contrast was carried by the product of the second main effect and mother's education, Morphcon X ME. In addition to the five variables ME, Phoncon, Morphcon, Phoncon X ME, and Morphcon X ME, Vocabulary from WISC-R was entered as a covariate. Vocabulary was significantly correlated with all the spelling measures and might be viewed as a control for verbal IQ in the presented analyses.

The six variables Vocabulary, ME, Phoncon, Morphcon, Phoncon X ME, and Morphcon X ME were entered into the regression in one block. Each independent variable was then evaluated in terms of what it added to the prediction of the spelling measure that was different from the predictability offered by the other independent variables (variables viewed as covariates included). The results from the regression analysis are presented in Table 3.

Table 3. The effects of vocabulary, mother's education,and training on spelling development.

Measure	Beta	t	p
Vocabulary	.379	6.245	.000
Me [a)]	.194	2.700	.008
Morphcon [b)]	.037	0.594	.554
Phoncon [c)]	.045	0.727	.468
Morpcon X ME [d)]	.176	2.553	.011
Phoncon X ME [e)]	-.166	-2.553	.011

a) ME = Mother's education; b) Morphcon = Morphological training group vs. control group; c) Phoncon = Phonological training group vs. control group; d) = Interaction between Morphcon and ME; e) = Interaction between the Phoncon and ME.

The R^2 for the total block was significant, $F (6,209) = 13.03$, $p=$.000. Vocabulary accounted for a significant and unique part of the variance. Mother's education also accounted for a significant and unique part of the variance for the spelling factor score. Significant interactions were found between training and mother's education. There were significant differences between the differences of means in both variables carrying the interaction contrasts. This means that the phonological training had an effect for those children in the Phonological Group who started the training period at a rather low cognitive and linguistic level. Children of poorly educated mothers in the Phonological Group developed their spelling abilities to the same level as children of highly educated mothers. This did not happen in the Control Group. The result was different when it came to the morphological training. The metamorphological training was most effective for those children who started out at a rather high cognitive and linguistic level. The children with highly educated mothers developed their spelling abilities at a faster speed and to a higher level than children of poorly educated mothers.   Children of highly educated mothers in the Control Group were also ahead of children of poorly educated mothers. The difference between the two groups, however, were not so clear as it was in the Morphological Group.

DISCUSSION

The preschool metalinguistic training clearly had an effect on the development of metalinguistic awareness and on the development of spelling. The results, however, differed in the two experimental groups. The training had effect in both the Phonological Group and in the Morphological Group on the measures of Identification of Word Length, Rhyme Identification, Syllable Identification, Segmentation of Sentences into Words, and Analyses of Compound Words. Children in the Phonological Group, however, developed their ability to segment words into phonemes and to master deletion tasks to a significant higher level than children in The Control Group and The Morphological Group.   The children in the experimental groups did not develop their ability to a significantly higher level than the control group children on the measures Memory for Word Sequences, Listening Comprehension, Sound Blending, Word Compounds, Homophones, and Knowledge of Compound Words.   Ceiling effects, however, might have covered up possible training effects for the measures Sound Blending, Word Compounds, and Knowledge of Compound Words.

The metaphonological training and the metamorphological training had different kinds of effects on spelling development for different groups of children. Children of poorly educated mothers in the Phonological Group, who entered the training program with a relatively low level of metalinguistic awareness, developed their spelling ability in the end of first grade to a significantly higher level than other children of poorly educated mothers. Children of highly educated mothers, on the other hand, who entered the training period with a relatively high level of metalinguistic awareness, profited the most from metamorphological training.   Spelling measure differences between children of highly and poorly educated mothers were substantial in the Morphological Group compared with differences in the Control Group.   Such differences were not present in the Phonological Group where those children who started out with a disadvantage were at the same level in spelling as those children who entered the program with a relatively high cognitive and linguistic level.   One explanation of these results is quite obvious to be found in the different effects the two pre-school training programs had on the development of different linguistic and metalinguistic factors.

The results of this study converge with findings in earlier studies. Children trained in the area of phonological and phonemic awareness enter school with a significantly higher level of linguistic awareness than children not given such training (Ball & Blackman, 1988; Bradley & Bryant, 1983; Lundberg et al. , 1988). Training in the area of morphological awareness had effects on spelling development in first grade only if the children had reached a certain level of phonological awareness.

The metaphonological training presented here seems to have been more effective than the training given by Lundberg and his colleagues (1988) if we consider the amount of intervention time in the two studies. Lundberg, Frost and Petersen did, however, only consider development in the total group and not different sub-groups in the sample. The exposure to print activities in the Phonological Group, which otherwise received training in line with the children in the Lundberg et al. study, might also explain differences in effect. The effect of training in the present study support the view that phonological awareness training is effective when run alongside reading and spelling instruction or is presented to the children alongside information about letters and print (Hatcher et al., 1994).

We cannot conclude from the results of this study that phonologically or morphologically based linguistic training in pre-school is generally superior to the other. Each of them are, however, superior to the training or activities in the control group when viewing sub-groups within the different experimental groups. The findings in this study give support to extend to spelling the theory that different metalinguistic knowledge has different importance at different stages of reading development (Tunmer & Bowey, 1984).

Implications for teaching and therapy

If the results from this study are taken into account, spelling instruction and remediation techniques should vary depending on the children's level of linguistic awareness and on the stage of spelling development reached by the children. A wide range of learner characteristics and attitudes may interact with instructional methods (See Cronbach & Snow, 1977). When children enter school they have reached a variety of stages, some are good spellers, some are beginning spellers and create their own spellings in line with Read's (1986) descriptions, some are pre-spellers and have very little knowledge and awareness of the links between a spoken word and its spelling, and some have not even reached the level of phonological awareness which in turn might be necessary for developing knowledge and awareness of the smallest phonological elements, the sounds or the phonemes. Given such a mixed group of first graders, informal spelling instruction compatible with a phonics approach and that "fits with the language experience and whole-language philosophies" (Treiman, 1993, p. 291) should be of great value. Such a group of children need to have the instruction tailored in different ways to different children.

Formal spelling instruction, however, allots more time and effort to the spelling of words children find difficult to spell. Most Norwegian children spell even very phonologically complex words in a correct way long before they finish first grade. Since some children, on the other hand, struggle with regular words, phonemic awareness training should be a formal part of the instruction. When children are able to analyze the sound structure in regular words and to spell regular words, even the more complex ones, they should be helped to be aware of the morphemic structure of the written language.

It should be possible to combine the two types of metalinguistic awareness training presented here in a way that gives support to children at different developmental levels in the same class. It seems important to identify the children who have problems developing a basic level of phonological awareness before they enter school. If we can help them to develop their phonological awareness, they will be better prepared for spelling instruction in school. Another way of helping these children will be to give phonological awareness training in school alongside reading instruction. A "whole- language" approach with little focus on the sound structure of words might be devastating for these children and take their attention away from the phonological parts of words. Children who, on the other hand, have reached the alphabetic level, but seem to be arrested at this stage, might be helped if a training program in the area of morphological and syntactic awareness is presented alongside reading instruction.

The different words presented to the children in the spelling tests had onsets and rimes of differing difficulties. Questions connected to intra-syllabic units and different levels of syllabic complexity should be put forward in training studies and should be taken into account in teaching. Treiman (1992, 1993) gives important insight into these questions and reports results from a longitudinal study of children's beginning spelling, which give us knowledge about the problems certain phonological structures create in spelling compared with other phonological structures. It seems important to take into account the different levels of children's spelling in devising words for a spelling test and its scoring system. In evaluating training effects, spelling development might not be discovered if we are not aware of the many different levels of spelling that children pass through before different words can be spelled correctly.

AUTHOR'S NOTE. This study was supported by grant 571. 92/007 from the Norwegian Research Council.

REFERENCES

Adams, M.J. (1990). *Beginning to read: Thinking and learning about print.* Cambridge, MA: MIT press.

Ball, E.W. & Blackman, B.A. (1988). Phoneme segmentation training: Effect on reading readiness. *Annals of Dyslexia, 38,* 208-225.

Blachman, B.A. (1991). Phonological awareness: Implications for prereading and early reading instruction. In S.A. Brady & D.P. Shankweiler (Eds.), *Phonological processes in literacy. A tribute to Isabelle Liberman* (pp. 29-36). Hillsdale, NJ: Lawrence Erlbaum.

Bradley, L. & Bryant, P. (1983). Categorizing sounds and learning to read - a causal connection. *Nature, 301,* 419-421.

Bradley, L. & Bryant, P. (1985). *Rhyme and reason in reading and spelling.* Ann Arbor, MI: The University of Michigan Press.

Bruck, M., & Waters, G.S. (1988). An analysis of spelling errors of children who differ in their reading and spelling skills. *Applied Psycholinguistics, 9,* 77-92.

Carlisle, J.F. (1987). The use of morphological knowledge in spelling derived forms by learning disabled and normal students. *Annals of Dyslexia, 37,* 90-108.

Cohen, J, & Cohen, P. (1983). *Applied multiple regression/correlation analysis for the behavioral sciences,* (2nd ed.). Hillsdale NJ: Lawrence Erlbaum.

Cronbach, L.J., & Snow, R. E. (1977). *Aptitudes and instructional methods. A Handbook for research on interactions.* New York: Irvington publishers.

Cunningham, A.E., (1990). Explicit versus implicit instruction in phonemic awareness. *Journal of Experimental Child Psychology, 50,* 429-444.

Cunningham, A.E., & Stanovich, K.E. (1990). Assessing print exposure and orthographic processing skills in children: A quick measure of reading experience. *Journal of Educational Psychology, 82,* 733-740.

Ehri, L. (1984). How orthography alters spoken language competence in children learning to read and spell. In J. Downing & R. Valtin (Eds.), *Language awareness and learning to read* (pp. 119-147). New York: Springer-Verlag.

Ehri, L.C., & Wilce, L.S. (1980). The influence of orthography on reader's conceptualization of the phonemic structure of words. *Applied Psycholinguistics, 1,* 371-385.

Ehri, L.C., & Wilce, L.S. (1985). Movement into reading: Is the first stage of printed word learning visual or phonetic? *Reading Research Quarterly, 20,* 163-179.

Elbro, C. (1990). *Differences in dyslexia.* Munksgaard, København.

Elbro, C., & Arnbak, E. (In press). The role of morpheme recognition and morphological awareness in dyslexia. *Annals of Dyslexia, 46,*

Ellis, N., & Large, B. (1987). The development of reading: As you seek so shall you find. *British Journal of Psychology, 78,* 1-28.

Gjessing, H.J. (1958). *En studie av lesemodenhet ved skolegangens begynnelse* (A study of reading readiness at school entrance). Oslo: J. W. Cappelens forlag.

Goswami, U., & Bryant, P. (1990). *Phonological skills and learning to read.* London: Lawrence Erlbaum.

Griffith, P.L. (1992). Phonemic awareness helps first graders invent spellings and third graders remember correct spellings. *Journal of Reading Behaviour, 23*, 215-234.

Hatcher, P., Hulme, C., & Ellis, A. (1994). Ameliorating early reading by integrating the teaching of reading and phonological skills: The phonological linkage hypothesis,*Child Development, 65*, 41-57.

Henry, M. K. (1989). Beyond phonics: Integrated decoding and spelling instruction based on word origin and structure. *Annals of Dyslexia, 38*, 258-275.

Henry, M.K. (1993). Morphological structure: Latin and Greek roots and affixes as upper grade code strategies. *Reading and Writing: An Interdisciplinary Journal, 5*, 227-241.

Juel, C., Griffith, P.L., & Gough, P.B. (1986). Acquisition of literacy: A longitudinal study of children in first and second grade. *Journal of Educational Psychology, 78*, 243-255.

Lie, A. (1991). Effects of a training program for stimulating skills in word analysis in first-grade children. *Reading Research Quarterly, 26*, 234-250.

Lundberg, I., Olofsson, Å., & Wall, S. (1980). Reading and spelling skills in the first school years predicted from phonemic awareness skills in kindergarten. *Scandinavian Journal of Psychology, 21*, 159-173.

Lundberg, I., Frost, J., & Petersen, O. (1988). Effects of an extensive program for stimulating phonological awareness in preschool children. *Reading Research Quarterly, 23*, 263-284.

Lyster, S.-A.H. (1995). *Preventing reading and spelling failure: The effects of early intervention promoting metalinguistic abilities.* Unpublished doctoral dissertation, Universoty of Oslo.

Lyster, S.-A.H., & Tingleff, H. (1991). *Ringeriksmaterialet: Kartlegging av språklig oppmerksomhet hos barn i alderen 5-7 år* (Linguistic awareness: Assessment and intervention for the 5-7 year olds). Hønefoss: Ø. Tingleff.

Mann, V.A. (1991). Are we taking too narrow a view of the conditions for development of phonological awareness? In S.A. Brady & D.P. Shankweiler (Eds.), *Phonological processes in literacy. A tribute to Isabelle Y Liberman* (pp. 55-64). Hillsdale, NJ : Lawrence Erlbaum.

Morais, J. (1991). Metaphonological abilities and literacy. In M. Snowling & M. Thomson (Eds.), *Dyslexia: Integrating theory and practice* (pp. 95-107). London: Whurr Publishers.

Morais, J., Cary, L., Alegria, J., & Bertelson, P. (1979). Does awareness of phones arise spontaneously? *Cognition, 7*, 323-331.

Morais, J., Bertelson, P., Cary, L., & Alegria, J. (1986). Literacy training and speech segmentation. *Cognition, 24*, 45-64.

Morais, J., Alegria, J., & Content, A. (1987). The relationships between segmental analysis and alphabetic literacy: An interactive view. *Cahiers de Psychologie Cognitive, 7*, 415-438.

Olofsson, Å. (1989, April). *Phonemic awareness training before reading instruction: Effects on learning to spell.* Paper presented at V Simposio escuelas de logopedia y psicologia del lenguaje, Salamanca, Spain.

Olofsson, Å., & Lundberg, I. (1985). Can phonemic awareness be trained in kindergarten? *Scandinavian Journal of Psychology, 24*, 35-44.

Raven, J.C. (1956). *Standard Progressive Matrices. Sets A, B, C, D, and E.* London: Lewis.

Read, C. (1986). *Children's creative spelling.* London: Routledge and Kegan Paul.

Schneider, W., and Näslund, J.C. (1993). The impact of early metalinguistic competencies and memory capacity on reading and spelling in elementary school: Results of the Munich longitudinal study on the genesis of individual competencies (LOGIC). *European Journal of Education, 8*, 237-287.

Skjelfjord, V.J. (1983). *Analysetrening i leselæringen: Treningsprogram og lærerveiledning* (Training in analyses when teaching reading: Trainign program and teacher's guide). Oslo: Universitetsforlaget.

Skjelfjord, V.J. (1987). Phonemic Segmentation: An Important Subskill in Learning to Read. *Scandinavian Journal of Educational Research, 31*, 42-57.

Snowling, M. (1994). Towards a model of spelling acquisition: The development of some component skills. In G.D.A. Brown & N.C. Ellis (Eds.), *Handbook of Spelling: Theory, process and intervention* (pp. 111-128). London: Wiley.

Snowling, M., & Perin, D. (1983). The development of phoneme segmentation skills in young children. In D.R. Rogers & J. Sloboda. (Ed.), *The acquisition of symbolic skills* (pp. 155-162). London: Plenum Press.

Stanovich, K.E. (1986). Matthew effects in reading: Some consequences of individual differences in the acquisition of literacy. *Reading Research Quarterly,21*, 360-407.

Stanovich, K.E., & Siegel, L. (1994). Phenotupic performance profile of children with reading disabilities: A regression-based test of phonological-core variable-difference model. *Journal of Educational Psychology, 86*, 24-53.

Stanovich, K.E., Cunningham, A.E., & Cramer, B.B. (1984. Assessing phonological awareness in kindergarten children: Issues of task comparability. *Journal of Experimental Child Psychology, 38*, 175-190.

Stanovich, K.E., & West, R.F. (1989). Exposure to print and orthographic processing. *Reading Research Quarterly, 24*, 402-433.

Taft, M. (1985). The decoding of words in lexical access: A review of the morphographic approach. In D. Besner, T.G. Waller, & G.E. MacKinnon (Eds.), *Reading research: Advances in theory and practice,* 5, (pp. 83-123). Orlando, FL: Academic Press.

Tornes, J. (1968). *Standpunktprøver i skolen. Matematikk. 1., 2. og 3. klasse.* Seksjon for skolepsykologi, NPF, Oslo: Universitetsforlaget.

Tornéus, M. (1983). *Rim eller reson: Språklig medvetenhet och läsning,studier av metafonologiska färdigheters betydelse för läs och skrivinlärningen* (Rhyme or reason: Linguistic awareness and reading). Unpublished doctorial dissertation, Department of Psychology, University of Umeå.

Tornéus, M. (1987, July). *The importance of metaphonological and metamorphological abilities for different phases of reading development.* Paper presented at the Third World Congress of Dyslexia, Crete, Greece

Treiman, R. (1992). The role in intrasyllabic units in learning to read and spell. In P.B. Gough, L.C. Ehri, & R. Treiman (Eds.), *Reading acquisition*, (pp. 65-106). Hillsdale, NJ: Erlbaum.

Treiman, R. (1993). *Beginning to spell.* Oxford: Oxford University Press.

Tunmer, W.E., & Bowey, J. (1984). Metalinguistic awareness and reading acquisition. In Tunmer, W.E., Pratt, C., & Herriman, M.L. *Language Awareness in Children* (pp. 144-168). New York: Springer-Verlag.

Tunmer, W.E., Herriman, M.L. (1984). The development of metalinguistic awareness: A conceptual overview. In W.E. Tunmer, C. Pratt, & M.L. Herriman (Eds.), *Language awareness in children: Theory, research and implications*, (pp. 12-35). New York: Springer-Verlag.

Tunmer, W.E., Herriman, M.L., & Nesdale, A.R. (1988). Metalinguistic abilities and beginning reading. *Reading Research Quarterly*, *23*, 134-158.

APPENDIX 1

Play and training activities in the Morphological Group

The children have play activities consisting of two words. If presented with the word *skoeske* (shoe box), they have to find the two words shoe and box. They also have to delete one word at the time to find what is then left, and to move the last word in the compound word to the front of the word to create the word *eskesko (box shoe)*. Then the children have to decide whether the new word is a real word and what meaning it has.

Other activities focus on prefixes and suffixes. An example is that the pre-school teacher puts a drawing (made by one of the children) on the board and says "Look here is a pei. " Pei is a non-word with an acceptable Norwegian orthography. "Look", the teacher goes on, "the pei is happy (glad is the Norwegian word). Can you see that he is smiling?" Then the teacher places the two written words under the drawing and says: " Look here is the word pei (points), and here is the word glad". Then the teacher puts another pei (even happier than the first one) beside the first one and asks the children if it is correct to say only pei and glad now. Then the children alone or with help from the pre-school teacher find out that there are two pei*er* (plural is expressed with -er in Norwegian) and they are glad*e* (adjective plural). The teacher and the children go on to the written word, listen to the sound structure of pei and glad and find out that these words are not correct anymore. They lack sounds in the "tail", the ending -er and the ending -e. The children with help from the teacher find the pieces of paper (among several) with -er and -e and place them at the end of the non-word pei and at the end of glad. The teacher says: "Look, we still have the word pei here, but we have added -er which tells us that we have more than one pei. The teacher goes on pointing to the pei that is crying the most and says: "What do you think about this pei? Is it as happy as the first pei?" Together the children the pre-school teacher find the answer that this one is even happier,- it is the happiest of the two peis. Then the superlative -est has to be added to glad instead of the -e (glad*est)*

The same procedures are used for many of the morphemic presentations. But presentations are also done with only words and no drawings. One example is the following: The teacher asks the children if they know what the word *lykkelig* (happy) means. The children and the teacher talk about the meaning of the word and the children are presented with the printed word on the board. Then the teacher asks if the children know a word that means the opposite of "happy". When they have found the word *ulykkelig (unhappy)*, the teacher asks if they can hear any difference between lykkelig (happy) and *u*lykkelig (*un*happy). Then they end up adding the prefix u- to lykkelig and focus on the part of the word that makes happy a word with opposite meaning.

APPENDIX 2

SPELLING TESTS

Spelling regular words at school entrance: is bil kone fisk strømpe

Spelling end of grade 1

I. *Regular words*: så far vi sol bare krok ark frisk spark aks kreps fløy plystre ripsbusker sprang struts* kringle

II. *Spelling irregular words*: er vov ei for der jeg det de nei god land også au regne hva gjøre tidlig haug

III. *Spelling complex regular words:* tavle støvler straks struts nifst mystisk klatrestativ leverpostei elektrisk

IV. *Spelling non-words*: aki søf vru tasit dadile prakto fakati mong burt

---

* The word struts is also used in Spelling Complex Regular Words. This is because it was decided to add the old tests from 1958 to the test battery immediately after the children had been presented Spelling Complex Regular Words.

WHAT CAN BE LEARNED ABOUT READING ACQUISITION IN THE FINNISH LANGUAGE

RIITTA-LIISA KORKEAMÄKI
Department of Education
University of Oulu
Fin-90570, Oulu
Finland

ABSTRACT. Three case studies investigated the process of learning to read and write in the Finnish language when emergent literacy principles were applied to literacy instruction in a first grade classroom and two kindergarten classrooms. The subjects were nine first graders (age 7) and 16 and 17 kindergarten children (ages 5-6). In contrast to typical beginning reading instruction which is characterized by synthetic drill instruction, letters and their sounds were introduced in the context of meaningful words. Also invented spelling was emphasized. The children were assessed prior to each intervention and after it. But observational notes, video and audio tapes were the main data source. The results revealed that children's strategies gradually changed from memory based strategies to alphabetic strategies. All the first graders and most of the kindergarten children learned to read by recoding. But some children used partial alphabetic strategies and one child recognized only a few familiar words. The findings suggest that the regular phonetic spelling of the Finnish language may allow children to acquire literacy without phonic drills.

In this chapter we outline the impetus for the three studies of learning literacy in a meaning based approach in Finland and report preliminary findings. The meaning-based approach described here contrasts sharply with the typical synthetic phonics approach to reading instruction in Finland. The findings focus on the first data collection in the Finnish first grade although preliminary findings of patterns of children's literacy behaviors that emerged in two subsequent kindergarten studies are also noted. In order for the reader to understand the meaning of the studies, necessary information on Finnish language and the typical reading instruction is provided first.

Characteristics of the Finnish language

The phonetic spelling of the Finnish language has been considered a reason for the relative ease in learning to read. In fact, the Finnish language is probably the most regular in use today (Venezky, 1973). There is only one sound that requires two optional spellings, but generally the pronunciation of a grapheme is straightforward. For example, the letter *a* is always pronounced /a/, and this sound is never marked by other vowels such as *u* and *o* in the English language (Kyöstiö, 1967). One special feature of the Finnish language

C.K. Leong and R.M. Joshi (Eds.), Cross-Language Studies of Learning to Read and Spell, 331–359.

is the long and short vowels and single and double consonants that must be indicated with double letters and are pronounced accordingly. Leaving out a phoneme or adding one changes the meaning, e.g., *tuuli* (wind), *tuli* (fire) and *tulli* (customs). Children must learn to distinguish these differences in duration especially for the correct spelling of the words. Also the word-initial consonant clusters *pr*, *tr*, *kr* are rare in Finnish words and occur only in loan words. Instead, three consonant clusters are common at the boundary between the first and second syllables (Sulkala & Karjalainen, 1992). The following examples represent these clusters: *mpp* in *lamppu* (lamp), *rkk* in *merkki* (mark), *lkk* in *tulkki* (interpreter), *rss* in *kurssi* (course).

Another special feature of the Finnish language is the various cases that substitute for prepositions in other languages. The whole word methods have been ignored because of the synthetic nature of the language (Linnakylä, 1993). The cases make the long stem words even longer. When children have learned basic decoding skills, preprimares have words with five and six syllables and consequently easily include more than ten letters. For instance, there are only ten words in the Finnish language with two letters, a consonant and a short vowel (Sarmavuori & Rauramo, 1984).

The Finnish alphabet has 28 letters but only 21 of them are needed for reading the Finnish words. The letter names capture the corresponding sounds of the vowels fairly well, but it is confusing to children that the letter names and long vowels are equal. The consonants are even more problematic since the letter names include extra vowel sounds. Teaching the letters and their sounds has been considered the first step in reading instruction. A typical reading method is delineated next.

Teaching reading in Finland

In Finland teaching reading and writing is based on the readiness perspective and synthetic phonics instruction (for a complete description see Korkeamäki & Dreher, 1993). Preprimaries include exercises for motor, visual, and auditory discrimination, as well as some exercises for phonological segmentation of words before the reading instruction starts. Segmenting the words into their syllables is essential not only before the actual reading instruction but all the way through up to the second grade.

After the readiness period the synthetic phonics starts, which means an extremely careful examination of each letter and its sound in isolation. The features of the letters and how to write them are also emphasized. It has been common to teach only upper case letters, but lately, both upper and lower case letters have been introduced. Teacher guide books recommend the investigation of sounds where in the mouth they are formed in front of a mirror. An essential part of the phonics program is to combine as soon as the students know a few letters and sounds to form syllables for drills. Students practice these meaningless drills and a few words that may make a simple isolated phrase. The understanding of letter-sound correspondences is controlled by dictating the practiced drills that students print by listening to the sounds. Teaching of letters and phonic drills is recommended to proceed slowly.

The concept of sight vocabulary is unknown in Finnish reading education and teacher guides, perhaps because the whole word methods have not been used, and because the regular letter-sound correspondence allows the application of the alphabetic principle to any word. Mature readers never come to a Finnish word they would not know how to pronounce.

In Finland, children begin reading instruction at the age of seven in the first grade. Although more than a half of six year olds enter kindergarten (Muuri, 1994), the children are not taught academic skills rather, the focus is on social skills and free play (In Finland the day-care represents kindergarten). Also, story reading, rhymes, songs, and games are popular activities. Most kindergartens prepare children for school with readiness activities such as drawing lines, cutting with scissors, and coloring pictures. However, a change for lowering the school age or starting some literacy instruction in kindergarten is underway.

Important issues in learning and teaching

Understanding of the complex process of learning to read and write would solve many instructional problems. Unfortunately, despite extensive efforts of researching teaching methods in English (Adams,1990; Bond & Dykstra, 1967; Chall, 1967), development of the ability to read words (e.g., Byrne, 1992; Ehri,1987; Ehri & Wilce, 1985; Hiebert, 1981; Mason, 1980), and strategies in storybook reading (Bissex, 1980; Clay, 1977; Doake, 1985; Sulzby, 1985) - there is very little research in these areas in the Finnish language - we still lack a comprehensive model on learning to read, including psychological, social, and instructional components (Juel, 1991; Mason, Peterman, Dunning & Steward, 1992; Valtin, 1989). Also, it is worthy to note that the process of learning to write is not incorporated in these models as a factor. The models that have been proposed in recent literature (Ehri, 1991; Juel, 1991; Mason,et al., 1992; Stanovich, 1991; Sulzby & Teale, 1991) lead to different instructional principles and practices.

Juel (1991) claimed that the focus of reading research should be moved from the method and teacher to the child. This change is very crucial (Lehmuskallio, 1983). However, we think that the child's learning depends on the learning environment, including methods, approaches, materials, and opportunities for learning, as well as interactions between teacher and peers in the classroom.

Therefore, these factors cannot be separated from each other, since the child's experience is a holistic one.

Despite disagreement on the reading model there seems to be more agreement that in alphabetic languages children must become aware of the alphabetic principle in order to become conventionally literate. But the question is: In what ways? Stanovich (1986) stated that there may be many roads to it. He wrote: "This principle may be induced; it may be acquired through direct instruction; it may be acquired along with or after the building-up of visually - based sight vocabulary..." (p. 363). Yet, this is the fact that causes the debate and disagreement between the whole language philosophers and code emphasis proponents (see the recent ones Adams, 1990; Fry, 1993; Goodman, 1992,1993; McKenna, Stahl & Reinking 1994; Yatvin, 1993). Therefore, all efforts to clarify the learning processes, especially information on processes that take place in the classrooms, have extremely important instructional implications.

In this study we drew on descriptions of literacy development by such researchers as Ehri (1991) and Sulzby (1985). In other words, the reading strategies are compared to children's strategies used in favorite storybook reading in Sulzby's developmental study and Ehri's descriptions of logographic, rudimentary alphabetic, alphabetic, and orthographic readers to represent children's literacy development.

Children's early literacy knowledge - Building the bridge to instruction

It is a well known fact based on the research of emergent literacy (for a review see e.g., Mason & Allen, 1986) that children start their literacy development far before formal instruction in highly literate societies where print is frequently used for communication. An increasing number of children who already have learned to read without formal instruction enter the first grade in Finland (Julkunen, 1990). Those children who do not read conventionally have been observed to possess an emerging knowledge of language, literacy elements, processes, and procedures both in Finland (Uusikylä, 1992) and other countries (e.g., Clay, 1985; Fahlén, 1994; Ferreiro & Teberosky, 1982; Harste, Woodward & Burke, 1984; Lomax & McGee, 1987). For example, they may know a few letters, they attempt to print their own name, parents' and peer's names, and they may recognize where a story starts and ends. However, children may not necessarily become aware of the alphabetic principle without help (Mason, et al., 1992). Rather, they may recognize familiar words based on salient features of the words, and their ability to read is limited to contextual constraints and memory (Ehri, 1991). Thus, it is important to consider all of these facts when we organize literacy instruction. For instance, children may know how to print their own names, but they don't necessarily know the names of the letters. Rather, they may use their own metalanguage to describe them such as a circle for an O, a snake for an S, or a walking stick for a J. However, the familiar context of a child's own name supports learning letters and their sounds in a meaningful word and enforces the developmental process in which available knowledge is used in the construction of new knowledge. Adams (1990) pointed out that it is important that children be interested in letters and that they must know what to use them for when they are learning the letter names. Yet the child might not discover the rules between the spoken and written language, letters and sounds, but needs the teacher's help to understand these highly abstract relationships and the structure of the language. Meaningful context supports learning the idea that reading and writing are means of communication which Finnish synthetic phonic drills completely ignore.

The core of this study was to investigate the nature of the environment, including letter-sound information which would support literacy learning. These questions lead to three different endeavors to reach the goal.

Rationale for alternate approaches in the Finnish language

Although Finnish children start formal reading instruction later than American and British children, the delay does not seem to hinder their learning. The IEA Study of Reading literacy in 32 countries (Elley, 1992) showed that the Finnish students outperformed children from other countries in almost all domains. One possible explanation for their success is the regular orthography of the Finnish language that may lead children to literacy more easily than other languages. Also, one could argue that the synthetic phonics is the appropriate approach to teach reading in a most regular letter-sound correspondence language such as Finnish, and as a result, students achieve high literacy levels. On the other hand, one could argue that because the Finnish orthography is so regular, intensive phonic drills are unnecessary. If the meaning-based approaches are successful in English (Holdaway, 1979; Stephens, 1991), then it seems likely that such approaches would work well in the more regular Finnish orthography. If so, then the teachers could use more meaningful approaches to reading instruction, since they have been worried about the meaningless and uninteresting exercises that the students do not regard as reading. Indeed, there is an increasing number of teachers who would like to shift to a more meaningful approach, despite the fact that most students achieve good decoding skills in the synthetic phonics programs, according to Julkunen (1984).

Since it is possible that the regular language offers a good account for implementing a meaning-based literacy instruction, we designed an approach for first graders that emphasized story reading and invented spelling and information of letter-sound association in a familiar context. The interesting results of this small scale study of nine children encouraged us to continue in designing an approach for kindergarten children which was important for upcoming curricular changes. We assumed that for younger children it is more important to offer meaningful opportunities for learning. Therefore, we organized an environment for activities that would enforce learning the alphabetic principle and reduced the focus on letters and their sounds in a whole group situation. The results led us to continue with another kindergarten group in the literacy rich environment without systematic introduction of letters and sounds. So far in the Finnish kindergarten, because children have not been expected to learn to read and write, we were free to try any approach to teaching without risking children's achievement. Instead of training kindergarten children's phonological awareness, as Lundberg, Frost, and Petersen (1988) did for nine months, we were interested in investigating whether or not children could do more than progress in phonological awareness. We raised important theoretical and practical questions for instruction. How do children acquire and learn to apply the necessary knowledge of the alphabetic writing system of the Finnish language without the teaching of systematic phonics drills? What role does letter-sound introduction in context play in the process of learning to read and write? We attempt to answer these challenging questions by describing three settings with slightly different approaches to instruction and by reporting the preliminary results.

Three alternate approaches

Each study is reported in turn so that first the approach is delineated, and then the results are reported. However, to save space only the changes made in each approach are described. The first grade study is reported first in more detail, and then the preliminary results of the kindergarten studies follow.

STUDY 1

We designed a meaning based approach for nine (six and seven year old) first grade children in the university training school, and the author functioned as a teacher. These children were part of the combined first and second grade classroom. This approach was designed to implement story reading and invented spelling. In addition, we introduced some letters and sounds in a meaningful context.

Setting and procedures. For story reading we made five big books by hand and borrowed some regular size, predictable books from the public library. The teacher read these books daily for about 20-25 minutes and followed her reading with a modified version of the shared-book-experience approach (Holdaway, 1979, 1989). She pointed to the words while reading and encouraged the children to do the same way when they read individually. In subsequent readings, she stopped at several points to give the students an opportunity to predict the next words and their initial letters, directing their attention to the fact that printed words are composed of different letters. Some of the frequent words were printed in large print, and the students identified and located them in the story. Also some features of these words, such as the initial, ending or double letters, as well as the length of the word were discussed.

Indeed, eleven letters - *a, u, i, e, s, r, l, o, k, m, n* - and their sounds were introduced in the context of story reading or children's own names. The words were articulated clearly and pointed to simultaneously, letter by letter, to demonstrate the letter-sound relationships. During the first weeks we focused on one letter and sound a week, but later a couple of letters a week were introduced. First the initial, ending sounds and letters were inspected, and then we moved to the medial letters and sounds of the words. The words were printed on a slip of paper or on the board, and they were read slowly in unison while the teacher pointed to letters by sliding her finger underneath. Then the students were asked what they heard by a specific letter and what the letter's name was. In subsequent days a special feature of the Finnish language, long vowels and double consonants were the focus of attention. The same words were reread and investigated according to the double letters the same way as described for single letters.

Although the words of stories were investigated, story reading for enjoyment and discussions were of crucial importance and were followed by the retelling of stories. The story reading also motivated students to author two big books. In addition, they memorized words from stories which they used in their writing.

The teacher modeled how to write words by listening to sounds. She pronounced the words slowly and wrote each letter accordingly. The students wrote frequently with invented spelling on assigned or their own topics such as letters to each other. Although letter formation was modeled and children practised handwriting in their workbooks according to their own motivation, mostly at home, handwriting was not the most important point in learning to write.

The classroom was organized around the rug that occupied a central place and was used for story reading and discussion as described above. For students' individual literacy activities there was a library corner with a "reading tower", a writing center with a variety of pens and paper always available. Close to the writing center was a billboard that also functioned as the students' individual mailboxes. An alphabet center included manipulative letters and a felt board, and a few games made by the teacher for identifying letter-sound associations and some games to identify familiar pictures and words from the big books. The students were free to choose any literacy activity they liked.

The study took place from mid September to February. Students' letter knowledge, phonemic awareness, and word recognition were assessed prior to literacy instruction. Students' reading of familiar and unfamiliar books was videotaped four times in October, November, December and February. The readings were coded and analyzed according to the reading miscues and the signs of the use of phonological strategies that inductively emerged from the data. The main categories used for this report were substitutions, omissions, additions, repetition, sounding out, elongating, and naming of letters. The following patterns of reading behaviors emerged.

FINDINGS. The preassessment revealed (Table 1) that none of the students read conventionally. However, they possessed a high level of letter knowledge, some degree of phonemic awareness and recognized a few words. In the fall children read familiar and unfamiliar books using a variety of different strategies, but in February they were much more likely to read familiar and unfamiliar books using mostly a recoding strategy. In the familiar book context in October, the children used their memory to support their reading. Therefore, the use of accurate graphic information was not necessary. Indeed, one student read a text that was extremely predictable and repetitive very fluently with extremely accurate pointing. Thus, his reading resembled fluent conventional reading, but he used the knowledge of the story and language as a strategy and succeeded in a way that was otherwise beyond his ability at this point. He demonstrated logographic reading by pointing to the words he pronounced, but he failed to recall a few words and refused to read them. Thus, the accurate pointing and speech matching the text, as well as non responses to the words he did not remember indicated a high level of print awareness; this is a critical factor and prerequisite in reading development (Downing, 1979; Lomax & McGee, 1987).

Four students used some familiar words and their initial letters to support their reading. These words, such as names, were the most frequent words in the text. Sulzby (1985) termed this reading behavior "aspectual reading" (p. 471). According to Ehri (1991), the partial use of letter-sound association is identified as rudimentary alphabetic reading. Knowing the letter names is regarded as a prerequisite for moving to alphabetic reading (Adams, 1990; Mason, et al., 1992). By the first videotaping all children had learned to recognize all the letters required for reading the Finnish words and could also recognize words (see Table 2). Substitutions for several words and the use of letter information suggest that these students' reading strategies were a combination of graphic and contextual information.

Two other students read the book with stronger attachment to letter-sound associations at different points of the story. When they came to a word they did not remember, they elongated the sounds. For example, the sounds of the word *erilaisia* (different) were stretched to *eerrriillaisia*. This behavior made their reading slow and cumbersome. Clearly, their reading was based on graphic information, and they were unable to use the context to ease their recoding the

Table 1. Students' pretest scores in Study 1.

					Students				
Pretest no. of items	1	2	3	4	5	6	7	8	9
Letter knowledge									
Uppercase (28)	28	27	17	16	24	23	28	22	26
Lowercase (28)	22	22	16	10	21	18	25	11	18
Letter writing (28)	28	26	14	22	29	26	26	26	21
Phonemic Awareness									
Initial sound (10)	10	10	2	9	6	10	10	9	4
Ending sound (10)	5	4	6	3	6	7	6	8	7
Consonant deletion (20)	12	0	0	0	0	4	0	8	8
Word recognition									
Familiar words (14)	9	9	3	6	9	9	10	4	4
Pseudowords (10)	2	4	0	3	2	3	6	0	2
Analogies (20)	10	8	4	5	9	8	10	10	1
Environmental print									
with logo (18)	6	14	6	6	4	4	12	10	14
Standard print	16	15	8	7	8	8	10	7	6

Table 2. Students' scores on retest of letter knowledge and word identification measures.

Retest no. of items	Students								
	1	2	3	4	5	6	7	8	9
Letter knowledge									
Uppercase (28)	27	27	28	26	27	27	28	28	28
Lowercase (28)	26	25	24	23	26	23	28	27	24
Word recognition									
Familiar words (14)	12	14	12	14	12	14	14	12	12
Pseudowords (10)	8	10	4	6	6	6	10	6	1
Analogies (20)	20	20	13	15	19	17	20	20	7

words. Recoding words phonologically means that these students had reached the alphabetic phase (Ehri, 1991), although their use of strategies was inflexible. Thus, these findings were similar to reading "strategies imbalanced" as noted by Sulzby (1985, p. 473). But two other students read the text with fluency, using the familiar context of the book and their recoding skill equally. According to the field notes these students read words independently in class. Thus, they were already alphabetic readers.

The findings of the first videotaping and retest information showed that the students had acquired the alphabetic principle and were able to apply it to familiar book reading. Therefore, we predicted that children would master the alphabetic principle with a little more practice and would be able to read a new book in subsequent videotapings.

In an unfamiliar context both in November and December, children were forced to use their emerging recoding skill, since the reading could not be supported by memory. Indeed, in both readings frequent sounding out and elongating were used to recode the words. Children demonstrated different abilities to do so. The students who excessively used the sounding out strategy produced many nonsense words. While sounding out the students often pronounced the names of the consonants, which was very confusing. In November, two students who read this way were puzzled and refused to read the story to the end. Only one of them did so in December. This showed that these students felt that they could not make sense of their reading. The elongating strategy seemed to work better. By elongating the students slowly blended the sounds together and did not lose the meaning of the words. In addition, the substitutions of the words which shared graphic similarities were common instead of substitutions with synonyms. However, the substituted words were also predicted from the semantic cues.

The shift in strategies was very similar to the change that occurred in Biemiller's study (1970) when he observed first grade students' reading from October to May. First the students read by using contextual information, but after a few months they read using graphic information. Researchers disagree on the importance of this phase. Some think that it is an unnecessary artifact of instruction, and some others interpret it as a necessity on the way to literacy in alphabetic languages (Juel, 1991). In the light of the findings on these readings, it seems that the use of phonic strategies was occasionally necessary for recoding new text at this point. The evidence of the use of phonic strategies in November and December is important to show that students had generalized their knowledge of a few letters and sounds to other letters and sounds. Moreover, although the students' reading was not yet fluent, they were able to apply their knowledge of alphabetic principle by recoding new words. Indeed, children's extensive use of sounding out and elongating was a surprising finding because phonic drills were not used. However, the teacher's reading slowly by pointing may have modeled the elongating strategy. In addition, it is possible that the students' elongating strategy reflected their writing strategies, since the students were encouraged to listen to the sounds while they wrote with invented spelling.

In February students read two books - one familiar book and one unfamiliar book. The new book included new words (the total number of words was 243) that the students recoded phonologically. This has been considered a major achievement in reading education (Ehri, 1991). Thus, the findings show that all children had learned how to decipher. There was not such a big difference in strategies children used with familiar and unfamiliar books because they used both context and graphic information in both readings. This developmental pattern, moving from contextual strategies to graphic strategies and finally using both, was suggested by Biemiller (1970).

Conclusions.   Our findings suggest that investigations of letter-sound correspondences in context of familiar words, and reading and rereading of predictable books in group and individually both stimulated and fostered children's understanding of the alphabetic principle. We think that the students learned to apply the alphabetic principle and recode words when they read and reread the books during the fall. One student put it this way: "...If I don't remember something, I'll read it." Frequent reading of books enabled the practice of decoding and increased fluency; the students started to read new books in class.

The research has demonstrated the importance of letter knowledge in learning to read (Bond & Dykstra, 1967; Clay, 1991; Mason & McCormick, 1979; Mutter, 1994). In fact, it has been considered the best predictor for learning to read (Ehri, 1991; Adams, 1990). It was possible that the students' high level of letter knowledge was such a supportive factor in the learning process that the students learned easily and quite fast the use of alphabetic principle and, as a result, learned to "crack the code". Therefore, we organized the second study in kindergarten, in order to investigate how a similar approach would work with younger children who would not know many letters. At the same time we also changed somewhat the introduction of letters and their sounds.

STUDY 2

Setting and procedures. The participants in this study were 16 five- and six-year old kindergartners, ten boys and seven girls. The children came from low socio-economic families and most of them were from single parent families. All parents were shift workers therefore the day care center was open 24 hours a day.

Five days a week at noon the children had one hour and forty minutes for literacy learning. The daily schedule consisted of about forty minutes of singing, story reading, nursery rhymes and games in a group. Then the children were engaged in individual activities that they could freely choose according to their own interests; e.g., they could draw and write letters (each child had a personal mailbox), play with manipulative letters or literacy games that went with the letters. The independent activity period was voluntary and was followed by sharing mail and individual silent book reading.

The purpose was to minimize the teacher centered lessons and rather offer opportunities for learning by children being active participants of their learning. The number of handmade big books was extended to 12 books. In addition, familiar nursery rhymes and songs were written in large print and were used in the same way as the big books described in the preceding section.

Although some children knew only a couple of letters, the letter introduction was much briefer than in the previous study and only eleven letters (a, i, o, s, ä, r, s, k, p, n, v) were focused. We started the letter introduction with the children's own names. On Mondays the names were investigated, and the target letter of a week was especially emphasized. The investigation occurred the same way by reading, pointing to large print (only capital letters were used), and listening to sounds as described above. However, long vowels and double consonants were not a central issue as they were only shortly noticed and discussed. Also the investigation of the target letter was restricted to one day a week. Children had no exercise books for letter writing; instead, they painted letters in all sizes to be displayed on the wall. Opportunities for functional writing e.g., in role plays were the main focus in learning to write.

Later during the term words from big books, songs and nursery rhymes emerged to be the focus of investigation. One popular nursery rhyme turned into a special vehicle for letter-sound investigation. For example, all the vowels were substituted with the letter I or all initial letters were substituted with the letter S, and the children read accordingly in unison. Then some of the words were investigated as to why they sounded funny and what letters they included. Children played with the language and formed more funny words and suggested letters to print them.

This study took place from late January to mid June for 17 weeks. The author helped two kindergarten teachers to implement the program. The children's literacy knowledge was assessed at the beginning similarly with the previous study. The data were collected by participant observations, video, and audiotaping, when children attempted to read books, play the word recognition games, or write. The writing samples were also collected. At the end children's reading of familiar or unfamiliar books was videotaped and/or other word recognition tasks were administered according to the children's ability. The data were coded and analyzed separately for reading and writing, although they are reciprocal and thus must be integrated for final analysis. We report the preliminary findings.

Findings. The pretest result (Table 3) showed that none of the children could read conventionally in January, but eleven children did so in the beginning of June as measured by reading a new book (Table 4). The preliminary analysis of the data showed that children's names played an important role in the learning process as found by Mason (1980). First, the names were recognized and printed from memory based on salient features of letters e.g., two S's in *Essi* or other visual signs such as the length of the word e.g., Aki. By recognizing the names the children often focused on the initial letters and consequently learned the letter names. When children printed the names over and over again by copying or from memory, they learned that the letters are not in random order in words. Children also wrote the names with invented spellings. Thus, the names served the goal of acquiring the alphabetic principle. Children who already knew many letters often unintentionally modeled the strategies to the other children and implicitly taught the letter names.

Similarly, the familiar words from big books became a vehicle to literacy. Both the names and the familiar words were frequently used in letter writing. Only one child regularly used random letter strings for her messages. She also used the names or the letters of the names to represent any word she needed. For example, her mother's name represented eggs in a shopping list or a label to represent the word "princess".

Scribbling was used very seldom in writing, except during the role plays. Even then, most children copied or wrote with invented spelling. Indeed, writing with invented spelling enforced the children's phonemic awareness and segmentation of words into their sounds as claimed by Juel (1991) and others. The adults and more knowledgeable children assisted those who were not yet able to write on their own. Consider the next example.

> Child 1 is writing the name of the restaurant (Mustakokki, Black Cook) for their game.
> Child 2 and two adults are assisting. Child one starts with the first part of the compound word, musta (black).
> Child 2: "Mus-"
> Child 1 writes the letter M.
> Adult 1: "What could the next one be? Mus-"
> Child 1: "U." He writes the letter U.
> Adult 1: "What's next? Mus-"
> Child 1: "S." He writes the letter S.
> Adult 2: "What comes then? Musta-"

Table 3. Students' pretest scores in Study 2.

Students

Pretest no. of items	1	2	3	4	5	6	7	8	9	10	11	12	13	14	15	16
Letter knowledge																
Uppercase (28)	0	4	2	18	5	5	1	3	18	10	18	21	25	17	23	27
Lowercase (28)	0	2	1	15	2	2	0	0	11	6	11	13	14	9	16	18
Phonemic Awareness																
Initial sound (10)	0	0	3	5	0	5	3	7	10	0	10	10	9	8	10	8
Ending sound (10)	0	0	0	1	0	0	5	9	10	0	0	9	5	0	10	5
Consonant deletion (20)	0	0	0	0	0	0	0	0	0	0	0	0	4	0	0	0
Word recognition																
Analogies (10)	0	0	0	0	0	0	0	0	0	0	0	0	0	0	0	7
Pseudo analogies (10)	0	0	0	0	0	0	0	0	0	0	0	0	0	0	0	6
Pseudowords (5)	0	0	0	0	0	0	0	0	0	0	0	0	0	0	0	0

Table 4. Students' posttest scores in Study 2.

								Students								
Posttest no. of items	1	2	3	4	5	6	7	8	9	10	11	12	13	14	15	16
Letter knowledge																
Uppercase (28)	10	28	21	28	21	24	9	15	28	23	24	28	28	26	28	28
Lowercase (28)	0	18	21	28	12	10	5	4	26	13	21	24	23	21	28	28
Phonemic Awareness																
Initial sound (10)	5	10	10	10	9	10	3	10	10	6	10	10	10	10	10	10
Ending sound (10)	7	9	10	10	7	7	5	10	10	10	10	10	10	10	10	10
Consonant deletion (20)	0	6	7	10	0	0	0	0	10	0	8	10	10	10	10	10
Word recognition																
Analogies (10)	7	10	10	10	5	8	0	9	10	10	10	10	10	10	10	10
Pseudo analogies (10)	0	10	0	10	0	7	0	9	10	10	5	10	10	10	10	10
Pseudowords (5)	0	0	0	5	0	0	0	0	5	0	5	5	2	5	5	5

Child 1: "... musta, K."
Child 2: "No, T."
Adult 1: "Musta"
Child 1: "T." He writes the letter T.
Child 1: "Musta, A." He writes the letter A.

The children learned to write new words with invented spelling before they were able to read new words (in the example above the spelling was correct). One child commented on her invented spelling: "I don't know how to read but I know how to write a few words."

By the first videotaping children's reading of familiar books followed the same patterns as in the preceding study. In other words, the children supported their reading from memory, but at the same time, they started to pay attention to initial letters or some other salient letters in the words. When they recognized the words for pictures in games, they said the name of the picture and then listened to the pronunciation. They distinguished some of the sounds, but they were not necessarily aware of whether it was an initial, ending sound or something else. Some children were surprisingly aware of their strategies, as evident from the following quote: "I listened to letters, in the beginning and ending of the word and something else such as R." In some words the medial sounds appeared so salient that children mistakenly considered them to be initial sounds. Typically it was the sound /r/ like in this example:

The child is searching for a word *karhu* (bear) to go with the picture in a game.
Child: "[r]. R,R it starts with an R."
Adult: "Hm."
Child: "[r,r]. With an R (convincingly). There is no word that has an R as initial letter."
Adult: "So, do you think that *karhu* starts with an R?"
Child. "[r]. I hear a sound like that."

It was also very confusing for them too when there were several words sharing the same initial letters, and even more so when the final letters also happened to be the same. Then their strategies often turned to random guessing before they noticed that some medial sound could help.

In five months, however, most children's strategies changed from arbitrary use of letters and sounds to systematic recoding of words. Indeed, all the six-year olds and four of the five year olds learned cipher reading (See Table 4 for word recognition). When they read a new book the same phonic strategies were observed as in the preceding study in February. Three children read the new book fluently by recognizing most of the words by sight and recoded phonologically only the longest words (more than ten letters). One child learned in a couple of weeks after we finished our program. We predicted in January that she would learn faster, since she demonstrated an emerging ability to distinguish the initial and ending sounds in spoken words quite well (See Table 3 # 8). Her difficulty in learning was the struggle with letters. She did not learn to remember the letter names, even her own initial. She was able to segment words into their sounds when she eagerly attempted to write with invented spelling, but she hardly ever managed to write anything without help. The next example describes a discouraging event:

> Children are writing an incentive for their play shop. The child intends to write *mansikka* (strawberry). She knows the initial sound but does not know how the corresponding letter looks. Then she distinguishes the medial /k/ sound but does not remember that letter either. She gives up writing that word and moves to another word, *appelsiini* (orange).

Although the lack in letter knowledge was an obstacle in her learning to read, learning letters was not enough to make some other children readers. Namely, two children who knew only five letters in the beginning but learned them during the course of the study did not yet become conventional readers (See Table 4 , child # 5 and 6). One of them wrote with invented spelling and read words based on letter-sound cues, whereas the other child relied on her memory in recognizing the words and printing them. She learned quite a range of words from memory in kindergarten, experiencing success, and was quite surprised at her inability to read at home.

Two other children learned approximately ten letters. One of them could recognize familiar words based on initial letters and was able to distinguish sounds in spoken words. The other one had difficulties in recognizing the familiar words and often limited his attention in words only to letters that he knew from his own name. Both of these children had problems remembering the letters. However, the strategies they used revealed that they may have moved from the logographic phase to the rudimentary alphabetic phase.

Conclusions. It is interesting to consider the findings in the light of our approach, the letter and sound introduction, and the development of letter knowledge and phonemic awareness. The pretest information showed that in general the six-year olds' letter knowledge was on a much higher level than the younger ones' with the exception of two five year old boys; they knew nearly all the letters they needed for reading the Finnish words. All these children learned to read as measured by reading a new book. Thus, letter knowledge was a good predictor of learning to read but did not always hold true - the rest of the children knew only a few letters. Yet, two of these children also learned to recode words. Letter knowledge seemed to be an important factor, but learning the letters was not necessarily linked to the introduction of letters and their sounds. Some children learned letters we did not have as the focus of investigation, and others did not even learn the letters we introduced.

Our understanding is that the introduction helped children more in capturing the idea of alphabetic principle than in remembering the letter names. For example, long before we introduced the letter K one child (she knew only five letters in the pretest) said: "I know which letter says /k/." Thus, what children learned about one letter they could generalize to others. It was obvious that letter knowledge was conducive to choosing alphabetic strategies, for reading the books and recognizing the words in games. By this process the children increased and tested their knowledge. Also, printing with invented spelling was an important contributor. Children were also constructing their knowledge of long and short vowels and double consonants when they wrote with invented spelling, they asked how many letters they should write, despite the fact that this structural feature of the language was not investigated systematically as in the previous study.

We concluded from the findings that it was not the weekly letter introduction that made children remember the letter names and forms but the active use of them both in reading and writing. The letter introduction may have helped the children become aware of the nature of the alphabetic principle. We reasoned that perhaps this nature could be acquired without letter introduction. Thus, we designed the next study.

STUDY 3

Setting and procedures. Seventeen five- and six-year old kindergarten children from middle class families were part of this study. The children spent about eight hours a day in the kindergarten, although four children were there only half a day. Three days a week in the morning, about one hour and a half was reserved for reading and writing activities in the group and individually. However, children's independent work was on voluntary basis. In addition, if they so liked, children could read and write throughout the day. From time to time a group of children spontaneously worked together or with the help of the teacher any time of the day.

In this study we did not introduce the letters and their sounds. Instead, we started in the following way. The teachers and children discussed about objects and what letter they start with. The children pulled out a random letter from a hat and named it. Then they named objects that start with that letter. Later, some children volunteered to draw pictures of things they had named. The teachers hung the pictures on the wall with a printed letter and word. These print-picture combinations were used as a source of letter information during the study. The letter formation was not practised.

On daily basis all through the study the teachers read to students the big books or nursery rhymes while pointing but did not print from books the words to be investigated. However, discussions about letters, sounds and words were initiated both by the teachers and children. In addition, the teachers wrote on the board the name of the weekday by pronouncing the sounds slowly while writing the corresponding letters. Then the children read the word and investigated the initial sound or any other sound of the word. In the same way the teachers also wrote and read the names of the day. (In Finland there are one or a few names in the calendar for each day to celebrate a name day.)

The kindergarten curriculum was based on thematic units, and each child had a file to collect drawings about each topic including copied labels or labels with invented spelling. Also during the spring term composing longer connected text for one's own story and for a big book about the world's animals were long term projects.

The same individual activities and materials were available for the children as in Study 2, although much less role play was used. The study took place from late September to mid-May for 28 weeks. The children were pretested similarly as in the two preceding studies. At the end the children were tested again. In addition to pretests the post-tests included reading a new book (the same book as in Study 2), according to each child's ability. The data collection and analysis were similar to Study 2.

Findings. The pretest information showed that children differed in their letter knowledge (See Table 5). The strategies reflected the emergent literacy knowledge as observed in Study 1 and 2, and the development followed the same patterns as in the two preceding studies although at different rates. In other words, in the beginning the names were frequently the focus of writing by copying them on the letters the children sent to each other. Later they began the letter-name strategy which was then applied to initial sound strategy. Consequently, by December the children's letter knowledge had increased substantially without the letter introductions described in the previous studies. Also, children wrote frequently on thematic units by listening to sounds when the teachers pronounced the words. When the teachers wrote the name of each day (a daily celebration name) on the board, children started to predict the upcoming words based on a couple of initial letters. When more letters were written they corrected their predictions accordingly. Some children analyzed these names and found that some included familiar names, e.g., *ANNIINA* included *NIINA*. Soon they extended this process to other names and words in big books, e.g., *ELEFANTTI* (elephant) included the name *ANTTI*. Ehri (1992) found that reading words by analogy to known words requires some decoding skill. Thus, children may have used both their sight word knowledge and emerging decoding skill in these situations.

Table 5. Students' pretest scores.

Students

Pretest no. of items	1	2	3	4	5	6	7	8	9	10	11	12	13	14	15	16	17
Letter knowledge																	
Uppercase (28)	19	13	0	10	16	18	7	7	12	16	4	13	24	27	0	20	28
Lowercase (28)	13	7	0	7	12	13	0	3	9	8	3	7	22	19	0	16	19
Phonemic Awareness																	
Initial sound (10)	9	5	5	8	8	8	0	8	4	5	8	4	8	9	0	10	9
Ending sound (10)	7	0	0	4	8	0	0	6	0	1	6	0	6	6	0	6	4
Consonant deletion (20)	0	0	0	2	0	0	0	3	0	0	0	0	0	0	0	0	0
Word recognition																	
Analogies (10)	7	0	0	5	0	0	0	6	0	0	0	0	10	0	0	0	8
Pseudo analogies (10)	0	0	0	0	0	0	0	0	0	0	0	0	10	0	0	0	0
Pseudowords (5)	0	0	0	0	0	0	0	0	0	0	0	0	0	0	0	0	0

Only one child was observed to write wavy scribbling during the fall term. The preassessment test showed that she did not recognize any letter in the beginning (See Table 5). Her stories were long and illustrated. However, she wanted her letters to be conventional when she wrote for other purposes. She also practiced letter writing extensively repeating the same letter in nice letter strings. Some others followed her model for a short period. This behavior disappeared after Christmas.

During the spring term writing and composing generated invented spelling and enforced children's phonemic awareness. In these events the teachers' scaffolding in segmenting the words into their sounds by pronouncing them slowly and encouraging the children to listen to the sounds was typical. The teachers accepted children's incomplete responses and allowed them to write with invented spelling. When the children's own understanding of letter-sound correspondence rules grew they became suspicious of their invented spelling and the adults' responses. Consider the next example.

> A child is composing a story of *Tiku* (Chip) and *Taku* (Dale). After listening to the words she writes TKU for both of the words and asks whether her spellings are correct or not. The teacher says that it is OK. The child stares at the words and starts wondering how they can be correct, since they look exactly the same and represent two different words. She listens to both of the words again and figures out the missing and differentiating vowels and corrects her spelling accordingly.

As a result of frequent writing attempts, it was evident that some children seemed to become literate through writing as much as through reading. Thus, Study 3 confirmed the findings of Study 2.

In fact, in May ten out of seventeen children were able to cipher read as measured by reading either a new book, new words or pseudo words, or all of them (See Table 6 for word recognition). One child read very fluently and had started to read books daily at home. At the end all these children wrote some dictated words with full invented spelling and a few of them with correct spelling.

The letter knowledge of four other children increased so that it was not an obstacle to reading, but these children did not quite yet know how to apply the alphabetic principle to unknown words. But they knew how to write with invented spelling which demonstrated their ability to distinguish the sounds in spoken words. Two children whose letter knowledge was minimal in the beginning still struggled with the letters. Since these children learned to recognize only a couple of words, they stayed in the phase of logographic reading.

Table 6. Students' posttest scores.

Students

Posttest no. of items	1	2	3	4	5	6	7	8	9	10	11	12	13	14	15	16	17
Letter knowledge																	
Uppercase (28)	26	28	10	24	28	28	22	26	25	27	15	28	28	28	12	28	28
Lowercase (28)	25	28	6	17	22	24	17	18	14	20	11	23	27	25	8	28	27
Phonemic Awareness																	
Initial sound (10)	10	10	9	10	10	10	10	10	10	10	10	10	10	10	10	10	10
Ending sound (10)	7	10	8	8	10	10	10	9	10	10	8	10	10	10	6	10	10
Consonant deletion (20)	9	10	0	5	2	10	0	8	0	0	0	10	0	10	0	10	10
Word recognition																	
Analogies (10)	10	10	0	9	10	10	6	10	8	10	10	10	10	10	4	10	10
Pseudo analogies (10)	9	10	0	0	9	10	0	10	6	10	3	4	10	9	0	10	10
Pseudowords (5)	2	5	0	0	5	5	0	0	0	0	0	0	5	5	0	5	5

Conclusions

The three studies described here emphasized the learning of letter-sound correspondences in the context of meaningful reading and writing instead of phonic drills. The purpose was to investigate how children induced the alphabetic principle in this context, and how they used this knowledge in their reading and writing. In fact, at the end of each study the majority of children could recode words which is the major achievement of reading instruction (Ehri, 1991). Some other children were able to apply alphabetic strategies to their writing and reading, but they were not yet independent. A couple of children did not apply their emerging letter knowledge in their reading attempts.

In all three studies children were read to with pointing, and the letters and their sounds were investigated in the context of familiar words. In Studies 1 and 2, eleven letters were introduced systematically, but the investigation of letter-sound relationships was more thorough in Study 1, focusing also on long vowels and double consonants. In Study 3, letter-sound associations were investigated by pointing to words letter by letter while reading and by articulating the sounds carefully when writing simultaneously the corresponding letters. Individual letters and sounds in printed and spoken words were also explored. Invented spelling was used in all three settings. The same patterns of reading and writing behaviors emerged in each study although at different rates. Some children used logographic reading and read stories and words, e.g., names from memory, but moved gradually to using rudimentary alphabetic strategies. Some other children started to use partial alphabetic cues, initial, ending, and salient medial letters - mostly consonants - from the very beginning.

Book reading with pointing helped children learn sight words and direct their attention to letters and sounds in words. Shared reading was powerful because it was supported by other activities that emphasized the learning of the alphabetic principle.

In acquiring the alphabetic principle, writing with invented spelling played an important role in both kindergarten groups. First, invented spelling enforced phonemic awareness. Segmenting the words into their sounds seemed to be easier than blending them to form words. Thus, the reciprocal processes had different requirements for children's development. Printing the words was useful for learning the letters and of crucial importance in the learning process. In fact, for many children who started with poor letter knowledge it was more difficult to learn to remember the letters than to understand the letter-sound relations. It seems that letter-sound introductions were more effective for learning the alphabetic principle than learning the letters themselves in kindergarten.

Also, the children's letter knowledge was important in choosing strategies for their reading attempts. Letter knowledge was useful at least in two ways. First, it helped to establish a sight vocabulary for frequent words. In other words, children remembered words based on letters they knew. Second, letter knowledge allowed the use of the initial and ending sound strategy to reason out the words instead of relying on memory and visual cues alone. Consequently, good letter knowledge forced children to capture the alphabetic principle and helped them understand the phonetic structure of their sight words.

On the other hand, good letter knowledge in the beginning was not necessary for success. In both kindergarten groups there were children who started with little letter knowledge and yet learned to recode new words. These children were active and intent to explore print, given the opportunity. It was typical for them to print their own names and extend them to other names and words and recognize familiar words from their initial letters and some other letters. In doing so, they used what they already knew to explore new things about print. But there were also children who started with little letter knowledge and learned enough letters to read the Finnish words but did not yet learn how to crack the code. They did not yet use the knowledge they had acquired about the alphabetic principle, in order to adopt more mature strategies.

It is also important to note a few children who showed the slowest development. These children learned about ten letters according to post-test information, and their phonemic awareness increased. But they could recognize only a few familiar words. Typically, when they attempted to write they were able to distinguish sounds from spoken words, but they did not remember the corresponding letters. Thus, it seems that their poor letter knowledge hindered them in learning sight words; poor sight word knowledge in turn hindered them in learning more letters. It is likely that letter knowledge is one of the most important factors in the learning process in alphabetic languages, as claimed by many researchers (see e.g., Adams, 1990; Ehri, 1991; Mason, 1984).

In short, the findings of this study confirmed on the one hand the patterns of reading behavior observed by Sulzby (1985). On the other hand, development followed the path proposed by Ehri (1991). This may mean that these two perspectives are complementary, because reading strategies seem to depend on what children read, words or stories, as well as the familiarity of the context. In Study 1, reading development was also very similar to Biemiller's (1970) findings from contextual reading to the use of graphic information and finally to the use of both graphic and contextual information. All these findings suggest that reading in different orthographies has universal features, although there are some features that are specific to each orthography, requiring different approaches in instruction.

Indeed, the findings of these three studies suggest that the regular phonetic spelling of the Finnish language may allow children to acquire the alphabetic principle in context without phonic drills. However, it seems that children needed active investigation of letter-sound relations and assistance from teachers to direct their attention to essential and relevant features of print. This was critical for development to take place. It is unlikely that these children could have discovered the secret of the code system just on their own. Instead of training children's phonological awareness as Lundberg and his colleagues did (1988), children were involved in literacy activities and learned more about the written language.

It is not clear why some children progressed slowly. Especially the difficulty to learn the letters must be carefully considered to develop new and better ways to ease this process. Furthermore, we need more research in this area, as well as follow-up studies on how these children progress in school. It is possible that these children need additional instruction in long vowels and double consonants to improve their correct spelling of words.

REFERENCES

Adams, M.J. (1990). *Beginning to read: Thinking and learning about print.* Cambridge, MA: The MIT Press.

Biemiller, A. (1970). The development of the use of graphic and contextual information as children learn to read. *Reading Research Quarterly, 6,* 75-96.

Bissex, G.L. (1980). *Gnys at wrk.* Cambridge, MA: Harvard University Press.

Bond, G., & Dykstra, R. (1967). The cooperative research program in first grade reading. *Reading Research Quarterly, 2,* 5-142.

Byrne, B. (1992). Studies in acquisition procedure for reading:Rationale, hypotheses and data. In P.B. Gough, L.C. Ehri, & R. Treiman (Eds.), *Reading acquisition* (pp. 1-34). Hillsdale, NJ: Lawrence Erlbaum.

Chall, J.S. (1967). *Learning to read: The great debate.* New York: McGraw-Hill.

Clay, M.M. (1977). *Reading: The patterning of complex behavior.* Portsmouth, NH: Heinemann.

Clay, M.M. (1985). *Early detection of reading difficulties* (3rd ed.) Portsmouth, N.H: Heinemann.

Clay, M.M. (1991). *Becoming literate: The construction of inner control.* Portsmouth, N.H: Heinemann.

Doake, D.B. (1985). Reading-like behavior: Its role in learning to read. In A. Jaggar, & M. Smith-Burke (Eds.), *Observing the language learner* (pp. 82-98). Newark, Delaware: International Reading Association.

Downing. J. (1979). *Reading and reasoning.* New York: Springer.

Ehri, L.C. (1987). Learning to read and spell words. *Journal of Reading Behavior*, *19*, 5-31.

Ehri, L.C. (1991). Development of the ability to read words. In R. Barr, M.L. Kamil, P.B. Mosenthal & P.D. Pearson (Eds.), *Handbook of reading research, Volume II* (pp. 383-417). New York:Longman.

Ehri, L.C. (1992). Beginners need some decoding skill to read words by analogy. *Reading Research Quarterly, 27*, 13-25.

Ehri, L.C., & Wilce, L.S. (1985). Movement into reading:Is the first stage of printed word learning visual or phonetic? *Reading Research Quarterly, 20*, 163-179.

Elley, W.B. (1992). *How in the world do students read? IEA study of reading literacy.* Hamburg, Germany:The International Association for the Evaluation of Educational Achievement.

Fahlén, R.M. (1994). *Perspektiv på läs- och skrivinlärning* [Perspectives on learning to read and write]. Lingköping, Sweden: Lingköping University Department of Education and Psychology.

Ferreiro, E., & Teberosky, A. (1982). *Literacy before schooling.* Portsmouth, NH: Heinemann.

Fry, E. (1993). Letter to the editor: Does whole language work? *The Reading Teacher, 47*, 182.

Goodman, K.S. (1992). I didn't found whole language. *The Reading Teacher, 46*, 188-199.

Goodman, K.S. (1993). Letter to the editor: Goodman's response. *The Reading Teacher, 47*, 182.

Harste, J.C., Woodward, V.A., Burke, C.L. (1984). *Language stories and literacy lessons.* Portsmouth, N.H.: Heinemann.

Hiebert, E.H. (1981). Developmental patterns and interrelationships of preschool children's print awareness. *Reading Research Quarterly, 16*, 236-259.

Holdaway, D. (1979). *The foundations of literacy.* Sydney: Ashton Scholastic.

Holdaway, D. (1989). Shared book experience:Teaching reading using favorite books. In G. Manning & M. Manning (Eds.), *Whole language: Beliefs and practices , K-8* (pp. 137-150). Washington, D.C.: National Educational Association.

Juel, C. (1991). Beginning reading. In R. Barr, M.L. Kamil, P. Mosenthal & P.D. Pearson (Eds.), *Handbook of reading research. Volume II* (pp. 759-788). New York: Longman.

Julkunen, M.L. (1984). *Lukemaan oppiminen ja opettaminen* [Learning to read and teaching reading]. (Publication in Education No. 1). Joensuu, Finland: University of Joensuu.

Julkunen, M.L. (1990). Koulun alku ja lukeminen [The beginning of school and reading]. In P. Linnakylä & S. Takala (Eds.), *Lukutaidon uudet ulottuvuudet* [New dimensions of reading] (pp. 73-83). (Publication series B. Theory into practice 61). Jyväskylä, Finland: Institute for Educational Research, University of Jyväskylä.

Korkeamäki, R.- L., & Dreher, M.J. (1993). Finland, phonics, and whole language: Beginning reading in a regular letter-sound correspondence language. *Language Arts, 70*, 29-36.

Kyöstiö, O.K. (1967). Reading research at the kindergarten level in Finland. In J. Downing & A.L. Brown (Eds.), *In the second international reading symposium* (pp. 71-79). London: Cassell & Company Ltd.

Lehmuskallio, K. (1983). *Mitä lukeminen sisältää* [What does reading involve]? Helsinki: WSOY.

Linnakylä, P. (1993). Exploring the secret of Finnish reading literacy achievement. *Scandinavian Journal of Educational Research, 37*, 63-74.

Lomax, R.G., & McGee L.M. (1987). Young children's concepts about print and reading: Toward a model of word reading acquisition. *Reading Research Quarterly, 22*, 237-256.

Lundberg, I., Frost, J., & Petersen, O.P. (1988). Effects of an extensive program for stimulating phonological awareness in preschool children. *Reading Research Quarterly, 23*, 264-284.

Mason, J.M. (1980). When do children begin to read: An exploration of four-year-old children's letter and word reading competencies. *Reading Research Quarterly, 15*, 203-227.

Mason; J. (1984). Early reading from developmental perspective. In R. Barr, M.L. Kamil, P.B. Mosenthal & P.D. Pearson (Eds.), *Handbook of reading research* (pp. 505-543). New York: Longman.

Mason, J.M., & Allen, J.B. (1986). A review of emergent literacy with implications for research and practice in reading. In E.Z. Rothkopf (Ed.), *Review of research in education*, vol. 13 (pp. 3-47). Washington, DC: American Educational Research Association.

Mason, J.M., & McCormick, C. (1979). *Testing the development of reading and linguistic awareness* (Tech. Report No 126). Urbana: University of Illinois, Center for the Study of Reading.

Mason, J.M., Peterman, C.L., Dunning, D.D., & Steward, J.P. (1992). Emergent literacy: Alternative models of development and instruction. In M.J. Dreher & W.H. Slater (Eds.), *Elementary school literacy: Critical issues* (pp. 51-67). Norwood, MA: Christopher- Cordon Publishers, Inc.

McKenna, M.C., Stahl, S.A., & Reinking, D. (1994). Critical issues: A critical commentary on research politics and whole language. *Journal of Reading Behavior, 26*, 211-233.

Mutter, V. (1994, October). *The nature of phonological awareness: How it interacts with letter knowledge to influence early literacy development - A longitudinal study.* Paper presented at NATO advanced study institutes programme cognitive and linguistic bases of reading, writing, and spelling, Alvor/Algarve, Portugal.

Muuri, A. (1994). *Lasten päivähoito* [Children's daycare]. (Tilastotiedote 1994: 6). Helsinki: STAKES.

Sarmavuori, K., & Rauramo, S.L. (1984). *Luokanopettajan äidinkielen käsikirja* [Class teacher's handbook of mother tongue]. Helsinki: Koulun erityispalvelu.

Stanovich, K.E. (1986). Matthew effects in reading: Some consequences of individual differences in acquisition of literacy. *Reading Research Quarterly, 21*, 360-407.

Stanovich, K.E. (1991). Word recognition: Changing perspectives. In R. Barr, M.L. Kamil, P.B. Mosenthal & P.D. Pearson (Eds.), *Handbook of reading research, Volume II* (pp. 418-452). New York: Longman.

Stephens, D. (1991). *Research on whole language: Support for a new curriculum*. Katonah, NY: Richard C. Owen.

Sulkala, H., & Karjalainen, M. (1992). *Finnish descriptive grammars*. London: Routledge.

Sulzby, E. (1985). Children's emergent reading of favorite storybooks: A developmental study. *Reading Research Quarterly, 20*, 458-481.

Sulzby, E., & Teale, W. (1991). Emergent literacy. In R. Barr, M.L. Kamil, P.B. Mosenthal & P.D. Pearson (Eds.), *Handbook of reading research. Volume II* (pp. 727-757). New York: Longman.

Uusikylä, A. (1992). *Varhaisen lukemisen diagnosoinnin alkumittausten kehittely* [The development of a test pattern for early reading assessment]. Unpublished Master's Thesis. Oulu: Department of Teacher education, University of Oulu.

Valtin, R. (1989). Dyslexia in the German language. In P. G. Aaron & R.M. Joshi (Eds.), *Reading and writing disorders in different orthographic systems* (pp. 119-136). London: Kluwer Academic Publishers.

Venezky, R.L. (1973). Letter-sound generalizations of first-, second-, and third-grade Finnish children. *Journal of Educational Psychology, 64*, 288-292.

Yatvin, J. (1993). Letter to the editor: Need for experimental research on whole language. *The Reading Teacher, 46*, 636.

PHONOLOGICAL AWARENESS AND LEARNING TO READ CHINESE

J. RICHARD HANLEY
Department of Psychology
University of Liverpool
Liverpool, L69 3BX
United Kingdom

H. S. HUANG
Dept. of Special Education
National Tainan Teachers College
Tainan, Taiwan

ABSTRACT. The research that is discussed here investigated the relationship between performance on tests of phonological awareness and learning to read Chinese. Eight-year-old children learning to read Chinese in Hong Kong and Taiwan were compared with children to read English in the UK. In Taiwan, all children are taught to read Chinese by first learning an alphabetic writing system ("Zhu-Yin-Fu-Hao"), but this is not the case in Hong Kong. The results showed that phonological awareness was significantly correlated with reading test scores in both Chinese and British children. However, in the Chinese children, although not in the British children, the relationship between reading and phonological awareness was no longer significant when the effects of vocabulary and non-verbal intelligence were partialled out. In a further study, six-year-old children from Taiwan were used as subjects in a longitudinal study. In these children, there was a significant correlation between pre-school phonological awareness scores and reading ability a year later. However, the predictive power of early phonological awareness disappeared once the effects of pre-school reading scores had been partialled out. The research also revealed that the nature of phonological awareness skills differed in the Chinese and British children. For example, children from Hong Kong performed better than the British children at deleting the initial phoneme from words that start with consonant clusters, but performed worse than the British children at deleting the initial phoneme from words that start with a single consonant. The results are explained in terms of the Chinese and British children's familiarity with different types of syllable structures, and with different types of alphabetic scripts.

In the last few years, we have conducted two detailed investigations of phonological awareness and reading skills in children who are learning to read Chinese (Huang & Hanley, 1995, in press). One of these studies has compared the performance of eight-year-old children learning to read English in Britain with eight-year-old children learning to read Cantonese in Hong Kong, and eight-year-old children learning to read Mandarin in Taiwan on a series of measures including tests of reading, phonological awareness and visual skills. The other investigation has followed the reading progress of a group of 6-year-old children during their first year at primary school in Taiwan. The purpose of the present chapter is to review and

C.K. Leong and R.M. Joshi (Eds.), Cross-Language Studies of Learning to Read and Spell, 361–378.
© 1997 *Kluwer Academic Publishers. Printed in the Netherlands.*

summarize our main findings and to bring together the results of the two investigations.

In both of these investigations we were interested in two key questions. The first of these was whether phonological awareness skills are as closely related to reading ability in Chinese children as they are in British children. For example, in our sample of 6-year-old Taiwanese children, we examined the extent to which reading performance at the end of the school year could be predicted by phonological awareness skills assessed at the start of the year. The second question was the extent to which phonological awareness skills themselves would differ in Chinese and British children. The syllabic structure of Chinese words is much simpler than those of English words; for example, there are no consonant clusters in Chinese. How would factors of this kind influence performance by the Chinese children on tests such as phoneme deletion?

The Chinese Writing System

The language that is spoken in China varies considerably from one region to another. For example, the official language Mandarin-Putonghua is spoken in the north of mainland China and in the capital, Beijing. There are regional dialects such as Min, Wu, Xiang, Hakka, Gan and Cantonese, that are spoken in the south of China. Like Mandarin, all of these dialects have their origins in Ancient Chinese, but may not be mutually comprehensible, having evolved their own vocabularies over the centuries (for further details, see Forrest, 1965). In Min, for example, which is the language that has traditionally been spoken in Taiwan, the word for death and the word for four are homophones but varying in tones. The effect of this is that there is no fourth floor in many Taiwanese hotels and department stores, and certainly no ward 4 in Taiwanese hospitals! Since the second world war, in an attempt to unify spoken Chinese, both the Republic of China in Taiwan, and the People's Republic of China in mainland China have adopted Mandarin (Putonghua) as the National Language or common language. Nevertheless, it will be some time before all the peoples of China are able to communicate fully with each other via spoken language.

It follows from this that it is not possible to introduce one single alphabetic writing system for Chinese that would simultaneously be phonetically transparent for all Chinese readers. In the Chinese writing system the written characters represent morphemes rather than units of spoken language. A word can therefore be consistently represented by the same written symbol or symbols regardless whether the pronunciation of that word changes from one area of China to another. This means that it is possible for a reader to understand the meaning of the words (although not necessarily syntax at times) in a sentence that has been written by someone who speaks a different Chinese language or dialect.

One of the difficulties associated with a logographic writing system is that it is difficult to recognize a character unless one has encountered (and learnt) that character previously. Nevertheless, there is one aspect of the Chinese writing system that does provide the reader with some information about how an unfamiliar character might be pronounced. Over 80% of Chinese characters are derived from the principle known as phonetic compounds and are usually divided into two parts, a meaning radical and a phonetic radical. The phonetic radical is phonologically related to the character that is being written, and thus provides a cue as to its possible pronunciation. Tzeng, Zhong, Hung, and Lee (1994) have recently argued that the occurrence of the phonetic in compound characters means that strictly speaking Chinese is not a logographic writing system. Some (e.g., Flores d'Arcais, 1992) have argued that such phonological information might be used by skilled Chinese readers when they are recognizing characters.

Unfortunately, the phonetic does not always provide a totally reliable guide to the pronunciation of the word to someone who has never seen the word before in print. First, the pronunciations of some words have changed over the centuries such that the phonetic no longer resembles the character phonologically. Second, although the phonetic usually appears to the right of the radical (in approximately 80% of phonetic compounds), this is not always the case. Consequently, the reader may attempt inappropriately to use that radical as the phonetic cue. Third, the nature of the relationship between the phonetic and the character that is being written varies; they may either rhyme with each other, or be homophonic.

Nevertheless, a common strategy adopted by Chinese readers when they encounter an unfamiliar character is to attempt to give a pronunciation that corresponds to the phonetic element (Fang, Horng, & Tzeng, 1986; Wang, 1973), even though this yields the correct pronunciation of at most 40% of phonetic compound characters (Zhou, 1978). Consistent with this, Lien (1985) showed that children made more errors when naming characters whose phonetic component did not give a reliable cue to the pronunciation of the character as a whole. Similarly Tzeng et al. (1994) have shown that children are faster at pronouncing compound characters whose phonetic component is homophonic with the pronunciation of the entire character. In adult reading, Flores d'Arcais, Saito and Kawakami (1995) have shown that the naming of compound characters can be inhibited by prior presentation of certain parts of the compound, but is facilitated by prior visual presentation of the phonetic compound.

Pinyin and Zhu-Yin-Fu-Hao

A second major problem that faces children who are attempting to master a logographic script is the considerable amount of learning that is required. Whereas an alphabetic system uses a small number of abstract elements to represent the phonemic structure of the language, Chinese words are represented by a large number of different visual symbols. It is estimated that a child should have learnt to recognize over 470 different characters by the end of their first year at school and at least 4000 different characters by the time they reach 12 years old.

Since the 1950's, in an attempt to make it easier for a child to learn to read Chinese, some young children have been introduced to the reading of Chinese via a phonetic system when they start schooling. All six-year-old children in the People's Republic of China are taught to read an alphabetic script (Pinyin) before beginning to learn Chinese characters. Similarly, pupils in Taiwan learn an alphabetic script known as Zhu-Yin-Fu-Hao during the first ten weeks of the first grade before they begin to learn to read Chinese characters.

Zhu-Yin-Fu-Hao (which literally means 'symbols of phonetic pronunciation') is a phonetic script similar to Pinyin in which a phoneme is represented by a unique symbol. There are 37 different symbols in Zhu-Yin-Fu-Hao. In Pinyin, the written symbols comprise letters from the Roman alphabet, but otherwise the two systems are similar. Although it is learnt during the first few weeks of the first year in school, children continue to use Zhu-Yin-Fu-Hao throughout their primary school years. Whenever a new character appears in a primary school textbook, it is always accompanied by its representation in Zhu-Yin-Fu-Hao. Knowledge of Zhu-Yin-Fu-Hao thus helps children to pronounce new characters via sublexical phonology without assistance from the teacher.

Investigation of the Relationship Between Phonological Awareness and Reading Test Scores in Chinese and English

The fact that some Chinese children have learnt a new phonetic system for representing spoken Chinese, in addition to the fact that many Chinese characters contain a phonetic component, suggested to us that it might be interesting to investigate the relationship between phonological awareness and learning to read Chinese. In our first study, we examined and compared the relationship between performance on tests of phonological awareness (rhyme ability and phoneme deletion) and reading in 50 eight-year-old children from Taiwan, 42 eight-year old children from Hong Kong and 45 eight-year-old children from Britain.

The link between phonological awareness and reading in children who are learning to read an alphabetic system such as English has been well documented. Children with superior reading skills consistently perform significantly better on tests of phonological awareness than less able readers (see Goswami & Bryant, 1990 for a review). Moreover, these differences remain significant even when the effects of variables such as vocabulary and non-verbal intelligence have been partialled out (Tunmer & Nesdale, 1985). We therefore expected to observe findings consistent with this in our British sample who were learning to read English. The critical question was whether similar results would be obtained with our sample of children who were learning to read Chinese.

As we mentioned above, Taiwanese children learn a phonetic system (Zhu-Yin-Fu-Hao) in their first few weeks at primary school as a means of simplifying the subsequent learning of Chinese characters. However, in Hong Kong the majority of children, including those that we studied, learn to read Chinese characters without being taught Pinyin or Zhu-Yin-Fu-Hao. We were therefore particularly interested in whether the relationship between reading and phonological awareness would differ in children from Hong Kong and Taiwan.

Studies using English and other alphabetic orthographies have demonstrated that there is a striking relationship between children's early phonological awareness and their subsequent reading success in an alphabetic writing system (e.g., Bradley & Bryant, 1983; Bryant & Bradley, 1985; Ellis & Large, 1987; Lundberg, Olofsson & Wall, 1980; Maclean, Bryant & Bradley, 1987; Mann, 1984; Mann & Liberman, 1984; Perfetti, Beck, Bell, & Hughes, 1987; Stanovich, Cunningham, & Cramer, 1984; Stuart & Coltheart, 1988; Wimmer, Landerl, Linortner, & Hummer, 1991). Such findings are particularly important if one wishes to argue that phonological awareness ability is a cause rather than a consequence of subsequent reading performance. In the second of our two studies, therefore, we employed a longitudinal design and examined the relationship between reading development and phonological skills in 40 six-year-old Taiwanese children during their first year at primary school. If phonological test scores, collected before children had started their reading instruction at school, could significantly predict their reading ability a year later, then this would be consistent with the view that these skills play a major role in determining how quickly a child will learn to read Chinese.

TEST MATERIALS

To assess reading skill in the British subjects, we used the Schonell reading test. For the Chinese children, we created a similar test using Chinese characters. Hence, one hundred characters in total were selected for the test, arranged with ten characters per line and in a sequence that increased in difficulty as the page went down. Subjects were given credit for each character that they read out correctly (in Mandarin for the Taiwanese children, and Cantonese for the children from Hong Kong).

The tests of phonological awareness consisted of both rhyme and phoneme deletion tests. The latter required subjects to work out how particular words would sound if they lost a specific phoneme. On one half of the trials, the child was asked to delete the first phoneme of a word (e.g., 'ku' becomes 'u', 'fan' becomes 'an'). On the other half of the trials, the child was asked to delete the last phoneme. The remaining set of phonological tests assessed the ability to recognize rhyme and alliteration in spoken words and were based on tests used in the UK by Bryant & Bradley (1985). Three versions of the test were used: an English word test, a Chinese Words Odd Man Out test and a Chinese Non-word Odd Man Out test. All of the items in the Chinese words test were real Chinese (Mandarin) words while the items in the non-word test were non-words in Chinese. In each test, the child heard four one-syllable words. Each test contained three parts: first sound difference (the child had to indicate which was the odd word out in terms of its first sound), middle sound difference, and last sound difference.

We also assessed the children's visual skills by examining their performance on the Visual Paired Associates (VPA) test, which is a sub-test of the Wechsler Memory Scale-Revised (Wechsler, 1987). This test requires the subject to learn the color associated with each of six abstract line drawings. Then, subjects are presented with each of the line drawings in turn, and are asked to point out from a color folder which color had appeared with that figure. Although memory for color is unlikely to be closely related to learning to read Chinese, it was felt that the ability to learn unfamiliar figures of the kind used in this test might be related to the ability to learn to recognize a new Chinese character.

RESULTS

There was evidence of strong correlations between reading and phoneme development in all of the groups of children that we tested. In the eight-year-old children, the correlations between phoneme deletion and the number of words read correctly aloud were: $r = .59$ ($p < .001$) for the British children; $r = .55$ ($p < .001$) for the Taiwanese children; $r = .41$ ($p < .01$) for the Hong Kong children.

In the six-year-old Taiwanese children, a fixed-order multiple regression was used in order to find out how much of the variation in the reading scores at the end of the year could be accounted for by early phonological awareness skills after the effects of differences in IQ and in vocabulary ability had been controlled. The stepwise regression focused on the predictive power of the phonological tests combined together. In other words, the Odd Man Out tests and the phoneme deletion tests were combined as a single phonological score. This was calculated by first converting each child's score on each test to a z score and then using the sum of the mean of each child's z scores from both phonological tests. The regression analyses revealed that there was a highly significant relationship between the combined phonological awareness score in the first two weeks of school and the number of words read correctly at the end of the school year. A similar result was obtained when the phoneme deletion test score replaced the combined score in the regression analysis. This was true even when the effects of IQ and vocabulary had been partialled out.

Initially, these findings appeared to us to be extremely exciting. However, it turned out to be the case that phonological awareness scores were not significant predictors of Chinese reading ability when some other variables were entered into the regression equations. In the eight-year-old children from Hong Kong and Taiwan, the relationship between phonological awareness and Chinese reading test score was no longer significant ($p > .05$) once the effects of visual skill, IQ [Raven's (1977) Colored Progressive Matrices], and vocabulary skill [Dunn, Dunn, and Whetton's (1982) British Picture Vocabulary Scale] had been partialled out. By contrast, the relationship between phonological awareness and English reading remained significant ($P < .01$) in the British sample even when the effects of IQ, visual skill and vocabulary skill had all been partialled out.

On the data from the six-year-olds in Taiwan, we conducted a regression analysis which examined the effect of phonological skills on predicting later reading ability after the influences of reading ability at the first testing session had been partialled out. This was because Taiwanese children have some ability to read Chinese characters before they go to school. The results revealed that reading ability before pupils received any formal instruction in primary school had a notable effect on later reading ability. The amount of the variance in reading ability at the end of the year that was accounted for was 51.07% ($p<.001$). Performance on the phonological tests played a nonsignificant role in predicting later reading ability after the effects of the early reading scores had been partialled out.

The finding that pre-school reading level was of overwhelming importance in determining subsequent reading performance is reminiscent of some results obtained by Wagner and Torgesen (1987) with an alphabetic writing system. They recalculated the data of Lundberg et al. (1980) and controlled for the pre-schooler's reading scores. They, too, found that the predictive ability of the phonological tests for subsequent reading ability dropped from a level of significance to near zero. This is not always observed in longitudinal studies of learning to read an alphabetic script, however. Wimmer et al. (1991) showed that performance on a phoneme awareness task at the start of the school year in Austria was a significant predictor of reading scores at the end of the first school year, even when the effects of pre-school reading scores were taken into account in the regression analysis.

Overall, our research failed to generate evidence that phonological skills are as important for learning to read Chinese as we and others have found that they are for learning to read an alphabetic system such as English. In our eight-year-old Chinese children, phonological awareness and reading ability were no longer significantly correlated once the effect of vocabulary and non-verbal intelligence had been partialled out (cf. Tunmer & Nesdale, 1985). In our six-year-old Chinese children, phonological awareness and reading ability were no longer significantly correlated once the effect of pre-school reading scores had been partialled out (cf. Wimmer et al., 1991).

Our conclusions are therefore somewhat different from those which have recently been drawn by Hu and Catts (1994) in an interesting study which also investigated the relationship between phonological awareness and reading in six-year-old children learning to read in Taiwan. Like us, Hu and Catts reported a highly significant correlation between the children's ability to read Chinese characters and their performance on a phonological awareness test. They concluded that "the relation between phonological processing skills and early reading success is not specific to an alphabetic language. This relation extends to a logographic language as well" (p. 2).

We believe that such a conclusion may be somewhat premature. Hu and Catts did not attempt to partial out the effects of potentially confounding variables such as IQ and vocabulary before they examined the relationship between phonological awareness and Chinese reading scores. In addition, as Hu and Catts acknowledge, because they employed a cross sectional design, their results do not allow one to determine whether there is a causal relationship between phonological awareness and success in learning to read Chinese (Wimmer et al., 1991).

One particularly interesting aspect of Hu and Catts' study was their finding that phonological awareness test scores were significantly correlated with children's performance on a test of reading in Zhu-Yin-Fu-Hao. Moreover, they found that the relationship between phonological awareness and learning to read Chinese characters remained significant even when the effect of reading skill in Zhu-Yin-Fu-Hao had been partialled out. This result is consistent with a link between phonological awareness skills and the ability to process the phonetic component of compound characters.

Consequently, this potentially important result is well worthy of further investigation in the future.

Our somewhat conservative conclusions about the relationship between phonological awareness and learning to read Chinese could be seen as having implications for theories about the relationship between phonological awareness and learning to read English. Even though this relationship has been demonstrated on many occasions, it is always possible that the effects of phonological awareness on reading might be in fact caused by a correlation between some as yet undetected variable and both reading and phonological awareness. If this was the case then one might have expected that this variable would produce an equally strong relationship between phonological awareness and the reading of a non-alphabetic writing system. Our findings are thus consistent with the view that phonolgical awareness is a primary cause of differences in reading ability amongst children who read an alphabetic script.

However, it must not be forgotten that our results did reveal significant correlations between phonological awareness scores and reading scores in children learning to read Chinese. In addition, the relationship that we observed between phonological awareness and reading in the six-year-old Taiwanese children was identical to that which has sometimes been reported with children learning an alphabetic script (Wagner & Torgesen, 1987). We would therefore like to see our results replicated by others in the future before they are taken as showing definitively that phonological skills are of less importance for learning to read Chinese than English.

Visual Skills

The fixed order regression analysis showed that performance on the test of visual skills was the most powerful predictor of reading ability in both the eight-year-old Taiwanese and the eight-year-old Hong Kong children. This suggests that the ability to learn unfamiliar figures of the kind used in the visual paired associates test is closely related to the ability to learn a new Chinese character and that a child with excellent visual memory skills is likely to have a significant advantage when he or she learns to read Chinese characters. Consistent with this, the effects of visual skills on learning to read were of much less importance in the data from the English children. There was a significant simple correlation between reading and visual form discrimination, but this was no longer significant when the effects of IQ were partialled out.

However, the relationship between performance on the visual skills test and learning to read Chinese was very different in our two investigations. In the data from the six-year-old children, by contrast, visual skill was not a significant predictor of Chinese reading when the effects of the Raven's IQ test were controlled. There are at least three possible reasons for the discrepancy between the two studies.

First, Hoosain (1986) claimed that learning to read the Chinese language facilitates visual form manipulation. If this is true, then children who are better readers may develop superior visual skills over time. However, this explanation is weakened by the fact that we found no significant increase in visual skill after children had been learning to read Chinese characters for a year.

Alternatively, visual skill may not be important for beginning readers, but may become critical in subsequent school years as the impact of the children's intense early training in the alphabetic system fades over time. Consistent with such a possibility, Hu and Catts (1994) found no correlation whatsoever between learning to read and performance on a visual memory test in their first grade Chinese readers. However, Hu and Catts' visual test was basically a spatial short-term memory test, which may not necessarily be sensitive to the same skills as the visual tests that were used in our study, and to those that may be involved in reading Chinese.

Finally, it is also possible that the Raven's (1977) test was itself picking up the visual skills which are critical for learning to read in these young children. Raven's test was chosen as a measure of general intellectual skills in order to maintain comparability with developmental studies of English reading which have frequently used this measure (Goswami & Bryant, 1990). However, the correlations that we observed in this study between Raven's scores and Chinese reading (e.g., 0.44 at the third testing session) were particularly high. Therefore, it might be preferable if future studies of the way that children learn to read Chinese were to use a different test to assess general intellectual ability. Without doubt, our results again suggest that the relationship between visual skills and reading Chinese requires further investigation from studies in the future.

Comparison of the Nature of Phonological Awareness Skills in Chinese and British Children

Do children perform better on phoneme deletion tests in their own language if they have learnt an alphabetic writing system?

The study also provided an opportunity to investigate the nature of phonological awareness skills in Chinese children. Read, Zhang, Nie and Ding (1986) claimed that phonological skill is not acquired naturally in the absence of learning an alphabetic script. They compared two groups of adult subjects. One of these had learned to read Chinese characters via

Pinyin. The other group had not learned Pinyin and were literate only in Chinese characters. The results showed that Chinese adults literate only in Chinese characters found it difficult to add or delete individual consonants in spoken Chinese words. In contrast, subjects in the Pinyin group could perform the same tasks readily and accurately.

Read et al.'s (1986) study provided strong evidence that phonological awareness skills are improved by learning an alphabetic script. The present study gave us an opportunity to replicate and extend their findings in two ways. First, we were able to examine whether their relative lack of familiarity with Zhu-Yin-Fu-Hao would lead to worse performance by the eight-year-old Hong Kong children on Chinese phoneme deletion tests than the Taiwanese children. Second, we predicted that the phonological awareness skills of the six-year-old Taiwanese children would improve dramatically immediately after they had learnt Zhu-Yin-Fu-Hao.

The results supported both of these predictions. After learning Zhu-Yin-Fu-Hao, the performance of the 40 Taiwanese children aged six years improved significantly on the phoneme deletion test ($p < .01$) from 7.1/20 (pre-test) to 12.1/20 (post-test). This improvement occurred despite the fact that there was a gap of only ten weeks between the two testing periods. This improvement is likely to be specific to the learning of Zhu-Yin-Fu-Hao rather than to greater maturity because there was no further improvement in performance on the phoneme deletion test when children were re-tested at the end of the school year. Consistent with these findings, the eight-year-old children from Taiwan, who had been taught Zhu-Yin-Fu-Hao two years earlier, performed significantly better ($p < .01$) on Chinese phoneme deletion (16.8/20) than the eight-year-old Children from Hong Kong (5.4/20), where Zhu-Yin-Fu-Hao is not taught.

It should be emphasized that the instruction of Zhu-Yin-Fu-Hao does not specifically teach these kinds of skills. As Read et al., (1986) pointed out, "there is not a classroom exercise like the deletion task" (p. 42). Our findings are consistent with the results of Read et al. (1986) in showing that people who have not learnt Pinyin had difficulty in adding or deleting individual consonants in spoken Chinese words. The findings are also consistent with the results of Mann (1986) which revealed relatively poor phoneme deletion ability in Japanese children who have not learnt an alphabetic script. Our results show that the phonological awareness of such children immediately increases once they have learnt an alphabetic system.

Are the improvements caused by learning an alphabetic script language specific?

When we administered the English phoneme deletion tests to the Chinese children, the results changed strikingly. It turned out to be the case that the children from Hong Kong knew some English. These children, now in the third grade, studied English as a second language for seven hours per week at school, having studied it for 5 hours a week in the first grade, and six hours a week in the second grade. They studied both written and spoken English, and were therefore familiar with the Roman alphabet.

Despite their poor performance on Chinese phoneme deletion tests, an analysis of variance revealed that the eight-year-old children from Hong Kong performed overall as well (32.4/40) as the British children (34.1/40) on the English phoneme deletion tests. By contrast, the eight-year-old children from Taiwan, who had little or no exposure to English, were quite unable to perform phonological awareness tests in English. None of the children that we tested were able to make a response of any kind, and we were forced to abandon testing to avoid distressing them.

It therefore appears to be the case that the advantages of learning an alphabetic script for performance on phoneme deletion tests are only present if the child has learnt an alphabetic script in the language in which they are being tested. The Hong Kong children have learned an alphabetic script for English but not for Chinese. Hence, they can perform relatively well on English phoneme deletion tasks but not on Chinese phoneme deletion tasks, even though their reading ability is clearly much better in Chinese than in English. Conversely, the Taiwanese children have learnt an alphabetic script for Chinese but not for English. Hence, they can perform well on Chinese phoneme deletion tests but not on English phoneme deletion tests.

One possible reason for this is that children might be implicitly generating a representation of the word's spelling from which they delete a letter, the task therefore entailing letter rather than phoneme deletion (Ehri & Wilce, 1980). On most of the trials, this would have produced the correct answer. In order to check whether this account is true, it would be interesting to use a set of words where such a strategy would not work (e.g., made > may) in future experiments. As the following section demonstrates, however, it may be differences in the phonotactic rules of Chinese and English that are primarily responsible for the differences in phoneme deletion test performance by the Hong Kong and Taiwanese children in the two different languages.

The qualitative nature of phonological awareness skills in children speaking different languages

In this section, we investigate whether differences in the phonemic structure of a language produces differences in the phonological awareness skills of children who speak that language. Children who speak English or French find phoneme deletion more difficult when they have to delete the initial phoneme from words with CCVC structures than from words with CVC structures (Morais, Cluytens & Alegria, 1984; Perfetti, et al. 1987; Stuart & Coltheart, 1988). It appears that these childen treat consonant clusters as single units. By contrast, Caravolas and Bruck (1993) observed that Czech children (aged six years) had no difficulty deleting a target phoneme when it was embedded in a cluster onset (CCV) either in the native language condition (Czech) or in the foreign language condition (English). The reason proposed by Caravolas and Bruck was that Czech and English differ at the level of syllable structure in that Czech has a higher frequency and a variety of complex onsets than English.

In Chinese, however, there are no consonant blends in syllables. This is the case for all Chinese languages including Cantonese, Mandarin, and Min. As Wang (1973) noted: "One striking feature of Chinese words in comparison with most European words is the lack of clusters of consonants before and after the nuclear vowel. When European words with consonant clusters are represented in Chinese, they are typically broken up so that each consonant has its own syllable" (p.57). The name "Clinton", for example, is rendered with three characters representing three syllables: [kuh]-[lin]-[ton]. It is therefore interesting to discover whether the ability to parse consonant clusters differs in Chinese and British children.

When the results were analyzed, it emerged that the British children were significantly better ($p<.01$) than the Hong Kong children only on first sound deletion from CVCC words. Conversely, the Hong Kong students were significantly better than the English children on CCVC first sound deletion ($p<.01$). End sound deletion did not differ in the 2 groups. In addition, CVCC first sound deletion was significantly more difficult than CCVC first sound deletion for the Hong Kong subjects ($p<.01$). For example, to delete /s/ from "stop" was easier than to delete /t/ from "task" for the Hong Kong group. In contrast, English children found first sound deletion to be significantly more difficult in CCVC words than in CVCC words ($p<.01$).

Relatively poor performance by English subjects when asked to delete a phoneme from an initial consonant cluster is consistent with the findings of Morais et al. (1984) and Perfetti et al. (1987). Morais et al. showed that normal French-speaking children in the first and second grades had less trouble deleting an initial consonant from a CVC item than from a CCVC item. Perfetti et al. (1987) showed that children performed better when the consonant was an onset (e.g., deleting /s/ from sit) rather than when it was part of an onset (e.g., deleting /s/ from star). Treiman (1985) argued that English speaking children always group the phonemes in a syllable into the onset and the rime and that initial consonant clusters are treated as single units. Stuart and Coltheart (1988) also suggested that their subjects treated initial consonant clusters as single units. They suggested that four-and five-year-olds considered that 'bread' began with /br/ not with /b/; that 'grapes' began with 'gr' not with 'g'; and that 'plum' began with /pl/ not with /p/. Consequently, they tended to delete the entire cluster when asked to delete the first phoneme. These facts suggest that English speaking children often only parse letter strings phonologically into single consonant and single vowel units. Therefore, CCVC, CVCC, and CCVCC words would all be parsed as simple CVC strings.

Caravolas and Bruck (1993) suggested that Czech children (aged six years) had no difficulty deleting a target phoneme when it was embedded in a cluster onset (CCV) because Czech has a higher frequency and variety of complex onsets than English. There are no consonant blends whatsoever in Chinese syllables, however. Bearing this in mind, it perhaps is surprising to note that the Hong Kong children performed so well on initial phoneme deletion of words containing consonant clusters. As was noted earlier with the example of "Clinton" however, the Chinese tend to introduce a vowel after the initial consonant in English words of this kind. If the Hong Kong children are implicitly doing something similar when they hear such words, then the phoneme deletion task in reality becomes a syllable deletion task. As a consequence, this may make it relatively easy for them to parse consonant clusters into separate units.

Why did the Hong Kong children performed worse than the English children when asked to delete the first phoneme from an English word with a single consonant before the vowel? Chinese words tend to be monosyllabic and typically have a *CV* structure. In CVC words, the range of consonants that can follow the vowel is very restricted. In Mandarin, only 2 nasal consonants /n/ and /h/ ever follow the vowel. In Cantonese, /p/, /t/, and /k/ are also possible endings. The fact that Chinese words typically consist of a consonant followed by a vowel or vowel combination may explain the results. It would not be surprising if their experience with words of a CV structure makes Chinese children show a tendency to treat a consonant followed by a vowel as a single unit.

If this is true, then it may explain why the children from Taiwan and Hong Kong performed so differently on phoneme deletion tests in Chinese and English, as reported in the previous section. The variety of consonants at the end of words and the existence of consonant clusters at the start and end of words must have made English seem very alien to the children from Taiwan who had virtually no previous exposure to the English language. This may have made it impossible for them to perform phoneme deletion on English words. The Hong Kong children's greater experience with English words may have made this less of a problem for them. However, knowledge of Zhu-Yin-Fu-Hao will confer upon the Taiwanese children the experience of decomposing Chinese syllables into distinct consonant-vowel units. Without similar experience of Zhu-Yin-Fu-Hao, the Hong Kong children may be much more likely to consider a Chinese CV syllable to be an indivisible unit. This would have made the Chinese deletion tests, which contained a large proportion of CV stimuli, comparatively difficult for them. The finding that the Hong Kong children had relative problems in deleting the first phoneme from a CVCC compared with a CCVC word in the English phoneme deletion test strongly supports such an interpretation.

Performance on the oddity tests, by contrast, appeared to be less affected by knowledge of Zhu-Yin-Fu-Hao than was phoneme deletion performance. The Taiwanese children did out-perform the Hong Kong children on the Chinese odd man out tests, but the differences were relatively small and were much less dramatic than for phoneme deletion. It might be argued that such a result is consistent with the claims of Goswami & Bryant (1990) that rhyme and alliteration skills are much less strongly influenced by learning to read an alphabetic script than is phoneme deletion.

However, it is not clear that one can talk about different levels of phonological awareness (knowledge of rhymes versus knowledge of phonemes) with Chinese as readily as one can with English. In English, vowels are typically followed by one or more consonants, and it is therefore possible to make a distinction between phonological awareness of vowel phonemes and awareness of rimes (Goswami & Bryant, 1990). In Chinese, because so many words comprise a consonant followed by a vowel, such a distinction can be made much less frequently. With many Chinese words, therefore, the ability to judge whether two words rhyme cannot be separated from the ability to judge whether they contain the same final phoneme, and on most of the trials in the phoneme deletion test, the phoneme was deleted at the boundary between the onset and the rime.

Conclusion

The view that phonological awareness skills play a key role in enabling children to learn to read an alphabetic writing system has emerged as a result of a vast research enterprise that has involved a wide variety of research techniques being employed by a large number of investigators from many different countries over a great many years. By contrast, the investigation of whether similar skills play a role in learning to read a logographic system such as Chinese has only just begun.

We must therefore emphasize that our results should be seen as preliminary, the precise nature of the relationship between reading Chinese and phonological awareness requires further clarification. Nevertheless, the fact that many Chinese characters do contain a phonetic component, and the fact that many Chinese children learn a phonological script at the start of their school-days means that this is a more important issue than many might have previously believed to be the case. Moreover, our results have shown that phonological awareness skills and reading ability are significantly correlated in children learning to read Chinese. Our conclusion at present, however, is that these skills may not be playing quite the same role in learning to read Chinese as they do in learning to read English. We have also shown that a comparison of British and Chinese children makes it possible to ask some very interesting questions about the effects of exposure to different writing systems and to words with different syllabic structures on phonological awareness skills. We anticipate that by the end of the century, a large number of detailed investigations of the skills that enable children to learn to read Chinese will have been conducted.

REFERENCES

Bradley, L., & Bryant, P.E. (1983). Categorising sounds and learning to read-A causal connection. *Nature, 301*, 419-421.

Bryant, P.E., & Bradley, L. (1985). *Children's reading problems--Psychology and education.* Oxford: Blackwell.

Caravolas, M., & Bruck, M. (1993). The effect of oral and written language input on children's phonological awareness: A cross-linguistic study. *Journal of Experimental Child Psychology, 55*, 1-30.

Dunn, L.M., Dunn, L.M., & Whetton, C. (1982). *British Picture Vocabulary Scale: Manual for Long and Short Forms.* Berkshire, England: NFER-Nelson.

Ehri, L.C. & Wilce, L.S. (1980). The influence of orthography on reader's conceptualization of the phonemic structure of words. *Applied Psycholinguistics, 1*, 371-385.

Ellis, N.C., & Large, B. (1987). The development of reading: As you seek so shall you find. *British Journal of Developmental Psychology, 78*, 1-28.

Fang, S.P., Horng, R.Y., & Tzeng, O. (1986). Consistency effects in the Chinese character and pseudo-character naming tasks. In H.S.R. Kao & R. Hoosain (Eds.), *Linguistics, psychology, and the Chinese language* (pp. 11-21) Hong Kong: University of Hong Kong.

Flores d'Arcais, G.B. (1992). Graphemic, phonological, and semantic activation of processes during the recognition of Chinese characters. In H.C. Chen & O.J.L. Tzeng (Eds.) *Language processing in Chinese* (pp. 37-66). Amsterdam: Elsevier.

Flores d'Arcais, G.B., Saito, H., & Kawakami, M. (1995). Phonological and semantic activation in reading Kanji characters. *Journal of Experimental Psychology: Learning, Memory and Cognition, 21*, 34-42.

Forrest, R.A.D. (1965). *The Chinese language.* London: Faber & Faber.

Goswami, U., & Bryant, P. (1990). *Phonological skills and learning to read.* East Sussex: Lawrence Erlbaum.

Hoosain, R. (1986). Language, orthography and cognitive processes: Chinese perspectives for the Sapir-Whorf hypothesis. *International Journal of Behavioral Development, 9*, 507-525.

Hu, C.F., and Catts, H.W. (1994). Phonological processing and children's reading of Chinese. *Unpublished manuscript, University of Kansas.*

Huang, H. S., & Hanley, J.R. (1995). Phonological awareness and visual skills in learning to read Chinese and English. *Cognition, 54*, 73-98.

Huang, H.S., & Hanley, J.R. (In Press). A longitudinal study of phonological awareness, visual skills and Chinese reading acquisition amongst first graders in Taiwan. *International Journal of Behavioral Development.*

Lien, Y.W. (1985). *Consistency of the phonetic cues in the Chinese phonograms and their naming latencies.* Unpublished Master's thesis, National Taiwan University, Taiwan.

Lundberg, I., Olofsson, A., & Wall, S. (1980). Reading and spelling skills in the first school years predicted from phonemic awareness skills in kindergarten. *Scandinavian Journal of Psychology, 21*, 159-173.

Maclean, M., Bryant, P., & Bradley, L. (1987). Rhymes, nursery rhymes, and reading in early childhood. *Merrill Palmer Quarterly, 33*, 255-281.

Mann, V.A. (1984). Longitudinal prediction and prevention of early reading difficulty. *Annals of Dyslexia, 34*, 117-136.

Mann, V.A.. (1986). Phonological awareness: The role of reading experience. *Cognition, 24*, 65-92. .

Mann, V.A., and Liberman, I. Y. (1984). Phonological awareness and verbal short-term memory. *Journal of Learning Disabilities, 17*, 592-599.

Morais, J., Cluytens, M,, & Alegria, J. (1984). Segmentation abilities of dyslexics and normal readers. *Perceptual and Motor Skills, 58*, 221-222.

Perfetti, C.A., Beck, I., Bell, L.C., & Hughes, C. (1987). Phonemic knowledge and learning to read are reciprocal: A longitudinal study of first grade children. Special Issue: Children's reading and the development of phonological awareness. *Merrill Palmer Quarterly, 33*, 283-319.

Raven, J.C. (1977). *Guide to using the colored progressive matrices.* (Reprinted) Dumfries, The Crichton Royal.

Read, C., Zhang, Y., Nie, H., & Ding, B. (1986). The ability to manipulate speech sounds depends on knowing alphabetic writing. *Cognition. 24*, 31-45.

Stanovich, K.E., Cunningham, A.E., & Cramer, B.R. (1984). Assessing phonological awareness in kindergarten children: Issues of task comparability. *Journal of Experimental Child Psychology, 38*, 175-190.

Stuart, M., & Coltheart, M. (1988). Does reading develop in a sequence of stages? *Cognition, 30*, 139-181.

Treiman, R. (1985). Onsets and rimes as units of spoken syllables: evidence from children. *Journal of Experimental Child Psychology. 39*, 161-181.

Tunmer, W.E., & Nesdale, A.R. (1985). Phonemic segmentation skill and beginning reading. *Journal of Educational Psychology, 77*, 417-427.

Tzeng, O.J.L., Zhong, H.L., Hung, D.L., & Lee, W.L. (1994). Learning to become a a conspirator: Tale of becoming a good Chinese reader. *Dokkyo International Review, 7*, 303-335.

Wagner, R. K., & Torgesen, J. K. (1987). The nature of phonological processing and its causal role in the acquisition of reading skills. *Psychological Bulletin, 101*, 192-212.

Wimmer, H., Landerl, K., Linortner, R., & Hummer, P. (1991). The relationship of phonemic awareness to reading acquisition: More consequence than precondition but still important, *Cognition, 40*, 219-249.

Wang, W. S.-Y. (1973). The Chinese language. *Scientific American, 228*, 50-63.

Wechsler, D. (1987). *Manual of Wechsler Memory Scale--revised.* New York: The Psychological Corporation Harcourt Brace Jovanovich.

Zhou, Y.G. (1978). [The efficiency of phonetization from the phonetic radicals in present day Chinese characters]. [Chinese Language Journal], *Zhongguo Yuwen, 146*, 172-177. [in Chinese].

PARADIGMATIC ANALYSIS OF CHINESE WORD READING: RESEARCH FINDINGS AND CLASSROOM PRACTICES

CHE KAN LEONG
Department for the Education of Exceptional Children
College of Education
University of Saskatchewan
Saskatoon, Saskatchewan
Canada, S7N 0X1

ABSTRACT. This chapter first examines the morphosyllabic or phonosemantic nature of Chinese, and discusses paradigmatic analysis in emphasizing a network of linguistic connections in analytic Chinese word reading. There is strong evidence from experimental psychology that the "universal" phonological principle also applies to lexical access in Chinese. Studies of phonological processing relating to manipulation of speech sounds by Chinese adults in Beijing, Chinese children in Taiwan and Hong Kong, and Chinese university students in Hong Kong are discussed. Careful analyses of these studies suggest the need to examine linguistic variables, especially the internal structure of the syllable pertaining to sonority contour in spoken word perception and production, intervocalic consonants, and to initial (onset) and final (rime) including tone assignment in Chinese syllables. The precise role of these variables in relation to learning to read and spell in Chinese still needs investigation. Chinese language, linguistics and classroom practices all emphasize the integrative nature in learning the shape, sound and meaning of characters. This integrative approach is supported by the psychological principles of redundancy and precision in promoting lexical representation.

As the author of the last chapter in this volume and as its coeditor, I take umbrage in these lines from T.S. Eliot's **Ash Wednesday**: "Let these words answer. For what is done, not to be done again. May the judgment not be too heavy upon us." More to the point, I attempt to integrate views on phonological and orthographic processing in word reading with special reference to Chinese. Specifically, I discuss what it is and how it is that Chinese children come to understand and learn Chinese characters and words in what Mattingly (1972) terms analytic reading. The emphasis is on the **productivity** of the language system (Mattingly, 1985), which refers to the transcribing of new or possible lexical items, including possible but non-occurring words.

C.K. Leong and R.M. Joshi (Eds.), Cross-Language Studies of Learning to Read and Spell, 379–417.
© 1997 *Kluwer Academic Publishers. Printed in the Netherlands.*

Linking Shape, Sound and Meaning in Chinese Word Reading

The focus of this chapter on the interplay of phonological and orthographic processing in learning to read Chinese is predicated on current research in experimental psychology, on contributions from Chinese language and linguistics, and "real-life" classroom practices. Specifically, the discussion draws on the "Universal" Phonological Principle as proposed and explicated in elegant psychological studies of processing Chinese by Perfetti and his colleagues (Perfetti & Zhang, 1991, 1995a, 1995b, in press; Perfetti, Zhang, & Berent, 1992; Zhang & Perfetti, 1993) and others. The nature of the phonology involved in Chinese word reading may revolve around the age-old **fǎnqiè** principle and its current versions in emphasizing the internal structure of **initials** (onsets) and **finals** (rimes) in lexical items.

While awareness of the syllable structure in speech and in writing is necessary to acquire reading in Chinese, it is not sufficient. Current classroom practices in China emphasize equally inter-related processes of what Halliday (1981) calls the complex of character-syllable-morpheme as the fundamental unit to access in analytical Chinese word reading. These practices integrating **xing** (shape), **shēng** (sound) and **yi** (meaning) in word reading and spelling are firmly rooted in linguistic theories of **hànyǔ** (Chinese language) and **hànzì** (Chinese script). These theories go back to the first systematic study of the Chinese language and script in the monumental dictionary **shuōwén jiězi** compiled by Xǔ Shèn and completed in AD 100 during the Hàn Dynasty.

The inquiry into teaching and learning Chinese began for me in the late 1960s while working on a Chinese type-token study of primary school children in Hong Kong (Leong, 1973). What solid research there was on applied aspects of Chinese reading psychology went back to the 1920s (Ai, 1950). Basic research on experimental aspects took shape during the 1950s to 1980s and flourished at universities in Taiwan, Hong Kong and, to a lesser extent, in China because of societal changes in the last-named (see, Kao & Cheng, 1982, for details).

The pioneering work on speech recoding in reading Chinese characters by Tzeng, Hung, and Wang (1977), and functional cerebral laterality of the Chinese language by the same group may be said to provide the impetus to enhance further systematic studies of information processing of Chinese. In the intervening years, there have been research studies of inter-related issues of cognitive processing of Chinese as discussed in edited volumes (Chen & Tzeng, 1992; Kao & Hoosain, 1984, 1986; Liu, Chen, & Chen, 1988), books (e.g., Hoosain, 1991), in addition to research papers (e.g., Liu, Zhu, & Wu, 1992). These various works have done much to explain the basic mechanisms involved in processing a writing system based more on meaning than on sound, and at the same time elucidate general principles which may apply to reading different writing systems or orthographies.

Paradigmatic and Segmental Analyses

The general question of learning to read in alphabetic or syllabic language systems centers around the question of making contact from the primary activities of listening and speaking to the secondary activities of deciphering print. The nature of this mapping mechanism may vary according to language and writing systems. Even with variations in languages and orthographies, the general principle for beginning readers is one of matching speech signals with lexical or sublexical entries in their abstract, internal lexicon. In alphabetic languages the word with its sublexical structure is usually taken as the starting point of contact because it is represented in print by a transcription of the underlying phonological representation of the speech signal (Liberman & Shankweiler, 1985).

Does the transcription mechanism apply similarly in learning to read Chinese? What is the nature of this mapping mechanism? What are the units of perception and processing for beginning readers and spellers? Is phonemic awareness or manipulation of speech sounds a precursor to, or necessary for, reading Chinese? Is such awareness or analysis mainly limited to learners or users of alphabetic languages or those learning to read and write alphabetically? Such proposals have been made by Read, Zhang, Nie and Ding (1986) in their oft-quoted "phoneme" (strictly nonsegmental phoneme or "speech sound") deletion study with two groups of adult Chinese, one group literate in the traditional Chinese writing system and the other group having learnt the phonetic system in school as well. Similar suggestions are implicit in the study of Hanley and his colleague (Hanley & Huang, this volume; Huang & Hanley, 1995) with children in Hong Kong using traditional Chinese and with children in Taiwan using romanizations of

Chinese known as **zhùyīn fúhào**.

Furthermore, is phonemic awareness or segmentation facilitated according to the degree in which the lexical segments or sublexical units map onto the underlying phonological representation, as asserted by Mann (1985, 1986, 1991) in her cross-language studies (English and Japanese)? If so, alphabets should transcribe phonemes and syllables with strong and weak stress; Japanese kana, morae (closest equivalent being syllables with approximately equal time duration); and Chinese characters, syllables/morphemes with their nonsegmental phonemes.

Morphosyllabic, Phonosemantic Nature of Chinese

To attempt even partial answers to some of the above questions, it is necessary to understand the nature and the characteristics of the Chinese language system. As a writing system, Chinese has been described as "morphemic" by Leong (1973) and Sampson (1985). The term **morphosyllabic** has been proposed recently by DeFrancis (1989) to emphasize the phonetic component of Chinese characters. While this term conveys correctly the "meaning-plus-sound" syllabic system of Chinese and is preferred over the term morphemic, it would appear that the much earlier proposal by Boodberg (1937) of **phonosemantic** could also be considered. Whereas morphosyllabic emphasizes the syllabic aspect of Chinese characters as primary; phonosemantic stresses the meaning part as important.

Strictly, the writing system making contact with the Chinese language is the complex of characters (configurations) plus syllables plus morphemes as explicated by such eminent linguists as Yen Ren Chao (1968), Li Wang (1985) and Michael Halliday (1981) from both synchronic and diachronic Chinese linguistics. While the term "complex of character-syllable-morpheme" favored by Halliday (1981) correctly conveys the shape-sound-meaning inter-relationship of Chinese characters, it is cumbersome. On balance, the term morphosyllabic may be preferred over phonosemantic, if only because the former term has found greater acceptance by scholars in the West.

To relate phonology to the Chinese language and the orthography, there is general agreement that the basic graphic unit is **zì** or the syllable, which almost always corresponds to a morpheme (Chao, 1968; DeFrancis, 1989; Norman, 1988). The graph or the spatial unit of writing in Chinese is termed a "frame" (lexeme) by Wang (1981), or "functional frame" by Chao (1968). It should be noted that Chao (1968) carefully distinguishes in Chinese the "sociological word" (zì) from the linguistic or "syntactic word" (**ci**). He states: "By the 'sociological word' I mean that type of unit, intermediate in size between a phoneme and a sentence, which the general, nonlinguistic public is conscious of, talks about, has an everyday term for, and is practically concerned with in various ways. It is the kind of thing which a child learns to say, which a teacher teaches children to read and write in school..." (Chao, 1968, p. 136).

This smallest unit zì or Chao's (1968) sociological word is "phonologically... the feature, which corresponds roughly to the independent gestures of the articulators" (Wang, 1981, p. 223). Wang goes on to dispute the myth that Chinese is "nonphonetic" and to emphasize that "A syllabary tells us that morpheme x should be pronounced as syllable 1, followed by syllable 2, followed by syllable 3, and so on rather than with morpheme x pronounced as segment 1, followed by segment 2, etc." (Wang, 1981, p. 232). As an early proponent for the term morphosyllabic for Chinese, Wang now prefers "semosyllabic" in that it is "the radical of a character that refers to a wide semantic area" and not so much the character itself referring to a particular morpheme (W.S.-Y. Wang, personal communication, May 3, 1996).

In his insightful writing on Chinese, Halliday (1981, p. 137) also stresses the syllabic nature of Chinese. He suggests that "the phonology [for Chinese] remained a phonology of the syllable, always analyzed into initial and final, with the initials classified by place and manner of articulation and the finals by rhyme, vowel grade, labialization and time" (Halliday, 1981, p. 137). The precise nature of the Chinese syllabary and its decomposition into initials and finals and their roles in early reading will be discussed in subsequent sections.

Segmental, Paradigmatic Analysis

In analyzing Chinese syllabary into constituent parts, could or should the same or similar segmental process as with alphabetic languages apply? According to Chomsky and Halle (1968/1991), the phonetic component of a language is a system arranged in conformity with transformation rules, where surface structures bracketing a string of minimum elements called formatives are mapped onto phonological representation. The formative consists of consonants and vowels and is analyzable into phonemes and morphophonemes which constitute its **segments**. On these views, Mattingly (1987, p. 5) argues that Chinese does not encourage segmental awareness, and "never achieved a true segmental analysis", even though traditional Chinese linguistics analyzes syllables into onset, rime and tone.

This disavowal of Chinese as not being strictly amenable to segmental analysis should be taken to mean that Chinese is not analyzable into discrete phonemes or morphophonemes. The alternative concept of **paradigmatic** word formation process advocated by another linguist Andrew Spencer (1991) may be appropriate for our purpose here. Spencer's general idea is that word formation relies on relationship between the items currently present in the internal lexicon and not on a syntagmatic process of compounding. The paradigmatic process is explained in terms of analogies made between members of a set of utterances sharing similar speech characteristics as in BEAK-PEAK (Mattingly, 1987). The process is defined more specifically as a "network of relationships, such that, if a language has an empty place at some point in the network, that place will normally be filled" (Spencer, 1991, p. 417).

Paradigmatic Analysis as "Slot-Filling"

This paradigmatic analysis of slot-filling of immediate linguistic constituents from a syntactic perspective has much to commend itself and is the preferred term here. To maintain that Chinese analytic word reading is paradigmatic is not to diminish the importance of the internal structure of the syllable. The phonological analysis of the syllable revolves around the hierarchical structure of onset and rime further analyzable into peak or nucleus and coda. Semantically, how morpheme complexes fill corresponding positions in the sentence constitutes the paradigmatic aspect of word analysis.

Chao's (1968, p. 183) "first approximation to a paradigmatic definition" of "a minimum form which has unlimited versatility in combination with a certain form class or form classes" emphasizes the productive aspect of Chinese lexical items.

This versatile or productive aspect is achieved through morphological reduplication, morphological affixation in accordance with Chao's other criteria of intelligibility and practicality (acceptance as spelling unit) (Leong, 1995). As an example, there are more "versatile" end morphemes or suffixes than prefixes to generate a number of new Chinese words.

The emphasis on the paradigmatic analysis of Chinese words is important for several reasons. One reason is that with the current phonetic system for beginning reading, what constitutes a syntactic word will determine the way that word is transcribed phonetically. The other reason is that in real classroom practices, learning to read Chinese integrates the phonological and orthographic components in parallel in building a network of related shape, sound and meaning components. This integrative view is well accepted in Chinese linguistics and pedagogy and is underscored by the concept of the complex of characters-syllables-morphemes emphasized by Halliday (1981).

To summarise this part of the discussion, Chinese is best described as a morphosyllabic language system; and is predominantly analytic (as compared with synthetic languages) in that the basic unit the character is coterminous with the syllable, which is basically a morpheme (hence the "monosyllabic myth" of Chinese). The analytic process of syllabification is best considered as paradigmatic, if not strictly segmental, in that the emphasis should be on analyzing and integrating the complex of the configuration, phonology and meaning inherent in the character as a lexical item. In emphasizing the syllabary nature of Chinese, whether it is morphosyllabic as proposed by DeFrancis (1989), or phonosemantic as suggested by Boodberg (1937), the rhythmic, alternating aspects of sounds of words are seen as forming the basis of syllables and as the point of contact from spoken to written language in learning to read and spell in Chinese.

Contribution from Experimental Psychology

The question of interest for our present purpose is the nature and mechanism of phonological processing of Chinese characters. Of particular significance are the research programs of Tzeng in both Riverside and Taiwan (Hung & Tzeng, 1981; Hung, Tzeng, & Tzeng, 1992; Tzeng, Hung, & Wang, 1977; Tzeng &

Wang, 1983), of Perfetti in Pittsburgh (Perfetti & Zhang, 1991, 1995a, 1995b, in press; Perfetti, Zhang, & Berent, 1992; Zhang & Perfetti, 1993), of Chen in Hong Kong (e.g., Chen & Tzeng, 1992), among others.

Pioneering Phonetic Recoding Study of Chinese

Of the growing and important literature on phonological processing of Chinese characters, it is instructive to outline the pioneering study by Tzeng, Hung and Wang (1977). In their Experiment 1 Chinese subjects were presented visually with four Chinese characters followed immediately by an oral interference task and were then asked to recall the previously presented four characters in their correct order. The interference task was either phonemically similar or dissimilar to the target characters. The hypothesis tested was that if phonetic recoding occurred, then the interference characters would disrupt the memory for the to-be-recalled items. The results confirmed the hypothesis. The second experiment of Tzeng et al. using sentences (normal and anomalous versions) with phonemically similar characters/words and phonemically dissimilar characters or words provided further support for the hypothesis. Phonemic similarity was found to affect not only short-term memory retention of unrelated Chinese characters but also the reading of meaningful sentences.

The pioneering study of Tzeng et al. (1977) is important for several reasons. One reason is that the results showing performance decrease because of phonemic similarity in the interfering characters and those to be recalled singly or in sentence frames, provide evidence for phonetic recoding in working memory in processing Chinese. This phonetic recoding in working memory suggests the phonological mechanism is postlexical in deriving meaning from lexical items; and serves "reference holding" purposes in sentence comprehension. The other reason is that this study was prototypical for subsequent studies; and alerted other researchers to the possibility of broadly common phonetic recoding mechanisms in lexical access of writing systems as disparate as Chinese from English.

"Universal" Phonological Principle of Chinese Word Reading

In a series of elegant studies of Perfetti in Pittsburgh (Perfetti & Zhang, 1991, 1995a, 1995b), of Chen in Hong Kong (e.g., Chen & Tzeng, 1992) of Liu in

Taiwan (e.g., Liu, Zhu, & Wu, 1992), among others, have proposed the **"Universal" phonological principle**, and have educed strong psychological evidence of processing English and Chinese to support their claim. In a tour de force paper, Perfetti, Zhang, and Berent (1992) raise several research questions of generalized phonological activation in processing Chinese and provide some detailed answers. These questions relate to the pre-and post-lexical activation; the generalized nature of the activation; the function of the activation; and the nature of the phonological properties involved. Discussion here is necessarily succinct and accents mainly that part of Perfetti et al's. research program pertaining to Chinese analytic word reading.

Priming, Backward and Forward Masking Studies

In essence, on the questions of "when" and "how general" Perfetti et al. show from their various studies using backward masking paradigm with word or pseudoword (for English only) targets and graphemic and phonemic masks exposed at very brief duration that the phonological activation is one of "lexical phonology", which occurs "at-lexically" or "lexically". Perfetti et al. (1992, p. 228) state that phonological activation is a component of word identification and "always plays some part in identifying the word, provided the writing system allows it to do so." The degree of generalized phonological activation varies according to different writing systems in terms of the chronometric or time course of retrieval. There is "increasing reason to believe that universal reading processes include phonological constituents as part of word identification." (Perfetti & Zhang, 1995a, p. 31).

In an earlier study in reading Chinese characters, Perfetti and Zhang (1991, Experiment 3) obtained a phonemic priming effect on target recognition when the prime was exposed at 50 ms, but not at 20 ms. Their Experiment 4 with unlimited exposure to the target and limited exposure to the prime further confirmed the priming effect for phonemic primes. These results led the authors to suggest that semantic and phonological information are activated as part of the word identification process in Chinese. More recently, Tan, Hoosain, and Peng (1995) focussed on semantic "fuzziness" and precision in a backward masking procedure with exposure duration of 60 ms and 40 ms respectively for the target `and mask, and found evidence for phonological activation before access to meaning in commonly used Chinese characters.

In reviewing their own and the Tan et al. (1995) results, Perfetti and Zhang (1995a, 1995b) suggest that phonemic mask reduction effect may emerge at sufficient exposure for targets, and reiterate the "at-lexical" phonological processing in Chinese lexical access. However, the notion of early activation of phonemic information, or at least its strong version, has not gone unchallenged. Wu and Liu (1995) point out that phonemic masking effects found by Perfetti and his colleagues may show only some activated phonemic information is reinstated. In three parallel naming experiments with hogh- and low-frequency phonetic compounds, Wu and Liu found slower latencies in naming phonetics than in naming characters and suggested that any strong versin of "at lexical" phonological processing of Chinese characters requires independent evidence that a character is not yet recognized when its phonology is activated (I.M. Liu, personal communication, June 28, 1996; Wu & Liu, 1995).

Tongue-Twister Studies

Another source of evidence comes from a study with two experiments by the Pittsburgh group of researchers using the visual "tongue-twister" paradigm in Chinese (Zhang & Perfetti, 1993). Specific, significant phonemic interference was observed in the time in reading orally and silently tongue twister passages as compared with control texts (Experiment 1). The tongue-twister texts were designed with these sets of nonsegmental phonemes: alveolar stops (/t/ & /d/), bilabial stops (/b/ & /p/), velar stops (/g/ & /k/), and alveolar fricatives (/s/, /z/, & /c/); while the control passages contained mixed phonemes. Furthermore, the interaction between remembering the phonemic contents of digits (beginning with bilabial stops and alveolar fricatives) while reading tongue-twister passages involving the same nonsegmental phonemes of bilabial stops and alveolar fricatives (Experiment 2) suggests interference in working memory.

The Zhang and Perfetti 1993 study replicated and extended the McCutchen, Bell, France, and Perfetti (1991) study using English tongue-twisters with word-initial phonemes differing in place of articulation for stop consonants and also alveolar fricatives. Taken together, these innovative tongue-twister studies with both English and Chinese materials show that automatic phonological coding applies to both English and Chinese; and that this phonological involvement serves working memory and reading comprehension.

In this connection, we should also note the study by Ren and Mattingly (1990), which shows that phonological similarity affects the performance of poor grade 2 readers of Chinese more than good readers under the visual condition. Xu (1991) provides evidence that sensitivity of short-term memory to phonemic similarity extends to tonal features in Chinese over and above underlying abstract phonological representation.

To summarize this section on phonological involvement in word reading in English and Chinese, there is strong evidence for generalized phonological activation across writing systems. Moreover, different language systems constrain the extent and time course of this activation. Perfetti, Zhang and Berent (1992, p. 231) are emphatic that theirs is "a principle-based theory of phonological activation during reading, with lexicon." Moreover, "... we believe it is useful to stay at the level of principle rather than at the level of algorithm in a theory of phonological activation, or word identification generally. Implementation of the principles can be along network activation lines. On the other hand, a lexicon may be needed, certainly for other reading processes and probably for identification as well." (Perfetti, Zhang, & Berent, 1992, p. 231).

Manipulation of Speech Sounds by Chinese Subjects

The necessarily succinct discussion in the preceding section explains that an analytic approach is applicable to Chinese word recognition and that phonological coding is also involved as a constituent process. The psychological studies using different experimental paradigms such as lexical access, naming, priming with stimulus onset asynchrony (SOA), forward and backward masking all converge to support the "'universal' phonological principle" of Perfetti, Zhang and Berent (1992) in accessing lexical items.

There is another aspect in phonological processing pertaining to phonemic awareness (Wagner & Torgesen, 1987) that is necessary for learning to read in alphabetic languages. Much has been written on the theory of and research into phonemic awareness (see Leong, 1987 chapters 6 & 7, 1991; Stanovich, 1988), and the efficacy of explicit training to help learning to read (e.g., Lundberg, Frost, & Petersen, 1988); and will not be pursued here.

For the purpose in this paper, the aspect of awareness and manipulation of speech sounds in studies of Chinese subjects is of direct relevance and will be discussed in some detail. Since acquisition of syllabary literacy refers to the morphosyllabic or phonosemantic Chinese, the appropriate term should be access to phonological or linguistic structure. Since the prototypic study by Read, Zhang, Nie and Ding (1986) of speech sounds manipulation by Chinese adults has spurred on subsequent research, the work will be briefly revisited as the starting point of our discussion.

Revisiting Study by Read et al. (1986)

In essence, Read et al. (1986) predicated their phonemic segmentation study on similar logic and tasks as used by the Brussels group of Morais and Bertelson (Morais, Bertelson, Cary, & Alegria, 1986; Morais, Cary, Alegria, & Bertelson, 1979). The Read et al. finding of performance difference in a phoneme deletion or addition task of real and pseudo English words by adult Chinese literates, exposed or not exposed to the Chinese pīnyīn (alphabetic) transliteration system, generally replicated the results of the Brussels study with Portuguese illiterates and ex-literates.

This work by Read et al., just as that by the Brussels group, is important in showing that segmental analysis of phoneme deletion and addition does not develop spontaneously and needs to be instilled in, if not taught explicitly to, learners. This is the puzzlement raised and partly answered by the authors in that their Chinese adult literates may have had many years of "reading and writing nonalphabetically in a language rich in implicit examples like rhymes, minimal pairs, and phonetic radicals, not to mention Spoonerisms..." (Read et al., 1986, p. 43); and yet the "nonalphabetic" group performed much below chance level.

With hindsight, readers may ponder the reasons for the almost ceiling performance of the pīnyīn group of 12 adults as compared with the almost floor performance of the nonalphabetic group of 18 adults in adding or deleting phonemes (Figures 1 & 2 of Read et al., 1986). The rather distinct bimodal distributions may pertain to subject characteristics, to the actual tasks used or to both.

On the stimulus materials of adding or deleting the phonemes of /d/, /s/, and /n/ in Read et al. (1986), it would appear that the extremely low performance by the 18 nonalphabetic adults may be explained in terms of the **sonority** principle. This principle relates to the alternating, rhythmic characteristics of succession of sound and was first articulated by Jesperson (1904), Bloomfield (1933/1962), and further elaborated by such theoretical linguists as Goldsmith (1990) and psycholinguists such as Treiman (1989), among others. The sonority principle and its effect on phonemic or syllabic analysis will be further discussed in subsequent sections. If it can be assumed that the sonority principle applies to the perception of initial consonants or consonant clusters (onsets), then /d/ as a voiced stop is extremely low in sonority, /s/ as an alveolar fricative and /n/ as a nasal stop also have medium to low "rating" on the sonority continuum. The medium to low sonority rating of the phoneme items obviously did not encourage the performance of the nonalphabetic group.

Still, the sonority principle of speech perception does not explain why the alphabetic group performed almost at ceiling level despite the two groups being "similar in education and experience" except for the reported alphabetic learning. Perhaps the nonalphabetic group was sensitive to phonological tasks other than the segmental analysis of phonemes. What I wish to draw attention to is the effect of linguistic structure on performance in segmentation or related phonological processing tasks. The Read et al. study and related studies by the Brussels group provide evidence that there is generalized, or global phonological ability as shown in rhyming tasks and this global phonological ability may differ from the more analytic segmental analysis. This distinction is also drawn in a recent study with preschool, kindergarten and grade school Brazilian children (Cardoso-Martins, 1994).

Study of Chinese Children's Phoneme Segmentation

There are other issues implicit in the Read et al. study. These are issues on the nature of accesss to the phonological structure in Chinese learners and the relationship to reading. Hanley and his colleague (Hanley & Huang, this volume;

Huang & Hanley, 1995) address some of these issues with well designed tasks. These researchers examined the effect of phonological awareness (rhyming and alliteration) in spoken words (the same tone for the Chinese items), English and Chinese phoneme deletion tasks for the respective subjects, and visual skills (discrimination and paired associates) on the reading ability of a total of 137 eight-year old primary school children in Taiwan, Hong Kong and England. It should be noted that children in Hong Kong use traditional Chinese orthography, while children in Taiwan use zhùyīn fúhào (a set of phonetic symbols along the lines of IPA transcription) in learning to read.

There are several interesting findings in the Hanley and Huang and Huang and Hanley studies. One main result is that when general ability and vocabulary were partialled out, the performance of the Chinese children on the phonological tasks did not relate significantly to their reading. The other finding is that the Taiwanese children's performance on the Chinese phoneme deletion task was "reminiscent" of the results of Read et al. (1986). Another main finding is that the English subjects outperformed their Chinese age-peers in deleting the first sound from CVCC words, whereas Hong Kong children did significantly better than their British peers in deleting first sounds from CCVC words. The explanation given by the researchers is that the consonant clusters were treated by the British children as single units; whereas the Hong Kong children performed well on consonant clusters because "there are no consonant blends whatsoever in Chinese syllables" (Huang & Hanley, 1995, p. 95). This is a strong statement as the aspirated affricate /ts/ in the consonantal onsets of some Chinese characters could be considered the closest to consonant clusters (Chao, 1968). Moreover, from their studies of syllables containing clusters and those not containing clusters, Treiman and Zukowski (1991) state that in terms of syllable structure on phonological awareness: "...the present results suggest that clusters are **not** always harder than single phonemes" (p. 76, original emphasis). It would thus be instructive to know the precise nature of the phoneme deletion tasks in both English and Chinese. In the last analysis, it is the linguistic status and structure that are critical in our understanding of access to linguistic structure.

Segmental and Syllabic Analysis by Chinese College Students

Recently, Sophia Hsia of the City University of Hong Kong (CityUHK) and I carried out a study on phonological and morphological processing of Chinese university students learning English along the lines of our earlier work and within a framework of componential analysis of reading (Hsia, 1992; Leong, 1992). Of relevance here is that part of the overall study dealing with segmental and syllabic analysis of English by 82 Cantonese speaking Chinese subjects completing their first year of English studies at CityUHK.

The hypothesis tested was that students in the Pǔtōnghuà language (PL) subgroup (n = 24 students) receiving Pǔtōnghuà (Common Language) segmental and syllabic training should perform better in phonological tasks than would their counterparts in the Cantonese language (CL) subgroup (n = 58 students) not receiving such training. These two subgroups were equated in their reading comprehension and memory span prior to the main study. Using the term training in the broad classroom sense, we put forward the "very tentative suggestion that the learning of Pǔtōnghuà and segmental training promote the learning of phonological and phonetic principles in English." (Leong & Hsia, 1996). This tentative suggestion still holds but needs to be refined. I now wish to report on further, fine-grained analysis of the relevant data, which may add to our understanding of segmental and syllabic analysis by adult learners.

Tasks and procedure.

To examine the segmental and syllabic analysis of the Pǔtōnghuà and Cantonese language subgroups, these tasks were given:

(1) Segmental analysis of English initial consonants or consonant clusters (EIC) and English final consonants (EFC). There were 16 English (c)cvc(c) pseudowords (4 to 7 letters) such as PRINGS /priŋz/, SHEEKS /si:ks/, THAVES /Qeivz/ and JAKE /dzeɪk/. The procedure for the EIC task was as follows: "If I say -ANK (for the pseudoword VANK), what is the *beginning sound* left out of the letter string?"; and for the EFC task for the same 16 pseudowords was: "If I say VAN- (for VANK) what is the *end sound* left out of the letter string?" All the items were randomized and the subjects were required to supply the deleted initial

consonant or consonant clusters or the deleted final consonants, as applicable.

(2) Segmental analysis of Cantonese initial consonants (CIC) in 25 Chinese characters/words across 3 Cantonese tones with Cantonese phonemes considered in positions of flux, such as liquids /l/ and nasals /n/, the velar stop /k/, and the guttural /h/. The linguistic basis of the design of the "written Cantonese" and written Chinese items was motivated by Bauer's (1988) detailed analysis of registers of spoken Cantonese. Subjects were required to say the Cantonese equivalent of English words such as NYLON, [a] PEAR (discrimination and production of critical initial /l/ and /n/ in Cantonese).

(3) Syllabic analysis of the phonetic category of intervocalic consonants of liquids, nasals, fricatives and stops with 30 items with stress on the first syllable (ES1) (e.g., MALICE, RELISH), and another 30 items with stress on the second syllable (ES2) (e.g., SARONG, EMERGE) adapted from Treiman and Danis (1988, Experiments 1 & 2). The 82 subjects were required to put a slash (/) to "break up the written word" for the "best" syllabification, although the latter term was not used (e.g., PA/TIENT, E/MERGE). The general idea is that every syllable contains a vowel or syllabic consonants and there are orthographically defined units of intervocalic consonants.

Deeper Linguistic Explanation of Results

In general, statistical analyses comparing the performance of the subgroup of 24 students with training in Pǔtōnghuà segmental analysis and the subgroup of 58 students without such training showed significant differences, task for task, with the exception of the English segmentation task for final consonants (EFC). The means and standard deviations of the performance of the two subgroups on the five tasks are shown in Figure 1.

On the surface, the above results as summarized in Leong and Hsia (1996) seem to support the findings of the prototypic Read et al. (1986) and the more recent Huang and Hanley (1995) and Hanley and Huang (this volume) studies in suggesting that segmental analysis is promoted in Chinese students who learn the phonetic system of Pǔtōnghuà or its variant zhùyin fúhào. Further analysis of the within-task data and the items themselves point to the critical role of linguistic variables that will add to the behavioral results. Leong and Hsia (1996) explain the differential performance of the 82 Cantonese-speaking students in the Pǔtōnghuà and non-Pǔtōnghuà subgroups in terms of typological markedness invoked by Eckman (1981) to account for the difficulty of his Mandarin-speaking Chinese subjects in pronouncing English word final-voiced obstruents. Further evidence comes from Flege, McCutcheon, and Smith (1987) who show that Chinese adults find it difficult to distinguish voiceless /p/, /t/, and /k/ from voiced /b/, /d/, and /g/, and are not effective in implementing /b/, /d/, and /g/ sounds.

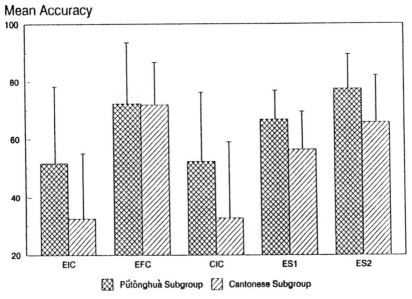

Figure 1. Performance of two subgroups of university students in Hong Kong on segmental analysis of English initial consonants or consonant clusters (EIC) and English final consonants (EFC), segmental analysis of Cantonese initial consonants (EIC), and syllabic analysis fo intervocalic consonants of English words with stress on the first syllable (ESI) and on the second syllable (ES2).

The above explanation of prototypic or "best fit" effects in Chinese students learning English still holds for the present set of data. However, I want to offer more fine-grained linguistic analysis to further explain the segmental and syllabic analysis findings as shown in Figure 1.

It should be noted that the performance of the Pŭtōnghuà subgroup on both the English initial consonant (EIC) and the Chinese initial consonant (CIC) tasks was at about the chance level (mean proportion correct of 51.8% & 52.3% respectively), while the Cantonese subgroup did much worse (32.4 & 32.7% respectively). The English final consonant (EFC) task did not discriminate between the two subgroups (72.4% & 72%). The more discriminating tasks were the syllabic analysis tasks with stress on the first syllable (ES1) and stress on the second syllable (ES2), both adapted from Treiman and Danis (1988). In examining individual differences for the subjects, which were considerable, and the tasks including intra-item differences, it would appear that the sonority principle offers a viable explanation for the chance performance on the initial consonant segmentation tasks for both English and Chinese.

Sonority Contour Principle as Explanatory

In emphasizing Chinese as morphosyllabic (DeFrancis, 1989) or as phonosemantic (Boodberg, 1937) the link between syllables and phonology is evident. The relationship between syllables and sonority contour was long emphasized by Jespersen (1904). In his classic book **Language**, Bloomfield (1933/1966) explains the sonority principle as follows: "In any succession of sounds, some strike the ear more forcibly than others: differences of **sonority** play a great part in the transition effects of vowels and vowel-like sounds. Thus, other things (especially, the stress) being equal, a low vowel, such as [a], is more sonorous than a high vowel, such as [i]; any vowel is more sonorous than a consonant; a nasal, trill, or lateral more than a stop or spirant; a sibilant [s, z], with its concentration of the breath-stream into a narrow channel, more than another spirant; a spirant more than a stop; a voiced sound more than an unvoiced. In any succession of phonemes there will thus be an up-and-down of sonority." (Bloomfield, 1966, p. 120, original emphasis).

The sonority contour principle relating the internal structure of segments to the measurable peaks of sonority could provide an explanation for such tasks as segmental analysis of initial and final consonants and syllabic analysis of stress assignment. For the English initial consonant task, 11 of the 16 items contained consonant clusters. Could this be the possible reason for the performance at 52% and 32% correct for the Pǔtōnghuà and the non-Pǔtōnghuà subgroups? We should also note the caution by Treiman and Zukowski (1991), discussed earlier, that consonant clusters may not necessarily be more difficult to perceive. Still, what might be the reason for the much lower performance of the Cantonese subgroup in perceiving and producing the missing initial consonants? Similar questions could be asked about the accuracy rate of 52% compared with the 33% in the performance of the Cantonese initial consonants. Could the sonority principle also explain the low performance because of the considerable number of items requiring the discrimination and production of the Cantonese liquid /l/ and nasal /n/, both of medium range in sonority?

In contrast, the overall performance for the English final consonants was at 72% accuracy for both subgroups and there was no significant difference. Closer examination of the 16 items reveals that of the 8 final <s>, 4 are voiceless /s/ and 4 voiced /z/; and as alveolar fricatives, these end /s/ and /z/ have medium sonority (Goldsmith, 1990). There are 2 items each of the alveolar stop /d/ and the labial stop /p/, 2 velar stop /k/, and 1 each for labial fricative /v/ and interdental fricative /q/. Results from psychological studies suggest a superioty for fricatives and in isolating final consonants, at least under certain conditions (Treiman & Weatherston, 1992). Moreover, Treiman (1989) has shown for her adult subjects that rimes containing vowels followed by stops or fricatives are easier to divide into phonemes than rimes followed by liquids. Of the 16 items 8 items end in fricatives and 6 in stops, the overall performance of 72% accuracy seem to support the Treiman (1989) and Treiman and Weatherston (1992) findings.

Syllabic Analysis of Intervocalic Consonants

Results of the syllabic analysis of the phonetic category of intervocalic consonants of liquids, fricatives and stops with stress on the first syllable or on the second syllable seem to be more felicitous (Figure 1). The written task of placing the critical intervocalic consonant was clearly affected by stress assignment and was performed better on the second syllable stress (e.g., E/MERGE rather than EM/ERGE). This pattern seems to be the result of the critical intervocalic consonant being more affected by the more sonorous neighboring vowels. This set of findings is in line with the results of Treiman and Danis (1988).

Moreover, the ambisyllabicity effect found by these researchers was also noted with this task. Many subjects seemd unsure about the syllabic division of such words as COMM/A, COMM/AND. They seemed vaguely aware of the illegality of beginning the second syllables of the above words as CO/MMA, CO/MMAND, but were unable to explain the reason and opted by dividing the double consonants as COM/MA, COM/MAND. These observations are also in line with the findings of Treiman and Danis (1988). The results outlined here point to the difficulty in defining truly ambisyllabic consonants. I would agree with Treiman and Danis (1988, p. 100) that "Sonority differences may need to be built into theories of syllabification as well as theories of the structure of individual syllables." In a recent study with disyllabic and trisyllabic stimulus materials, Treiman, Fowler, Gross, Berch, and Weatherston (1995) further show syllabic-based and word-based structures play a role in the processing of spoken English words.

To summarize this part of the report on the segmental and syllabic analysis of initial and final consonants and intervocalic consonants by Chinese university students, detailed study of the linguistic structure has added more explanatory power to the behavioral results as shown in Figure 1 and as outlined in Leong and Hsia (1996). On the surface, the different sets of results seem to lend support to the work with Chinese adults by Read et al. (1986) and to the study with Chinese children by Huang and Hanley (1995) and Hanley and Huang (this volume). Deeper, fine-grained linguistic analysis suggests the need to incorporate more linguisitc principles as advocated by Treiman (1989) and that the sonority contour principle may explain such phonological processing tasks as segmental and syllabic analysis.

However, the question as to why the Cantonese subgroup performed so much poorer than their Pŭtōnghuà counterparts still remains. While Leong and Hsia (1986) are tentative in suggesting possible "training" effect, I would now add that perhaps other aspects of phonological processing should be examined in our quest to understand the role of phonemic awareness and segmentation in Chinese learners. Should we even look for segmentation of phonemes in initial and final positions and its possible link to reading? By its very nature, Chinese syllables emphasize initials (onsets) and finals (rimes) subserved by peaks and codas. The phonological processing of what Chao (1968) terms sociological words may lie more in syllabification as shown with English children and adults by Treiman and her colleagues (Treiman, 1989; Treiman & Danis, 1988; Treiman & Zukowski, 1990, 1991). Furthermore, we should be examining the integral aspects of character complexes of shape, sound and meaning in Chinese word reading.

Language Principles and Classroom Practices

To attempt to answer even part of the above questions, we will need to hark back to the underlying notion of segmentation, explicit in much of the research into access to phonological structure in relation to early reading in English, and implicit in reading Chinese (see Leong, 1991, for discussion). It seems much of the work on manipulation of sounds or segmentation has focussed on the "units of perception". The main candidates for such units are the phoneme and, as discussed here, the syllable along the lines of the research program of Treiman and her colleagues.

In this connection, Cutler and her colleagues (Cutler & Norris, 1988; Norris & Cutler, 1985) have argued convincingly for the search for **classification**, rather than speech segmentation, to develop word identification strategies. Classification refers to "identifying units occurring in the signal" and segmentation means "making a division at some point in the signal" (Cutler & Norris, 1988, p. 114). Furthermore, "It is possible to segment speech without classifying it. That is, the recognizer could segment the signal by choosing points at which to begin lexical access attempts, without necessarily constructing any prelexical representation of the signal as a sequence of specific phonetic segments, syllables, or feet." (Cutler & Norris, 1988, p. 114). Thus the extraction from the speech signal to determine the lexical boundaries or juncture helps in lexical access.

Phonology in Chinese and Unit of Perception - Fǎnqiè Principle

In relating experimental studies of phonemic awareness in Chinese and Chinese students to the concepts of classification and segmentation, we should also be guided by knowledge of Chinese linguistics and language. The main question in our context is the way in which individual Chinese characters are "pronounced" or mapped onto the sound form. The **fǎnqiè** principle going back to the sixth century AD relies on the glossing of heterographic homophones with variations in the tones (primarily variation in pitch contour); and provides a practical and powerful means for pronouncing the characters for many centuries (Chao, 1968; Leong, 1995; Wang, 1985).

Very briefly, the fǎnqiè principle involves the combination of two and only two characters in such a way that the final (rime) of the first character and the initial (onset) of the second character are elided and that the tone of the to-be-pronounced character is the same as that of the second character. In other words, the initial (onset) of the first character and the final (rime) of the second character are blended to provide the pronunciation of the new character. An examples is: [t'u] + [l'iau] = [t'iau] (for the to-be-pronounced character).

The **tones** in Chinese are defined in terms of the rhythmic rise and fall of pitch, or the pitch contour of the voiced part of the character, such that if the initial is voiced, the tone begins with the initial and spreads over the whole syllable; and if the initial is voiceless, the tone is spread over the final only. As examples, the tone for NIAN begins with the voiced /n/, but for the voiceless /p/ in PIAN the tone begins with /i/ or strictly /ia/. The four classical tones are **píng** (even or level), **shǎng** (rising), **qǔ** (going or departing), and **rù** (entering). The modern tones (in Pǔtōnghuà) divide the classical even or level tone into **yīnping** (voiceless) and **yángping** (voiced), giving rise to first and second tones. The Pǔtōnghuà third and fourth tones correspond approximately to the classical rising and going tones respectively.

Thus syllables could alliterate by sharing the same onset syllabics. Syllables could also rhyme by sharing the same **yùn** (rime), or strictly the same **yùnfù** (main vowel), or **yùnwěi** (syllabic ending). It must be emphasized that while the Chinese syllable structure also consists of onset and rime, as with English syllables, the absolute minimum constituents are the yùnfù (main vowel) and the tone.

The tones are important in reading and spelling because they carry phonemic information and different tones change the meaning of the characters. An example is the syllable LIANG, which means "to measure" when pronounced with the second tone, and "quantity" when pronounced with the fourth tone. Another examples is MAI, meaning "to buy" in the third tone and "to sell" in the fourth tone. The differentiation of tones often baffles foreign learners of Chinese and it is largely both local and global contexts of the syntactic word, phrase or sentence that help to decide the correct tone, and also the pronunciation. Pronouncing a Chinese character with the wrong tone is analogous to pronouncing the wrong consonant or vowel in English. Thus studies of phonological processing of Chinese need to incorporate the phonemic aspects especially with the rime elements, and also the tonemic aspects.

Evolution from Fǎnqiè -- Zhùyīn Fúhào and Pīnyīn Systems

It cannot be emphasized too strongly that the fǎnqiè principle going back to the sixth century AD has served well the pronunciation of syllables in classical literary Chinese language (wényán). This long utility is all the more remarkable despite the lack of clear demarcation of consonantal and vocalic segments, and the limitation of the glossing or blending of two and only two syllabics.

Given this background, the zhùyīn fúhào introduced in the 1920s in China provides more flexibility in "pronouncing" Chinese syllables. The zhùyin fúhào consists of a set of phonetic symbols and is designed along the lines of International Phonetic Association (IPA) together with tonal information. The zhùyin fúhào phonetization system integrated with traditional Chinese characters enhances pronunciation and is used in primers for learning to read and spell in Taiwan.

Still more flexible and versatile is the pīnyīn alphabet system used to represent and pronounce different sounds in Pǔtōnghuà (Common Language). Pǔtōnghuà is the standard national language of the People's Republic of China and is based on the Beijing pronunciation. The pīnyīn phonetization system consists of 25 letters (including the half- or semi-vowel of /y/ and /w/) of the alphabet and the four modern tones of yīnping (voiceless), yǎngping (voiced), shǎng (rising) and qǔ (going) shown respectively with the diacritical marks of -, /, v, \ placed above the yùnfù or the main vowel. Space limitation preclude detailed discussion; and interested readers are referred to such sources as Chao (1968), Wang (1985), and Norman (1988), among others.

The general alphabetic principle of pīnyīn and zhùyīn fúhào is illustrated in the three sets of doublets of tongue-twister (ráo kǒu lìng) sentences shown in Figure 2. Take (1a) which means "Ten is (equals) ten.", the same onsets and rimes are used, except for the assignment of the second or voiced tone to denote "ten" and the fourth or the going tone to mean "is". Sentence (1b) means "Ten [does] not equal four." with "bù" (tone 4) to mean "not". The doublet (2a) and (2b) means "Four equals four" and "Four [does] not equal ten." respectively. The parallel sentences (3a) and (3b) refer to "Eating (not eating) pútáo (a fruit) and spitting out (not spitting out) the skin (seed)." The final voiced continuant is a retroflex ending. The retroflex ending of -l or -er, is the only non-syllabic morpheme in Pǔtōnghuà. According to Chao (1968, p. 46), the general principle is "the tendency for articulators to be telescoped together if they are not compatible." Figure 2 showing sentences in traditional Chinese characters (line 1) and the corresponding pīnyīn and zhùyīn fúhào (lines 2 & 3 of each sentence) transliteration illustrates the ways in which characters are pronounced and learned by Chinese learners in their literacy acquisition.

Importance of Onset-Rime Internal Structure for Experimental Studies of Chinese Segmental and Syllabic Analyses

The necessarily succinct discussion of the phonological structure inherent in the morphosyllabic Chinese, and the utilization of zhùyīn fúhào and the more versatile pīnyīn alphabetic principle in early reading, both derivable from fǎnqiè, raise a number of issues for research. As shown in psychological studies by Perfetti and his colleagues (Perfetti & Zhang, 1991, 1995a, 1995b, in press; Perfetti, Zhang, & Berent, 1992; Zhang & Perfetti, 1993), phonology IS involved in analytic word reading of Chinese. This is the "unity in diversity" principle or "the diverse oneness of writing systems" discussed by DeFrancis (1989) in his linguistic treatise. The unity or oneness is the generalized phonological activation

繞口令 （急口令） ráo kǒu lìng

1a) 十是十。

shí shì shí.
ㄕ　ㄕ　ㄕ

1b) 十不是四。

shí bù shì sì.
ㄕ　ㄈㄨ　ㄕ　ㄙ

2a) 四是四。

sì shì sì.
ㄙ　ㄕ　ㄙ

2b) 四不是十。

sì bù shì shí.
ㄙ　ㄈㄨ　ㄕ　ㄕ

3a) 吃葡萄吐葡萄皮兒。

chī pútáo tǔ pútáo pí(er).
ㄐㄧ　ㄅㄟ　ㄊㄠ　ㄊㄨ　ㄅㄟ　ㄊㄠ　ㄆㄧ　ㄋㄧ

3b) 不吃葡萄不吐葡萄皮兒。

bù chī pútáo bù tǔ pútáo pí(er).
ㄈㄨ　ㄐㄧ　ㄅㄟ　ㄊㄠ　ㄈㄨ　ㄊㄨ　ㄅㄟ　ㄊㄠ　ㄆㄧ　ㄋㄧ

Figure 2. Doublets of Chinese tongue-twisters (ráo kǒu lìng) showing pīnyīn plus tonal features and zhùyīn fúhào respectively in the second and third lines for each sentence.

inherent in alphabetic and syllabic writing systems, including Chinese. The pertinent questions to ask are the nature of the phonology involved, the mechanism in processing and if sensitivity to the phonology is the main means to acquiring literacy in Chinese.

From the early study of Read et al. (1986) with Chinese adults, to the Hanley study (Hanley & Huang, this volume; Huang & Huang, 1995) with Chinese children in Hong Kong and Taiwan, and the further analysis of the study with Chinese university students in Hong Kong as summarized in Leong and Hsia (1996), it is reasonable to ask if phoneme segmentation is the best way to tap the access to the structure of the Chinese phonology. Since Chinese is morphosyllabic or phonosemantic with initial (onset) and final (rime) and further decomposable into peak (nucleus) and coda along not dissimilar linguistic lines to English, more fruitful results may emerge from examination of the hierarchical structure of the Chinese syllable and the effect on reading. This aspect has been argued forcefully by Treiman (1989, p. 49). She raises the rhetorical question as to whether or not onset/rime is also a psychological universal in addition to "speculations" of onset/rime being a linguistic universal. Furthermore, studies of intervocalic consonants such as the role of rhyme (yùn) in Chinese in relation to the main vowel, medial glide and syllabic ending, from speech errors and word games (e.g., tongue-twisters), are all relevant and important.

Surface Phonetic Features of Chinese Tones

The integral component of the standard Chinese four tones either in isolation or in context also plays a role in memory and reading. Typically, when the third (rising) tone occurs before another third tone, the first third tone changes to the second tone. This morphophonemic change (not just allophonic change because the second tone is a separate phoneme) is known as tone sandhi (Chao, 1968). This notion of tone sandhi in Chinese was utilized by Xu (1991) in a study of the effect of tonal similarity on short-term memory (STM) for Chinese characters presented visually on the computer screen.

In Xu's Experiment 1 the stimulus materials rhymed (sharing the same final or rime) but differed in the initial (onset); and in Experiment 2 the heterographic disyllabic Chinese nonsense words varied in syllabic structure and tones (either the third or second tone).   The results show that sensitivity of STM to phonological similarity also applies to Chinese, as suggested by the earlier study by Tzeng et al. (1977).   Furthermore, tonal features have a strong effect on STM for the materials.   Xu claims that phonological representation for Chinese characters includes surface phonetic features in speech perception and production analogous to stress assignment in English.   However, Taft and Chen (1992) in their study of homophony judgment by Pǔtōnghuà-speaking and Cantonese-speaking Chinese subjects suggest that tonal information is hard to represent in working memory even though they accept Xu's claim of tonal features as part of phonological representation in distinguishing Chinese morphemes.

Classroom Practices

In his insightful chapter in the Festschrift in honor of Paul Bertelson, Brian Byrne (1992) emphasizes that phonemic awareness combined with letter-phoneme knowledge is necessary, though not sufficient, for acquiring alphabetic literacy. He draws attention to the multitude of processes in reading and to the complexity of "real life" classroom situations beyond experimental psychology.   It is with the same spirit that I examine briefly principles and current practices of teaching beginning Chinese reading and spelling.   From these principles and practices, experimental psychologists can also draw ideas for further experimentation.

Emphasis on Explicit, Systematic Teaching of Word Knowledge

In a recent symposium on curriculum changes and challenges for Chinese communities in Southeast Asia (China, Taiwan, Hong Kong and Singapore), the symposiasts on teaching and learning Chinese in elementary grades all emphasize the integration of the primary linguistic activities of listening, speaking; and the secondary linguistic activities of reading and composing including spelling (Lam, Wong, & Fung, 1993).   These curriculum specialists all stress explicit and systematic instruction of "sociological" and "syntactic" words (Chao, 1968), then proceeding to text materials in their linguistic environment.   Emphasis on morphosyllabic or phonosemantic processes of Chinese is aimed at enhancing both quantitative and qualitative aspects of word knowledge as necessary for reading comprehension.   The foundational aspects of teaching and learning both sociological and syntactic Chinese words in meaningful linguistic and real-life contexts is shown in Figure 3.

Figure 3. Sample page from an early lesson in grade one Chinese primer.

The sample page is from an actual lesson in the early weeks of teaching and learning primary one Chinese in China (People's Education Publishing, 1994). Several features should be noted. First, the characters taught are carefully controlled and sequenced in terms of iconicity (few strokes), and meaningfulness in real-life situations. The characters are the numerals "yí" (one), "sān" (three), "wǔ" (five), "qī" (seven) and "jiǔ" (nine) with their very simple (from one to four) strokes. Second, the children learn in the form of a song and as a game these five characters, first from pīnyīn with tone assignment as shown in the top five lines ("One piece [of leaf], one piece [of leaf], yet one more piece [of leaf]" as in line 1, "two piece(s), three piece(s), four, five piece(s) as in line 2, and in the picture of falling leaves). Parenthetically, numerals in Chinese expressing quantity are bound morphemes and are generally followed by "measures" to yield free morphemes as in the present examples of "yí piàn", "liǎng piàn..." Third, the children are guided in their recognition of these characters and are taught to write these characters almost simultaneously with their word reading. In their writing (spelling) in their workbooks, they are given help in the correct sequence of strokes. This help in the form of writing one stroke, two, then three and subsequent strokes in the correct sequence to the full character is in accordance with the scaffolding principle.

While phonology is emphasized in teaching and learning through pīnyīn, it is only one aspect of acquiring word knowledge. All the aspects of xing (shape), shēng (sound) and yi (meaning) are equally stressed from Chinese language, linguistics, pedagogy and even "folk psychology" going back hundreds of years.

The sequential, systematic and explicit teaching of Chinese sociological and syntactic words, first through pīnyīn, then through character learning both from guided reading and guided writing, is shown in Figure 4 adapted from Ding, Li, & Bao (1985). The instructional goals in the early grades are representative of the aims of Chinese language learning in China. The integrative aspect always emphasizes the combination of oral language with phonological and morphological learning of the characters before moving into reading annotated [with pīnyīn], then unannotated, text materials and composing.

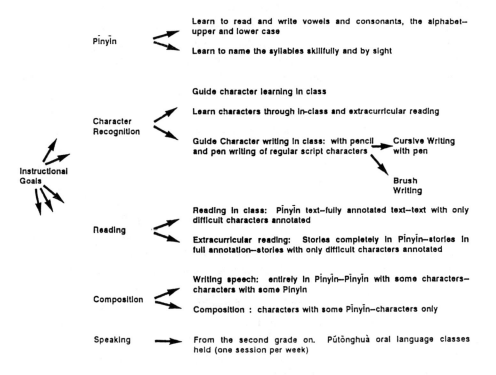

Figure 4. Instructional goals and sequence in learning to read and write in Chinese (from Ding, Li, & Bao, 1985)

Principle of Redundancy and Precision

To summarize this part of the discussion of learning to read and spell Chinese in China and generalizable to other Asian regions, real-life classroom practices are much more complex. Phonological and orthographic processing; reading and composing including spelling are all equally emphasized in game-like formats for beginning readers/spellers (see examples of tongue-twisters in Figure 2, & sample page in Figure 3). This integrative approach is supported by the redundancy principle articulated by Byrne (1992), Seidenberg (1989), and Perfetti (1992).

Byrne (1992) considers reading and literacy acquisition as complex systems, which require backup systems and also backups for backups to minimize breakdowns in a manner analogous to the complex systems in modern passenger aeroplanes. Seidenberg (1989) discusses redundancy in reading complex English words in terms of "orthographic redundancy" or the connection structure of the lexicon, and not so much in terms of syllables or morphemes.

Perfetti (1992) explicates the issue of representation in reading acquisition and emphasizes autonomous aspects of word recognition while allowing for interactive processes in his restricted-interactive model. Perfetti suggests that lexical representation is characterized by the principles of redundancy and precision. Redundancy is provided by the interplay of phonetic strings and orthographic strings and the "bonding" of orthographic with phonological representations. Precision is concerned with fully specified representations as compared with partial or variable representations. Perfetti (1992) states that both the redundancy and precision principles enhance the quantity and quality of words that children know in their becoming proficient readers and spellers. He further suggests that reading and spelling may draw on the same lexical representation.

Thus from a different route, the integrative approach in emphasizing shape, sound and meaning in accessing the linguistic structure of Chinese is in accord with current theories of reading psychology and psycholinguistics. Liberman and Shankweiler (1985, p. 10) emphasize the "understanding of linguistic structure", "awareness of linguistic structure", "metalinguistic awareness of the internal structure of words" and "becoming aware of sublexical structure for the purpose of developing word recognition strategies". Ehri (e.g., 1984, 1994) in her research program has argued forcefully that written language (spelling) provides a powerful visuospatial representation analogous to the temporal-sequential representation of speech, particularly at the phonetic and lexical levels. Ehri proposes that acquiring spellings as symbols of pronunciation helps children to learn phonetic segments of words, when graphemes in the spellings represent slightly different sounds from those in the pronunciation. Ehri's "phonetic symbolization" or amalgamation theory of word reading is in accord with Perfetti's (1992) explication of lexical representation of words according to both the redundancy and precision principles. Classroom practices in teaching and learning reading and spelling in Chinese may be seen along similar dimensions.

Conclusion

One central question in learning to read (and to spell) in alphabetic and syllabic languages is the involvement of phonological and orthographic processes and their interplay. There is general agreement from the research literature that phonology is an integral part in the access to the linguistic structure by learners, and this phonological involvement is constrained only by variations in language or orthography systems.

Chinese is morphosyllabic or phonosemantic and has a phonological basis in analytic word reading. If such analysis is not strictly segmental, divisible into discrete phonemes or morphophonemes, then a paradigmatic analysis in emphasizing a network of linguistic connections is a potent approach to examine the access issue. The "universal" phonological principle proposed by the Pittsburgh group of Perfetti and his colleagues (Perfetti & Zhang, 1991, 1995a, 1995b, in press; Perfetti, Zhang, & Berent, 1992; Zhang & Perfetti, 1993) is supported empirically by studies using different experimental paradigms such as priming, forward and backward masking with Chinese stimulus materials and Chinese tongue-twisters.

The other aspect of phonological processing in Chinese learners, that of manipulation of speech sounds, has been studied by Read et al. (1986) with Chinese adults in China, Hanley and his colleague (Hanley & Huang, this volume; Huang & Hanley, 1995) with Chinese children in Taiwan and Hong Kong, and Leong and Hsia (1996) with Chinese university students in Hong

Kong. These studies are revisited. Further fine-grained analysis of the Leong and Hsia data suggests the strong effect of linguistic variables on segmental analysis of initial consonants in both English and Chinese words and final consonants in English and intervocalic consonants in English words differing in stress assignment. From these studies and from both the linguistic and psychological literature, it is suggested that internal structures of the syllable with its onset (initial in Chinese syllables) and rime (final in Chinese syllables) further decomposable into peak (nucleus) and coda are particularly relevant for analytic Chinese word reading. The sonority contour principle seems to play an important role in perceiving and analyzing speech and lexical units of processing necessary for reading acquisition in English and probably in Chinese. The assignment of Chinese tones has been shown experimentally to be part of the phonological representation, although the precise nature of such representation still needs to be mapped out.

While phonology is integral in learning to read alphabetic and syllabic languages or orthographies and is demonstrated experimentally from studies of lexical access and speech sounds segmentation, real-life classroom situations are much more complex. Chinese analytic word reading is traditionally predicated on the integration of word structure, sound and meaning and this integrative approach is delineated in Chinese language and linguistics, in "folk psychology" and in pedagogy. Current curriculum and classroom practices in teaching Chinese in primary schools are emphatic on explicit, systematic instruction to promote knowledge of sociological and syntactic words (Chao, 1968), beginning with pīnyīn before progressing to text materials with scaffolding to guide learners. This integrative approach involving understanding of the sounds of words, their internal structure, their meaning in local and global contexts and the simultaneous teaching and learning of listening, speaking, reading and writing including spelling is in accord with the morphosyllabic or phonosemantic characteristics of Chinese. Furthermore, the integrative classroom practices are supported by the psychological principles of redundancy and precision to achieve higher quality lexical representation.

REFERENCES

Ai, J.W. (1950). A report on psychological studies of the Chinese language in the past three decades. *The Journal of Genetic Psychology, 76,* 207-220.

Bauer, R.S. (1988). Written Cantonese of Hong Kong. *Cahiers de Linguistique Asie Orientale, 17,* 245-293.

Bloomfield, L. (1933/1962). *Language.* London: George Allen & Unwin.

Boodberg, P.A. (1937). Some proleptical remarks on the evoluation of archaic Chinese. *Harvard Journal of Asiatic Studies, 2,* 329-372.

Byrne, B. (1992). Experimental psychology and real life: The case of literacy acquisition. In J. Alegria, D. Holender, J.J. de Morais, & M. Radeau (Eds.), *Analytic approaches to human cognition* (pp. 169-182). Amsterdam: North-Holland.

Cardoso-Martins, C. (1994). Rhyme perception: Global or analytical? *Journal of Experimental Child Psychology, 57,* 26-41.

Chao, Y.R. (1968). *A grammar of spoken Chinese.* Berkeley, CA: University of California Press.

Chen, H.-C., & Tzeng, O.J.L. (Eds.). (1992). *Language processing in Chinese.* Amsterdam: North-Holland.

Chomsky, N., & Halle, M. (1968/1991). *The sound pattern of English.* Cambridge, MA: The MIT Press.

Cutler, A., & Norris, D. (1988). The role of strong syllables in segmentation for lexical access. *Journal of Experimental Psychology: Human Perception and Performance, 14,* 113-121.

DeFrancis, J. (1989). *Visible speech: The diverse oneness of writing systems.* Honolulu: University of Hawaii Press.

Ding, Y., Li, N., & Bao, Q. (1985). A report on an experiment in "phonetically annotated character recognition shortens the time needed to learn to read and write". *Chinese Education, 18(2),* 57-85. (R. Thomas, Trans. Original work published in Chinese in *Jiàoyù Yánjiu,* Nov., 1983).

Eckman, F.R. (1981). On the naturalness of interlanguage phonological rules. *Language Learning,* 31, 195-216.

Ehri, L.C. (1984). How orthography alters spoken language competencies in children learning to read and spell. In J. Downing & R. Valtin (Eds.), *Language awareness and learning to read* (pp. 119-147). New York: Springer-Verlag.

Ehri, L.C. (1994). Development of the ability to read words: Update. In R.B. Ruddell, M.R, Ruddell, & H. Singer (Eds.), *Theoretical models and processes of reading* (4th ed., pp. 323-358). Newark, DE: International Reading Association.

Flege, J.E., McCutcheon, M.J., & Smith, S.C. (1987). The development of skill in productive word-final English stops. *Journal of the Acoustical Society of America, 82,*

433-447.

Goldsmith, J.A. (1990). *Autosegmental and metrical phonology*. Oxford: Basil Blackwell.

Halliday, M.A.K. (1981). The origin and early development of Chinese phonological theory. In R.E. Asher & E.J.A. Henderson (Eds.), *Towards a history of phonetics* (pp. 123-140). Edinburgh: Edinburgh University Press.

Hanley, J.R., & Huang, H.S. (this vol.). Phonological awareness and learning to read Chinese.

Hoosain, R. (1991). *Psycholinguistic implications for linguistic relativity: A case study of Chinese*. London: Lawrence Erlbaum.

Hsia, S. (1992). Developmental knowledge of inter- and intraword boundaries: Evidence from American and Mandarin Chinese speaking beginning readers. *Applied Psycholinguistics, 13*, 341-372.

Huang, H.S., & Hanley, J.R. (1995). Phonological awareness and visual skills in learning to read Chinese and English. *Cognition, 54*, 73-98.

Hung, D.L., & Tzeng, O.J.L. (1981). Orthographic variations and visual information processing. *Psychological Bulletin, 90*, 377-414.

Hung, D.L., Tzeng, O.J.L., & Tzeng, A.K.Y. (1992). Automatic activation of linguistic information in Chinese character recognition. In R. Frost & L. Katz (Eds.), *Orthography, phonology, morphology, and meaning* (pp. 119-130). Amsterdam: North-Holland.

Jesperson, O. (1904). *Lehrbuch der Phonetik* [Dictionary of phonetics]. Leipzig & Berlin: B.G. Teubner.

Kao, H.S.R., & Cheng, C.M. (Eds.). (1982). [*Study of the psychology of the Chinese language*]. Taipei, Taiwan: Wenshe Publishing (in Chinese).

Kao, H.S.R., & Hoosain, R. (Eds.). (1984). *Psychological studies of the Chinese language*. Hong Kong: The Chinese Language Society of Hong Kong.

Kao, H.S.R., & Hoosain, R. (Eds.), (1986). *Linguistics, psychology, and the Chinese language*. Hong Kong: Centre of Asian Studies, University of Hong Kong.

Lam, C.C., Wong, H.W., & Fung, Y.W. (Eds.). (1993). *Curriculum changes for Chinese communities in Southeast Asia: Challenges of the 21st century*. Hong Kong: The Chinese University of Hong Kong Faculty of Education (Part in Chinese & part in English).

Leong, C.K. (1973). Hong Kong. In J. Downing (Ed.). *Comparative reading: Cross-national studies of behavior and processes in reading and writing* (pp. 383-402). New York: Macmillan.

Leong, C.K. (1987). *Children with specific reading disabilities*. Lisse, The Netherlands: Swets & Zeitlinger.

Leong, C.K. (1991). From phonemic awareness to phonological processing to language access in children developing reading proficiency. In D.J. Sawyer & B.J. Fox

(Eds.), *Phonological awareness in reading: The evolution of current perspectives* (pp. 217-254). New York: Springer-Verlag.

Leong, C.K. (1992). Cognitive componential modelling of reading in ten- to twelve-year-old readers. *Reading and Writing: An Interdisciplinary Journal, 4,* 327-364.

Leong, C.K. (1995). Orthographic and psycholinguistic considerations in developing literacy in Chinese. In I. Taylor & D.R. Olson (Eds.), *Scripts and literacy: Reading, and learning to read alphabets, syllabaries and characters* (pp. 163-183). Dordrecht: Kluwer Academic Publishers.

Leong, C.K., & Hsia, S. (1996). Cross-linguistic constraints on Chinese students learning English. In M.H. Bond (Ed.), *The handbook of Chinese psychology* (pp. 63-78+ref.). Oxford: Oxford University Press.

Liberman, I.Y., & Shankweiler, D.P. (1985). Phonology and the problems of learning to read and write. *Remedial and Special Education, 6(6),* 8-17.

Liu, I.-M., Chen, H.-C., & Chen, M.J. (Eds.). (1988). *Cognitive aspects of the Chinese language* (Vol. 1). Hong Kong: Asian Research Service.

Liu, I.-M., Zhu, Y., & Wu, J.-T. (1992). The long-term modality effect: In search of differences in processing logographs and alphabetic words. *Cognition, 43,* 31-66.

Lundberg, I., Frost, J., & Petersen, O.-P. (1988). Effects of an extensive program for stimulating phonological awareness in preschool children. *Reading Research Quarterly, 23,* 263-284.

Mann, V.A. (1985). A cross-linguistic perspective on the relation between temporary memory skills and early reading ability. *Remedial and Special Education, 6(6),* 37-42.

Mann, V.A. (1986). Phonological awareness: The role of reading experience. *Cognition, 24,* 65-92.

Mann, V.A. (1991). Phonological awareness and early reading ability: One perspective. In D.J. Sawyer & B.J. Fox (Eds.), *Phonological awareness in reading: The evolution of current perspectives* (pp. 191-215). New York: Springer-Verlag.

Mattingly, I.G. (1972). Reading, the linguistic process, and linguistic awareness. In J.F. Kavanagh & I.G. Mattingly (Eds.), *Language by ear and by eye* (pp. 133-147). Cambridge, MA: The MIT Press.

Mattingly, I.G. (1985). Did orthographies evolve? *Remedial and Special Education, 6(6),* 18-23.

Mattingly, I.G. (1987). Morphological structure and segmental awareness. *Cahiers de Psychologie Cognitive, 7,* 488-493.

McCutchen, D., Bell, L.C., France, I.M., & Perfetti, C.A. (1991). Phoneme-specific interference in reading: The visual tongue-twister effect revisited. *Reading Research Quarterly, 26,* 87-103.

Morais, J., Bertelson, P., Cary, L., & Alegria, J. (1986). Literacy training and speech segmentation. *Cognition, 24,* 45-64.

Morais, J., Cary, L., Alegria, J., & Bertelson, P. (1979). Does awareness of speech as a sequence of phones arise spontaneously? *Cognition, 7,* 323-331.

Norman, J. (1988). *Chinese.* Cambridge: Cambridge University Press.

Norris, D., & Cutler, A. (1985). Juncture detection. *Linguistics, 23,* 689-705.

People Educational Publishing (1994). [*Yuwen Vol. 1: Teachers' manual*]. Beijing: Author (in Chinese).

Perfetti, C.A. (1992). The representation problem in reading acquisition. In P.B. Gough, L.C. Ehri, & R. Treiman (Eds.), *Reading acquisition* (pp. 145-174). Hillsdale, NJ: Lawrence Erlbaum.

Perfetti, C.A., & Zhang, S. (1991). Phonological processes in reading Chinese characters. *Journal of Experimental Psychology: Learning, Memory and Cognition, 17,* 633-643.

Perfetti, C.A., & Zhang, S. (1995a). Very early phonological activation in Chinese reading. *Journal of Experimental Psychology: Learning, Memory and Cognition, 21,* 24-33.

Perfetti, C.A., & Zhang, S. (1995b). The universal word identification reflex. In D.L. Medin (Ed.), *The psychology of learning and motivation* (Vol. 33, pp. 159-189). San Diego: Academic Press.

Perfetti, C.A., & Zhang, S. (in press). What it means to learn to read. In M.F. Graves, B.M. Taylor, & P. van den Broek (Eds.), *The first R: A right of all children.* New York: Teachers College Press.

Perfetti, C.A., Zhang, S., & Berent, I. (1992). Reading in English and Chinese: Evidence for a "universal" phonological principle. In R. Frost, & L. Katz (Eds.), *Orthography, phonology, morphology, and meaning* (pp. 227-248). Amsterdam: North-Holland.

Read, C., Zhang, Y.-F., Nie, H.-Y., & Ding, B.-Q. (1986). The ability to manipulate speech sounds depends on knowing alphabetic writing. *Cognition, 24,* 31-44.

Ren, N., & Mattingly, I.G. (1990). Short-term serial recall performance by good and poor readers of Chinese. *Haskins Laboratories Status Report on Speech Research, SR-103/104,* 153-164.

Sampson, G. (1985). *Writing systems.* Stanford, CA: Stanford University Press.

Seidenberg, M.S. (1989). Reading complex words. In G.N. Carlson & M.K. Tanenhaus (Eds.), *Linguistic structure in langauge processing* (pp. 53-105). Dordrecht: Kluwer Academic Publishers.

Spencer, A. (1991). *Morphological theory: An introduction to word structure in generative grammar.* Oxford: Blackwell Publishers.

Stanovich, K.E. (Ed.), (1988). *Children's reading and the development of phonological awareness.* Detroit, MI: Wayne State University Press.

Taft, M., & Chen, H.-C. (1992). Judging homophony in Chinese: The influence of tones. In H.-C. Chen & O.J.L. Tzeng (Eds.), *Language processing in Chinese* (pp. 151-172). Amsterdam: North-Holland.

Tan, L.H., Hoosain, R., & Peng, D.-L. (1995). Role of presemantic phonological code in Chinese character identification. *Journal of Experimental Psychology: Learning, Memory, and Cognition, 21,* 43-54.

Treiman, R. (1989). The internal structure of the syllable. In G.N. Carlson & M.K. Tanenhaus (Eds.), *Linguistic structure in language processing* (pp. 27-52). Dordrecht: Kluwer Academic Publishers.

Treiman, R., & Danis, C. (1988). Syllabification of intervocalic consonants. *Journal of Memory and Language, 27,* 87-104.

Treiman, R., Fowler, C.A., Gross, J., Berch, D., & Weatherston, S. (1995). Syllable structure or word structure? Evidence for onset and rime units with disyllabic and trisyllabic stimuli. *Journal of Memory and Language, 34,* 132-155.

Treiman, R., & Weatherston, S. (1992). Effects of linguistic structure on children's ability to isolate initial consonants. *Journal of Educational Psychology, 84,* 174-181.

Treiman, R., & Zukowski, A. (1990). Toward an understanding of English syllabification. *Journal of Memory and Language, 29,* 66-85.

Treiman, R., & Zukowski, A. (1991). Levels of phonological awareness. In S.A. Brady & D.P. Shankweiler (Eds.), *Phonological processes in literacy: A tribute to Isabelle Y. Liberman* (pp. 67-83). Hillsdale, NJ: Lawrence Erlbaum.

Tzeng, O.J.L., Hung, D.L., & Wang, W.S.-Y. (1977). Speech recoding in reading Chinese characters. *Journal of Experimental Psychology: Human Learning and Memory, 3,* 621-630.

Tzeng, O.J.L., & Wang, W.S.-Y (1983). The first two R's. *American Scientist, 71,* 238-243.

Wagner, R.K., & Torgesen, J.K. (1987). The nature of phonological processing and its causal role in the acquisition of reading skills. *Psychological Bulletin, 101,* 192-212.

Wang, L. (1985). *Zhōngguó xiàndài yǔfǎ* [Modern Chinese grammar]. Beijing: Shangwu Yinshuguan.

Wang, W.S.-Y. (1981). Language structure and optimal orthography. In O.J.L. Tzeng & H. Singer (Eds.), *Perception of print: Reading research in experimental psychology* (pp. 223-236). Hillsdale, NJ: Lawrence Erlbaum.

Wu, J.-T., & Liu, I.-M. (December, 1995). *Phonological activation in pronouncing characters.* Paper presented at the Seventh International Conference on the Cognitive Processing of Chinese and Other Asian Languages, The Chinese University of Hong Kong, Hong Kong.

Xu, Y. (1991). Depth of phonological recoding in short-term memory. *Memory &* *Cognition, 19,* 263-273.

Zhang, S., & Perfetti, C.A. (1993). The tongue-twister effect in reading Chinese. *Journal of Experimental Psychology: Learning, Memory, and Cognition, 19,* 1082-1093.

Author Note

The preparation of this paper was assisted in part by the John Ranton McIntosh research grant, a grant from the University of Saskatchewan President's Social Sciences Research Fund, and a research grant from the Social Sciences and Humanities Research Council of Canada (SSHRC 410-96-0186). I am grateful for the assistance. Over the years I have benefitted from the work of H.-C. Chen, R. Hoosain, H.S.R. Kao, I.-M. Liu, and O.J.L. Tzeng on the cognitive processing of the Chinese language. I alone am responsible for any shortcomings in this paper.

Footnote

The tonal marks for the Chinese terms are shown in the pīnyīn transliteration.

AUTHOR INDEX

A

Aaron, P.G., 2, 23
Adams, M.J., 8, 10, 71, 76, 196, 206, 253, 289, 307, 333, 334, 335, 338, 342, 355
Ai, J.W., 380
Akkerhuis, G.W., 255
Alegria, J., 5, 15, 31, 32, 34, 140, 142, 150, 306, 373, 390
Alexander, A.W., 72, 73, 78
Allen, J. B., 334
Andersen, H. G., 72
Anderson, W.G., 199
Arnbak, E., 9, 308
Aronoff, M., 9
Atkins, P., 18, 23, 197

B

Backman, J., 196
Baddeley, A. D., 98
Ball, E.W., 72, 74, 290, 307, 324
Balthazar, M., 35,
Bao, Q., 407, 408
Baron, J., 31
Bassich, C., 92
Beasley, D.S., 90
Beck, I., 34, 150, 365
Beck, M., 143
Becker, G., 37, 38
Beech, J.R., 196
Beers, J.W., 175
Bell, L. C., 388
Bell, N., 21
Bentin, S., 32
Berch, D., 398
Berent, I., 20, 380, 386, 387, 389, 402, 410
Berninger, V.W., 24
Berrian, R.W., 199
Bertelson, P., 5, 31, 32, 34, 140, 142, 150, 306, 390

Bertoncini, J., 12
Biddle, K., 13
Biemiller, A., 341, 342, 355
Bilger, R., 37, 38
Bishop, D.V.M., 92
Bissex, G. L., 333
Bjaalid, I.K., 5
Blachman, B.A., 72, 74, 144, 290, 306, 307, 324
Black, R. S., 74
Blaesser, B., 290
Blennerhassett, A., 140, 143
Bloom, L., 76
Bloomfield, L., 391, 396
Blum, L., 143, 145
Blumenthal, S., 34
Bond, G., 333, 342
Boodberg, P.A., 382, 385, 396
Bosman, A.M.T., 251, 278
Bowers, P.G., 104
Bowey, J., 324
Bradley, L., 31, 32, 36, 37, 72, 140, 142, 143, 144, 148, 150, 155, 196, 290, 300, 306, 307, 310, 324, 365, 366
Brady, S., 289, 290, 300
Brooks, L., 216, 220
Brown, G.D.A., 23
Brown, I., 37
Bruck, M., 67, 76, 81. 83, 105, 118, 196, 218, 220, 307, 373, 374
Brügelmann, H., 145, 163, 181, 190
Brus, B.Th., 240, 272
Bryant, B., 37
Bryant, B.R., 92
Bryant, P.E., 11, 31, 36, 37, 72, 104, 140, 142, 143, 144, 148, 150, 155, 196, 290, 300, 306, 307, 310, 324, 365, 366, 370, 375
Burgemeister, B., 143, 145